MW01030563

Logic as a Liberal Art

Logic as a Liberal Art

An Introduction to Rhetoric & Reasoning

R. E. Houser

The Catholic University of America Press | Washington, D.C.

Copyright © 2020
R. E. Houser
All rights reserved
The paper used in this publication meets the minimum requirements of
American National Standards for Information Science—Permanence
of Paper for Printed Library Materials, ANSI Z39.48-1984.
∞

Design and composition by Kachergis Book Design

Library of Congress Cataloging-in-Publication Data
Names: Houser, R. E., author.
Title: Logic as a liberal art : an introduction to rhetoric and reasoning
/ R.E. Houser.
Description: Washington, D.C. : The Catholic University of America
Press, 2020. | Includes bibliographical references and index. | Summary:
"This textbook for a first course in logic takes a verbal rather than
symbolic approach, based on the student's natural language. It starts by
discussing grammar, rhetoric, and the essential nature of logic; formal
logic is then taken up following Aristotle's division of the three acts of
the mind"—Provided by publisher.
Identifiers: LCCN 2019035083 | ISBN 9780813232348 (paperback) |
ISBN 9780813232355 (ebook)
Subjects: LCSH: Logic—Textbooks. | Rhetoric. | Reasoning.
Classification: LCC BC108 .H68 2020 | DDC 160—dc23
LC record available at https://lccn.loc.gov/2019035083

To M. C. S. and C. J. H. C.
who are one with me in the love
of the Catholic Liberal Arts

What is madness? To have erroneous perceptions, and to reason correctly from them.

—Voltaire, *Philosophical Dictionary*

Contents

Part 1. Grammar, Rhetoric, and Logic

Part 4. The Logic of Arguments

Acknowledgments

First and foremost, I would thank the numerous logic students I have taught over the years. They are too many to name, but my debt to them is immeasurable, as well as my pleasure in being included within the journey of their formal education.

Two of my own teachers, however, I must mention. I received an excellent education in the public schools of Dallas, especially at the junior high and high school levels. The post-Sputnik era saw the development of honors programs in science and mathematics, but the humanities by no means were neglected, as has recently become the trend. For my first two years in high school, however, I was exposed for the first time to the Catholic tradition of education, at two different high schools run by the Christian Brothers (FSC). And though I have taught logic—both verbal and symbolic—for many years, I never took a course in logic, in high school or university, as an undergraduate. I did not need to do so, because of the teaching of two men.

Br. Leonard, FSC, taught me how to reason deductively while leading me through plane geometry at Mullen High School in Denver. His course opened up the world of deductive argument like no one had, before or since. Our textbook covered a good portion of Euclid's *Elements*, I think. But we did not read Euclid's proofs; Br. Leonard had us do the proofs ourselves, using a book that contained only a few sample proofs in the chapters and no answers in the back. Clear, precise, and absolutely rigorous "sweet reason" was his guiding principle, in the class and out. So when it came time for our presidential election debates in 1960—one debate at each class level—I was tapped for the freshmen debate and chose to support Mr. Nixon. There were comments from my friends and strained looks from some teachers; it was, after all, a Catholic school and Mr. Kennedy his opponent. But Br. Leonard's only comment to me was, "Strong arguments."

The next year, at Bishop Kelley High School in Tulsa, Oklahoma, I met Br. Kilian Bernardine, FSC, who had helped found the school the year before and taught there for thirty-five years. A large man, vigorous in body and mind, in Algebra 2 he extended the range of reasoning beyond what I had heretofore imagined. The abstract problems, like quadratic equations, I loved; but word problems proved more difficult. To help us out, Br. Bernardine suggested searching the used bookshops of Tulsa for older math books, circa 1880–1920, with harder problems than those in our own textbook. So under him I not only learned to love the hard problems but also took my very first steps in academic research, courtesy of my mother, who drove me to the shops. A tough grader, Br. Bernardine rearranged our seats in order from the highest to the lowest grade in the previous quarter, something that might now be thought harassment, but was an inducement to harder study. The class consisted in Brother questioning individual students, and when he approached you, his giant hand took hold of your upper arm in a squeeze that started gently and became more and more severe until you came up with the right answer or he had mercy on your arm, but not on your mind. When parents complained about so many low grades in his classes, Br. Bernardine replied that a student of his, who had never gotten more than a C in math, had been accepted into the U.S. Military Academy at West Point the previous year. Until he died, my father, whose command of math made him a highly decorated bombardier/navigator in World War II, complained about Br. Bernardine giving me the only B I ever received in math. My reply: "But Daddy, he taught me how to think about everything under the sun."

In sum, I esteemed Br. Leonard, and I loved Br. Bernardine. And between them they set me on my intellectual journey: to math and science, followed by the liberal arts, and culminating in philosophy. It took me a long time to realize that my intellectual journey simply followed the path that had been taken for centuries: quadrivium, trivium, humanities, philosophy.

Let me add one final note of deep appreciation. On several points that come up in this book, one of the readers appointed by the Catholic University of America Press corrected a mistake or taught me a truth I did not know before. The book is better, much better, for the extensive and insightful comments of Dr. Brian Carl. His review was superb, an exemplary professional job. And I thank him.

A Note to the Logic Instructor

In the twenty-first century there are two ways to study logic. The minority approach, which held universal sway in the West for centuries, is what we might call the "verbal" way, or learning logic in what is nowadays called a "natural" language. This way of learning and teaching logic was invented, of course, by Aristotle and developed by later ancient, medieval, Renaissance, and early modern logicians. It was considered so fixed and perfected that Kant confidently used the logic of judgments, as found in what Aristotelians call the "second act of the mind," as an absolutely firm foundation for the transcendental deduction of his own categories.

The more recent approach was invented in the last part of the nineteenth century by the German mathematician Gottlob Frege and popularized in the early twentieth century by the British philosophers Bertrand Russell and Alfred North Whitehead, in their *Principia Mathematica* (we should add *Logicae*, since their title was an homage to Newton's *Philosophiae Naturalis Principia Mathematica*). This approach to logic resulted from Frege's studies of the foundations of arithmetic. He found that mathematics is built on certain basic logical truths; and because Frege approached logic through mathematics, the way logicians like Russell and Whitehead presented logic itself was in a format employing mathematical-style symbols. Their way of presenting logic by using the language of mathematical-style symbols, rather than the verbal language of ordinary discourse, was highly original and powerful. It has proven particularly useful in the study of science for the simple reason that mathematics has become the common language of science itself. And its utility in technological advances, such as computers, is beyond question.

Symbolic logic, however, is not without its drawbacks as a means of teaching and learning logic as a systematic academic discipline in a first logic course at the undergraduate level. Let me mention three reasons. First, because it uses the language of abstract symbols, it is often hard to learn, especially for those people who, for good reasons or bad ones, shy away from mathematics. The second and far greater problem is one of applying logic to real, verbal discourse. This application is necessary, but it requires repeated *translations* from the highly abstract language of symbolic logic into the ordinary language of verbal speech and writing and back again. The last and perhaps greatest problem with symbolic logic is that it tends to separate the logic we have already learned during our normal intellectual development from the logic we learn in logic class. For the logic presented in a logic course is not the first logic the student learns; we start learning logic when we start learning our native language. All too often, then, symbolic logic is treated as an alien discipline one learns for the course, with little or no connection to the student's intellectual life outside the logic classroom. And this result in turn can undercut belief that logic or reasoning of any form can result in our acquiring truth, which feeds directly into the widespread skepticism in our culture and especially its academic sphere.

For these reasons, if we look at the history of using symbolic logic to teach college courses in logic for the last century, we can discern a definite but very odd trend. Before World War II, symbolic logic was pretty well limited to graduate education and to the domain of mathematicians. Alfred North Whitehead's career path is a fine illustration. During his tenure at Cambridge (1884 to 1910) he wrote primarily in mathematics and logic, publishing with Bertrand Russell *Principia Mathematica* (1910, 1912, 1913). At the University of London (1910 to 1924) he was appointed professor of applied mathematics and wrote in the areas of logic and philosophy of science, then expanded into philosophy of education. It was not until he went to Harvard (1924–1937) that he moved fully into philosophy proper, founding the metaphysical movement known as "process philosophy." This was a development stemming from his symbolic approach to logic, where a "natural language" statement like "there are two chairs" is analyzed into a series of more abstract and relational claims: "There is an x which is a chair; and there is a y which is a chair; and x is not identical with y; and if there is a chair z, then z is identical to either x or y."[1] This logical analysis led Whitehead to reverse the Aristotelian priority of substance over relation, which had committed "the fallacy of misplaced concreteness," and affirm the universe is made up of "actual occasions" fundamentally constituted by sets of relations.

In North America, teaching logic courses in the symbolic way began in earnest shortly after World War II and by the 1960s was used in many undergraduate logic courses. I myself have taught logic in both its symbolic and verbal (or Aristotelian) modes. Beginning in the 1970s, many factors, but in my view primarily the difficulties experienced by undergraduate students in learning logic in the symbolic way, led first to the movement called "informal logic," which understood formal logic to mean symbolic logic, and tried to come up with a more easily understood alternative, but could not bring itself to "retreat" back to Aristotelian logic. Then after a few years the step was made to "critical thinking," which tended to empty logic of the rigor it has in both its verbal and symbolic forms. At this point, the teaching of logic expanded beyond the Philosophy and Mathematics departments and was justified on the grounds that faculty in all departments can think critically, so they should be able to teach what they do. These developments can be traced by tracking the changes in the editions of popular logic textbooks, such as Copi. Most such textbooks are still structured around symbolic logic, conceived as the *real* logic, but with verbal logic appended, as a shortcut to syllogistic, since the means of teaching syllogistic in symbolic logic, the predicate calculus, is normally studied after propositional calculus. This long and arduous approach has produced textbooks of huge size that can hardly be accommodated in a one-semester course. In short, insistence on teaching logic in the symbolic way that "professionals" like to pursue their own researches has had the perverse effect of pulling students away from mastering the logical rigor that symbolic logic was supposed to impart in the first place. What has resulted is a kind of logical hippogriff, whose eagle head and wings are like symbolic logic, flying through the aery heights of abstract thought, and trailing behind it the horse's body of verbal logic, for use when the mythical beast touches its hooves to the ground of everyday experience.

Because of such difficulties, in this book I have wholeheartedly embraced

---

1. Ronald Desmet and Andrew David Irvine, "Alfred North Whitehead," in *The Stanford Encyclopedia of Philosophy*, ed. Edward N. Zalta (Fall 2018 edition), https://plato.stanford.edu/archives/fall2018/entries/whitehead/.

the verbal approach to logic, primarily in order to position the study of logic in its natural setting, much as a scientist might study tropical plants or polar bears in their natural habitats. The natural habitat of logic is the verbal and written language of ordinary human discourse, taken in its full range, including the high-level verbal discourse that can be encountered in university courses. The *problem sets* are designed to mirror this wide range. While they normally begin with elementary problems of the textbook variety, a serious effort has been made to reach up to real problems, taken from real authors, in their own words. One cannot deal with the logic of Plato's arguments apart from reading Plato's own writings. And here the verbal approach has a genuine advantage. Discourse in ordinary or natural language often contains clues that help us to understand its logic. Such clues, of course, are missing from the mathematical-type language used in symbolic logic. While mathematical-style symbols do on occasion offer insightful help in seeing logical relations, and we will employ symbols from time to time in this book, by using ordinary or natural language to study logic we can avoid the large headache of translating from the language of mathematical-style symbols to ordinary language and back again. So we content ourselves with the smaller but real headaches involved in searching out the logic contained within verbal or natural language.

Now I have criticized other textbooks for being too large, so I must admit that this textbook also contains more material than can normally be taught in a one-semester logic course. In class I usually cover about twenty-eight of the thirty-three lessons, though on two occasions, with particularly excellent classes, I did manage to get in all the lessons. So choices do have to be made. As a result, this book has been designed consciously to offer a number of different ways of teaching the first (and usually only) course in logic students will take. Of course, I myself prefer to situate logic within the trivium. But I have myself tried all five of the other modes listed here:

1. *Skipping grammar and rhetoric*: Too many teachers of philosophy are dismissive of grammar and really despise rhetoric, in the way Plato despised its creators, the sophists. (But Aristotle was more even-handed.) Teachers who choose to skip over grammar and rhetoric will probably want to start with lesson 6, or perhaps lesson 7. But hard choices still will have to be made. And in defense of keeping some rhetoric, let me add that the "information revolution" makes it more necessary than ever to distinguish *ethos*, *pathos*, and *logos*. So please consider cutting lessons from later in the book rather than cutting lesson 4.

2. *Purely formal logic*: The few logic books that take a verbal approach almost inevitably omit most of the logic of terms (lessons 7–12). This part of logic is sometimes dismissed as being neo-scholastic or importing too much metaphysics into logic, though Aristotle himself used the categories, predicables, and causes throughout his logical books. I tried for a few years omitting this section entirely. The problems with doing so are practical, not theoretical. My utilitarian criterion is this: does a student understand a classical definition like "a human is a rational animal" or "a triangle is a three-sided plane figure"? Teachers tend to think they do, because the students have heard these formulae so often; but a bit of probing shows most students do not. If they do not understand such definitions after taking the class, then I have failed in my task as a teacher. The topics covered in part 2 are all designed as preparation for lesson 12. So I tend to cut lessons in part 3 or 4 more than in part 2. But if you want a purely formal logic course, it would focus on lessons 13 and beyond.

3. *Analysis of problems*: a course that focuses on giving students maximum practice in logical analysis of problems, which is helpful in their other classes. For this course I would concentrate on teaching theory by doing problems in class. Please don't skip diagramming sentences in lesson 1. Then I would focus on lessons 8–12, 13–16, 25–26, 28–29, and 32.

4. *Even-handed logic*: a course purely in logic, but that gives equal treatment to the logic of all three acts of the mind. You might focus on lessons 8, 11–12, 13–16, 23–29, and 32.

5. *Logic of argumentation*: a course for good to excellent students that concentrates on increasing skills in argument through extensive engagement with the more difficult problems probably would begin with lesson 13. You would want to reserve a lot of time to do a large number of problems in lessons 26 to 33, something I have never succeeded in doing to my satisfaction.

Good luck with using this book. Please do give me your personal outcomes assessment.

A Note to the Student

In the very first chapter of his *Politics*, Aristotle notes that humans are the only animals "endowed with speech." He makes this point in an interesting argument that connects this definition of humans with another of his famous definitions of humans:

> It is evident that the city-state (*polis*) is one of the kinds of things that exist by nature, and that *by nature man is a political animal*.... The reason why man is the kind of being designed for political association, in a higher degree than the bees or other gregarious animals ever can associate, is evident. Nature, we say, does nothing in vain. But *man alone among the animals is endowed with speech*. Making sounds indicates pleasure and pain, and so belongs to animals in general. Their nature enables them to get to the point where they perceive pleasure and pain, and they signify these perceptions to one another. But speech declares what is *useful* and what is not, and therefore it serves to declare what is *just and unjust*. It is peculiar to man, in comparison with the rest of the animals, that he alone has perception of good and evil, of the just and unjust, and like things. And it is association in these things that makes a family and a city-state.[1]

Other animals—bees and birds and buffaloes—form communities, but only humans form genuine families and political communities, because only humans have speech. Speech is not only characteristic of humans, it is arguably their greatest invention, because it is the basis for so many others. Au-

1. Aristotle, *Politics* 1.2, 1253a1–17; translated by R. E. Houser.

gustine noted, however, that speech is lost to the past almost as soon as it's produced. So once we got around to inventing writing in order to capture and preserve speech, the systematic study of speech gradually developed.

Consider the following memorable speech by one of the finest orators of the twentieth century:

[handwritten: sense, persuasion, logos]

[handwritten in margin: matching an argument]

Hitler knows that he will have to break us in this island or lose the war. If we can stand up to him, all Europe may be free, and the life of the world may move forward into broad, sunlit uplands. But if we fail, then the whole world, including the United States, and all that we have known and cared for, will sink into the abyss of a new dark age made more sinister, and perhaps more prolonged, by the lights of a perverted science. Let us therefore brace ourselves to our duty and so bear ourselves that if the British Commonwealth and Europe lasts for a thousand years men will still say: This was their finest hour.[2]

In this passage we find three things that work together. First, Mr. Churchill knows the right form of a word to use, how to put words into sentences, and how to put sentences into paragraphs. In short, he had mastered what from the time of the Greeks was called "the art (*techne*) of grammar." Second, he chooses words, sentences, and a paragraph that are effective in persuading us that what he says is true, important, even inspiring. During a time when Britain was actively trying to avoid impending defeat by Nazi Germany, Mr. Churchill's intention was to persuade the leaders of Great Britain, and of the United States and other world leaders, to oppose Hitler. Third, while Mr. Churchill's speech rouses our emotions—even so many years later—it also contains an argument, one meant not just to persuade our hearts, but to convince our minds, that the task ahead not only needed to be done, but could be done.

In order to make this speech, Mr. Churchill was the beneficiary of a long tradition of what is called the study of the "liberal arts." Three of these arts are exhibited in this kind of speech and writing: the liberal arts of grammar, rhetoric, and logic. All human discourse—from the loftiest to the most mundane—has grammatical, rhetorical, and logical features. This is why, although the ancients distinguished these three arts and generally taught them separately, they understood that it is the task of the speaker and writer to use all three together in speech and writing. In this book, we shall focus on the art of

---

2. Winston Churchill, "Speech in the House of Commons, 18 June 1940," in *Winston S. Churchill: His Complete Speeches, 1897–1963* (New York: Chelsea House, 1974), 6:6238.

logic. But since logic is so closely connected in real discourse with grammar and rhetoric, we shall start with them. *Lesson 1* covers a bit of grammar, and *Lessons 2–4* present a few central points of rhetoric. The topics developed there are important for our study of logic, which will make up the remainder of the book.

The Seven Liberal Arts

Although the Greeks began the process of creating the liberal arts as early as the fifth century B.C., it was not until quite late in the ancient period that the Roman Martianus Capella (ca. 400 A.D.) limited the "liberal arts" to the seven that became standard in the Middle Ages. They cover the basic knowledge and intellectual skills that a "free (*liber*)" man should understand, a sort of minimum for education. They were arranged into two groups: four arts in the *quadrivium* (coming from the Latin words for "four" and "way") and three arts of the *trivium* (coming from the Latin words for "three" and "way").

The *quadrivium* contained two areas of mathematics—arithmetic and geometry—and two areas of science—astronomy, which makes use of geometry, and music (which meant not so much learning to play a musical instrument as understanding and appreciating it through seeing its mathematical character)—that uses arithmetic. A memorable example of music in this sense was the discovery, attributed to Pythagoras, that shortening the length of a lyre string by half produces a note one octave higher, while doubling the length produces a note one octave lower.

The *trivium*, with which we are concerned, consisted in three arts necessary to be an effective speaker and writer—namely, grammar, rhetoric, and logic. Knowledge of grammar gives one the skill (*ars*) to put together words, sentences, and paragraphs according to the rules governing each language, whether Latin or Greek, English or Spanish, Arabic or Chinese. In fact, the art of grammar consisted primarily for the ancient grammarians in learning what these rules were, for the rules of correct grammatical usage were only implicit in spoken or written language before the development of grammar as an art. Grammar was the last of the three arts of the trivium to be systematized. The earliest Greek grammarian, whose works still exist, was Dionysius Thrax, who taught in Alexandria in the first century B.C. Other major Latin grammarians came later, such as Donatus (fourth century A.D.) and Priscian (sixth century A.D.).

It was the great scientist and philosopher Aristotle who invented the art of logic. Of course, speakers and writers before Aristotle used logic: witness his teacher Plato, one of the great writers of world culture. However, it was Aristotle who first created logic as a systematically organized art. He invented logic in reply to his beloved teacher Plato, who had held, incorrectly according to Aristotle, that knowing the *matter* and the *manner* of reasoning about some subject, say, politics or human nature, necessarily go together; you can't know one without the other. On the contrary, Aristotle said they could be separated. So a thinker can make mistakes about the *matter* or content of what he says while still speaking and writing in a correct *manner*—that is, using correct grammar, rhetoric, and logic. Aristotle also wrote the oldest surviving work of rhetoric. But he let us know that he did not invent rhetoric—there were earlier rhetoricians, some of whom he named. We will meet them in *Lesson 2*. And, surprisingly enough, books on grammar came last, even though it might seem logical that grammar ought to have been written down first, since before our discourse can be logical or rhetorically effective, it needs first to be grammatically correct in order to be intelligible at all.

Two Approaches to Studying Logic

In the twenty-first century there are basically two ways to study logic. The more recent approach was invented in the last part of the nineteenth century by the German mathematician Gottlob Frege and popularized in the twentieth century by the British philosophers Bertrand Russell and Alfred North Whitehead. This approach to logic resulted from Frege's studies of the foundations of arithmetic. He found that mathematics is built on certain basic logical truths; and because Frege approached logic through mathematics, the way that logicians like Russell and Whitehead presented logic itself was in a highly symbolic, mathematical format. At the time, it was thought that Frege and his followers had discovered something completely new and revolutionary. Further research into the history of logic has since shown that some of these "discoveries" were actually known by late medieval (fourteenth- to sixteenth-century) logicians. But what was genuinely original in Frege's approach was the attempt to present logic using the language of mathematical-style symbols rather than the verbal language of ordinary discourse. This symbolic approach to logic has proven particularly useful in the study of science, where its abstract mathematical-style language is particularly useful, for the simple reason that mathematics has become the common language of science itself. Mathematical logic and science, then, share the same kind of language, the language of abstract mathematical-style symbols. Symbolic logic has also been extremely useful for technological advances, for instance, in the development of computers.

Symbolic logic, however, is not without its drawbacks as a means of learning logic. First, because it uses the language of abstract symbols, it is often hard to learn, especially for those people who, for good reasons or bad ones, shy away from mathematics. With regard to mathematical proficiency in their students, symbolic logicians tend to follow the lead of Plato, who is said, so the story goes, to have put a sign in front of his school—the Academy—that read, freely translated, "You may not enter without a credit in geometry."

The second and greater problem is one of applying logic to real life. Mathematical logic focuses on statements of logical relations set out in an abstract language of symbols. But when we apply logic to areas of thought outside of mathematics and some areas of science, as we do in everyday life, the symbolic language of logic has to be applied to ordinary verbal discourse, to everyday speech and writing. This "application" of symbolic logic requires an act of translating the symbolic language of logic into the ordinary language of verbal speech and writing. Learning how to perform this act of translation turns out to be quite difficult, as anyone who has tried to act as an interpreter can easily understand. The source of the difficulty is the need to translate from the language of mathematics to the everyday language of ordinary discourse, somewhat like constantly needing to translate from, say, English into Spanish.

The last and perhaps greatest problem with mathematical logic is that it tends to separate the logic we have already learned during our normal intellectual development from the logic we learn in logic class. For the logic presented in this book, or any logic book of whatever sort, is not the first logic you will learn. You have been learning logic from the time you started thinking and speaking, and then reading and writing, in your own native language, and any other "natural" languages you have picked up. This book, then, is not designed to teach you something you have never studied. Learning to think includes learning logic, though not as a formal course. What this book is designed to do is to improve your success rate in logic, no matter how poor or how good your logical skill presently is. Everyone, including your instructor, has room to improve.

Because of these difficulties, among others, we will take the other approach to the study of logic. This approach is to study logic in its "natural" setting, much as a scientist might study tropical plants or polar bears in their natural habitats. The natural habitat of logic is the verbal and written language of ordinary human discourse, including the high-level verbal discourse that occurs in university courses. The man who invented this approach to logic was Aristotle, who wrote the first textbooks in logic in the fourth century B.C. The main reason why this approach is preferable for most people is that it avoids the two problems that have plagued the teaching of symbolic logic during its heyday and up to the present. First, the verbal approach is clearly preferable for those who have math phobia. The problems used in the verbal approach are set out in ordinary language, language that often contains clues that help us to understand the logic of verbal discourse. Such clues, of course, are missing from the mathematical symbols used in symbolic logic. Second, the verbal study of logic has the advantage of avoiding the problem of needing to translate back and forth between abstract logical symbols and the more concrete verbal symbols we call words. While mathematical symbols do on occasion help us see logical relations, and we will employ some elementary symbols from time to time in this book, by using ordinary or "natural" language to study logic we can avoid the large headache of translating from the language of symbols to ordinary language, and then back again. So we content ourselves with the smaller but real headaches involved in searching out the logic contained within verbal or "natural" language.

The Verbal Approach to Logic: Studying Rhetoric and Logic Together

The verbal approach to logic has yet another advantage, one not very often admitted even by its proponents. We can see this one by looking at history. The verbal approach to logic and the discipline of rhetoric were invented by the Greeks, those early masters of the spoken and written word. In fact, rhetoric was invented slightly before Aristotle invented logic. Aristotle conceived of rhetoric and logic as correlative, noting that "rhetoric is the analogue of dialectic," a subfield of logic. (One of Aristotle's books of logic, the *Topics*, covers dialectical or probable arguments, as we will see in *Lesson 5*.) If you don't pursue the verbal form of logic, then you probably won't see the importance of rhetoric, dialectic's twin. Following the inspiration of Aristotle, therefore, we shall begin by reviewing a couple of useful points of grammar and then turn to rhetoric before setting out on our journey through logic.

How to Use This Book

Each chapter of this textbook is divided into four sections: "The Essentials," "A Deeper Look," "Primary Sources," and a "Problem Set." Unlike many of your other courses, including philosophy courses, the most important section is the problem set. You may be tempted to try to do the problems before reading the text, but this is not advisable. Look at the topics covered, then read "The Essentials" carefully. Then try the problem set. If you get stuck there, go back to where your question is taken up, either in "The Essentials" or, for more difficult problems, in "A Deeper Look."

For those interested in where the main ideas in each chapter come from and for a more "philosophical" explanation of them, try the "Primary Sources" and the footnotes in each lesson. Here you will need to find the works cited, all of which are available in printed books and on the internet. A glance at the "Chronology of Logicians and Their Logical Works," at the end of this textbook, shows that over the centuries many first-class minds have contributed to the development of logic. But as often the case in intellectual endeavors, it is best to begin with the pioneers, followed by their finest followers. This is the reason why, with a few exceptions, I have limited the footnotes and "Primary Sources" in each chapter to Aristotle and the man universally acknowledged to be best commentator on his works over the centuries, Thomas Aquinas.

Part 1

Grammar, Rhetoric, and Logic

A Grounding in Grammar

The Essentials

The Eight Parts of Speech

The ancient grammarians divided grammar into two parts: grammar proper, the study of the kinds of words; and syntax, the study of how to put words together properly. Both are important for the study of logic. From grammar it is understood that words fall into different categories called "the parts of speech." So we first review the parts of speech. Positioning a word within the scheme of the eight parts of speech is analogous to determining where a term falls within the logical scheme of categories, predicables, and causes. Developing our grammatical skill at placing words within the parts of speech is excellent practice for learning to analyze terms in logic. If we can't recognize what part of speech a word is, this undermines our understanding of the terms, propositions, and arguments we will study in logic.

Syntax studies how to assemble different parts of speech correctly to form sentences. One way of learning syntax is to diagram sentences; in fact, it is the best way, because diagramming forces us to concentrate on how the words of a sentence function in relation to each other. And this skill is invaluable in logic when we are learning to recognize different kinds of propositions based on how their parts are related to each other. These two skills—diagramming sentences and analyzing propositions—are very much analogous to each other, even though the notions used in grammatical analysis of a sentence and in logical analysis of a proposition are not the same. Learning to diagram sentences pays great rewards when we come to analyze propositions and then go further to evaluate arguments. The way a grammarian analyzes a sentence is not exactly the same way a logician analyzes a proposition, but skill in grammar helps us develop our skills in logic.

According to the ancient Latin grammarians Donatus and Priscian,[1] there are eight parts of speech: nouns, pronouns, verbs, adverbs, participles, conjunctions, prepositions, and interjections. Over the centuries, this list has remained the same apart from one exception. Participles are a verbal form, like the present participle "walking" and the past participle "walked." In many of the ancient languages, most words English grammar calls "adjectives" were formed from the verb, as participles are. Over time, "adjective" came to replace "participle" as one of the eight parts of speech. Grammarians have devoted a lot of time to very precise definitions of these parts of speech and have come up with different lists. But we shall follow the simple and traditional list derived from these two Romans, since it is essential to recognize the different parts of speech. Here are very brief descriptions and examples.

Part of Speech	Description	Examples
Noun	person, place, or thing	dog, rabbit, road
Verb	action, passion	barked, was chased, is, were
Adverb	modify verbs or adjectives	certainly, suddenly
Pronoun	stands in for a noun	us, she, we, her, him, they
Adjective	modifies a noun	the, red, fun, little
Preposition	introduces a descriptive phrase	into, down, from
Conjunction	connection	and, or, but
Interjection	added for emphasis	Oh! Yes! Say,

Here is a sentence that contains every part of speech:

"Well, she and young John walk to school slowly."

interjection	pron.	conj.	adj.	noun	verb	prep.	noun	adverb
Well,	she	and	young	John	walk	to	school	slowly.

1. Aelius Donatus (ca. 350), *Ars grammatica*, *Ars minor* (Eight Parts of Speech); Priscian (ca. 500), *Institutiones grammaticae*.

Definitions of the Parts of Speech

Noun: The word "noun" comes from the Latin word *nomen*. It is a word that describes a subject or object of discourse, something about which we are talking. Nouns are the most important part of the subject of a sentence, which says what it is that performs the action described in the predicate.

Types of Nouns

Proper nouns: name a particular thing: Joan, John, America.

"*Joan* is running to the store."
"A nation of high ideals describes *America*."

Common nouns: name a class or type of thing: *horse, jacket*.

"Abe Lincoln, with his *jacket* buttoned against the cold, rode his horse into town."

Abstract nouns: name a feature of things, apart from individuals: *justice, humanity, reasonableness*.

"The Muslim philosopher Avicenna famously said, '*Horseness* is only horseness.'"
"*Liberty* is what most American immigrants seek."

Collective nouns: name of a group of the same kind: *team, jury, flock*.

"Our school's *baseball team* won the tournament."

Adjective: A word that modifies a noun, further clarifying the kind of thing the noun describes: *a fast* horse, *true* justice, *a fair* jury; *this* jacket; *the* team.

The ancient grammarians noted that adjectives often are formed from nouns. The Latin grammarian Priscian described adjectives as a subtype of noun, the *nomen adjectivum* or "added noun."

"The *fast* horse won the race."
"Black is *beautiful*."

Pronoun: a word that stands in for or is a placeholder for a noun: *he, she, it, who, which*.

"*She* is fast."
"*It* seems to be an antelope, but I can't yet see *it* clearly."

Verb: The word "verb" comes from the Latin word *verbum*; a verb is a word that describes some action or passion. Verbs are the most important part of the predicate of a sentence, which says what the subject does or undergoes.

Types of Verbs

Transitive verbs: verbs that describe an action affecting an object: *build, destroy.*

Intransitive verbs: verbs that describe an action or passion that does not require an object: *to sleep, to snore.*

Some verbs can be either transitive or intransitive: *to run, to hide.*

"He is *running* down the street."

"She *runs* the Accounting Department."

"I *am hiding* from my sister."

"Writers sometimes *hide* the true meaning of their words."

Adverb: a word that modifies a verb—that is, gives further clarification of the kind of action or passion involved or modifies another modifier, like an adjective.

"He runs *quickly*."

"Your daughter is *very* vivacious.

Preposition: A word that introduces an explanatory phrase.

"He runs quickly *to* the store."

"I hid the book *in* my room."

"Do you take this man, *for* richer and *for* poorer, until death you do part?"

Conjunction: A word that connects two different parts of a sentence, often two different clauses in the sentence: *and, or, unless, because.*

"We need to study logic *because* we use it every day."

"You don't really know the three angles of a triangle equal two right angles, *unless* you can prove it."

Interjection: The word "interjection" comes from two Latin words, *jacio*, which means "throw," and *inter*, which means "between" or "among" or "in." An interjection is a word that is thrown into a sentence, usually simply to give emphasis: Oh! Really! My goodness!

"*Oh, my goodness*, did the Athenians *really* execute the first great philosopher, Socrates, in 399 B.C.?"

There are many subdivisions falling under these eight basic parts of speech. Some English grammar books add one or two other parts of speech, and of course, the parts of speech can vary among languages. But what is important for the study of logic is to be able to ask yourself what *kind* of word each word in a sentence is, and to get the right answer. This is the first step in understanding how it contributes to the meaning of the sentence.

Syntax and Diagramming Sentences

Syntax is the second, more complicated, and more interesting part of grammar. The term comes from the Greek words meaning "with" or "together" (*syn*) and "arrangement" or "order" (*taxis*). Syntax concerns how words of a sentence are related to each other within the sentence. An interesting way to test whether you understand the syntax of a sentence is to diagram it. Sentence diagramming was popularized by Alonzo Reed and Brainerd Kellogg, in their book *Higher Lessons in English*, published in 1877. Sentence diagramming has gone in and out of fashion over the years, but it is a fine way to learn how to analyze the grammar and syntax of a sentence. And this grammatical analysis is an excellent preparation for the logical analysis that is the main focus of this book. Let's start with some basics and learn through examples. The different lines in the diagram are designed to indicate different kinds of functions the words in a sentence perform. Here are some of the features of the Reed-Kellogg system.

1. John runs.

This is a simple sentence. The diagram begins with a base line. The subject of the sentence is separated from the predicate by a vertical line extending through the base. The predicate contains a verb.

2. Students quietly read books.

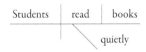

This sentence adds a direct object of the verb and a modifying adverb.

3. Teachers are effective leaders.

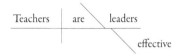

This sentence adds a predicate noun to the verb, and a modifying adverb.

4. I heard you were leaving.

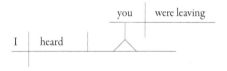

This sentence adds a clause as a direct object.

5. Children read books and emails.

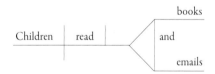

This sentence has two direct objects.

6. The fact is, you are not ready.

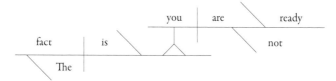

This sentence has a clause as a predicate nominative.

~~~~~~

7. Give the man your wallet.

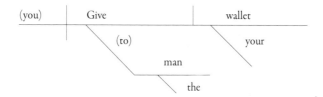

This sentence has an understood subject and an indirect object.

~~~~~~

8. Dawn, my cat, ate her food.

This sentence has an appositive.

~~~~~~

9. The stunned crowd watched the bridge falling into the river.

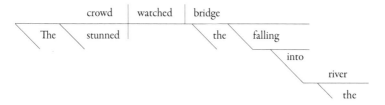

This sentence has a participle, a verbal form used as adjective.

~~~~~~

10. Studying hard can be profitable.

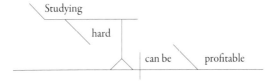

This sentence has for its subject a gerund, a verbal form used as a noun.

~~~

11. Pedro hit the ball well, but he ran to the wrong base.

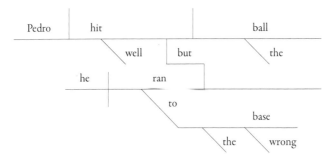

This is a compound sentence, composed of two clauses that could stand on their own. In logic, we will learn that, while simpler sentences contain only one proposition, a compound sentence contains two (or more) propositions.

~~~

12. St. Augustine said that sinning is easy.

This is a much-used kind of compound sentence called "indirect dis-course." In it, "that" is not a demonstrative adjective (like "that man") but is a conjunction. "That" comes as a translation of the Latin words *quod* and *quia*, which were used in sentences like this one. "That" functions as an opening quotation mark.

~~~

1 3. The man whom the grand jury indicted was arrested in Biloxi.

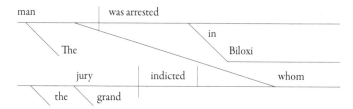

This is a complex sentence, composed of two clauses, but they cannot stand on their own, because one is subordinate to the other.

~~~

1 4. I want to meet a man who will treat me well.

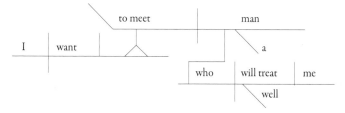

The direct object is a clause with an infinitive and direct object. The rest of the sentence is a subordinate clause explaining what kind of man he should be.

~~~

15. When the train goes through, the windows rattle noisily, and the whole house shakes.

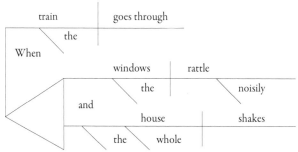

This is a compound-complex sentence. It begins with a subordinate clause saying when everything happens. After "through" we have a compound sentence with two independent clauses.

~~~

16. "I really do not know that anything has ever been more exciting than diagramming a sentence." (Gertrude Stein, 20th cen. English writer)

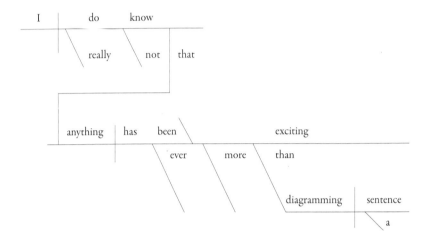

This sentence in indirect discourse is interesting on its own; but what makes it fun is that the author was a very eccentric English lady. She did many other things one might think are "more exciting."

It is possible to diagram much more complex sentences.

17. We the people of the United States, in order to form a more perfect Union, establish justice, insure domestic Tranquility, provide for the common defence, promote the general Welfare, and secure the Blessings of Liberty to ourselves and our Posterity, do ordain and establish this Constitution for the United States of America.

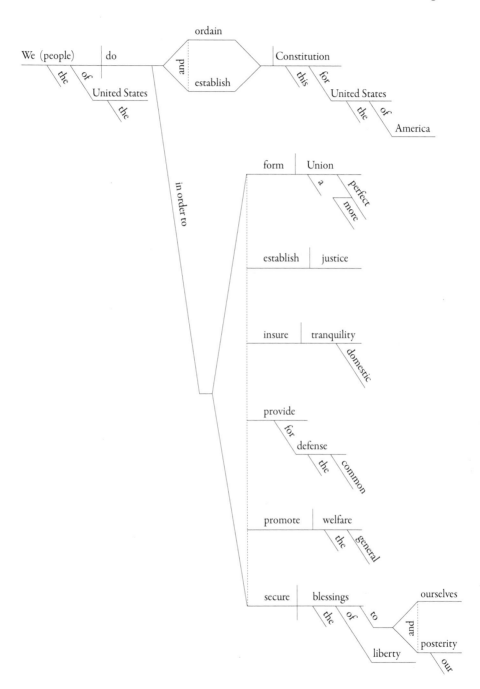

Some Helpful Websites and Webpages about Grammar and Syntax

Guide to Grammar and Writing, http://grammar.ccc.commnet.edu/grammar/index.htm.

"Basic Sentence Parts, Phrase Configurations," Guide to Grammar and Writing, http://grammar.ccc.commnet.edu/grammar/diagrams2/diagrams_frames.htm.

"500 Sentence Diagrams: English Grammar and Usage," *German—Latin—English*, http://www.german-latin-english.com/diagrams.htm.

"Sendraw," *University of Florida Department of English*, http://sendraw.ucf.edu/.

"Parts of Speech," *English Club*, http://www.englishclub.com/grammar/parts-of-speech_1.htm.

"How to Diagram a Sentence," *ThoughtCo*, http://homeworktips.about.com/od/englishhomework/ss/diagram.htm.

Problem Set 1: Grammar Review

Identifying the Eight Parts of Speech

Noun	Adjective	Adverb	Conjunction
Pronoun	Verb	Preposition	Interjection

Instructions

Identify examples of the parts of speech in ten of the sentences to be diagrammed in "Diagramming Sentences," below. Then take a few sentences from Gorgias, *Encomium of Helen* (from Problem Set 2) and identify each word's part of speech.

Diagramming Sentences

Instructions

Using the traditional method of diagramming sentences as introduced by A. Reed and B. Kellogg in *Higher Lessons in English Grammar* (1877) and recently popularized by Kitty Burns Florey in *Sister Bernadette's Barking Dog* (2006), diagram the following sentences:

1. John runs.
2. Students quietly read books.
3. Teachers are effective leaders.

4. I heard you were leaving.
5. Students read books and articles.
6. The fact is, you are not ready.
7. Give the man your money.
8. I jumped when he popped the balloon.
9. Eve, my cat, ate her food.
10. The dog barked.
11. The dog chased the rabbit.
12. The dog was tired.
13. The dog chased the rabbit into the woods down the road.
14. The dog gave us her paw.
15. Stop that loud barking!
16. The dog is doing what?
17. As she chased the rabbit down the road, Mildred wondered why she bothered, when she could be home eating dog food from her yellow bowl.
18. Trotting down the road in a red collar, I spotted the dog.
19. Chasing rabbits is fun.
20. Tuffy is a good dog, but maybe he needs obedience school or some plain old-fashioned discipline.
21. "Death is the black camel which kneels at every man's gate." (Arab proverb)[2]
22. "Time flies like an arrow but fruit flies like a banana." (Groucho Marx, 20th-cen. American comedian)
23. "His attention was called to her by the conduct of his dog, who had suddenly darted forward with a little volley of shrill barks, in which the note of welcome, however, was more sensible than that of defiance." (Henry James, 19th-cen. American novelist, *The Portrait of a Lady*)
24. "It is a truth universally acknowledged, that a single man in possession of a good fortune, must be in want of a wife." (Jane Austen, 18th cen. English novelist, *Pride and Prejudice*)
25. "So we beat on, boats against the current, borne back ceaselessly into the past." (F. Scott Fitzgerald, 20th-cen. American novelist, *The Great Gatsby*)

2. Jon R. Stone, *Routledge Book of World Proverbs* (Oxfordshire and New York: Routledge, 2006), 92.

26. "I could see the achieved sentence standing there, as real, intact, and built to stay as the Mississippi State Capitol at the end of my street." (Eudora Welty, 20th-cen. Southern American writer and photographer, *On Writing*)

27. "Sir Walter Elliot, of Kellynch Hall, in Somersetshire, was a man who, for his own amusement, never took up any book but the Baronetage; there he found occupation for an idle hour, and consolation in a distressed one; there his faculties were roused into admiration and respect, by contemplating the limited remnant of the earliest patents; there any unwelcome sensations, arising from domestic affairs changed naturally into pity and contempt as he turned over the almost endless creations of the last century; and there, if every other leaf were powerless, he could read his own history with an interest which never failed." (Jane Austen, 18th-cen. English novelist, *Persuasion*)

28. "The logician does not care particularly about this or that hypothesis or its consequences, except so far as these things may throw light upon the nature of reasoning." (Charles Sanders Peirce, 19th-cen. American philosopher)

Rhetoric: An Introduction

The Essentials

Historical Setting: The Invention of Rhetoric by the Greeks during the Fifth Century B.C.

The way that rhetoric and logic were born tells a lot about what these two crafts or arts are like. We will look here at the origins of rhetoric, the first of the two to be developed, then in Lesson 5 we will look at the invention of logic.

We begin with a historical fact. In 467 B.C. the people of Syracuse, a Greek colony in Sicily, deposed the political strong-man (*tyrannos*, from which we get the term "tyrant") ruling them, whose name was Hieron I. The Syracusans replaced Hieron's form of one-man rule with democracy, which literally means "rule by the common people" or "rule by the many." Two institutions central to Greek democracies quickly grew up in Syracuse and other Greek city-states that followed its lead in developing democratic forms of government: a popular assembly (*ekklesia*) designed to pass laws and make political decisions for the community and a law court designed to deal with those who broke the laws, where citizens decided guilt or innocence. The way decisions were made in both of these new institutions was through discussion and majority rule.

Traditionally Greeks had called a person who was most knowledgeable about the most important matter a "wise man" or "sage" (Gk. *sophos*). To be effective in this new political environment, a person needed to be skilled in delivering persuasive speeches. So there quickly sprang up a new kind of teacher who would teach the skills needed to carry the day in assembly or courtroom. Since what such men taught was good speaking (Gk. *rheo* or *ero*), the craft they taught was called the "art of rhetoric (*rhetorike techne*)" or just "rhetoric." Aristotle then defined rhetoric as "the art of observing in any given case the available means of persuasion." And to underscore how they were teaching this new kind of knowledge for a new kind of political life in a democracy, the teachers of rhetoric put a new ending on this traditional word and called themselves "sophist" (Gk. *sophistes*), from which we get, among other things, the English word "sophisticated."[1]

The Three Kinds of Rhetorical Discourse

The first of the Sicilian teachers of rhetoric, or sophists, was named Korax, and his student was Tisias. Both focused on teaching people how to be effective in the law courts and wrote textbooks on rhetoric that used sample scenarios to teach effective speaking. These books (called *technai*—that is, "technical manuals") have been lost, but they seem to have been organized around "topics." This word comes from the Greek word *topos* which means "place." So a topic in a rhetorical manual was a place in the book where one could find examples of the different rhetorical skills one could learn by imitation. In one place you would find examples of engendering the emotion of pity in the audience, in another you could see how to produce fear; one place would show you how to highlight your own qualities (*ethos*), while another would show how to "turn the tables" on your opponent.

Aristotle records this argument taken from the manual of Korax: "If an accused person is *not* open to the charge, for example, if a weak man is tried for violent assault, the defense is that he was not *likely* to do such a thing. But if he *is* open to the charge, for example, if he is a strong man, the defense is still that he was not *likely* to do such a thing, since he could be sure people would think he was likely to do it. And so with any other charge: the accused must be either open or not open to it, and there is in either case an appearance of *probable* innocence."[2]

1. For an introduction to Greek history and culture, see H. D. F. Kitto, *The Greeks* (New Brunswick, N.J.: Aldine, 2007).

2. Aristotle, *Rhetoric* 2.24, 1402a23–29.

This argument is not designed to show with absolute certainty that the accused is innocent, but is designed to point out an argumentative strategy, one that argues for innocence based on what is "probable" or "likely (Gk. *eikos*)," because such a "likely story" should be sufficient to have the jury render a finding of innocent. Familiarity with this scenario allows the student of rhetoric to adapt it to other cases. Over the centuries, this focus on probable or persuasive arguments that Tisias and Korax gave to legal rhetoric has remained a central technique in the lawyer's rhetorical arsenal.

Another Sicilian, a sophist named Gorgias, from the town of Leontini, applied rhetoric to a second area, the realm of political debate. In 427 B.C., just after the beginning of the Peloponnesian War between Sparta and Athens, he came to Athens as ambassador from Syracuse and was greatly applauded for his brilliant speeches He was especially prized by the Athenians for his sophisticated and ornate style of speaking.

In addition to speaking about political matters, Gorgias set up in Athens a popular school for teaching rhetoric, where Athenians could learn rhetorical skills useful in law court or political assembly. His *Encomium of Helen*, however, is not directly about legal or political matters, but concerns a mythical character, Helen of Troy, wife of the Spartan king Menelaus and reputedly the most beautiful woman in the world. She had left Sparta and her husband with a Trojan prince named Paris, and so the Greeks blamed her as the cause of the bloody Trojan War. Gorgias seems to have written his *Encomium* as a kind of advertisement for his school, since the implication of his speech is that rhetoric powerful enough to convince the Greeks, who hated Helen, of her innocence was certainly rhetoric worth paying good money to learn from him.

With Gorgias's *Encomium of Helen*, we complete the number of the kinds of rhetoric the Greek rhetoricians recognized. They set out three kinds of rhetorical discourse, based on three different kinds of speeches given:

1. *deliberative or political rhetoric*, which studies political speech and writing;
2. *forensic or legal rhetoric*, which studies legal speeches and writing; and
3. *display or ceremonial rhetoric* (*epideiktikos*) which studies ceremonial speeches and writing, as well as other persuasive discourse that is not directly political or legal.

The Wide Extent of Rhetoric

The Greek rhetoricians knew that these three areas studied by rhetoric do not exhaust the wide range of speaking and writing. They recognized poetry in many forms, history, and descriptions of the universe that Plato and Aristotle came to call "philosophy" (meaning "love of wisdom") and also called "science," a term we limit to only some of the disciplines one can study, say, in college. None of these forms of discourse are directly concerned with speaking (or writing) in a way that persuades, or tries to persuade, our fellow humans about how to act on a particular matter of practical life. This is why rhetoric as the Greeks understood it is a different art from these other studies. However, it is true that *all discourse*—whether written or spoken or just in the mind, whether designed directly to persuade someone of something or to narrate a tale or tell an abstract truth—**does have certain rhetorical features.** In a wide sense, then, all human discourse has rhetorical characteristics as well as grammatical and logical features. Consequently, the essentials of Greek rhetoric, as well as the verbal logic the Greeks invented, can help us in all our discourse, not just when we are trying to persuade our fellow citizens or the traffic cop or our mothers about some pressing practical matter. **Aristotle recognized the wide scope of both rhetoric and logic.** After noting that rhetoric is the counterpart of dialectic, he went on to say, "Both are concerned with things that come, more or less, within the general concern of all humans, and they do not belong to some limited discipline. Consequently, all humans make use, more or less, of both; for to some extent all attempt to discuss statements and maintain them [the concern of logic] and to defend themselves and attack others [the concern of rhetoric]."

The Three Rhetorical Appeals

As you read Gorgias's *Encomium of Helen*, you can see a second important feature of rhetorical discourse. Gorgias introduces his speech with a few general truths—the Greeks called them "maxims"—that you can easily accept. By beginning with some ideas with which his audience agrees, Gorgias presents himself as the kind of person to whom we should be willing to listen. This is a way of trying to persuade his audience not based on the content of the speech to come, but on the kind of character or skill or knowledge or qualifications of the speaker—Gorgias himself. The Greek rhetoricians called this mode of persuasion "ethical appeal" because it persuades the audience based on the qualities (*ethos*) of the speaker himself. Such ideas dispose us to listen to him. Then Gorgias sets out a few facts about Helen, lets us know from the beginning that he will "refute those who rebuke Helen," and presents four lines of reasoning that attempt to prove through reasoning that Helen is innocent. This kind of persuasion is called "rational appeal." Gorgias ends his speech by focusing on the powerful emotion of love, which appeals to the emotions of those in his audience and so is called an "emotional appeal." In Gorgias's *Encomium*, then, not only do we see an example of one of the three kinds of speeches the classical rhetoricians recognized, but we also see examples of the three appeals they taught.

So the three modes of rhetorical appeal are:

1. Ethical appeal (*ethos*)
2. Rational appeal (*logos*)
3. Emotional appeal (*pathos*)

In Lesson 3 we will learn how a persuasive speech should be organized, according to the ancient Rhetoricians. And in Lesson 4, we will go more thoroughly into these three appeals.

Primary Sources

1. Aristotle, *Sophistical Refutations*, c. 34, 183b17-33: For in the case of all discoveries the results of previous labors that have been handed down from other have been advanced bit by bit by those who have taken them on, whereas the original discoveries generally make an advance that is small at first, though much more useful than the development that later springs out of them. For it may be that in everything, as the saying is, the first start is the main part: and for this reason also it is the most difficult; for in proportion as it is most potent in its influence, so it is smallest in its compass and therefore most difficult to see: whereas when this is once discovered, it is easier to add and develop the remainder in connection with it. This is in fact what has happened in regard to rhetorical speeches and to practically all the other arts: for those who discovered the beginnings of them advanced them in all only a little way, whereas the celebrities of today are the heirs, so to speak, of a long succession of men who have advanced them bit by bit, and so have developed them to their present form, Tisias coming next after the first founder [that is, Korax], then Thrasymachus after Tisias, and Theodorus next to him, while several people have made their several contributions to it: and therefore it is not to be wondered at that the art has attained considerable dimensions.
2. Aristotle, *Rhetoric* 1.2, 1355b26: Rhetoric may be defined as the art of observing in any given case the available means of persuasion.

3. Aristotle, *Rhetoric* 1.3, 1358a36–b11: Rhetoric falls into three divisions, determined by the three classes of listeners to speeches. For of the three elements in speech-making—speaker, subject, and person addressed—it is the last one, the hearer, that determines the speech's end and object. The hearer must be either a judge, with a decision to make about things past or future, or an observer. A member of the assembly decides about future events, a juryman about past events, while those who merely decide on the orator's skill are observers. From this it follows that there are three divisions of oratory: (a) *political*, (b) *forensic*, and (c) the *ceremonial oratory of display*. Political speaking urges us either to do or not to do something: one of these two courses is always taken by private counselors, as well as by men who address public assemblies. Forensic speaking either attacks or defends somebody: one or the other of these two things must always be done by the parties in a law case. The ceremonial oratory of display either praises or censures somebody.

Problem Set 2: Rhetorical Analysis

Identifying the Rhetoric of Gorgias's *Encomium of Helen*

Instructions

Read the following speech composed by the sophist and rhetorician Gorgias. Then answer the following questions:

1. What *kind* of oratory is this speech: (a) deliberative or political oratory? (b) forensic? (c) display?
2. What is Gorgias's main conclusion or thesis?
3. Identify the parts of the speech (by using section numbers in parentheses) where Gorgias uses each of the three different *rhetorical appeals*:
   a. Ethical appeal
   b. Rational appeal
   c. Emotional appeal
4. What are the main *lines of argument* that Gorgias uses to prove his main conclusion? How many are there? Simplify each of these arguments, putting Gorgias's arguments in your own words.

Giorgias, *Encomium of Helen*

(1) What is becoming (*kosmos*) to a city is manpower, to a body beauty, to a soul wisdom, to an action virtue, to a speech truth, and the opposites of these are unbecoming. Man and woman and speech and deed and city and object should be honored with praise if praiseworthy and be blamed if blameworthy, for it is an equal error and mistake to blame what should be praised and to praise what should be blamed. (2) It is the duty of one and the same man both to speak

rightly about what is needed and to refute what is not spoken rightly. Thus it is right to refute those who rebuke Helen, a woman about whom the testimony of inspired poets has become as unanimous as the bad omen of her name, which has come to remind us of misfortunes. For myself, by introducing some reasoning into my speech, I wish to free the accused of blame and, having reproved her detractors as liars and proved the truth, to free her from their ignorance.

(3) Now it is not unclear, not even to a few, that in her nature and race the woman who is the subject of this speech is preeminent among humans. For it is well-known that her mother was Leda, and her father was actually a god, Zeus, but was thought to be a mortal, Tyndareus. (4) Born from such stock, her beauty was godlike, which lasted; no mistake about that. In many she produced great desire for her love, and her one body was the cause that drove off together many bodies of men, thinking great thoughts for great goals. For some the greatness of wealth, others the glory of ancient nobility, others the vigor of their own skills, and others the power acquired by knowledge. And all came because of a passion that loved to conquer and loved unconquerable honor. (5) Who it was and why and how he sailed away, taking Helen as his love, I shall not say. To tell the knowing what they know seems right but brings no delight.

I shall set forth the causes through which it was likely (*eikon*) that Helen's voyage to Troy should take place.

(6) For either by will of Fate and decision of the gods and vote of necessity did she do what she did, or taken by force, or seduced by words [or captured by love].

Now if in the first way, it is right for someone responsible to be held responsible; for a god's predetermination cannot be stopped by human premeditation. For it is the nature of things, not for the strong to be hindered by the weak, but for the weaker to be ruled and drawn by the stronger, for the stronger to lead and the weaker to follow. A god has more power than a mortal, in strength and mind, and many other ways. So if one must place blame on fate and a god, one must free Helen from disgrace.

(7) But if she was violently abducted or illegally assaulted or victimized unjustly, it is clear that the abductor, the assaulter, and the victimizer, did the wrong, and she who was abducted, assaulted, and victimized, did the suffering. So the barbarian abductor deserves to meet with a barbarous response, in speech and law and deed: blamed in speech, sentenced in law, and punished in deed. She who was forced, and removed from her homeland, and separated from her friends, is she not to be pitied rather than reviled? For he did terrible things; she was the victim; it is accordingly right to pity her and to hate him....

(12) Now if speech persuaded her soul, which it moved and compelled to believe the things said and to agree to the things done, he who persuaded, like an abductor, did wrong; but she who was persuaded, like one abducted, is wrongly blamed. (13) Persuasion, when added to speech, shapes the soul at will. This we can see: first, in the explanations of those who study nature, who, by discarding one opinion in favor of another, make what used to seem unbelievable and obscure become clear to the eyes of opinion; second, in powerful discourse, where a speech, written with art but not spoken with truth, delights and persuades the many; and third, in the competing arguments of philosophers [lovers of wisdom], in which quick thought is displayed, but makes believing an opinion something easy to change.

(14) The effect of speech upon the condition of the soul is comparable to the power of drugs over the physiology of the body. For just as different drugs draw off different humors from the body, and some kill disease and others kill life, the same is true of speeches: some distress, others delight; some cause fear, others induce courage; and some drug and bewitch the soul with a kind of evil persuasion. (15) This explanation means that if she was persuaded by speech, she did no wrong but was not favored by fortune.

Now I turn to the fourth cause. If it was because of love she did these things, there it will not be difficult to escape the charge alleged. For things we see do not have the nature we wish them to have, but the nature each one actually has. Through sight the soul receives an impression, even in its own way.

(16) When soldiers in war buckle on their martial bronze and steel, some for defense, others for attack, when sight sees this, immediately it is alarmed and it alarms the soul, so that often men flee, panic-stricken, from future danger, as though it were present. As strong as the custom of obeying the law is, it retreats because of fear that comes from sight, which causes a man no longer to care about what is thought honorable because of the law and advantageous because of victory.

(17) And it has happened that after seeing what is terrifying, they have lost their presence of mind about the immediate problem. This is how fear extinguishes and destroys thought. So many have fallen victim to useless deeds and frightful diseases and incurable madness. In this way, sight engraves on the mind images of things seen; many frightening impressions linger; and what lingers is exactly like what is spoken. . . .

(19) Consequently, if the eye of Helen, pleased by the figure of Alexander [Paris], that presented to her soul erotic desire and the embraces of love, what is so wondrous in that? If love, as a god, has the divine power found in the gods, how could a lesser being reject and refuse it? On the other hand, if love is a disease of human origin and a fault of the soul, it should not be blamed as an evil, but regarded as an affliction.

(20) How then can you think blaming Helen is just, since she did what she did from love or was persuaded by speech or abducted by force or because of fate? Whatever way, she is completely acquitted. (Gorgias, *Encomium of Helen*)[3]

---

3. Gorgias, *Encomium of Helen*, sec. 1–20, trans. R. E. Houser, in *Early Greek Philosophy*, ed., trans. André Laks and Glenn W. Most (Cambridge, Mass.: Loeb Classical Library, 2016), 8:166–85.

The Canon of Five Rhetorical Skills and the Five Parts of a Classical Speech

The Essentials

Rhetoric Concerns Argumentative Discourse

The classical Greeks initiated the idea that the educated person master three sets of verbal and writing skills, three "arts," governing the use of language, whether the language be spoken, written, or in the mind: grammar, rhetoric, and logic. Grammar is concerned with putting language in the proper form, following the rules for forming words, sentences, and paragraphs correctly; logic is concerned with formulating language rationally; and rhetoric concerns formulating language persuasively, as we have noted. The earliest rhetoricians were concerned with speech about practical matters—political and legal disputes—that were the focus of attention in the political assemblies and law courts of Greek democracies and the Roman republic. In this realm of life, knowledge is important because it leads to action. In the practical sphere, we do not seek knowledge for its own sake, as we do in the theoretical sphere, say, in geometry or poetry or philosophy.

To distinguish these two kinds of knowledge, Aristotle called political and legal knowledge, where it is supposed to lead beyond itself to action, "practical knowledge," which he contrasted with "theoretical" or "speculative" or "contemplative" knowledge, where our goal is just to understand something.[1] From the beginning, then, rhetoric was thought of as a kind of practical knowledge. Once Aristotle invented the discipline of logic, he thought of it as an instrument serving theoretical knowledge, and so he said, "Rhetoric is the counterpart of logic," rhetoric being the instrument (*organon*) we use to develop ideas in the practical sphere, while logic is the instrument we use in the theoretical sphere. But in fact, Aristotle slightly overemphasized the separation between rhetoric and logic, since every form of discourse has rhetorical characteristics as well as grammatical and logical ones. All three of the language arts work together.

Since they were primarily concerned with the political sphere of life, the early rhetoricians focused on the kind of discourse where the speaker's purpose is practical, trying to convince the audience with a call to action about some political or legal matter. Such speeches range from whether the Athenians should send a fleet to attack the people of Syracuse in Sicily, who were allies of the Spartans during the Peloponnesian War (they did, but were defeated); to George Washington's "Farewell Address," which tried to convince Americans not to form political parties or alliances with other countries (too often ignored); to Winston Churchill's speeches rallying the British and Americans during World War II (successful at the time, but too easily forgotten since). Such speeches are examples of what is called "argumentative" discourse. Argumentative discourse can be seen in contrast with three other forms of discourse.

One of these is narrative, where the author's purpose is to say what happened, to narrate a story, whether real or fictional, such as the kind of writing found in histories like those of Herodotus and Thucydides or the epic poems of Homer. Another is descriptive discourse, whose purpose is to set out the facts, as Pausanias did in his *Description of Greece*, a second-century A.D. tour guide of Greece, or Pliny's *Natural History*, an early description of the phenomena of nature. A third kind is expository, where one "exposes" the truth by giving an *explanation* of some matter or some position or view one has. Expository discourse adds to simple narration of events or description of facts an explanation that begins to answer the question *why*?

In the highly charged political and legal realm where the Greek and Ro-

---

1. Aristotle, *Nicomachean Ethics* 1.1.1094a1–17, 6.1–8.1138b18–1142a31.

man rhetoricians plied their arts, however, simply narrating or describing the facts, or even offering an explanation, was not enough; nor is it today. The reason is that in this realm there are competing views—Socrates is guilty vs. Socrates is innocent; slavery is acceptable vs. slavery is not; the United States should attack enemies militarily vs. the United States should not. So argumentative discourse adds attempts to prove both that your view is true and that other views are false or that the course of action you propose is the best while others are inferior.

The Canon of Five Rhetorical Skills

The early rhetoricians found that their art incorporates skills in five different but related areas. These skills are essential to delivering a persuasive speech in a law court or political assembly, but they are also required to speak or write effectively in other areas of life. The term "canon" comes from the Greek word *kanon*, a "straight rod" that masons and carpenters could use as a rule or ruler. The canon of rhetorical skills consists in five skills necessary to deliver a persuasive speech.

The five skills are:[2]

1. **invention** or **discovery**, finding what you need to say (Greek: *heuresis*, from which we get "heuristic"; Latin *inventio*);

2. **disposition** or **arrangement**, organizing the discourse appropriately (Greek: *taxis*, from which we get "taxonomy," the classification of living things into genera and species, and "taxidermist," who arranges the skin of the animal to look real; Latin: *dispositio*);

3. **style**, that is, using the best vocabulary and syntax for the audience (Greek: *lexis*, from the word for speaking; Latin: *elocutio*);

4. **memorization**, remembering what you want to say (Greek: *mneme*; Latin: *memoria*); and

5. **delivery**, learning the voice modulation, clarity, and emphasis that distinguish the good speaker, as well as all the body language that is involved (Greek: *hypokrisis*; Latin: *pronuntiatio*). The ancient rhetoricians distinguished these five skills because they recognized that proficiency in one does not ensure proficiency in the other skills, but proficiency in all five is required if you want to be a great speaker.

---

2. For a fuller treatment, with examples, see Edward P. G. Corbett, *Classical Rhetoric for the Modern Student* (New York: Oxford University Press, 1971).

Demosthenes, the great orator who in the fourth century B.C. warned the Athenians that Philip of Macedon was preparing to move south to conquer them, provides a memorable example of how different these five canonical skills really are. As a young man he had mastered the first four skills, but he could not overcome a natural stutter that ruined his delivery. His solution to this problem was to practice speaking by the seashore, putting a few of the smooth pebbles he found there into his mouth, until he could deliver a good speech with such "marbles in his mouth." Sadly, the Athenians did not listen. They were conquered by Philip, whose son Alexander then conquered the known world and came to be called "the Great."[3]

When he wrote his own textbook, which is the oldest one to survive intact, Aristotle organized his *Rhetoric* around the first three canonical skills—invention, arrangement, and style. Take a look at the outline of Aristotle's *Rhetoric* at the end of this chapter. Better yet, go to the library, find a translation of Aristotle's *Rhetoric*, and spend an hour reading the first two chapters, then look here and there in the book.

Rhetorical Invention

In the outline of his *Rhetoric*, you can see that Aristotle emphasizes discovery, to which books I and II are devoted, while book III covers both style and arrangement. His treatment is organized by topics. If you read a few chapters of Aristotle's book you can see that for each topic he offers a number of examples illustrating effective rhetorical skills and occasionally showing mistakes to avoid.

Rhetorical Arrangement

After treating discovery in books I and II, Aristotle turned to the style of speeches at the beginning of book III, and then he finished his book with the arrangement of the parts of a speech. He was familiar with the ideas of the earliest rhetoricians that a good speech should contain five parts.[4] They are:

1. **Prologue** introducing the speaker: (Greek: *prooimion*; Latin: *exordium*).
2. **Statement of the topic** or case under consideration, which included a narration of the relevant facts (Greek: *diegesis*; Latin: *narratio*) as well as a preliminary statement of the speaker's thesis (Greek: *prothesis*).

3. Plutarch, *Lives of the Noble Greeks and Romans*, "Demosthenes," sec. 6.
4. Aristotle, *Rhetoric* 3.13–19.

3. Speaker's proof or argument (Greek: *pistis*, which means "persuasion"; Latin: *confirmatio*), which often began with a preliminary outline or division of the points to be made (Greek: *diairesis*; Latin: *divisio*).

4. Refutation of the opponent (Latin: *confutatio*, which could take the form of a direct reply to the opponent, in Greek: *to pros ton antidokon*), or an interrogation of the opponent or his ideas (*erotesis*), or occasionally just some sort of Aside.

5. Conclusion (Greek: *epilogos*; Latin: *peroratio*). Aristotle recognized these five parts of a speech, but in the interests of simplicity he said that only two of them are absolutely essential for all kinds of speeches: "You must state your case (*prothesis*), and you must prove it (*pistis*)"; all the other parts are icing on the cake, as it were.

Applications

If you reread Gorgias's speech in Problem Set 2 entitled *Encomium of Helen*, you can see how he used the idea of the parts of a speech. Many famous later speeches have followed this five-part model. Learning this arrangement from classical rhetoric should help you see how discourse is organized. Start looking for the organization of everything you read, which will help you organize your own speech, writing, and thinking.

A Deeper Look

More on Invention

Aristotle's use of rhetorical topics reflects earlier rhetoricians, for whom a topic is a place in the textbook for memorizing important and striking examples, what we might call an ancient "sound-bite." The way to discover something to say, then, is to remember something memorable someone else said and then adapt it to your present speech or writing. In covering discovery, Aristotle first presents ideas based on the three kinds of speeches we saw in Lesson 2—deliberative, forensic, and display oratory. He calls the topics he covers there "special" or "specific" topics because they are specific to each one of these three types of speech. The rest of the topics he calls "general" because they are generally applicable to *all* kinds of speech and writing. Some of the general topics do not fall within the art (*techne*) of rhetoric, so Aristotle calls them "nontechnical." These include useful information coming from (1) authorities, (2) testimonies, (3) moral maxims, (4) the law, and (5) precedents. Such information does not come from knowing the art of rhetoric but from elsewhere, but it is important in order to speak persuasively. The rest of the topics he covers, which are more important, he calls "technical" because they are part of the art (*techne*) of rhetoric. They are organized according to the three appeals. The general topics Aristotle put together were somewhat haphazard and were further organized by later Greek and Roman rhetoricians. Many of Aristotle's general topics in rhetoric overlap with subjects studied by later Aristotelian logicians in their treatment of logic. This historical overlap shows the close connection between rhetoric and logic.

Look under Primary Sources for a couple of rhetorical topics taken from the twenty-eight topics Aristotle lists in his *Rhetoric,* bk. 2, c. 23. We will learn about a number of these general topics when we study the logic of terms. This is because rhetoric and logic both cover some of the same material—human verbal discourse—which has grammatical, rhetorical, and logical characteristics. It is the task of the three arts of the trivium to distinguish these features and study them systematically. Since these three arts all apply to the same thing, it is not surprising that they sometimes overlap. Over the centuries, this overlap has caused some rhetoricians to try to eliminate logic as a separate study, and it has caused many philosophers to dismiss rhetoric as unimportant or even downright harmful. Aristotle's moderate position was that both logic and rhetoric are important, and he explicitly rejected the ideas of both Plato and the Greek sophists that one of these disciplines should usurp the legitimate territory of the other.

Primary Sources

Aristotle, *Rhetoric*: Outline of the Contents

Since we don't cover the whole of Aristotle's *Rhetoric,* look over this outline to see its full scope. You can correlate the subdivision under "Discovery" with material in this lesson. If you find something especially interesting, use the outline to find where to go in Aristotle's book.

Topic (book/chapter)

I. Introduction: basic definition and scope of rhetoric (I.1–3)
II. Discovery or invention (Gk. *heuresis*; Lat. *inventio*)
   A. Special topics useful in one area of rhetoric (I.4–14)

        1. in *political* (deliberative) rhetoric (I.4–8)
        2. in *display* (*epideiktic*) rhetoric (I.9)
        3. in *forensic* (legal) rhetoric (I.10–14)
    B. General topics useful in all areas of rhetoric (I.15–II.26)
        1. nontechnical means of persuasion (I.15)
        2. The technical means of persuasion: three appeals
          a. ethical appeal I (II.1)
          b. emotional appeal: rhetorical study of the human emotions
            (II.2–11)
          c. ethical appeal II: rhetorical study of human character
            (II.12–18)
          d. rational appeal (II.19–26)
            (1) four general topics (II.19)
            (2) two general modes of persuasion: example (inductive) and
               enthymeme (deductive) (II.20)
            (3) moral maxims: general rules of good conduct (II.21)
            (4) using enthymemes (II.22)
            (5) twenty-eight useful types of rational topics (enthymemes)
               (II.23)
            (6) nine fallacious enthymemes (II.24)
            (7) enthymemes for refutation: counter-arguments and objec-
               tions (II.25)
III. Style (Gk. *lexis, hermeneia, phrasis*; Lat. *elocutio*) (III.1–12)
IV. Arrangement (Gk. *taxis*; Lat. *dispositio*) (*III.13–19*)
    A. Introduction (III.14–15)
    B. Narration of facts (III.16)
    C. Argument: in favor of your thesis and counterargument against
       opponent (III.17)
    D. Reply to your opponent (counterargument or interrogation) or
       Aside (III.18)
    E. Peroration (III.19)
V. Memorization (Gk. *mneme*; Lat. *memoria*) [not in Aristotle's book]
VI. Delivery (Gk. *hypokrisis*; Lat. *pronuntiatio*) [not in Aristotle's book]

Aristotle, *Rhetoric* 2.23, 1397a6–11; 1398a3–9.

Two of many rhetorical topics that help you discover something to say in your speech:

> 1. One topic is based upon looking at the opposite of the thing in question. Observe whether that opposite has the opposite quality. If it does not, you refute the original proposition; if it does, you establish this opposite. Example: "Temperance is beneficial; for licentiousness is hurtful." Or, as in the Messinian speech: "If war is the cause of our present troubles, peace is what we need to put things right again."
>
> 6. Another topic is to apply to the other speaker what he has said against you. It is an excellent reversal to give to a debate.... It was employed by Iphicrates in his reply to Aristophon. "Would you," he asked, "take a bribe to betray the fleet?" "No," said Aristophon. And Iphicrates replied, "Very good: if you, who are Aristophon, would not betray the fleet, would I, who am Iphicrates?" Only we must remember beforehand that the other man is more likely than you are to commit the crime in question, otherwise you will make yourself ridiculous.

Problem Set 3: The Rhetoric of Socrates in the *Apology*

The Kind of Rhetoric Socrates Uses

Instructions

Read Plato, *Apology of Socrates* (there are many adequate translations you can use). Then answer the following questions about this work:

1. What is the primary conclusion for which Socrates is arguing?
2. Assuming that Socrates is using one of the three types of rhetoric outlined by the Greek rhetoricians, which of the three fundamentally describes his speech: deliberative rhetoric, forensic rhetoric, ceremonial rhetoric?

The Parts of Socrates' Speech

Instructions

Divide Socrates' speech into parts, using the Stephanus numbers (the page numbers found in most editions of Plato) for dividing the speech. See how your parts compare with the five parts of a good speech recognized by the Greek rhetoricians:

a. introduction
b. narration or statement of facts,
c. proof or confirmation of the case,
d. refutation or aside discrediting the opposition,
e. peroration

The Three Rhetorical Appeals

The Essentials

topic

*The Triangle of Relations
Involved in Rhetoric*

speaker   audience

All persuasive speech and writing are designed to persuade some audience of something. This means that all rhetorical discourse involves three, not just two, factors. It involves the speaker and his audience, to be sure, but it also involves the subject the speaker addresses. We can envision these three factors as the three angles of a rhetorical triangle made up of speaker, topic, and audience. Each of these three parts of the triangle is an image of a different way of trying to convince the audience of something. This is why the core of the art of rhetoric is what Aristotle called the "three appeals"—that is, the three ways a persuasive speaker or writer appeals in his speech to his audience. A speaker skilled in the art of rhetoric can use any of the three. But very good speakers (or writers) will use all three, though in different ways.

The three types of appeal flow out of the three angles of this triangle.

Ethical Appeal (*Ethos*)

Ethical appeal focuses on the speaker himself. The term "ethical" comes from the Greek word *ethos*, which means "character," "ability," "skill," and, above all, the "knowledge" of the speaker. So ethical appeal consists in whatever the speaker says—explicitly or implicitly—that *tells us something about himself*. You use ethical appeal to communicate to the audience the qualities that you—as speaker (or writer)—have, the qualities that are the reason the audience should listen to you and believe what you say. If you are speaking about baseball, you might indicate the experiences that make your message worthwhile. The same goes for a rock star, a politician, a soldier, a lawyer, or simply the man on the street. A good speaker does this self-consciously; a great speaker does it spontaneously, because the art or skill of rhetoric is so engrained in him that it has become, as it were, second nature to him. So said the Roman orator-philosopher Cicero. Sometimes the ethical appeal is made very overtly: "When I received the bronze star for service with the Tenth Mountain Division in Afghanistan ...," or "In my book about Islam I said this about *sharia* law." But it is usually better to make the ethical appeal in more subtle ways, especially in a democratic society like the United States.

One mistake often made is to think of ethical appeal as only dealing with the part of philosophy called "ethics" or "morality." But this is *not* correct. It is based on confusing two Greek works: *ethos* and *ethikos*. The first term refers to a person's skills or habits and *is not limited to the topic of morality*. The second word, however, refers precisely to morality, right and wrong, good and bad behavior. So *don't* think that ethical appeal is limited to that area. Indicating you are an experienced painter has nothing to do with your personal morality, but is very important in advertising your house-painting business. This is an example of ethical appeal as the term is used in rhetoric.

Finally, let's note that ethical appeal is often misused. Over the last couple of decades in our increasingly interconnected and celebrity-driven culture, it has become fashionable for someone to claim to know something in one area—politics is a favorite—based on having become well-known in another. This is not something new. In Plato's *Apology*, Socrates made exactly this criticism of the Athenian leaders of his day. Movie stars are notorious for doing this, and they get away with it because of the increasing gullibility of an increasingly uneducated American public. One can be a fine actor—whose job it is to deliver convincingly lines someone else has written—even while being completely ignorant about the topic one is addressing.

Emotional Appeal (*Pathos*)

Emotional appeal concentrates not on the speaker but on the audience, and in a very particular way. The members of the audience who listen to the speaker have both minds and hearts—intelligence and emotions. The audience will be impacted by the words of the speaker in both ways. In using emotional appeal, the speaker attempts to say things in a way that will unleash in the hearts of the audience the "right" emotions—that is, the emotions that go hand in hand with the conclusions the speaker is attempting to have them draw. In this way, emotional appeal uses such emotions as the instrument or means for attaining conviction in the audience members. Sometimes the speaker himself shows emotions in order to elicit emotions in the audience. It is not the speaker's emotions, however, but the audience's emotions that are the focus of an emotional appeal. Such emotions are very effective in getting the audience to follow the call to action that the speaker asks for, especially in political and forensic oratory. World War II in the twentieth century saw the rise of two extraordinary orators—on opposing sides of the conflict—who used the new medium of radio to extraordinary effect. Winston Churchill, the British prime minister and war leader, was a tremendously effective speaker. "Never have so many owed so much to so few," he said of the pilots who saved his homeland during the air "Battle of Britain" early in the war. After the war, when the facts about the Jewish Holocaust came out, it became popular to think of Adolf Hitler as a madman, a sort of incarnation of the devil. But such a caricature makes it impossible to understand his rise to power. Evil though he would prove to be, Hitler was an extraordinary speaker. It was based in part upon the speeches he gave at the Nuremburg rallies in the 1930s that he took the Nazis from a marginal movement to running the German government. "One Folk, one Fatherland, one Führer," was one of Hitler's many effective slogans. While these two examples of effective rhetoric use more than emotional appeal, it is the emotional appeal of patriotism—the love of country—that drives them and makes them memorable, even this many years later.

Rational Appeal (*Logos*)

According to Aristotle, the most important of the three appeals concentrates on the message about the topic at hand that the speaker (or writer) is trying to deliver. Here the speaker is appealing to the audience again, but to the mind of the audience, trying to show that facts and arguments about the topic—its content, not its emotional power or his own qualifications—are persuasive. Most of the *content* of persuasive discourse is concerned with this appeal. Here the speaker organizes his facts and makes his arguments. But the presentation of facts and the kind of arguments one makes should depend upon the audience you have in mind. A physicist will speak very differently to a room full of professional physicists at an academic meeting than to his Physics 1 class. Rational appeal is where rhetoric and logic come together. In fact, one could say the logic simply *is* a major part of rational appeal. Of course, for a rational appeal to work, the speaker (or writer) must understand his subject—and logic alone cannot produce this understanding. But we have all heard very learned scholars talk about fields they know quite well—perhaps they are world experts on the topic—but are so rhetorically inept that they are not at all convincing, especially when the audience is not other experts but the public at large.

This is a constant problem in our society, where technical expertise has the upper hand over broad education in the liberal arts. And it leads to the situation we've all experienced: you should believe me, or worse, you *must do* what I say, simply because I am the so-called expert in the field and hold a position of power in our society. Lawyers, judges, doctors, and yes, professors, are especially inclined toward this attitude, which is simply an exercise of the powerful over the powerless.

A Deeper Look

Using and Distinguishing the Three Appeals

Additional points about the three appeals are worth noting. First, quite often (though not always), ethical appeal is used at the beginning of a speech in order to make the audience receptive to the speaker's message; a good speech usually ends with an emotional appeal that will still be "ringing in their ears" as the audience departs the speech or puts down the pamphlet or newspaper; rational appeal makes up most of the content and the middle part of most good persuasive discourse. It is a shame that over the centuries rhetoric often was reduced to concerning itself with emotional appeal and style, which is part of the reason it is now studied far too little. But the examples of Churchill, Hitler, and modern advertising show how influential rhetorical appeals can be.

Second, in really fine persuasive speaking and writing, a given passage will combine two or even all three of these modes of appeal. Very succinct speeches—like Lincoln's *Gettysburg Address*—always combine appeals in this way. With discourse that combines two or three appeals together, however, it is always possible to distinguish the three appeals and note which appeal is *predominant* in a particular passage of the speech or writing. In fact, it is necessary to do so. For if one does not distinguish different forms of appeal, an emotional or ethical appeal can lead us to accept a conclusion and then lead us to do a very illogical thing to accept the speaker's reasoning, even if it is wrong, because it is built on bad principles.

This is the way bad ideas can come to be accepted by us and our society (much to our detriment), through what I call "the iron rule of logic." First one accepts—perhaps with hesitation—a dubious principle that leads to a much-desired conclusion. Then over time the principle is fully embraced, but leads to other conclusions, ones you would have rejected when the principle was first hesitantly accepted, but is now accepted as correct, based on embracing that very principle. History is rife with examples. Mussolini "made the trains run on time," but involved Italy in wars they could not win on their own, even in alliance with Nazi Germany. Hitler himself came to power because he promised to clean up the terrible economic and political mess created in Germany after World War I by the economic punishment handed out to Germany under the Treaty of Versailles and by the extreme democracy of the German Weimar Republic. But then Hitler's political principles led directly to World War II and the Jewish Holocaust, at a time when "sophisticated" opinion held that World War I had been "the war to end all wars." And the same thing has happened in the United States. The Supreme Court in *Brown v. Board of Education* struck down segregation—an excellent result; but to do so the Court used the principle "separate is inherently unequal" and therefore bad, which in turn produced many controversial results. For instance, in the field of education, most of the women's colleges that used to exist in the United States have become co-ed or have shut down on the grounds that "separate is inherently unequal."

Whatever your reaction to these kinds of cases, they clearly show the importance of making distinctions—rhetorical and logical distinctions in addition to grammatical ones. This is ultimately one of the main reasons for studying rhetoric and logic. If we don't make such distinctions, then we will swallow persuasive discourse whole, say, supporting "change" without knowing what kind of change involved, or rejecting "change" as something always bad. And such attitudes are the definition not of the liberally education person—the "free" man—but of the slave, a slave first to discourse and then to raw power; for the second follows necessarily—that is, logically—from the first.

Primary Sources

Aristotle's *Rhetoric* 1.2: Definition of Rhetoric and the Three Appeals

> Rhetoric may be defined as the faculty of observing in any given case the available means of persuasion. This is not a function of any other art. Every other art can instruct or persuade about its own particular subject-matter: for instance, medicine about what is healthy and unhealthy, geometry about the properties of magnitudes, arithmetic about numbers; and the same is true of the other arts and sciences. But rhetoric we look upon as the power of observing the means of persuasion on almost any subject presented to us; and that is why we say that, in its technical character, it is not concerned with any special or definite class of subjects. . . .
>
> Of the modes of persuasion furnished by the spoken word there are three kinds. The first kind depends on the personal character (*ethos*) of the speaker; the second on how it affects the audience (*pathos*); the third on the proof, or apparent proof, provided by the words of the speech itself (*logos*). (*Rhetoric* 1.2, 1355b26–36, 1356a1–3)

Three Factors in the Orator's Character Relevant to Ethical Appeal

> There are three things which inspire confidence in the orator's own character (*ethos*) the three, namely, that induce us to believe a thing apart from any proof of it: good sense, good moral character, and good will. (*Rhetoric* 2.1, 1378a6–9)

Factors about the Human Condition That Apply to the Speaker (Relevant to Ethical Appeal) or to the Audience (Relevant to Emotional Appeal)

> Age: youth, the prime of life; old age. Status: birth; wealth; power. (*Rhetoric* 2.12–17)

Aristotle's List of the Human Emotions That the Good Speaker Must Understand and Can Use

> Anger and calmness; friendship and hatred; fear and confidence; shame and shamelessness; kindness and unkindness; pity and indignation; envy and emulation. (*Rhetoric* 2.2–11)

Problem Set 4: The Three Appeals

Finding the Predominant Kind of Rhetorical Appeal

Instructions

For each of the following selections, answer these questions:

a. What is the *primary* point or conclusion?

b. Which of the three appeals—ethical, emotional, or rational—is *predominantly* used?

c. Give two reasons for your answer to (b).

1. Benjamin Franklin, *Speech in the Constitutional Convention on the Subject of Salaries*, June 2, 1787

> It is with reluctance that I rise to express a disapprobation of any one article of the plan, for which we are so much obliged to the honorable gentleman who laid it before us. From its first reading, I have borne a good will to it, and, in general, wished it success. In this particular of salaries to the executive branch, I happen to differ; and, as my opinion may appear new and chimerical, it is only from a persuasion that it is right, and from a sense of duty, that I hazard it. The Committee will judge of my reasons when they have heard them, and their judgment may possibly change mine. I think I see inconvenience in the appointment of salaries; I see none in refusing them, but on the contrary great advantages.

2. Edmund Burke, *Reflections on the Revolution in France* (1790)

> It is now sixteen or seventeen years since I saw the queen of France, then the dauphiness, at Versailles; and surely never lighted on this orb, which she hardly seemed to touch, a more delightful vision. I saw her just above the horizon, decorating and cheering the elevated sphere she just began to move in—glittering like the morning-star, full of life, and splendor, and joy. Oh! What a revolution! And what a heart must I have to contemplate without emotion that elevation and that fall! Little did I dream when she added titles of veneration to those of enthusiastic, distant, respectful love, that she should ever be obliged to carry the sharp antidote against disgrace concealed in that bosom; little did I dream that I should have lived to see such disasters fallen upon her in a nation of gallant men, in a nation of men of honor and of cavaliers. I thought then a thousand swords must have leaped from their scabbards to avenge even a look that threatened her with insult. But the age of chivalry is gone. That of sophisters, economists, and calculators, has succeeded; and the glory of Europe is extinguished forever. Never, never more, shall we behold that generous loyalty to rank and sex, that proud submission, that dignified obedience, that subordination of the heart, which kept alive, even in servitude itself, the spirit of an exalted freedom. The unbought grace of life, the cheap defense of nations, the nurse of manly sentiment and heroic enterprise is gone! It is gone, that sensibility of principle, that chastity of honor, which felt a stain like a wound, which inspired courage whilst it mitigated ferocity, which ennobled whatever it touched, and under which vice itself lost half its evil, by losing all its grossness.

3. Arnold Toynbee, *Civilization on Trial* (1948)

> Does history repeat itself? In our Western world in the eighteenth and nineteenth centuries, this question used to be debated as an academic exercise. The

spell of well-being which our civilization was enjoying at the time had dazzled our grandfathers into the quaint pharisaical notion that they were "not as other men are"; they had come to believe that our Western society was exempt from the possibility of falling into those mistakes and mishaps that have been the ruin of certain other civilizations whose history, from beginning to end, is an open book. To us, in our generation, the old question has rather suddenly taken on a new and very practical significance. We have awakened to the truth (how, one wonders, could we ever have been blind to it?) that Western man and his works are no more invulnerable than the now extinct civilizations of the Aztecs and the Incas, the Sumerians and the Hittites. So today, with some anxiety, we are searching the scriptures of the past to find out whether they contain a lesson that we can decipher. Does history give us any information about our own prospects? And, if it does, what is the burden of it? Does it spell out for us an inexorable doom, which we can merely await with folded hands, resigning ourselves, as best we may, to a fate that we cannot avert or even modify by our own efforts? Or does it inform us, not of certainties, but of probabilities, or bare possibilities in our own future? The practical difference is vast, for, on this second alternative, so far from being stunned into passivity, we should be roused to action. On this second alternative, the lesson of history would not be like an astrologer's horoscope; it would be like a navigator's chart, which affords the seafarer who has the intelligence to use it a much greater hope of avoiding shipwreck than when he was sailing blind, because it gives him the means, if he has the skill and courage to use them, of steering a course between charted rocks and reefs.

4. William Shakespeare, *Julius Caesar* III.2 (ca. 1599)

Mark Antony's speech after Julius Caesar has been killed:

You all do know this mantle. I remember
The first time ever Caesar put it on.
'Twas on a summer's evening, in his tent,
That day he overcame the Nervii.
Look, in this place ran Cassius' dagger through.
See what a rent the envious Casca made.
Through this the well-beloved Brutus stabbed,
And as he plucked his cursed steel away,
Mark how the blood of Caesar followed it,
As rushing out of doors, to be resolved
If Brutus so unkindly knocked, or no.
For Brutus, as you know, was Caesar's angel.
Judge, O you gods, how dearly Caesar loved him.

This was the most unkindest cut of all,
For when the noble Caesar saw him stab,
Ingratitude, more strong than traitors' arms,
Quite vanquished him. Then burst his mighty heart,
And, in his mantle muffling up his face,
Even at the base of Pompey's statue,
Which all the while ran blood, great Caesar fell.

5. Leonard S. Spector, *Nuclear Proliferation Today* (1984)

The spread of nuclear weapons poses one of the greatest threats of our time and is among the most likely triggers of a future nuclear holocaust. It is sobering, for example, to reflect on how the superpowers might have responded if Israel had used nuclear weapons against Soviet-backed Egyptian forces in the 1973 Middle East War, a course Israel reportedly considered.

Even if nuclear cataclysm were avoided, the use of nuclear arms in a regional war could cause untold devastation. A handful of nuclear weapons could destroy any country in the Middle East as a national entity, cause hundreds of thousands of casualties in the densely populated cities of India or Pakistan, or, if used against the Persian Gulf oil fields, undermine the economies of the West.

6. Jane Austen, *Pride and Prejudice* (1813), Chapter 19

In which Mr. Collins proposes marriage to Elizabeth Bennett:

My reasons for marrying are, first, that I think it a right thing for every clergyman in easy circumstances, like myself, to set the example of matrimony in his parish; secondly, that I am convinced it will add very greatly to my happiness; and thirdly—which perhaps I ought to have mentioned earlier—that it is the particular advice and recommendation of the very noble lady whom I have the honor of calling patroness [Lady Catherine de Burgh]. Twice has she condescended to give me her opinion, unasked too! on this subject: and it was but the very Saturday night before I left Huntsford—between our pools at quadrille, while Mrs. Jenkinson was arranging Miss de Bourgh's footstool, that she said, "Mr. Collins, you must marry. A clergyman like you must marry. Choose properly, choose a gentlewoman for *my* sake; and for your *own*, let her be an active, useful sort of person, not brought up high, but able to make a small income go a good way. This is my advice. Find such a woman as soon as you can, bring her to Huntsford, and I will visit her." Allow me, by the way, to observe, my fair cousin, that I do not reckon the notice and kindness of Lady Catherine de Bourgh as among the least of the advantages in my power to offer. You will find her manners beyond anything I can describe: and your wit and vivacity, I think, must be acceptable to her, especially when tempered with the silence and respect which her rank will inevitably excite.

Thus much for my general intention in favor of matrimony: it remains to be told why my views were directed to Longbourn instead of my own neighbourhood, where I assure you there are many amiable young women. But the fact is that being, as I am, to inherit this estate after the death of your honored father, who, however, may live many years longer, I could not satisfy myself without resolving to choose a wife from among his daughters, that the loss to them might be as little as possible, when the melancholy event takes place, which, however, as I have already said, may not be for several years. This has been my motive, my fair cousin, and I flatter myself it will not sink me in your esteem. And now nothing remains for me but to assure you in the most animated language of the violence of my affection. To fortune I am perfectly indifferent, and shall make no demand of that nature on your father, since I am well aware that it could not be complied with; and that one thousand pounds in the four percents, which will not be yours till after your mother's decease, is all that you may ever be entitled to. On that head, therefore, I shall be uniformly silent; and you may assure yourself that no ungenerous reproach shall ever pass my lips when we are married.

7. *Genesis* **18–19 (selections): Sodom and Gomorrah, RSV, abridged and with emendations.**

(18:1) And the LORD appeared to Abraham by the oaks of Mamre, as he sat at the door of his tent in the heat of the day. (2) He lifted up his eyes and looked, and behold, three men stood in front of him. When he saw them, he ran from the tent door to meet them, and bowed himself to the earth.... (9) They said to him, "Where is Sarah your wife?" And he said, "She is in the tent." (10) The LORD said, "I will surely return to you in the spring, and Sarah your wife shall have a son." And Sarah was listening at the tent door behind him. (11) Now Abraham and Sarah were old, advanced in age; it had ceased to be with Sarah after the manner of women. (12) So Sarah laughed to herself,...

(16) Then the men set out from there, and they looked toward Sodom; and Abraham went with them to set them on their way. (17) The LORD said, "Shall I hide from Abraham what I am about to do, (18) seeing that Abraham shall become a great and mighty nation, and all the nations of the earth shall bless themselves by him? (19) No, for I have chosen him, that he may charge his children and his household after him to keep the way of the LORD by doing righteousness and justice; so that the LORD may bring to Abraham what he has promised him." (20) Then the LORD said, "Because the outcry against Sodom and Gomor'rah is great and their sin is very grave, (21) I will go down to see whether they have done altogether according to the outcry which has come to me; and if not, I will know." (22) So the men turned from there, and went toward Sodom; but Abraham still stood before the LORD.

(23) Then Abraham drew near, and said, "Wilt thou indeed destroy the righteous with the wicked? (24) Suppose there are fifty righteous within the city; wilt thou then destroy the place and not spare it for the fifty righteous who are in it? (25) Far be it from thee to do such a thing, to slay the righteous with the wicked, so that the righteous fare as the wicked! Far be that from thee! Shall not the Judge of all the earth do right?" (26) And the LORD said, "If I find at Sodom fifty righteous in the city, I will spare the whole place for their sake." (27) Abraham answered, "Behold, I have taken upon myself to speak to the Lord, I who am but dust and ashes. (28) Suppose five of the fifty righteous are lacking? Wilt thou destroy the whole city for lack of five?" And he said, "I will not destroy it if I find forty-five there." (29) Again he spoke to him, and said, "Suppose forty are found there." He answered, "For the sake of forty I will not do it." (30) Then he said, "Oh let not the Lord be angry, and I will speak. Suppose thirty are found there." He answered, "I will not do it, if I find thirty there." (31) He said, "Behold, I have taken upon myself to speak to the Lord. Suppose twenty are found there." He answered, "For the sake of twenty I will not destroy it." (32) Then he said, "Oh let not the Lord be angry, and I will speak again but this once. Suppose ten are found there." He answered, "For the sake of ten I will not destroy it." (33) And the LORD went his way, when he had finished speaking to Abraham; and Abraham returned to his place.

(19:1) The two angels came to Sodom in the evening; and Lot was sitting in the gate of Sodom. When Lot [a nephew of Abraham] saw them, he rose to meet them, and bowed himself with his face to the earth, (2) and said, "My lords, turn aside, I pray you, to your servant's house and spend the night, and wash your feet; then you may rise up early and go on your way." They said, "No; we will spend the night in the street." (3) But he urged them strongly; so they turned aside to him and entered his house; and he made them a feast, and baked unleavened bread, and they ate. (4) But before they lay down, the men of the city, the men of Sodom, both young and old, all the people to the last man, surrounded the house; (5) and they called to Lot, "Where are the men who came to you tonight? Bring them out to us, that we may know them." (6) Lot went out of the door to the men, shut the door after him, (7) and said, "I beg you, my brothers, do not act so wickedly. (8) Behold, I have two daughters who have not known man; let me bring them out to you, and do to them as you please; only do nothing to these men, for they have come under the shelter of my roof." (9) But they said, "Stand back!" And they said, "This fellow came to sojourn, and he would play the judge! Now we will deal worse with you than with them." ... (15) When morning dawned, the angels urged Lot, saying, "Arise, take your wife and your two daughters who are here, lest you be consumed in the punishment of the city." (16) But he lingered; so the men seized him and his wife and his two daughters by the hand, the LORD being merciful to him, and they brought him forth and set him outside the city. (17) And when they had brought them forth, they said, "Flee for your life; do not look back or stop anywhere in the valley; flee to the hills, lest you be consumed." ... (23) The sun had risen on the earth when Lot came to Zo'ar. (24) Then the LORD rained on Sodom and Gomor'rah brimstone and fire from the LORD out of heaven; (25) and he overthrew those cities, and all the valley, and all the inhabitants of the cities, and what grew on the ground. (26) But Lot's wife behind him looked back, and she became a pillar of salt. (27) And Abraham went early in the morning to the place where he had stood before the LORD; (28) and he looked down toward Sodom and Gomor'rah and toward all the land of the valley, and beheld, and lo, the smoke of the land went up like the smoke of a furnace.

8. From *Sahih Muslim*, by Muslim ibn al-Hajjaj al-Nisaburi

(d. 875), compiler of hadiths, stories and sayings about the prophet Muhammad (d. 632), bk. 1 (on Faith), chapter 1, number 1:

It is narrated on the authority of Yahya b. Ya'mur that the first man who discussed about *Qadr* (= divine predestination) in Basra was Ma'bad al-Juhani. I along with Humaid b. 'Abdur-Rahman Himyari set out for pilgrimage or for 'Umrah and said: "Should it so happen that we come into contact with one of the Companions of the Messenger of Allah (= Muhammad), peace be upon him, we shall ask him about what is said about *Taqdir* (= predestined fate). Accidentally we came across Abdullah ibn Umar ibn al-Khattab (= son of Umar ibn Khattab, the second of the first four 'rightly guided' caliphs of the Muslims), while he was entering the mosque. My companion and I went up to him, one of us on his right and the other stood on his left. I expected that my companion would authorize me to speak. I therefore said: 'Abu Abdur Rahman, there have appeared some people in our land who recite the Holy Qur'an and pursue knowledge.' And then after talking about their affairs, he (=my companion) added: 'They claim that there is no such thing as *Qadr* (= divine predestination) and that events are not predestined.' He (= Abdullah ibn Umar) said: 'When you happen to meet such people tell them that I have nothing to do with them and they have nothing to do with me. And verily they are in no way in accord with my (belief).' Abdullah ibn Umar swore the Lord: 'If any one of them had with him gold equal to the bulk of Mt. Uhud, then, Allah would not accept it unless he affirmed his faith in *Qadr* (= divine predestination).'

"'He further said: 'My father, Umar ibn al-Khattab told me:

"'One day we were sitting in the company of Allah's Apostle (= Muhammad), peace be upon him, when there appeared before us a man dressed in pure white clothes, his hair extraordinarily black. There were no signs of travel on him. None amongst us recognized him. At last he sat with the Apostle, peace be upon him. He (= the visitor) knelt before him, placed his palms on his thighs, and said:

"'Muhammad, inform me about al-Islam (= duties required of Muslims; Islam = submission).' The Messenger of Allah, peace be upon him, said: '*Al-Islam* includes that (1) you testify that there is no god but Allah and that Muhammad is the messenger of Allah, and (2) you say your daily prayer, (3) pay *Zakat* (= alms), (4) observe the fast of Ramadan, and (5) perform pilgrimage to Mecca, if you are solvent enough for the journey.' He (= the visitor) said: 'You have told the truth.' He (Umar ibn al-Khattab) said: 'We were filled with wonder that he would put the question and then he would himself verify the truth.'

"'He (= the visitor) said: 'Inform me about *Iman* (faith).' He (= Muhammad) replied: 'That you affirm your faith (1) in Allah, (2) in His angels, (3) in His Books, (4) in His Apostles, (5) in the Day of Judgment, and (6) you affirm your faith in the *Qadr* (= divine predestination) about good and evil.' He (= the visitor) said: 'You have told the truth.'

"'He (the visitor) again said: 'Inform me about *al-Ihsan* (= performance of good deeds).' He (= Muhammad) said: 'That you worship Allah as if you are seeing Him, for though you don't see Him, He, verily, sees you.' He (= the visitor) again said: 'Inform me about the hour (of the end of the world).' He (= Muhammad) remarked: 'The one who is asked knows no more than the one who is inquiring.' He (the visitor) said: 'Tell me some of its signs. He (= Muhammad) said: 'That the slave-girl will give birth to her mistress and master, that you will find barefooted, destitute goat-herds vying with one another in the construction of magnificent buildings.'

He (the narrator of the story, Umar ibn al-Khattab, second caliph) said: "Then he (= the visitor) went on his way but I stayed with him (= Muhammad) for a long while. He then, said to me: 'Umar, do you know who this visitor was?' I replied: 'Allah and His Apostle knows best.' He (= Muhammad) remarked: He was *Jibril* (= the angel Gabriel). He came to you in order to instruct you in matters of religion.'"

9. Abraham Lincoln, *Gettysburg Address* (1864)

Four score and seven years ago our fathers brought forth, upon this continent, a new nation, conceived in Liberty, and dedicated to the proposition that all men are created equal.

Now we are engaged in a great civil war, testing whether that nation, or any nation so conceived, and so dedicated, can long endure. We are met here on a great battlefield of that war. We have come to dedicate a portion of it as a final resting place for those who here gave their lives that that nation might live. It is altogether fitting and proper that we should do this.

But in a larger sense we cannot dedicate—we cannot consecrate—we cannot hallow this ground. The brave men, living and dead, who struggled here, have consecrated it far above our poor power to add or detract. The world will little note, nor long remember, what we say here, but can never forget what they did here.

It is for us, the living, rather to be dedicated here to the unfinished work which they have, thus far, so nobly carried on. It is rather for us to be here dedicated to the great task remaining before us—that from these honored dead we take increased devotion to that cause for which they here gave the last full measure of devotion—that we here highly resolve that these dead shall not have died in vain; that this nation shall have a new birth of freedom; and that this government of the people, by the people, for the people, shall not perish from the earth.

10. Barack H. Obama, "State of the Union Address" (2015)

2014 was the planet's warmest year on record. Now, one year doesn't make a trend, but this does—fourteen of the fifteen warmest years on record have all fallen in the first fifteen years of this century.

I've heard some folks try to dodge the evidence by saying they're not scientists; that we don't have enough information to act. Well, I'm not a scientist, either. But you know what—I know a lot of really good scientists at NASA, and NOAA, and at our major universities. The best scientists in the world are all telling us that our activities are changing the climate, and if we do not act forcefully, we'll continue to see rising oceans, longer, hotter heat waves, dangerous droughts and floods, and massive disruptions that can trigger greater migration, conflict, and hunger around the globe. The Pentagon says that climate change poses immediate risks to our national security. We should act like it.

That's why, over the past six years, we've done more than ever before to combat climate change, from the way we produce energy, to the way we use it. That's why we've set aside more public lands and waters than any administration in history. And that's why I will not let this Congress endanger the health of our children by turning back the clock on our efforts. I am determined to make sure American leadership drives international action. In Beijing, we made an historic announcement—the United States will double the pace at which we cut carbon pollution, and China committed, for the first time, to limiting their emissions. And because the world's two largest economies came together, other nations are now stepping up, and offering hope that, this year, the world will finally reach an agreement to protect the one planet we've got.

11. Ivar Giaevar, Nobel Prizewinner in Physics (1973), on Global Warming (2015)

As part of the 62nd Lindau Nobel Laureate Meeting, Giaever referred to agreement with the evidence of climate change as a "religion" and commented on the significance of the apparent rise in temperature when he stated, "What does it mean that the temperature has gone up 0.8 degrees [in 150 years]? Probably nothing." Referring to the selection of evidence in his presentation, Giaever stated, "I pick and choose when I give this talk just the way the previous speaker (Mario Molina) picked and chose when he gave his talk." Giaever concluded his presentation with a pronouncement: "Is climate change pseudoscience? If I'm going to answer the question, the answer is: absolutely."

12. Teresa of Ávila, from *Interior Castle*

(d. 1582), Spanish mystic, reformer of the Carmelite Orders of both women and men, mentor of St. John of the Cross:

There is a secret place. A radiant sanctuary. As real as your own kitchen. More real than that. Constructed of the purest elements. Overflowing with the ten thousand beautiful things. Worlds within worlds. Forests, rivers. Velvet coverlets thrown over featherbeds, fountains bubbling beneath a canopy of stars. Bountiful forests, universal libraries. A wine cellar offering an intoxication so sweet you will never be sober again. A clarity so complete you will never again forget. This magnificent refuge is inside you. Enter. Shatter the darkness that shrouds the doorway.... Believe the incredible truth that the Beloved has chosen for his dwelling place the core of your own being because that is the single most beautiful place in all of creation.

Aristotle Invents Logic—Twice

The Essentials

Aristotle (d. 323 B.C.) invented logic. This does not mean that he was the first man to reason logically. As long as there have been humans on earth they have reasoned, and their reasoning has been a combination of logical and illogical reasoning. Nor does it mean that Aristotle was the first man to reason with great logical acuity. His teacher Plato (d. 347 B.C.) and before him his teacher Socrates (d. 399 B.C.) used logic with a great degree of accuracy, far beyond the degree most of us can achieve. And great thinkers in other traditions did so as well, such as K'ung Fu-tzu (Confucius; ca. 500 B.C.), who said, "Ignorance is the night of the mind, and a night without moon and stars," and Gautama Buddha (d. ca. 410 B.C.), who said, "All that we are is the result of what we have thought." While they *used* logic; they did not *invent* logic as a systematically organized subject that one could study and write about on its own. To note the difference between using logic in our thought, speech, and writing and logic as a subject to be studied, much later in history, Western medieval logicians distinguished *logica utens* (logic as it is used by thinkers) from *logica docens* (logic as a subject for teaching and studying). It was *logica docens*—logic as a discipline taught and studied, such as we are doing in this book—that Aristotle, for the first time in history, invented. In short, Aristotle invented logic as an "art" or skill to be learned from a teacher and a book, which means he wrote the first logic textbook. In point of fact, however, even a thinker as brilliant and creative as Aristotle did not get everything right on his first try. He had to invent logic twice, a fact that is recorded in the textbooks he wrote on the subject.

Aristotle's First Try: Topical Logic

In Aristotle's first attempt at writing a logic textbook, he named the book *Topics*, from the Greek word for "place" (*topos*), because in his book he collected useful examples of different types of persuasive techniques, which he organized into sections or "places." Earlier rhetoricians used this term to organize their rhetorical textbooks, so Aristotle used it for his first logic textbook. He lined up literally hundreds of examples of effective arguments used by earlier thinkers, as the writers of rhetorical textbooks had done. In this respect, his first logic was backward looking: it used memorable arguments of others to use as models for one's own arguments. But his *Topics* had a different focus from his *Rhetoric*. It left out ethical and emotional appeal and focused only on rational appeals, those that were "probable" because they took off from the "common opinions" of the time. In his language, such arguments are dialectical—that is, they give likely or probable conclusions, but not necessary ones. Look at the Primary Sources at the end of the chapter for a brief outline of the *Topics*. There you can see that the book's organizing principle was the sentence, for the *Topics* is divided into parts based on how the predicate of a sentence is logically related to its subject. This relationship is defined by Aristotle's doctrine of the "predicables," which means "ways things can be predicated" or the different relations possible between the predicate and subject of a sentence. We will study this subject in Lesson 9.

Aristotle's Second Try: The Logic of Discovery and Proof

Aristotle's first attempt at organizing logic focused too much on cataloging a set of effective arguments someone else had already devised. But that information wouldn't necessarily help us by ourselves to devise arguments and solve problems as yet unsolved. He soon recognized the need for a forward-looking way of organizing logic, one that uses the *structure* of reasoning to solve problems, to find a truth that is new (new at least to the one solving the problem). This is very different from a database of examples, which is helpful only if we already know what we want to say. Since what we can call "the logic of discovery" focuses on the structure of our thinking, it is different from the other disciplines (or "sciences," as he used this term) that he set out in his many other books. His other books focus on content, on the truths to be found about a particular subject matter, such as arithmetic, which studies numbers, biology, which studies living beings, ethics, which studies human action, and so on. To develop logic, he no longer concentrated on *what* we think about; he reserved that for the different disciplines. Logic, Aristotle said, was not a "science" focused on just one area of knowledge, but only an "art" or skill (*techne*; *ars*) that focuses on *how* we reason in using arguments to discover the truth. If we can improve how we reason, then we can use those improved skills in any and every area of study. Aristotle saw another benefit of focusing on the structure of our reasoning. Once we ensure our that reasoning is correct in structure and that our conclusions follow necessarily from our premises, we have taken the first step to achieving conclusions that are not just "likely" or "probable," like the "dialectical" arguments found in the *Topics*; we make it possible to take a further step and achieve conclusions that are true, and necessarily so (reasoning Aristotle called "demonstrative").

In order to focus on *how* we reason the *structure or form* our reasoning, speaking, and writing should take—Aristotle now realized he had to concentrate on three different acts of the mind, ones that produce three different types of thought, speech, and writing. The study of these three areas makes up what came to be called *formal* logic because it concentrates on the form or structure of our reasoning. (We will look at these three areas of logic more closely in Lesson 6.) For the time being, suffice it to say that Aristotle's second attempt at inventing logic focused on logic as a *tool for problem solving*, for acquiring *new* knowledge. In this way, Aristotle's logic became a technique for learning rather than merely for developing skill at persuading. This is why Aristotle gave his logic the name *organon*, which means "instrument." (Using the term "logic" to describe logic was initiated by the later Greek philosophers, called Stoics.) Aristotle now thought of logic as the instrument for solving problems and discovering the truth, analogous to the seamstress's needle or the carpenter's saw.

A Deeper Look

The Logic of Discovery: Steps in Logical Problem Solving

Opinion and Knowledge

In the Platonic dialogue that bears his name, Meno was reminded by Socrates that there is a great deal of difference between knowing and simply having an opinion about, say, how to travel the long road from Athens to Meno's hometown of Larisa, far to the north of Athens in Thessaly. (Please remember that this road was no interstate highway: no asphalt, no curbs, no markers. Knowing this road was more like knowing how to walk through the forest, from New York to Lake Huron, in a James Fenimore Cooper novel.) Meno had traveled that road to get to Athens, but it is doubtful Socrates ever had. Following his sophist teachers, Meno had said that the best the human mind can attain is opinion; but in order to show him that true knowledge is different from simply having a correct opinion, Socrates uses this example. A man like Meno who has traveled that road is much less likely to get lost than a man like Socrates, who only has instructions given to him by someone else. And Aristotle followed Socrates in saying that *opinion* is different from *knowledge* and inferior to it.

Ignorance and Wonder

Suppose you were to take the long walk from Athens to Larisa. The dusty plains of Thessaly would make you thirsty, and once you became thirsty you would be on the lookout for water. If you saw what looked like a well off in the distance, you would wonder if it is a well and whether or not there was any water in the well. Now philosophy, which literally means "love of wisdom," begins when our experience of the world generates *wonder*, for we wonder when we don't yet know something, but are capable of knowing it. (This is the reason for the saying "animals and God don't wonder"; animals can't know things as well as humans can, and God's knowledge is infinitely superior to ours.)

Questions

Wonder usually generates *questions*. Once we recognize our ignorance, we can move from a condition of wondering to the next step on the road to knowledge—in this case, asking questions about the dimly seen well and the water it might contain. Several questions might pop into our mind: Is the well something real, or an illusion caused by our exhaustion? Is it really a well? Does it have water? Can we drink it? Ever the systematic thinker, Aristotle organized the multitude of questions we can ask whenever we wonder about something into four general types of questions.[1]

---

1. Aristotle, *Posterior Analytics* 2.1.89b22–90a4.

1. In this case, the first question that comes to mind is Aristotle's question *"Is it?"* Is there something real there? As soon as we are close enough to see it is real, we have answered this question. If it still looks like a well, we speed up to make sure it is.

2. Here we ask Aristotle's question "What is it?" When we are close enough to see it clearly, we touch it, look down inside, and perhaps throw a few pebbles in, to see if it is deep. We have now answered Aristotle's second question. Now we look down more carefully or throw in some more pebbles to hear if they make a splash.

3. We are now asking if there is water in the well. This is Aristotle's third question: *"Whether?"* or *"Whether it is a fact?"* Once we hear the pebbles splash, we have good reason to think the well does contain water. So we ask another "Whether?" question: "Is the water potable (or drinkable)?" We might then test the water by pulling up a bucket, conveniently attached with a rope. (Let's assume we don't have to climb down into the well. Then we look at the water and take a taste on our tongue or use a water-testing kit. Once we determine to our satisfaction that the water is potable, we would normally stop our questions and just take a nice, long drink.)

4. If we were really curious we might proceed to the fourth and last of Aristotle's questions: *"Why?,"* or *"Why is it so?,"* or *"Why is S P?"* Here we are looking for an explanation or cause to show us, or perhaps reassure us if we are very hesitant, by determining the *reason why* the liquid in the well is water, or why the water is potable, or why impure water tastes one way, drinkable water another.

Some of these questions may seem similar. But when analyzed logically (that is, with an eye on the differences among terms, propositions, and arguments), we can see that the **first two questions deal with a single *term*.** These questions could be restated generally as, first, "Does X exist?" and, second, "What is the essence or nature of X?" **The second two questions deal with** *propositions* and consequently involve two terms. These questions could be restated as "Is it a *fact* that X is Y?" and "What is the *cause* or *reason why* X is Y?" While there are literally an unlimited number of questions we could ask about the universe, **Aristotle has helped us tremendously by narrowing them down to these four general types of questions.** (If Aristotle's conclusion is not obvious to you, do what he did. Be empirical and ask yourself some *specific* questions. Then try to see what *general* types of questions there are. You will probably come up with the same answer he did, because his four types are determined by the *structure* of the kinds of answers that are possible.) Being able to identify the type of question we ask helps us better understand the question itself; and this, in turn, helps us answer it.

Answering Questions: Problem Solving

A question is simply an answer turned inside out. So asking a question sets up our search for an answer. Some questions are rather easy to answer, some are exceedingly hard. But what Aristotle recognized was that searching for answers involves *reasoning* from one point to another. Reasoning first yields provisional answers. Further reasoning sometimes shows us how to prove that our preliminary guess is correct through coming up with an argument that proves the point. There are many kinds of arguments and many levels of proof. But what they all have in common is that answers are found through argument, argument that weaves together facts (or propositions) to prove a conclusion. What made Aristotle the inventor of logic is that he saw there was a difference in structure or form between those arguments that prove their conclusions and those that don't.

To take the first step in learning why logic is problem solving, please turn to the problems contained in Problem Set 5 and try to figure out what the answers are and how you get to those answers.

Primary Sources

Aristotle, *Posterior Analytics*, esp. 2.1.

Plato, *Meno*.

Aristotle, *Topics*: an outline. His first attempt at inventing logic.

   I. The nature of dialectical reasoning (bk. I)
  II. Topics for finding arguments: built on the structure of categorical propositions: "S is/is not P."
     A. Topics falling under accident (where P is unrelated to S) (bk. II-III)
     B. Topics falling under genus (where P is the genus of S) (bk. IV)
     C. Topics falling under property (where P is a property of S) (bk. V)
     D. Topics falling under definition (where P is the species of S) (bks. VI–VII)

(We will cover Aristotle's "predicables," which include genus, accident, and property, in Lesson 10.)

III. Practice in dialectics
    A. How to put questions in debate (bk. VIII, cc. 1–3)
    B. How to answer questions in debate (bk. VIII.4–14)

Compare these topics with the topics covered in Aristotle's *Rhetoric,* outlined in Lesson 3. Then compare them with the organization of Aristotle's second attempt at inventing logic, outlined in Lesson 6.

Problem Set 5: Problem Solving

Finding Conclusions and Arguments

Instructions

For the following problems:

a. Put the question in your own words.
b. What is the answer? Put your reply in the form of a *statement*.
c. What is the *reason* for the answer? Give a reason or argument for your answer.

1. Travelers in the tropics often notice that the climate is very hard on machinery. In fact, someone touring by taxi is amazed at how susceptible the car is to rust. Why?
2. A stack of magazines tied in a bundle does not burn up very easily. Why?
3. Snowshoes or skis help you to walk on snow. Why?
4. Mother Earth contains a great variety of living things—many kinds of plants and animals. What feature of the earth's atmosphere makes this possible?
5. A bedroom with a large south window gets very hot. But the glass in the window stays cool, so the glass is not the reason the bedroom gets hot. Why does it get so hot?
6. Is grass green? Why?
7. Are electrons visible? Why or why not?
8. Aristotle noticed that puncture wounds (like from a spear) heal much more slowly than gash wounds (like from a knife or sword). Why?

9. "I was particularly anxious to learn why the Nile, at the beginning of the summer solstice, begins to rise and continues to increase for a hundred days—and why, as soon as that number is past, it recedes and contracts its flow, continuing low during the whole of the winter until the summer solstice comes around again. On none of these points could I obtain any explanation from the Egyptians. Some of the Greeks, however, wishing to get a reputation for cleverness, have offered explanations of the annual flooding of the river. One thinks that the Etesian winds [coming from the north] cause the rise of the river by preventing the Nile water from running off into the Mediterranean Sea. But if the Etesian winds produced the effect, the other rivers which flow in a direction opposed to those winds ought to exhibit the same floods as the Nile, and more so, as they are all smaller streams and have a weaker current. But these rivers, of which there are many, both in Syria and Libya, are entirely unlike the Nile in this respect. (Herodotus, *History*, 2.20)

Aristotle Organizes the Logic of Discovery and Proof

The Essentials

We must define a premise, a term, and a syllogism; the nature of a perfect and an imperfect syllogism, including or not including one term in another as in a whole; and what we mean by predicating one term of all, or none, of another.

A *premise* is a sentence affirming or denying one thing of another; and this is either universal or particular or indefinite....

I call a *term* that into which a premise is analyzed—that is, both the predicate and that of which it is predicated, and "is" means added and "is not" means taken away.

A *syllogism* is discourse in which, when certain things have been laid down, something other than what was stated follows necessarily from their being so. This last point means the premises produce a consequence, in this way, that nothing further is required in addition in order to make the consequence necessary. I call that a "perfect syllogism" that needs nothing other than what has been stated to make clear what follows necessarily, while a syllogism is imperfect if it needs one or more propositions that are necessary consequences of what has been laid down, but have not been expressly stated as premises.[1]

---

1. Aristotle, *Prior Analytics* 1.24a10–24b26, trans. A. J. Jenkinson emended, in *The Basic Works of Aristotle*, ed. Richard McKeon (1941; repr. New York: Modern Library, 2001).

Aristotle's Second Attempt to Invent Logic

We have seen in the previous lesson that Aristotle's writings contain two attempts to organize logic. In his first attempt, where he closely followed the approach of organizing rhetoric around topics, he organized a large collection of dialectical arguments—that is, arguments from common opinions that reason to "probable" or "likely" conclusions around topics arranged according to the different ways the predicate of a proposition can be related to its subject. Aristotle himself recognized a significant problem with this work on logic: it is too unwieldy to read straight through, in great measure because it's like reading through a telephone directory or a database. You go from one example to another to a third.

As we saw, Aristotle's *Topics* did spark in his mind how to organize his second attempt at logic. First, as we saw in Lesson 5, his second attempt at logic focused on problem solving: finding truth that is new (at least new to me). Second, Aristotle realized that logic is different from the other disciplines he set out in his many other books because it is an absolutely universal "art," useful in all the disciplines. Its scope is wider than any of those disciplines because logic focuses on the structure or "form" our thinking takes rather than on the content.

Logic and the Three Acts of the Mind

Once Aristotle recognized that logic should focus on the structure or form our thinking takes rather than its content, the way to organize logic as a systematically presented art (*ars*, *techne*) followed quite naturally. To see this, consider the following three sentences:

> "Socrates is a man. All men are mortal. Therefore, Socrates is mortal."

This argument has been used by teachers of logic for almost two and a half millennia. We will put ourselves in that long tradition by beginning with it.

These three sentences, when taken together, make up a deductive *argument*. How does it work? The argument contains the three sentences, two of which, when taken together, have the combined impact of leading our mind to the conclusion. As quite often happens, there is a verbal marker—"therefore"—to help us see that the conclusion is "Socrates is mortal"; he will die.

Of course, Socrates is long since dead. But you can use the same argument about your classmate or yourself. The claim the argument is making is that it is more than just a probability that you, who are presently alive, will die; it is a certainty. And, what is more, you know this truth for sure, even though it is a truth about a still-living person, one that has not yet happened.

Aristotle recognized that this form of argument (we will learn to call it a "categorical syllogism") always consists in three propositions; that two are premises; and that they lead necessarily to a third proposition, the conclusion. The conclusion, then, flows from the premises. In thinking this way, our mind is engaging in what came to be called "the third act of the mind," the acting of reasoning from one point to another. In doing so, our mind produces within itself an argument. And there is more. This argument allows us to discover something true about the nature of the world around us, something so important that we don't keep this truth to ourselves. Rather, being naturally social animals, humans have invented languages to express the reasoning going on in their minds. The language of argument leads us to discover truths about the world.

Aristotle also recognized that the task of producing each of the three propositions in our mind that are contained in this argument is quite a different task from combining the propositions together to produce the argument itself. Here he identified what came to be called "the second act of the mind," the act of making a mental judgment about the way things are in the world. Once we make that judgment, in our mind, we formulate that judgment in a mental statement or proposition (we'll learn the difference between statements and propositions later). Each of the three sentences in the problem set contains one proposition, so the whole argument contains three propositions. If logic, when organized in terms of the *structure or form* of our thinking, studies arguments, it must also study the immediate component parts out of which arguments are constructed. These are propositions. So a second part of logic is devoted to the study of *propositions*.

Finally, Aristotle noted that each of the kinds of propositions in his argument—we'll learn to call them *categorical propositions*—is made up of yet smaller parts called *terms*. While three propositions can contain a total of six terms—two terms for each proposition—the three propositions in the problem set contain only three terms: "Socrates," "man" (or "human" in more recent English), and "mortal." This fact is not happenstance; it is necessary for a categorical syllogism to be made up of three propositions, and those three propositions must contain three and only three terms. But if we are to understand the propositions, and through them the argument, the terms first must be understood. The way we think in the process of coming to understand terms is again quite different from the way we think in formulating propositions or in mounting arguments. Here Aristotle had discovered what came to be called "the first act of the mind," the one by which we apprehend what things are, by which we formulate in our minds concepts in which we try to capture the meaning of our apprehensions, and that allows us to develop language to enunciate in spoken or written words the concepts in our minds. This "first act of the mind" is the ultimate building block for our reasoning.

We have just used a logical technique called *analysis* in which we analyze or "break up" some whole into its parts. This kind of mental analysis is similar to chemical analysis of compounds in chemistry, or mathematical analysis in analytic geometry, or the kind of detective analysis Sherlock Holmes used to solve crimes. In this case, the whole is an argument, which we first analyzed into three propositions, and then we analyzed each proposition into terms. Perfecting our powers of analysis is one of the main goals of studying logic, and for this reason Aristotle gave his most famous and important logic book the title *Analysis*. But we can also proceed the other way around, beginning with the parts and moving to the whole. This is called *synthesis*, because we are "putting the parts together." The organization of the side of logic that studies the structure of our thinking—what is now called "formal logic"—came quite naturally from Aristotle's discovery of the three acts of the mind. Aristotle wrote several logic textbooks; later Aristotelian logicians gave them the organization we will follow in this book, which follows the synthetic way of thinking logically.

In this logic book we will begin with the first act of the mind, apprehension or conceptualization, and study concepts, terms, and words. Then we will cover the way in which we put together concepts or terms to formulate statements or propositions. Finally, we will study the way we put together propositions into premises and conclusions to form arguments. But we should remember that we already perform all of these mental acts and make use of all of these kinds of signs. So if we start from our end of the whole, reasoning and arguments, we can see that they are composed of judgments and propositions, which in turn are composed of acts of conceptualization and concepts, words, and terms.

CHART OF THE THREE ACTS OF THE MIND

Mental Act	*Spoken or Written Discourse*	*Focus*
1. Conceptualization	word, term	definition
2. Judgment	proposition	truth
3. Reasoning	argument	valid proof

A Deeper Look

Aristotle's Works on Logic

The way Aristotle's logic books were organized after he died reflects this organization. The *Categories* (probably written by Aristotle but possibly the work of one of his students) presents part of the logic of the first act of the mind. Aristotle's *On Interpretation* gives a fairly full presentation of the logic of the second act of the mind. His *Prior Analytics* (the first half of the book Aristotle himself simply called *Analytics*) gives a comprehensive account of the formal logic of the syllogism, the most important kind of argument, in Aristotle's view.

Aristotle did not stop writing when he had finished his account of formal logic. He was even more interested in how logic is used in the various disciplines (which he called "sciences," using this word in a wider sense than we now do, where it is limited to the empirical sciences that follow the scientific method invented in the early modern period of Western history, about two millennia after Aristotle). Aristotle recognized that when we reason correctly in a formal sense, though our conclusions follow necessarily from our premises, there can be several degrees of truth in our conclusions, depending upon the degree of truth found in the premises of the arguments we use to prove those conclusions. He wrote several important books covering the differences among reasoning to necessary and certain truths (*Posterior Analytics*), to probable or likely truths (*Topics*), and to conclusions that only seem to be true but are not (*On Sophistical Refutations*). This second part of logic was called "material logic" by his medieval Latin followers because it is not confined to studying the "form" of our thinking, but considers how the "matter" or content of our arguments affects the quality of our conclusions. Aristotle's most influential logic book—*Posterior Analytics*—is among the books he wrote about this area of material logic. Nowadays, this area of logic is often studied when taking up a particular subject, going by the name of "methodology."

Since study of the methodology of the various disciplines includes logic as well as content from the discipline under consideration, it really is part of logic.

The outline in the Primary Sources shows that the various component parts of the kind of logic presented do fit into a consistent whole—like seeing a mountain from a distance first, before attempting to climb it.

Primary Sources

Aquinas, *Exposition of Aristotle's On Interpretation*, Lesson 1.

Aquinas, *Exposition of Aristotle's Posterior Analytics*, Prologue.

Outline of Aristotle's Works on the "Arts" of Logic and Rhetoric

A. **Formal logic:** focuses on the form or structure of theoretical discourse, where our purpose or "end" is knowledge; but applies to all types of human thought.

   1. *Categories*: The first act of the mind; apprehension of terms; definitions of the ten most general terms or "categories."

   2. *On Interpretation*: The second act of the mind. Judgments that produce statements and propositions. "Interpretation" here means understanding the meaning of sentences and seeing their truth or falsity.

   3. *Prior Analytics*: The third act of the mind. The structure or form of correct human reasoning (valid reasoning), as well as how human reason can be wrong or incorrect in its structure (invalid reasoning). Concentrates on deductive reasoning using syllogisms, rather than inductive reasoning.

B. **Material logic:** Called "material," as distinct from "formal," because it focuses on how certain or uncertain the conclusion derived by reasoning is.

   1. *Posterior Analytics*: Demonstrative reasoning: the strongest kind of reasoning that produces the necessary and certain deductive conclusions found in a "science." For Aristotle, the "sciences" span the full range of theoretical and practical knowledge. He divided theoretical knowledge into three areas: the physical sciences, the mathematical sciences, and metaphysics, which deals with things

beyond the physical realm. Practical knowledge he divided into ethics, focused on the individual, economics, focused on the family and tribe, and politics, focused on the largest social unit, the *polis* or "city state." Beginning in the nineteenth century, the term "science" has been limited to the physical sciences that employ the "experimental method" to draw conclusions.

2. *Topics*: As noted previously, this early book was Aristotle's first attempt at a logic textbook, but after writing his book on "formal" logic he came to recognize that the first book really only covers dialectical reasoning, which produces probable or likely conclusions. But this reasoning is important, because it is how we reason when learning the fundamental principles guiding our study of a discipline or, on Aristotle's understanding, a "science."

3. *On Sophistical Refutations*: What is wrong with sophistical reasoning—that is, the erroneous reasoning of the "sophists."

4. *Poetics*: Literature for Aristotle is fundamentally theoretical, designed to teach us truths, especially about human life and the difference between the morally good and bad, rather than teaching us practical skills in how to be good. A study of the structure and techniques of poetry, focused on Greek drama.

5. *Rhetoric*: A study of what makes practical discourse persuasive, as we have seen. Included in this list because Aristotle used the distinction between the form and content of discourse.

Problem Set 6: Three Acts of the Mind

Identifying Terms, Propositions, and Arguments

Instructions

In the following passages, identify examples of (a) terms, (b) propositions, and (c) arguments. Be sure you distinguish the terms, propositions, and arguments in each passage. Then consider how the differences among these three things are important for understanding the passage.

1. Socrates is a man. All men are mortal. Therefore, at some point Socrates will die.
2. Cars are vehicles for travel. Vehicles for travel are manmade. Therefore, cars are manmade.

3. "The human soul is immortal. The human soul is not the kind of thing subject to destruction by separating it into its parts. All things not subject to destruction in this way are immortal." (Simplified from Plato, *Phaedo*)

4. "All things that exist, therefore, seeing that the Creator of them all is supremely good, are themselves good. But because they are not, like their Creator, supremely and unchangeably good, their goodness may be diminished and increased." (Augustine, d. 430, Roman bishop and theologian, *On the Trinity*)

5. The following ad appeared in a London newspaper at the beginning of the twentieth century. The next day, 5,000 men answered the ad, which was designed to recruit men for an Arctic expedition. It has been called one of the most successful ads in history. Indicate how it uses the *first act of the mind* effectively:

   MEN WANTED—for dangerous undertaking. Poor working conditions, bad food, long hours, constant and great danger. Survivors, if any, are guaranteed lasting fame. Apply....

6. "Living in society is clearly a necessity of human nature. For all other animals, nature has prepared food, hair as a covering, teeth, horns, claws as a means of defense or at least speed in flight, while humans alone were made without any natural provisions for these things. Instead of all these, a human was endowed with reason, by the use of which he can procure all these things for himself by the work of his hands. Now, one man alone is not able to procure them all for himself, for one man could not sufficiently provide for life, unassisted. It is therefore natural that humans should live in the society of many."[2] (Thomas Aquinas, d. 1274, Italian philosopher and theologian)

7. "There are three distinctions in the kinds of bodies, or three states, which have more especially claimed the attention of philosophical chemists: namely, those which are marked by the terms "elastic fluids," "liquids," and "solids." A very familiar instance is exhibited to us in water, a body, which, in certain circumstances, is capable of assuming all three states. In steam we recognize a perfectly elastic fluid, in water a perfect liquid, and in ice a complete solid. These observations have tacitly led to the conclusion which seems universally adopted, that all

---

2. Aquinas, *On Kingship*, c. 1.

bodies of sensible magnitude, whether liquid or solid, are constituted of a vast number of extremely small particles."[3] (John Dalton, d. 1844, English chemist)

8. "Those who plead their cause in the absence of an opponent can invent to their heart's content, can pontificate without taking into account the opposite point of view and keep the best arguments for themselves, for aggressors are always quick to attack those who have no means of defense." (Christine de Pizan, d. 1430, French moralist, member of the court, and author of "mirror of princes" works such as *The Book of the City of Ladies*)

9. "Then it looks as though this [democracy] is the finest or most beautiful of constitutions, for, like a coat embroidered with every kind of ornament, this city-state, embroidered with every kind of character type, would seem to be the most beautiful. And many people would probably judge it to be so, ... as do children when they see something multicolored. (557c) ... But if someone tells him [the extreme democrat] that some pleasures belong to fine and good desires, while others to evil ones, and that he must pursue and value the first, but restrain and enslave the second, he denies all this and declares that all pleasures are equal and must be valued equally (561c)." (Plato, d. 347 B.C., Greek philosopher; his *Republic* traces the rise and demise of the city-state and the citizen, and here he describes the attractions and also the vices of extreme democracy, which leads to tyranny)

3. John Dalton, "Experimental Essays," Essay 2, in *Memoirs of the Literary and Philosophical Society of Manchester*, 2nd ed. (1802).

Part 2

The Logic of Terms

Language, Thought, and Reality

The Essentials

As spoken words are symbols of perceptions received in the soul, so are written words symbols of spoken words. And just as written words are *not* the same for all humans, so likewise spoken words are not the same for all. But the perceptions in the soul, of which spoken words are the first signs, *are* the same for all, and likewise the real things, of which the perceptions in the soul are *likenesses*, are also the same for all.

And just as perceptions received in the soul sometimes are neither true nor false, but at other times must be one or the other, the same thing is true about spoken words. For false and true require composition and division. So nouns and verbs by themselves resemble thoughts without composition or division; for example, "man," or "white," with nothing added, are neither true nor false. Here is a sign of this: "Goat-stag" signifies something, but nothing true or false, unless "is" or "is not" is added, in the present or another tense.[1]

Language Signifies Thought, Which in Turn Signifies Things

We live in two different worlds—the world of *facts* and that of their *symbols*. In order to acquire knowledge of ourselves, we utilize both observation

1. Aristotle, *On Interpretation*, c. 1., 16a1–18. See also Aquinas, *Exposition of Aristotle's On Interpretation*, Lessons 1–3.

and scientific abstractions. But the abstract may be mistaken for the concrete. In such an instance, facts are treated as symbols and the individual is likened to the human being. Most of the errors made by educators, physicians, and sociologists come from such confusion. Scientists, accustomed to the techniques of mechanics, chemistry, physics, and physiology and unfamiliar with philosophy and intellectual culture, are liable to mingle the concepts of the different disciplines and not to distinguish clearly the general from the particular. However, in the concept of *man*, it is important to define exactly that part of the human being and that of the individual. Education, medicine, and sociology are concerned with the individual. They are guilty of a disastrous error when they look upon him *only* as a symbol, as a human being. Indeed, individuality is fundamental in man. It is not merely a certain aspect of the organism. But it permeates our entire being. It stamps its mark on the whole of body and consciousness and, although remaining indivisible, on each component of this whole. It makes the self a unique event in the history of the world.[2]

The world in which we live and act and think is a world made up of individual things: this tree, that dog, the other thing, which is a rose, and above all, ourselves—individual humans. What we do affects individuals—we help our grandmother up the stairs or we clean out our hamster's cage. But human actions are guided by human thought, and our thought is communicated through language—mainly spoken and written language, but even what is sometimes called "body language." What Alexis Carrel is noting in this passage is that there is a difference between the world of concrete individual things, in the midst of which we live, and the world of symbolic or abstract language and thought, which we use to describe our world and ourselves. The terms we use—whether mental terms or spoken terms or written terms—signify the reality we are trying to describe. Most of the terms we use are signs of reality; they point to real things and in this way help us to understand them.

A few of the terms we use signify individuals: Socrates, my black dog, the hummingbird now at Miguelito's bird feeder, the present king of France (a philosophical joke—there isn't one). But most of the terms we use to describe reality, terms that point to or signify things, are broad or abstract terms, ones that can apply to more than one individual: human, black, dog, hummingbird, bird feeder, king of France. These are what Alexis Carrel calls "symbols,"

2. Alexis Carrel, French, Nobel Prize for Medicine (1912), *Man, the Unknown* (New York and London: Harper and Brothers, 1939 [1935]).

Aristotle calls "perceptions on the soul" (*pathemata en psychei*) and "likeness-es" (*homoiomata*), and philosophers normally call "universal" terms, because they are usually general or abstract, covering more than one individual. The concepts, terms, and words that we use and will study in this section of log-ic are, in a broad sense, signs of some sort of reality. In order to understand them, we need to understand how they function as *signs*.

Concepts, terms, and words are not the only signs we encounter or use. Our world is filled with signs. The medieval Franciscan theologian and phi-losopher St. Bonaventure built his whole understanding of reality around signs. And in the twentieth century there developed a philosophical move-ment devoted to understanding reality in terms of how signs function in the world, called "semiotics" from the Greek word for "sign" (*semeion*). In order to understand the logic of mental and linguistic signs, we will start with how signs function in nature, beyond the realm of human thought and language. This will help us understand what kind of signs human concepts, words, and terms are.

Signs in Nature

Signs point to or signify other things. Let's start with signs in nature. There are many such signs, independent of the realm of human thought. Smoke is a sign of fire, whether anyone sees the smoke or not. Birds flying south is a sign of winter approaching. Such signs, in which one thing "points to" another, even if there is no one to recognize they are signs, involve *two* things: the thing that "points," which is the sign that signifies something (in Latin, the *signum* or *significans*); and the object or thing "pointed to," the thing signified (*significatum*). So the first step in understanding signs is to rec-ognize the difference between the sign that signifies or points to something else and the thing signified by the sign. In the case of smoke being a sign of fire, the smoke is the sign, and the fire is the thing signified. Here both things exist together at the same time, even if an observer first sees the smoke and then reasons to the fire, its cause. This is the way the "sign relation" works most of the time. Occasionally, however, the signification runs the other way around. If you are cooking in the kitchen and notice a grease fire flare up on top of the stove, you will see the fire first, not the smoke it gives off. Quite often we don't notice the smoke until we go outside, then return to the house and notice how smoky it is. At that point we realize that the fire was a sign of the smoke, even when we hadn't noticed the smoke. In the case of the birds, their flying south is the sign, while winter approaching is the object signified. In this case, the object signified does not yet exist; it is in the future.

A famous use of signs found in nature, but unusual signs, is where Jesus prophesies the end of the world:

> And there will be signs in sun and moon and stars, and upon the earth distress of nations in perplexity at the roaring of the sea and the waves, men fainting with fear and with foreboding of what is coming on the world; for the powers of the heavens will be shaken. And then they will see the Son of man coming in a cloud with power and great glory. Now when these things begin to take place, look up and raise your heads, because your redemption is drawing near.
>
> And he told them a parable: "Look at the fig tree, and all the trees; as soon as they come out in leaf, you see for yourselves and know that the summer is already near. So also, when you see these things taking place, you know that the kingdom of God is near. Truly, I say to you, this generation will not pass away till all has taken place. Heaven and earth will pass away, but my words will not pass away."[3]

Recognizing Logical Signs: The Semiotic Triangle

While signs in nature exist whether or not someone realizes it, the full meaning of "sign" involves more than one thing pointing to another, it involves the *realization* that one thing is pointing to another. This third factor we can call the sign-perceiver or reader or interpreter or "interpretant." Consider the case of a diploma: a diploma is a sign of education. Here the sign is the diploma; what is signified is the fact that the person named on the diploma has an education. The sign reader is the person who reads the diploma and recognizes the sign relationship, as you do when you read the diploma in your doctor's office, which helps give you confidence in his medical knowledge. Being a sign reader may involve some skill; and it may involve recognition that what the sign signifies is not always true. A person who has a diploma ought to have knowledge commensurate with that level of education; but we have all met people for whom this is not true. And we've all met wise people who have never been to college. Moreover, there are those people who have bought their diploma, or stolen one, or gotten one from a "diploma mill." The point of problem 1 of "Identifying Signs," in Problem Set 7, is that, while humans are

---

3. Luke 21: 25–33 RSV.

good sign readers of pictures, dogs are not. They don't see the picture as a sign.

This fact about dogs, however, does not mean that animals cannot make use of signs, and sometimes even recognize signs.

> When a brown hare spots a fox approaching in the open landscape, the hare stands bolt upright and signals its presence instead of fleeing. The explanation for this behavior,... is that a hare can easily escape a fox simply by running—a fact the fox seems to "know" (whether by learning or instinct). Apparently, then, what is happening in this behavior is that the hare is telling the fox: "I have seen you"—and as a result, they can both be spared the effort of running.[4]

If a brown rabbit tries to hide in the brown dirt of the field until the fox gets very near, he will have to run for his life; and the fox will pursue him, at least for a while, and maybe even catch him. But since the rabbit "knows" he can outrun the fox, he behaves in a different way. He stands up to let the fox see him. By doing so, the rabbit is sending the fox a sign: "I'm here. But I can outrun you; so what is the use of you coming over here to try to catch me?" The fox will send a sign in return: either he'll continue approaching the rabbit, which lets the rabbit know he has to run away; or he'll veer away in another direction, letting the rabbit know he won't have to run. Most of the time, Hoffmeyer tells us, the fox will turn away, unwilling to chase a prey he knows he can't catch. The behaviors of both hare and fox are signs of one to the other, signs the other seems able to "read."

Once we add the reader or interpreter of the sign, we add a third factor to the "sign relation." The three parts of this relation are: (1) the sign; (2) the object signified; and (3) the sign-perceiver or "interpretant." This triple relation is sometimes called the "semiotic triangle."[5] It can be diagrammed thus:

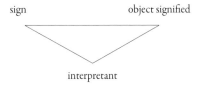

sign   object signified

interpretant

4. Jesper Hoffmeyer, *Biosemiotics: An Examination into the Signs of Life and the Life of Signs* (Scranton: University of Scranton Press, 2008), xiii.

5. John Deely, *The Basics of Semiotics* (South Bend, Ind.: St. Augustine's Press), 88–89.

Types of Signs

There are two divisions of types of signs that are especially important for logic, because they help us pinpoint what kinds of signs the concepts, words, and terms we use in logic actually are. The **first division** is that between *natural* signs and *conventional* signs. *Natural* signs are signs that do *not* depend upon humans deciding they are signs; they occur independently of human choice. The smoke signifies fire, independently of humans.

Conventional signs, by contrast, are called "conventional" because they depend upon human convention or choice. A stop sign is a conventional sign; there is no reason in nature why a red metal octagon should signify that you should stop your car. Humans decided this would be the sign for stopping. Another good example of conventional signs is the words—both vocal utterances and written signs—found in human languages. Different languages have different words for the same thing, as Aristotle points out, because languages have been created by humans, by human agreement or convention.

A **second division**, one that is important for logic, is the **distinction** between *instrumental* signs and *formal* signs. An instrument is normally a tool one uses to perform some task, such as a doctor's scalpel, a toothbrush, or a shovel. Such a tool exhibits two features also found in *instrumental signs*. First, an instrument, say, a toothbrush, is something that exists in its own right that you then use in order to do something else, like brush your teeth. Second, we see the instrument first, then become aware of what it can be used to do. To see the point of the second feature of an instrument, think of archeologists who dig up ancient sites in order to try to understand early cultures. Often they dig up human artifacts without knowing what they are or what they are for. Anyone visiting a museum housing such treasure troves can play the fun game of looking at the object first and trying to guess what it is before reading the card that explains what it is, where it comes from, and when it was made. **All *instrumental* signs have the same characteristics.** Now some instrumental signs are natural signs, like smoke and fire, while other instrumental signs are conventional signs, like a stop sign.

Formal signs have the opposite characteristics. They are *not* something in their own right first and then, second, a sign of something built on top of that. Their fundamental reality is that they are signs of something else. It is their nature or form (using a Platonic word) to be signs, which is why they are called *formal signs*. Second, we don't recognize them as things first and then become aware that they signify something else. Rather, our awareness goes in the opposite direction. We are first aware of the object signified, not of the sign that signifies it. Only afterward, and sometimes through a long process of analysis, do we become aware of formal signs.

Consider a predatory animal like a bear. It sees its prey, say, a salmon, only by means of some sensory process that involves its eyes, nervous system, and brain. That complex sensory process points to or is a sign of the salmon. Without it, the bear could never notice the salmon. But the bear is aware first of the salmon; and, in fact, the bear never reflects on his process of perception enough to become aware of the signs he uses to become *aware* of the salmon. He uses sensation and even a sense judgment akin to when a human thinks, "I want salmon," but he never recognizes that some operations within him are signs. Even the brown rabbit who sends a sign to the fox does not know what a sign is or that he is sending a sign, even though he knows he should sit up to let the fox see him. (And it doesn't matter whether he knows how to behave by instinct or "learned" behavior.) There are no philosopher-bears or psychologist-hares, but there are philosopher-humans. And in a way, we all are.

Linguistic and Mental Signs

There are, then, four possible kinds of signs, three of which actually exist. There are natural and instrumental signs, like the birds flying south. There are conventional and instrumental signs, like a handshake as a sign of friendship. There are natural and formal signs, like the operations of the sense powers and our intellectual powers in humans. But there cannot be conventional and formal signs, since every conventional sign has to be something on its own first before humans can decide it is a sign of something, and its sign value is decided by human choice; but formal signs don't work that way.

What kind of signs, then, are the linguistic signs—the written and spoken languages—humans use? And what kind of signs are the mental signs—the concepts, mental "words," ideas, judgments, and reasonings—that humans use?

Human *languages* are sets of *conventional* signs; witness the multiplicity of languages and the need for common agreement about the basic meaning of linguistic terms. And human languages are *instrumental* signs. We hear or see a language before we come to know what its words mean.

By contrast, the *mental* signs we use—concepts, judgments, reasoning, and mental signs related to them, like terms, propositions, and arguments—

are quite different. Their fundamental reality is to be a sign pointing to objects or features of things we are thinking about. We are aware first of what they signify, then only later do we come to recognize there must be interior and mental signs in our mind that we use in order to know things. Such mental signs are *formal* signs. And our using such signs is not up to us. We do not decide one day, "I'll use mental signs to signify things." We use them naturally first and only gradually become aware that we are using them at all. Therefore, they are *natural* signs.

In short, a written or spoken term is a conventional and instrumental sign; a mental term is a natural and formal sign.

These relations can be summed up in the following diagram:

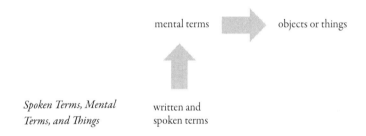

mental terms   objects or things

Spoken Terms, Mental   written and
Terms, and Things   spoken terms

A Deeper Look

Signs of Individuals, Universals, and Collections

Humans become cognizant of reality at two distinct levels, Alexis Carrel has told us. First is the level of sensation. With our five external senses we see, hear, smell, touch, and taste individual things in the world: this white chair; that black dog; the other odiferous flower. And we can also remember and imagine individual things with what are called our "internal" senses, such as memory and imagination (internal because they work with what we have already sensed). And sometimes we invent words and terms to signify such individual things. The most prominent of these are the names we give humans, like "Ed," though sometimes we name other individual things, like pets, such as the horse "Mr. Ed" on an old television show.

Most human language, however, operates at the general level, pointing out the common or universal features of things, such as "white" or "black" or "black dog," or "sunflower" or "flower" or "plant" or "living thing" or just "thing." Such terms are universal terms because they can be said of or predicated of many things, as in the propositions "Tuffy was a black dog" and "All black dogs are living things." Here we have to be careful, however, to distinguish universals from collections. "This logic class" is not an individual thing, but is made up of individuals. But neither is it a universal, because you cannot say of any individual in the class that he (or she) *is* the logic class; each is only a member of the group or collection. And the features of the logic class are not necessarily true of a given member of the class. The class may be good at logic, but it doesn't follow that a certain member of the good class must be good at logic. But everything that falls under the universal "flower" *is* a flower and has the attributes that go along with being a flower. The same thing holds for other collections, like a baseball team or the present student body of the University of St. Thomas (where I teach).

Primary Sources

Aristotle, *On Interpretation*, c. 1., 16a1–18. Signification.

Aristotle, *Prior Analytics*, bk. 1, c. 1, 24a10–24b31. Terms, propositions, arguments.

Thomas Aquinas, *Exposition of Aristotle's On Interpretation*, Lessons 1–3. Signification.

Thomas Aquinas, *Summa Theologiae* 1.85.1–2. Universals and particulars.

Problem Set 7: Signs

Kinds of Signs

Instructions

Identify whether the following signs are: (a) natural or conventional, and whether they are (b) formal or instrumental.

1. A diploma is a sign of a college education.
2. Groaning is a sign of pain.
3. A red light is a sign of danger.
4. Dark clouds are a sign of an approaching storm.
5. A word, spoken or written, is a sign of what we are thinking.
6. A footprint in the snow is the sign of the animal that made it.
7. A salute is a sign of respect for a superior.
8. Radioactivity is the sign of uranium or some similar radioactive substance.
9. A wedding ring is a sign of marriage.

10. An idea is a sign of what we are thinking about, and a sense image of what we are sensing.

Identifying Signs in Prose

Instructions

Analyze the use of signs in the following passages. (a) Be sure you can distinguish the sign (*signum*) from its object or thing signified (*significatum*). (b) Then identify the reader or interpretant of the sign relation. (c) Identify what kind of sign it is. (d) If there is *more than one sign* described in the passage, answer the three previous questions for *each one* of the signs you find.

1. "Beasts do not read symbols; that is why they do not see pictures. We are sometimes told that dogs do not react even to the best portraits because they live more by smell than by sight, but the behavior of a dog who spies a motionless real cat through the window glass belies this explanation. Dogs scorn our paintings because they see colored canvases, not pictures. A representation of a cat does not make them conceive one." (Suzanne K. Langer, d. 1985, American philosopher, *Philosophy in a New Key: A Study in the Symbolism of Reason, Rite, and Art*)

2. "In the very beginnings of modern physics, in Galileo, we find the metaphor that the 'book of nature' is written in mathematical ciphers. And since then, the entire development of exact natural science shows that every step forward in the formulation of its problems and concepts has gone hand in hand with the increasing refinement of its system of signs. (Ernst Cassirer, d. 1945, German philosopher, *The Philosophy of Symbolic Forms*. Vol 1, *Language*)

3. "There will be striking phenomena in sun and moon and stars; on the earth throes will grip the nations, perplexed by the roar of sea and surge; men will faint away from fright and expectation of what is yet to befall the world; for the foundations of the universe will rock. At last they will see the Son of Man riding upon a cloud with great might and majesty. When these phenomena are well underway, raise your heads and look up, for then your redemption is close at hand. He also told them a parable: 'Look at the fig tree, or any of the trees: the moment they begin to shoot, you need but open your eyes to know that summer is near. Apply this to yourselves: as soon as you see these events in progress, you know that the kingdom of God is at hand.'" (Luke 21:25–33 RSV)

Individuals, Collections, and Universals

Instructions

Are the following words or phrases signs of (a) individual things, (b) collections of individual things, or (c) universals?

1. John Paul Jones's Navy
2. the president of the United States from 1992 to 2000
3. dog
4. Gen. Ulysses S. Grant
5. the secretary of the treasury of the United States
6. color
7. our solar system
8. triangle
9. justice
10. the Milky Way
11. the 2015 American Women's Soccer Team
12. the eastern grey kangaroo
13. pronouns
14. argument
15. Queen Elizabeth II
16. Amazon.com
17. Ford Motor Corporation
18. scientist
19. pickle
20. sweet pickles

Categories

Working toward Definitions by Answering
the "What?" Question

The Essentials

The purpose or goal of studying the logic of terms is to be able correctly to *define* the concepts, terms, and words we use in the process of discovering and arguing for truths in all the other disciplines we study. In this lesson we will encounter Aristotle's doctrine of the categories. This first step can provide us with a way of organizing and understanding the matter or content of our definitions.

Logical categories are the general or universal concepts, terms, and words we use to describe things. All the universal terms we use to describe things are what the Greeks called "categories." The term "category" comes from the Greek word *kategorein*, a legal term for making an accusation, whether positive ("He's a *robber*") or negative ("He did not *betray the Athenians*"). But categories don't just apply to concepts, terms, and words. We use intellectual and verbal categories because they are designed to describe the attributes of *things in the world*, what we can call "ontological" or "real" categories. The concept of category describes both the ideas we use to think about things and features of the things we are thinking about. There are different levels of categories, from the *specific categories* we use every day to describe things—oak, rose, white, round, good, fast, computer—to **Aristotle's ten most** *general or universal categories*—substance, quantity, quality, relation, when, where, position, equipment, action, and passion.

Using Universals in Descriptions

In Lesson 7, we learned that most of the terms we use to describe things are universals, though a few of them are individual terms. Individual terms are usually proper names limited to one individual, and we limit proper names to very important individual things: humans, human institutions, and some animals. Socrates, the name of the famous Greek philosopher who was executed by the Athenians in 399 B.C., is often used in logic as an example of such an individual term. Let's use Socrates as an example. When we try to describe Socrates, or anything else, we invariably use *universal* terms, because the essence or "core" of anything, or any feature of anything, is not confined to that one thing; it is found in other things of the same sort. Here are some examples about Socrates:

Socrates was (1) a philosopher, (2) ugly, (3) snub-nosed (his nose was "smashed in"), and (4) looked to the Greeks like a satyr (look up this interesting word if you don't already know it).

Socrates also (5) talked to people, (6) he did so in the agora (the marketplace in Athens), (7) though sometimes he was a soldier, (8) on the battlefield, (9) where he suffered cold weather, (10) without complaining, and (11) he was heroic.

In addition, Socrates was (12) a husband (his wife was named Xanthippe), (13) a father, (14) friendly, (15) old (as portrayed in Plato's *Apology*), (16) with a bit of gray hair, (17) that was cut short, (18) dressed poorly (as befits a poor philosopher), (19) was often stooped over when he walked, (20) though in Plato's *Symposium* he was lying on a dinner couch, (21) next to the young tragic poet Agathon. (22) In the morning after the drinking party he was standing straight up (the only one left standing), and (23) then he walked back to the agora to follow his daily routine.

In describing Socrates, however, we seem to have left out some important but fairly obvious points. Socrates was (24) Greek, (25) a human (or man, in older English), (26) an animal, (27) a living thing, (28) a physical thing, and (29) a substance, (30) a thing, and (31) a being.

While a proper noun such as "Socrates" signifies an individual, when we use general terms like "old" or "man" or "old man," we often add the indefinite article "a" (or "an"), such as in the sentence "Socrates is an old man." The indefinite article points out that Socrates is one among many old men, to all of whom the universal term "old man" applies. Sometimes we use the definite article "the" to emphasize individuality, as in "Socrates is the philosopher over in the agora." In this sentence, what "the" points out is that Socrates is the single person who is "the philosopher over in the agora." On the other hand, when we say, "The kangaroo is an animal," usually we are not referring to just one kangaroo but to all kangaroos. The whole species of kangaroos are animals. In thought and language, we use universals to describe individual things through what they have in common with other things *of the same sort*. But such common traits can also be used to distinguish individuals from each other by focusing on the traits where they differ from each other. The vast majority of thinkers down through the ages have thought that there are such natural "sorts" or "kinds" of things; our assertions are true when our minds conform to those "kinds" and are false when they don't. When I think a dog really is a dog, my thought is true; but when I think it is a cat, my thought is false. (More on truth and falsity in Part 3: "The Logic of Propositions," Lessons 13–22.)

Specific Categories and General Categories

Aristotle noticed that the universal terms we use cluster together in *two* revealing ways. First, terms cluster into similar groups. In our example, Socrates (5) "talked" and (23) "walked." These are actions he performed. Socrates was (7) "in the battlefield," but he also spent a lot of time (6) "in the agora." These are places where he was. There are also a large number of terms used that are not quite as obviously similar as these examples, yet they do fit together by describing *what kind or quality of man* Socrates was: (1), (2), (3), (4), (11), (14), (16), (17).

Especially interesting is the way the most important cluster of traits works: Socrates is (23) a "human," (24) an "animal," (25) a "living thing," (26) a "physical thing," and (27) a "substance." All of these traits are similar by telling us what Socrates is *fundamentally*, in the unchanging "core" of the complex reality we call Socrates. They are quite different from things like (21) "walking" or (15) "old" or (1) a "philosopher," traits that come and go and that are, so to speak, built on top of these core traits. The core traits of Socrates, from "human" through "physical thing," all cluster together because they point out the fundamental character or nature of Socrates. Consequently, if we want to define Socrates—and definition is the goal of the logic of the first act of the mind—we would define him using these traits, because definitions are designed to distinguish the fundamental character of something from its additional traits. Socrates is a physical thing, a living thing, an animal, and a human.

Socrates or "this human" is an independently existing thing, while *walking* is something a substance does and *old* is something a substance is. Since such nonsubstantial traits depend upon substances, Aristotle called them "accidents." The etymology of this word tells us they "go along with" or "happen to" substances. Just as substance is the widest concept describing the fundamental nature of something, Aristotle also discovered nine accidental categories, the widest concepts that characterize the non-substantial features of things. Let's hear Aristotle himself describe all ten categories, because he gave good examples of each:

> Of those enunciations [written or spoken terms] that are not composite, each signifies either *substance* or *quantity* or *quality* or *relation* or *where* or *when* or *posture* or *being equipped* or *acting* or *undergoing*. There is *substance* in the ordinary meaning of the term, for example, man or horse; *quantity*, for example, being two or three cubits large; *quality*, for example, being white or being grammatical; *relation to something*, for example, double or half or greater; *where*, for example, being in the grove or in the market place; *when*, for example, tomorrow or the day before yesterday; *posture*, for example, reclining or standing; *being equipped*, for example, wearing shoes or being armed; *action*, for example, cutting or burning; *passion or undergoing*, for example, being cut or being burned.[1]

Here is a convenient list of Aristotle's ten categories:

1. Substance: independently existing things; fundamental natures of things.

[the nine accidental categories]
2. Quantity: how much?
3. Quality: what kind?
4. Relation: what is it like in relation to another?
5. Place: where?
6. Posture: how configured at its place?

---

1. Aristotle, *Categories*, c. 4, trans. Houser.

7. **When**: at what time?
8. **Being equipped, clothing**: limited to humans and domesticated animals.
9. **Action**: what is it actively doing?
10. **Passion/undergoing**: what is it passively receiving?

Aristotle's theory of the ten general categories, in sum, is this: every specific term we use to describe any individual thing in the universe, like "man" or "horse" or "grammatical" or "cutting" or "being cut," ultimately will fall under one or another of the ten most general categories, such as substance or quality or action or passion, as in these examples. Problem Set 8, in the section Terms and their "Aristotelian Categories," asks you to determine under which of the ten categories each more specific term (or category) that is listed falls. In order to answer these questions about logical categories correctly, you have to base your answer on the real or ontological categories into which the real things signified fall.

A Deeper Look: Some Important Categories

Let's look a bit closer at some of the more important of Aristotle's ten categories—substance, quantity, quality, and relation. In doing so, we'll be guided by what Aristotle himself said in his book *Categories*, where he distinguished different subdivisions of these important categories in order to explain them.

Substance

Substances have three features that are important for logic (other characteristics will take us too far into philosophy).

First, the substance of a thing describes what it is in its "core" or fundamental nature. It answers the question "what is it fundamentally?" or, more simply, "what is it?" Though Socrates is "walking" or "old" or even "a philosopher," none of these terms describe his fundamental nature in the way that "human" or "animal" or "living thing" does.

Second, individual substances are the independently existing things in the world. The nonsubstantial terms mentioned, like "walking" or "old" or "in the agora," describe traits that depend upon something already being a substance. They *exist in* a substance and depend upon that substance in order to exist. They do not exist independently of Socrates or some other individual substance. This is why Aristotle called them "accidents," not in the sense of something unexpected happening, but in the sense that they are "added to" substances. When he is walking to the agora, Socrates remains Socrates, but "walking" is "added to" and "exists in" his substance. But "walking" ceases to be added when he stops.

Third, Aristotle lived in a world very close to nature, so most of his examples of substances come from the natural world. But what about some artifact that is manmade, like a house or a statue? Such things are like Socrates and unlike his walking in being independently existing things. In this sense they are substances. But what makes a statue independently existing? The bronze or marble it is made out of. It is a statue, however, because of its shape, which is an accident, a kind of quality: it looks like Zeus or the emperor Augustus Caesar. It is both a substance and an accident; different features of it fall into different categories. But what is it fundamentally? The best answer depends upon what question you are asking. If you are asking why it is an independently existing thing, the reason why is because of the material it is made from, say, bronze. But in this sense it is just a bronze thing; that it is a statue of Zeus is irrelevant. But if you are asking why it is a statue, why we use this term to describe it, that is based upon the shape it has—a quality. Perhaps the best answer is that the statue fundamentally falls under the category of quality, but it must be made out of some substance in order to be a statue in the first place.

Quantity

If substance answers the question "what is it?," quantity answers the question "how much of it is there?" Aristotle noted that physical substances or bodies have size in terms of physical parts spread outside one another. They are extended in place (or space) along three dimensions, having height (which makes one dimension), width (which makes two dimensions), and depth (which makes three dimensions). (It would take over two millennia for scientists to come up with the hypothesis that there really might be more than three dimensions, but that argues for more quantity, not less.) Aristotle recognized that having size in three dimensions is something added onto the substance of a thing; size does not determine the kind of substance a thing is, so the category "quantity" must be different from "substance."

Aristotle also recognized two subdivisions of quantity. The first is the kind of quantity that bodies have, which he called "continuous quantity" because the lines, planes, and solids that make up the three dimensions of things are all continuous amounts. If we look at a baseball and don't concern ourselves with the stuff it is made of (its substance) or how it is used in playing the game, we can focus just on its quantity, which is what we do when we study spheres or circles in geometry. The other kind of quantity, according to Aristotle, is "discrete quantity," the discrete numbers we use in counting: 1, 2, 3, 4, and so on. This is what arithmetic studies, also without reference to the kind of substances we are counting. While there have been many developments in mathematics since the days of Aristotle, his insight that the quantitative features of things are different from their substantial features has stood the test of time.

Quality

The qualities of something answer the question "what is it like?" or "what kind is it?" Here we are not talking about the fundamental nature of something—dog, cat, whale, human—but other, less central features of a substance that fill out our view of what it is like. Often these can change without the substance of something changing. To give a better view of quality, Aristotle subdivided this category into four kinds of qualities.

(1) First are the qualities of things we can perceive with our five senses: *colors, sounds, tastes, odors, textures*. Each of these we take in with only one of our senses: sight, hearing, taste, smell, and touch, respectively. (2) *Figure* or *shape* is different. Unlike the first subdivision of quality, shape is a quality we can take in using more than one sense, as we can take in quantitative features of things with more than one sense. These first two kinds of quality are features of things we become aware of by perceiving them with our senses.

The other two kinds of quality we do not directly perceive on the surface of other things, though they exist within other things, as well as ourselves. (3) One kind Aristotle called "habit" (*hexis*) from the verb "to have" (*echein*), because habits are attributes something can come to have through development. For humans, here are some examples of habits: skill at bike riding (which is different from actually riding a bike); or being good at a game like soccer; or at an art like dancing; or having learned geometry or Spanish literature or chemistry. Also included are moral habits like being a just or courageous person. What makes all these traits to be habits is that we are born with the capacity or power to develop them, but that is different from having become good (or bad) at them through work, like we can build up our muscles through weight training or running. (4) The last kind of quality Aristotle mentions is the innermost, the basic *powers* or *capacities* that go along with being the kind of substance something is. Dogs, for example, have a better basic sense of smell than humans, while we have a better natural capacity to think. In sum, powers are what make it possible for us to develop habits, and habits are what make it possible for us to act in a proficient and reliable way.

Relation

The last of the four most important categories is relation. While substance, quantity, and quality describe something intrinsically or on its own, relation contains reference to something else. So being a *mother*, a *child*, *equal to*, *to the right of*, *to the left of*, being *sensible*—that is, "able to be sensed," or *knowable*, "able to be known"—are all relations. In relation, something is described in comparison with something else. While important on its own, relation has added significance because it forms the basis for the other six categories Aristotle listed: *when* (a temporal relation); *where* (a spatial relation); *posture* (the relation of the parts of a body at the place where it is); *equipped* (the relation between a person and his most immediate environment, his clothing or equipment); an *action*, such as making something with Legos, a *transient action* that produces an effect in the Legos when they become, say, a starship, or an immanent action, like thinking, which need not affect anything else; and its opposite, *passion*, where something else affects us, the thing that undergoes the passion, as when we see or hear something.

Some Conclusions

Universals are the normal way of thinking about things; proper names limited to one individual are the odd kind of names. We limit proper names to very important things: humans, some animals, human institutions.

In thought, humans use universals to describe things in terms of what they have in common with other things of the same sort. There are natural sorts of things to which our minds attempt to conform themselves.

For universal terms connected to each other, one universal term fits under another, both of which are true of the subject in question. For instance, Socrates is human, animal, living thing, physical thing, and substance.

Aristotle found empirically that all things or objects—both real or imaginary, actual or merely possible—fall into ten highest or most general groups—his ten categories. This is why we recognize both specific categories and Aristotle's ten most general categories.

Aristotle's ten categories and how he described them:

1. Substance: independently existing things; fundamental natures of things [the nine accidents].
2. Quantity: how much?
3. Quality: what kind?
4. Relation: what is it like in relation to another?
5. Place: where?
6. Posture: how configured at its place?
7. When: at what time?
8. Being equipped, clothing: limited to humans and domesticated animals.
9. Action: what is it actively doing?
10. Passion/undergoing: what is it passively receiving?

To understand anything, the first "what" question to ask is, "Which of the ten categories does the thing fall into?" Then we can proceed to more and more specific or precise categories used to describe it.

Primary Sources

Substance

Aristotle, *Categories*, c. 5, 2a11–4b19.

Aquinas, *Commentary on Aristotle's Metaphysic*, bk. 7, lec. 2, n. 1273–75.

Accidents

Aristotle, *Categories*, c. 6–9, 4b20–11b14.

Aquinas, *Commentary on Lombard's Sentences,* bk. 1, d. 8.4.3c.

Quantity

Aquinas, *Commentary on Aristotle's Metaphysics*, bk. 5, lec. 15.

Quality

Aquinas, *Commentary on Aristotle's Metaphysics*, bk. 5, lec. 16.

Relation

Aquinas, *Commentary on Aristotle's* Metaphysics, bk. 5, lec. 17.

Problem Set 8: Recognizing and Using Categories

Terms and their Aristotelian Categories

Instructions about Aristotle's *Categories*

Into which of Aristotle's ten general categories do the following terms fit?

1. the present millennium
2. leader
3. cat
4. wearing a baseball uniform
5. singing
6. kneeling
7. statue
8. rectangle
9. mile
10. in the desk
11. neutron
12. swimming
13. capable of swimming
14. risible (able to laugh)
15. to be humiliated
16. metal
17. seeing
18. being oval
19. mayor
20. upside-down
21. in the phonebook
22. a laptop computer
23. red
25. a fast runner
26. being categorized
27. thinking

Finding Terms in Prose

Instructions about using Aristotle's *Categories*

In the following passages, underline the five most important words in each passage. Then place each word in one of Aristotle's ten category.

1. "The next day he woke up late. Going over the impression of the past, what he recalled most vividly was that he was to be presented to the Emperor Francis. He remembered the Minister of War, the ceremonious Adjutant, Bilibin, and the conversation of the previous evening. He dressed for his attendance at court in full court dress, which he had not worn for a long

time, and fresh, eager, and handsome, he walked into Bilibin's room with his arm in a sling. Four gentlemen of the diplomatic corps were already there. With Prince Ippolit Kuragin, who was a secretary to the embassy, Bolkonsky was already acquainted. Bilibin introduced him to the others." (Leo Tolstoy, 19th-cen. Russian novelist, *War and Peace*)

2. "And what did it profit me that when I was barely twenty years old, there came into my hands, and I read and understood, alone and unaided, the book of Aristotle's ten *Categories*, a book I had longed for as for some great and divine work, because the master who taught me Rhetoric at Carthage, and others held learned, mouthed its name with such evident pride? I compared notes with others, who admitted that they had scarcely managed to understand the book even with the most learned masters not merely lecturing upon it but making many diagrams in the dust. And they could not tell me anything of it that I had not discovered in reading it for myself. For it seemed to me clear enough what the book had to say of substances, like man, and of the accidents that are in substances, like the figure of a man, and what sort of man he is, and of his stature, how many feet high, and of his family relationships, whose brother he is, or where he is placed, or when he was born, or whether he is standing or sitting or has his shoes on or is armed, or whether he is doing something or having something done to him—and all the other countless things that are to be put either in these nine categories of which I have given examples, or in the chief category of substance." (Augustine, d. 430, Roman bishop and theologian, *Confessions*)

3. "I had three chairs in my house: one for solitude, two for friendship, three for society. When visitors came in larger and unexpected numbers, there was but the third chair for them all; but they generally economized the room by standing up. It is surprising how many great men and women a small house will contain. I have had twenty-five or thirty souls, with their bodies, at once under my roof. And yet we often parted without being aware that we had come very near to one another." (Henry David Thoreau, 19th-cen. American essayist, *Walden*)

4. "The Crow and the Pitcher"

"Once there was a thirsty crow. She had flown a long way looking for water to drink. Suddenly she saw a pitcher. She flew down and saw it held a little water, but it was so low in the pitcher that she could not reach it.

"'But I must have that water,' she cried. 'I am too weary to fly farther.

What shall I do? I know! I'll tip the pitcher over.' She beat it with her wings, but it was too heavy. She could not move it. The she thought a while. 'I know now! I will break it! Then I will drink the water as it pours out. How good it will taste!' With her beak and claws and wings she threw herself against the pitcher. But it was too strong.

"The poor crow stopped to rest. 'What shall I do now? I cannot die of thirst with water close by. There must be a way, if I only had wit enough to find it out.'

"After a while the crow had a bright idea. There were many small stones lying about. She picked them up one by one and dropped them into the pitcher. Slowly the water rose, until at last she could drink it. How good it tasted!

"'There is always a way out of hard places,' said the crow, 'if only you have the wit to find it.'" (Aesop, Greek, ca. 600 b.c., *Fables*)

Identifying Specific Categories

Instructions

Consider the following very *specific* categorical terms. Describe what these terms mean by identifying at least two other, broader terms under which they fit and that help to describe their nature (whether the two terms are specific categories or Aristotle's most general categories).

1. sky blue
2. Shetland pony
3. ten
4. middle C
5. second cousin
6. running
7. tarantula
8. murder
9. larger than
10. being eaten
11. Miriam is a *pleasant* person.
12. sea shell

Clarifying Concepts through Division and Collection of Terms

The Essentials

Division and collection of terms are important techniques for analyzing the concepts, words, and terms we use, techniques that serve as a preparation for accurate definitions. When using terms, in order to find a full answer to the "what?" question, we should be able to understand how one term is different from terms that fall under the other nine categories. For instance, in a "green hopping toad," what are the differences among "toad," and "hopping," and "green"? And we should also understand how a term is related to other terms *within* the category under which it falls. For example, what kind of substance is a toad? Or what kind of quality is green? Or what kind of relation is being a daughter?

Extension and Comprehension of Terms

To answer questions like these, it helps to understand that each term we use has two features that work in tandem with each other: the first is what logicians call "extension," and the second is called "comprehension" (or "meaning" or "intension"). Extension is simply how wide the term extends, the range of the things to which it applies. We have already seen that "living thing" has a much wider extension than does "human." When we learn the meaning of terms, we normally learn their extension first. Aristotle has a memorable example: "A child begins by calling all men father, and all women mother, but later on distinguishes each of them." The child in Aristotle's example initially thinks that "mother" has the same extension as the much wider term "woman," and at first thinks that "father" has the same extension as "man," but then learns better. The comprehension of a term is its meaning; and through experience, we come to understand or comprehend it. The comprehension of a term is the basis for its extension. But we normally learn the comprehension of a term by first becoming aware of its extension, as in Aristotle's example of the child. The way to do this is to look at what we might call the term's "logical inferiors and superiors." The logical inferiors below it are the narrower terms that fall under it, as "red" and "green" and "yellow" fall under "color." Its logical superiors are the wider terms that stand over the term we are trying to understand, as "red" falls under the wider term "color," and "color" falls under the wider term "sensible quality," and sensible quality falls under the category "quality." Problem Set 9 focuses on using the extension of terms to get at their meaning by identifying their logical inferiors and superiors.

Logical Inferiors and Superiors

Looking for the logical superiors and inferiors of a term is not a haphazard business. Even before Aristotle, Plato had identified two techniques for this search. When looking for a logical superior, we use the technique of *collection*, where we collect examples of the logical inferiors of the term we are after until they lead us to that term. Moving from "red," "green," and "yellow" to the term "color" is an example of collection. When moving in the opposite direction, from the wider to the narrower term, we use the technique of *division*, dividing the wider term into its parts. If we start with "color," we can divide it into specific colors, like "red" or "blue" or "orange." And then we might further divide a specific color, say, brown, into what we normally call "shades" of brown. Division of concepts or terms is really the fundamental technique here, because when we move down we divide our original concept, and when we move up we follow the same division, but in the upward direction.

How Division of Terms Is Useful

Since Aristotle's ten categories are the most general terms or categories, they are very useful for beginning to understand what something is by asking, "What category does it fit into?" But fully understanding something means you need to find the more specific categories that describe it. Once you sort through these, you will be in position to give a good definition of the thing; and being able to define something—whether a shoe, a car, a beetle, or atomic energy—is the only way to be sure you know what it is. All of us use words that we don't really understand very well; and the clearest sign that our knowledge isn't so good is that we can't really define them very well. Consequently, the way to improve our logical skills involved with the first act of the mind is to improve our ability to define things.

One great aid in defining things—you might say the initial step of developing good definitions—is to be able to divide the terms related to the term being defined: its logical inferiors and superiors, or what we called in Lesson 8 the "specific categories" falling under the "general category" of the term. There we saw a number of features of Socrates that describe what he is fundamentally, in his substance: "human," "animal," "living thing," "physical thing," and, finally, "substance." But how do we know these terms describe him accurately? And how do we discover them? This is where division and collection come into play. We try to arrange these fundamental or essential features of Socrates in order, going from the narrower or more specific features to the wider or more general features, until we arrive at the general category of substance. In Lesson 10 we'll see that a narrower grouping or class is called a "species," while a wider one is a "genus."

An Example of Using Division and Collection

Let's look at how a philosopher explains what a human being is by dividing and collecting concepts, by examining the work of the English philosopher John Locke (d. 1704), whose division we'll consider here. (In Lesson 10 we'll look at an earlier philosopher, Porphyry [d. ca. 300], tackling the same problem.) Locke's thought was influential on the American founding fathers, the men who devised the American Constitution. Here Locke reasons using the technique of collection, starting with individual humans like Socrates, compared with individual horses. He then says:

General natures are nothing but abstract and partial ideas of more complex ones. That this is the way whereby men first formed general ideas, and general names to them, I think is so evident, that there needs no other proof of it but the considering of a man's self, or others, and the ordinary proceedings of their minds in knowledge.... For let any one effect, and then tell me, wherein does his idea of man differ from that of Peter and Paul, or his idea of horse from that of Bucephalus, but in the leaving out something that is peculiar to each individual, and retaining so much of those particular complex ideas of several particular existences as they are found to agree in?

Of the complex ideas signified by the names *man* and *horse*, leaving out but those particulars wherein they differ, and retaining only those wherein they agree, and of those making a new distinct complex idea, and giving the name *animal* to it, one has a more general term, that comprehends with *man* several other creatures. Leave out of the idea of *animal*, sense and spontaneous motion, and the remaining complex idea, made up of the remaining simple ones of body, life, and nourishment, becomes a more general one, under the more comprehensive term, *vivens* [*living thing*]. And, not to dwell longer upon this particular, so evident in itself; by the same way the mind proceeds to *body*, *substance*, and at last to *being*, *thing*, and such universal terms, which stand for any of our ideas whatsoever.[1]

In order to explain the meaning of "man," Locke uses the technique of collection to proceed upward to more and more universal terms that describe human nature: from an individual, like Socrates, to "man," and then on to "animal," "living" thing, "body," "substance," and ending with two correlative notions that are even more universal than substance: "being" and "thing." It is usually helpful to put a division into a diagram, because most descriptions of divisions, including Locke's, leave out some concepts that help us understand the procedure (see p. 96).

Such a diagram helps us to see several things. First, collection and division help us arrange these terms in the right order, going from the narrowest in extension at the bottom to the most universal at the top. Second, these terms fit together like the mixing bowls your mother probably has, the kind that "nest together" with the smallest bowl fitting inside the next larger one, and so on until you get to the largest bowl on the outside. We can see that Socrates is a human, and every human is an animal; but there are more animals than humans, because there are irrational animals. And every animal is a living thing,

---

1. John Locke, *Essay Concerning Human Understanding*, bk. 3, c. 3, sec. 9.

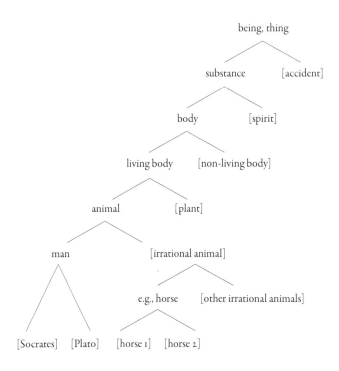

but there are living things that are not animals—namely, plants. Third, such a division is a good way—but not the only way—to try to define Socrates. And fourth, there is a basis for each division. For example, why are humans distinct from all the other animals? Because their thinking is rational, whereas the thinking of other animals is not based on rational, universal concepts, as human thinking is, but "irrational." See if you can figure out the *basis* Locke had for each of his divisions.

Unfortunately, after all his good logical divisions, **Locke's main conclusion here was wrong**: he thought that the "general natures" of things, like horse or man, are not real features of real things, but "nothing but abstract and partial *ideas*," existing *only* in our minds, not in reality, a conclusion his divisions in no way prove. Moreover, if these "natures" aren't a feature of real things in the world, then there is no *basis in reality* for our "ideas."

A Deeper Look

Kinds of Divisions

Locke's division of terms is very important for logic, but it is not the only kind of division. In explaining the moral virtues and vices, Thomas Aquinas (d. 1274) distinguished three ways we can divide a whole into its parts: "There are three kinds of parts, namely, an integral part, such as wall, roof, and foundation are the parts of a house; a subjective part, such as ox and lion are parts of animal; and a potential part, such as the nutritive power and the sensory power are parts of the soul."[2] The third sense of dividing a whole into parts is not directly relevant to our logical concerns here, but it is real. A car, for example, has the power to start and the power to stop, and the human soul, according to Aquinas, contains several different kinds of powers, including the powers of nutrition and growth, as well as the power of sensation, each of which is further divided into other powers, like sight and hearing and touch. But the other two kinds of wholes and parts are directly relevant to logical divisions.

Division of an Integral Whole into Its Parts

The word "integral" refers to the parts that must combine to form the whole thing. Every independently existing thing in the physical universal is this kind of whole, as Aquinas's example of the house makes clear. The roof, walls, and foundation are all required for a house to exist; but it is important to note that none of them are the house; they are only parts of the house. Looking forward to Problem Set 9, a second example is the republican type of government James Madison supported in his essay. It has a federal government divided into three parts we call branches: legislative, executive, and judicial. Taken together, these three parts make up the federal government, but none of them *is* that government; they are its separate, integral parts.

Division of a Universal Whole into Its Subjective Parts

Locke's division of a more universal concept or whole into its parts is even more important for logic, but this kind of division (or collection) is quite different from a house or government. Following Locke's collection of terms describing Socrates, we can see that he is a man, every man is an animal, all

---

2. Aquinas, *Summa Theologiae* II-II, q. 2, a. un. 2–2.49, un.c.

animals are living things and have bodies, which are one kind of substance. But if we go in the opposite direction, starting from the category of substance and dividing terms, we see that the very meaning or nature of the higher term flows down into its subordinate. This is why Aquinas calls these kinds of parts "subjective parts," because each part of this kind is a subject for propositions whose predicates are the terms above it. So "Socrates is a man," and "Socrates is an animal," because "all men are animals." In addition, at each step of this division, for the term divided there is a basis for the division Locke employs. These features of Socrates cluster together to make it possible for us to define his fundamental nature based on this division. The term "government" also provides examples of this kind of division, as when we divide government into monarchy, oligarchy (or aristocracy), and democracy. Or we might think of triangles as equilateral, isosceles, and scalene. These examples also reveal the three distinct "essential predicables" we'll see in Lesson 10: species, genus, and difference.

Rules for Divisions

We can even devise some rough-and-ready rules for divisions.

Rule 1: A good division must be a *real* division. This means that each part must be narrower (in extension) than the whole. In Locke's division, the range of *humans* and the range of *irrational animals* are each less that of *animal*.

Rule 2: A good division must be *exhaustive*. Nothing contained within the term being divided should be left out of the parts. When considered together, the parts must have an extension equal to that of the whole. Here, animals and plants exhaust the range of living bodily substances.

Rule 3: A good division must be *exclusive*. The parts cannot overlap. This is the reason why the basis for the division is often a negative notion, in order to separate the concepts divided. For example, we do so in the case of rational humans in contrast to all the other animals, which are described as irrational.

Rule 4: In the case of the division of a universal whole into its subjective parts, the parts of each division must fall into the same category. In the case of Locke's division, the category is the most basic one, substance. So all the terms arrived at through the division of substance are themselves kinds of substances.

Finally, collection and division are not limited to defining terms like "human being" or "animal," but they can be used in explaining more complicated concepts. Problem Set 9 is devoted to a famous argument in *Federalist*

No. 10, written by James Madison. It does not concern how to define a term like "faction," but offers an argument for why a "republic," such as that proposed by the as yet unpassed Constitution, would be the best way of preventing the problems that factions can cause. Madison's argument is as relevant to American life today as it was when first published in 1790.

Primary Sources

Aristotle: *On Interpretation*, Prior *Analytics* 1.31, 2.23–24.

Aquinas, *Summa Theologaie* I-II, q. 18, a. 7c, *Commentary on Aristotle's On Interpretation*, Lesson 3.

Problem Set 9: Argument Using Division

James Madison's Argument in *Federalist* No. 10

Instructions

The techniques of *division and collection* of concepts can be employed in arguments that use specific categories. Read the essay *Federalist No. 10*, by James Madison. Then answer the following questions to see how division and collection of concepts play a part in this work.

1. What is the *subject* under discussion?
2. What is Madison's *thesis*?
3. Madison presents his basic argument through a *division* of the main ideas or specific categories in the passage. *Diagram* this division of ideas. Be sure the words and phrases you use to label the ideas are clear. But don't try to repeat in a diagram *everything* Madison says in the text; just concentrate on dividing the main ideas.
4. Write down *four* of Madison's most important *definitions*. Do you think his definitions are good ones?
5. Write out your answers in order to turn in this homework in class.

Federalist No. 10

"The Same Subject Continued"
(The Union as a Safeguard against Domestic Faction and Insurrection)
From the *New York Packet*
Friday, November 23, 1787
James Madison

To the People of the State of New York:

1. AMONG the numerous advantages promised by a well-constructed Union, none deserves to be more accurately developed than its tendency to break and control the violence of faction. The friend of popular governments never finds himself so much alarmed for their character and fate, as when he contemplates their propensity to this dangerous vice. He will not fail, therefore, to set a due value on any plan which, without violating the principles to which he is attached, provides a proper cure for it. The instability, injustice, and confusion introduced into the public councils, have, in truth, been the mortal diseases under which popular governments have everywhere perished; as they continue to be the favorite and fruitful topics from which the adversaries to liberty derive their most specious declamations. The valuable improvements made by the American constitutions on the popular models, both ancient and modern, cannot certainly be too much admired; but it would be an unwarrantable partiality, to contend that they have as effectually obviated the danger on this side, as was wished and expected. Complaints are everywhere heard from our most considerate and virtuous citizens, equally the friends of public and private faith, and of public and personal liberty, that our governments are too unstable, that the public good is disregarded in the conflicts of rival parties, and that measures are too often decided, not according to the rules of justice and the rights of the minor party, but by the superior force of an interested and overbearing majority. However anxiously we may wish that these complaints had no foundation, the evidence of known facts will not permit us to deny that they are in some degree true. It will be found, indeed, on a candid review of our situation, that some of the distresses under which we labor have been erroneously charged on the operation of our governments; but it will be found, at the same time, that other causes will not alone account for many of our heaviest misfortunes; and, particularly, for that prevailing and increasing distrust of public engagements, and alarm for private rights, which are echoed from one end of the continent to the other. These must be chiefly, if not wholly, effects of the unsteadiness and injustice with which a factious spirit has tainted our public administrations.

2. By a **faction**, I understand a number of citizens, whether amounting to a majority or a minority of the whole, who are united and actuated by some common impulse of passion, or of interest, adverse to the rights of other citizens, or to the permanent and aggregate interests of the community.

3. There are two methods of curing the mischiefs of faction: the one, by removing its causes; the other, by controlling its effects.

4. There are again two methods of removing the causes of faction: the one, by destroying the liberty which is essential to its existence; the other, by giving to every citizen the same opinions, the same passions, and the same interests.

5. It could never be more truly said than of the first remedy, that it was worse than the disease. Liberty is to faction what air is to fire, an aliment without which it instantly expires. But it could not be less folly to abolish liberty, which is essential to political life, because it nourishes faction, than it would be to wish the annihilation of air, which is essential to animal life, because it imparts to fire its destructive agency.

6. The second expedient is as impracticable as the first would be unwise. As long as the reason of man continues fallible, and he is at liberty to exercise it, different opinions will be formed. As long as the connection subsists between his reason and his self-love, his opinions and his passions will have a reciprocal influence on each other; and the former will be objects to which the latter will attach themselves. The diversity in the faculties of men, from which the rights of property originate, is not less an insuperable obstacle to a uniformity of interests. The protection of these faculties is the first object of government. From the protection of different and unequal faculties of acquiring property, the possession of different degrees and kinds of property immediately results; and from the influence of these on the sentiments and views of the respective proprietors, ensues a division of the society into different interests and parties.

7. The latent causes of faction are thus sown in the nature of man; and we see them everywhere brought into different degrees of activity, according to the different circumstances of civil society. A zeal for different opinions concerning religion, concerning government, and many other points, as well of speculation as of practice; an attachment to different leaders ambitiously contending for pre-eminence and power; or to persons of other descriptions whose fortunes have been interesting to the human passions, have, in turn, divided mankind into parties, inflamed them with mutual animosity, and rendered them much more disposed to vex and oppress each other than to co-operate for their common good. So strong is this propensity of mankind to fall into mutual animosities, that where no substantial occasion presents itself, the most frivolous and fanciful distinctions have been sufficient to kindle their unfriendly passions and excite their most violent conflicts. But the most common and durable source of factions has been the various and unequal distribution of property. Those who hold and those who are without property have ever formed distinct interests in society. Those who are creditors, and those who are debtors, fall under a like discrimination. A landed interest, a

manufacturing interest, a mercantile interest, a moneyed interest, with many lesser interests, grow up of necessity in civilized nations, and divide them into different classes, actuated by different sentiments and views. The regulation of these various and interfering interests forms the principal task of modern legislation, and involves the spirit of party and faction in the necessary and ordinary operations of the government.

8. No man is allowed to be a judge in his own cause, because his interest would certainly bias his judgment, and, not improbably, corrupt his integrity. With equal, nay with greater reason, a body of men are unfit to be both judges and parties at the same time; yet what are many of the most important acts of legislation, but so many judicial determinations, not indeed concerning the rights of single persons, but concerning the rights of large bodies of citizens? And what are the different classes of legislators but advocates and parties to the causes which they determine? Is a law proposed concerning private debts? It is a question to which the creditors are parties on one side and the debtors on the other. Justice ought to hold the balance between them. Yet the parties are, and must be, themselves the judges; and the most numerous party, or, in other words, the most powerful faction must be expected to prevail. Shall domestic manufactures be encouraged, and in what degree, by restrictions on foreign manufactures? are questions which would be differently decided by the landed and the manufacturing classes, and probably by neither with a sole regard to justice and the public good. The apportionment of taxes on the various descriptions of property is an act which seems to require the most exact impartiality; yet there is, perhaps, no legislative act in which greater opportunity and temptation are given to a predominant party to trample on the rules of justice. Every shilling with which they overburden the inferior number, is a shilling saved to their own pockets.

9. It is in vain to say that enlightened statesmen will be able to adjust these clashing interests, and render them all subservient to the public good. Enlightened statesmen will not always be at the helm. Nor, in many cases, can such an adjustment be made at all without taking into view indirect and remote considerations, which will rarely prevail over the immediate interest which one party may find in disregarding the rights of another or the good of the whole.

10. The inference to which we are brought is, that the CAUSES of faction cannot be removed, and that relief is only to be sought in the means of controlling its EFFECTS.

11. If a faction consists of less than a majority, relief is supplied by the

republican principle, which enables the majority to defeat its sinister views by regular vote. It may clog the administration, it may convulse the society; but it will be unable to execute and mask its violence under the forms of the Constitution. When a majority is included in a faction, the form of popular government, on the other hand, enables it to sacrifice to its ruling passion or interest both the public good and the rights of other citizens. To secure the public good and private rights against the danger of such a faction, and at the same time to preserve the spirit and the form of popular government, is then the great object to which our inquiries are directed. Let me add that it is the great desideratum by which this form of government can be rescued from the opprobrium under which it has so long labored, and be recommended to the esteem and adoption of mankind.

12. By what means is this object attainable? Evidently by one of two only. Either the existence of the same passion or interest in a majority at the same time must be prevented, or the majority, having such coexistent passion or interest, must be rendered, by their number and local situation, unable to concert and carry into effect schemes of oppression. If the impulse and the opportunity be suffered to coincide, we well know that neither moral nor religious motives can be relied on as an adequate control. They are not found to be such on the injustice and violence of individuals, and lose their efficacy in proportion to the number combined together, that is, in proportion as their efficacy becomes needful.

13. From this view of the subject it may be concluded that a pure democracy, by which I mean a society consisting of a small number of citizens, who assemble and administer the government in person, can admit of no cure for the mischiefs of faction. A common passion or interest will, in almost every case, be felt by a majority of the whole; a communication and concert result from the form of government itself; and there is nothing to check the inducements to sacrifice the weaker party or an obnoxious individual. Hence it is that such democracies have ever been spectacles of turbulence and contention; have ever been found incompatible with personal security or the rights of property; and have in general been as short in their lives as they have been violent in their deaths. Theoretic politicians, who have patronized this species of government, have erroneously supposed that by reducing mankind to a perfect equality in their political rights, they would, at the same time, be perfectly equalized and assimilated in their possessions, their opinions, and their passions.

14. A republic, by which I mean a government in which the scheme of representation takes place, opens a different prospect, and promises the cure for which we are seeking. Let us examine the points in which it varies from pure democracy, and we shall comprehend both the nature of the cure and the efficacy which it must derive from the Union.

15. The two great points of difference between a democracy and a republic are: first, the delegation of the government, in the latter, to a small number of citizens elected by the rest; secondly, the greater number of citizens, and greater sphere of country, over which the latter may be extended.

16. The effect of the first difference is, on the one hand, to refine and enlarge the public views, by passing them through the medium of a chosen body of citizens, whose wisdom may best discern the true interest of their country, and whose patriotism and love of justice will be least likely to sacrifice it to temporary or partial considerations. Under such a regulation, it may well happen that the public voice, pronounced by the representatives of the people, will be more consonant to the public good than if pronounced by the people themselves, convened for the purpose. On the other hand, the effect may be inverted. Men of factious tempers, of local prejudices, or of sinister designs, may, by intrigue, by corruption, or by other means, first obtain the suffrages, and then betray the interests, of the people. The question resulting is, whether small or extensive republics are more favorable to the election of proper guardians of the public weal; and it is clearly decided in favor of the latter by two obvious considerations:

17. In the first place, it is to be remarked that, however small the republic may be, the representatives must be raised to a certain number, in order to guard against the cabals of a few; and that, however large it may be, they must be limited to a certain number, in order to guard against the confusion of a multitude. Hence, the number of representatives in the two cases not being in proportion to that of the two constituents, and being proportionally greater in the small republic, it follows that, if the proportion of fit characters be not less in the large than in the small republic, the former will present a greater option, and consequently a greater probability of a fit choice.

18. In the next place, as each representative will be chosen by a greater number of citizens in the large than in the small republic, it will be more difficult for unworthy candidates to practice with success the vicious arts by which elections are too often carried; and the suffrages of the people being more free, will be more likely to occur in men who possess the most attractive merit and the most diffusive and established characters.

19. It must be confessed that in this, as in most other cases, there is a mean, on both sides of which inconveniences will be found to lie. By enlarging too much the number of electors, you render the representatives too little acquainted with all their local circumstances and lesser interests; as by reducing it too much, you render him unduly attached to these, and too little fit to comprehend and pursue great and national objects. The federal Constitution forms a happy combination in this respect; the great and aggregate interests being referred to the national, the local and particular to the State legislatures.

20. The other point of difference is, the greater number of citizens and extent of territory which may be brought within the compass of republican than of democratic government; and it is this circumstance principally which renders factious combinations less to be dreaded in the former than in the latter. The smaller the society, the fewer probably will be the distinct parties and interests composing it; the fewer the distinct parties and interests, the more frequently will a majority be found of the same party; and the smaller the number of individuals composing a majority, and the smaller the compass within which they are placed, the more easily will they concert and execute their plans of oppression. Extend the sphere, and you take in a greater variety of parties and interests; you make it less probable that a majority of the whole will have a common motive to invade the rights of other citizens; or if such a common motive exists, it will be more difficult for all who feel it to discover their own strength, and to act in unison with each other. Besides other impediments, it may be remarked that, where there is a consciousness of unjust or dishonorable purposes, communication is always checked by distrust in proportion to the number whose concurrence is necessary.

21. Hence, it clearly appears, that the same advantage which a republic has over a democracy, in controlling the effects of faction, is enjoyed by a large over a small republic, is enjoyed by the Union over the States composing it. Does the advantage consist in the substitution of representatives whose enlightened views and virtuous sentiments render them superior to local prejudices and schemes of injustice? It will not be denied that the representation of the Union will be most likely to possess these requisite endowments. Does it consist in the greater security afforded by a greater variety of parties, against the event of any one party being able to outnumber and oppress the rest? In an equal degree does the increased variety of parties comprised within the Union increase this security. Does it, in fine, consist in the greater obstacles opposed to the concert and accomplishment of the secret wishes of an unjust and interested majority? Here, again, the extent of the Union gives it the most palpable advantage.

22. The influence of factious leaders may kindle a flame within their particular States, but will be unable to spread a general conflagration through the other States. A religious sect may degenerate into a political faction in a part of the Confederacy; but the variety of sects dispersed over the entire face of it must secure the national councils against any danger from that source. A rage for paper money, for an abolition of debts, for an equal division of property, or for any other improper or wicked project, will be less apt to pervade the whole body of the Union than a particular member of it; in the same proportion as such a malady is more likely to taint a particular county or district, than an entire State.

23. In the extent and proper structure of the Union, therefore, we behold a republican remedy for the diseases most incident to republican government. And according to the degree of pleasure and pride we feel in being republicans, ought to be our zeal in cherishing the spirit and supporting the character of Federalists.

—*PUBLIUS.*

Aristotle's Predicables

The Essentials

In this lesson we meet Aristotle's predicables. There are **three** *essential* predicables—genus, species, and difference—and two *nonessential* predicables—property and accident.

What "Predicable" Means

The predicables concern the relation of one term to another. The term "predicable" is taken from the Latin words *praedico*, which means "to speak publicly," and *praedicatio*, a "public speech." When we speak publicly we are trying to convince someone of something by asserting a grammatical "predicate" (*praedicamentum*) of a grammatical "subject," as in the proposition "Aristotle was the first great scientist." (He really was.) In "Socrates is a philosopher," "Socrates" is the *subject* of the proposition, while "philosopher" is the *predicate* of the proposition. In a proposition, then, "predicable" refers to how one term—a predicate—*can* be "predicated" or "said of" another—a subject. Aristotle found that while there are literally an unlimited number of concepts we might use to describe things, there are a very limited number of ultimate or highest terms we can used for describing things—his ten categories. Likewise, while there are an unlimited number of "predications" or sentences we can formulate, there are a very limited number of *ways* any given predicate can be related to a given subject in a categorical proposition. And we can make the same point without worrying about propositions: there are a very limited number of ways one *thing* can be related to another.

To see how the predicables work, let's use the example that many of Aristotle's followers (called Aristotelians) over the centuries have used, because it is so familiar to us: *human* (or *man* in older English, *l'homme* in French, *anthropos* in Greek, *Mensch* in German, *al-insan* in classical Arabic). First, draw up a list of terms that accurately describe someone you know, perhaps your sister or the person sitting next to you in class. Following a very long tradition of logicians, we'll use some of the examples, used in Lesson 8, of predicates asserted of our friend and teacher Socrates.

Predicates of Socrates

As we have seen, when we try to describe Socrates, we invariably use *universal* terms. Here are some of the terms used in Lesson 8 to describe Socrates, using the same numbers we used there. He was (1) a philosopher, (2) ugly, (3) snub-nosed, (4) looked like a satyr. Socrates also (5) talked to people, (6) he did so in the agora, (7) sometimes he was in the battlefield, (8) a soldier, (9) suffered cold weather, (10) without complaint, (11) and he was heroic. Socrates was also (12) a husband, (13) father, (14) friendly, (15) old, (16) with a bit of gray hair, (17) that was his hair's color. (18) He dressed poorly (as befits a poor philosopher), (19) often stooped over when he walked, (20) was lying on a dinner couch, (21) next to the young tragic poet Agathon, (22) was the only one left standing the morning after the symposium, and (23) then walked back to the *agora* to follow his daily routine. We also saw that Socrates could be described as (24) Greek, (25) a human, (26) an animal, (27) rational, or able to reason, (28) a living thing, and (29) a physical thing.

Essential vs. Nonessential Predicates

Aristotle noted that some terms describe the "essence" or "nature" or intelligible core of another term as distinct from terms that describe nonessential features. In our example of Socrates, (25) human, (26) animal, (27) rational, (28) living thing, and (29) physical thing all describe the essence or fundamental nature of Socrates, an essence that falls within the category of substance. We must be careful to note, however, that essence or fundamental nature is not confined to the category of substance. "Ugly" and "talking" and "soldier" and "suffering" and "color" and "lying" and "tragic," each of these has an essence, one outside the category of substance. To understand the essences of these traits, then, we can begin by determining which of the ten categories they fit in. "Talking" is a kind of *action*, "suffering" a kind of *passion*, "color" a kind of *quality*, and "lying" a kind of *position or posture*. But how do we come to understand that these statements are true about Socrates? Aristotle developed his idea of the predicables to answer this question as a kind of framework for developing definitions. The very first step toward defining something, whether Socrates or his talking or the shape of his snub nose, is to try to begin to define its essence by comparing it to other things, which are either essential to it or nonessential—that is, "accidental." Once we distinguish the essential from the nonessential traits, then we can look among the essential traits to find a definition, as Locke did in his division of concepts in Lesson 9. Since substance is the most important category, let's return to Socrates and distinguish essential and nonessential features of him. This time, however, we'll turn back the clock about 1,400 years, to the work of the philosopher Porphyry (d. ca. 300), who was born in the city of Tyre, in what is now Lebanon, but spent much of his life in Rome, which was then the center of the world.

The Essential Predicables: Genus, Species, Difference

Porphyry does not reason through collection but through division, moving downward from the most general term he considers, the category of substance, to more specific terms subordinated to it, and ending with individuals. The picture he draws in words has since become known as "Porphyry's Tree," because if you make a diagram of what he says, it will look something like a pine tree, the kind that grows in Italy. Porphyry's reasoning is more complete than Locke's, and most importantly he uses distinguishes three parts, so to speak, of the essence: genus, species, and difference:

> In each category there are the highest classes, the lowest classes, and some which are between the highest and the lowest. There is a highest genus beyond which there can be no other superior genus; there is a lowest species after which there can be no subordinate species; and between the highest genus and the lowest species there are some classes which are genera and species at the same time, since they include comparisons with the highest genus and the lowest species.

Let us make the meaning clear with reference to one category—substance. *Substance* is itself a genus; under this is *body*; and under body is *animate body*; and under this is *animal*; under animal is *rational animal*; and under this is *man*; and under man are *Socrates, Plato,* and individual men.

Of all these, *substance* is the highest genus, and it is only a genus, while *man* is the lowest species, and it is only a species. Body is a species of substance, but it is a genus of animate body. Animate body is a species of body, but it is a genus of animal. Animal is a species of animate body, but a genus of rational animal. Rational animal is a species of animal, but a genus of man. Man is a species of rational animal, but it is not also a genus of individual men, it is only a species. Every species, which is predicated immediately above individuals, will be only a species, never a genus.

Therefore, just as *substance* is highest because there is nothing superior to substance and is the highest genus, so too *man* is a species below which there is no species nor anything able to be divided into species. Of individuals—Socrates, Plato, and this white thing are individuals—there can only be a species, namely, the last species and, as we called it, the lowest species. The intermediate classes will be species of higher classes, but genera of lower classes.[1]

Porphyry's Tree is a little more complicated than Locke's description. But what is remarkable is how similar the two divisions are, even though written at an interval of 1,400 years. To see this, let's look at the diagram of Porphyry's division (facing page).

The main difference in language between Locke and Porphyry is that Porphyry uses terms that Aristotle had invented to describe logical superiors and inferiors—genus, species, and difference. You may be familiar with these terms from biology, so let's build on that and focus on how they are used in logic. An individual human, like Socrates, has an essence or fundamental nature that causes him to be human, having the same essence as other humans, like Plato and Aristotle. Socrates's essence, however, can be described at different levels of universality, more general or more specific; and this is where genus, species, and difference come in. Indeed, the word "general" comes from the term "genus," and the word "specific" comes from the term "species." The terms used for describing the essence—genus, species, and difference—do not describe different real parts of the individual thing being defined, such as Socrates. They don't exist as different features of things in reality.

Rather, genus and species exist in the mind, so the difference between

1. Porphyry, *Introduction* [to Aristotle's *Logic*], sec. 2, "Species."

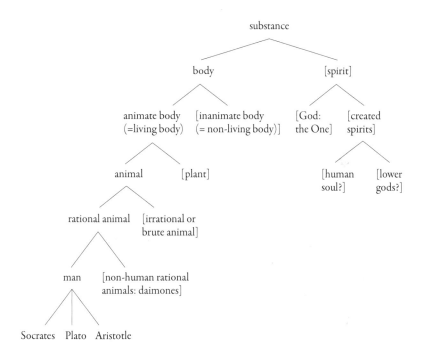

them is a difference in the concepts or terms we use to describe the essence of something. Each signifies a distinct feature of one and the same essence. But what kind of difference? The distinction is that between what is more determinate or delimited, the species, and the more indeterminate or unlimited, the genus, as Thomas Aquinas says in his book *On Being and Essence*. This is a difference among universal concepts we use to understand the essence of Socrates. The difference is designed to try to pinpoint the exact basis for distinguishing the species falling under the genus (here, "human being" falling under "animal"), in comparison to other species falling under the same genus (here, "animal"). This is why genus and species are relative terms: genus always refers to a wider universal term and species to the narrower universal term that falls under it. (Please note that while many of us misuse "specific" by using it to mean the same thing as "individual," "specific" describes a lower universal term, not a term describing individuals.) Finally, since genus and species are relative to each other, speaking logically, each of the steps in this series is both a species, in relation to the next higher genus, and a genus in relation to the next lower species, as Porphyry says.

One final point. You may have noted that Porphyry lists a genus between "man" and "animal"—namely, "rational animal"; but Locke does not. The reason why is that Porphyry thought humans are not the only rational animals. This is because, as a polytheist and anti-Christian, Porphyry believed in the existence of rational beings that were not humans, things he called *daimones*, a term from which the English word "demon" is derived. He was interested in the interactions among humans, the daimones, the gods, and the One or Highest God.

Nonessential Predicables: Property and Accident

Nonessential terms divide into two very important groups: property and accident. An accident is a predicate term that is wholly disconnected from the essence of its subject. Consider "Socrates is *talking in the agora* (or marketplace) today." Actually, *talking* is wholly disconnected from the essence of Socrates; he doesn't have to be talking in order to be a human being, though he can do so. The same thing holds for being "in the agora" and "today." Such terms, therefore, are "predicable accidents" in relation to Socrates's essence as a rational animal.

The other kind of nonessential predicable is called a "property" or sometimes a "proper accident" or an "essential accident." These features of things are far more important than accident. Consider the following terms in relation to Socrates: social, political, language-using, and the classic example in the Aristotelian tradition, risible (which means "able to laugh"). None of these terms describe the very essence of Socrates, so they are nonessential in relation to him. Yet they all are *necessarily connected* with him because they all necessarily result from his human essence. For every human is *by nature* social, political, a language user, and risible. These traits don't constitute or *cause* the essence of Socrates, but they *flow from* it as *necessary effects* flow from their causes. This is why they are called properties. His human nature is the cause of these properties. In short, an accident is wholly unconnected with the essence of its subject, which is why it must be caused by something other than essence. By contrast, while a property is different from that essence, it is necessarily connected with it, because it is caused by that essence.

A property, in short, flows from the essence or nature of the subject, as being risible flows from Socrates's essence but "talking in the agora today" does not. You can see why if you ask yourself what causes a man like Socrates to be "able to laugh." In order to laugh you have to be able to sense what is happening around you, and living things with senses are *animals*. But not all animals laugh. To be able to laugh, you have to have reason in order to understand that what you are presently seeing is odd, unusual, not happening as it normally does. In short, in order to be able to laugh you need to be a rational animal, which is the very definition of a human. So "being able to laugh" (and cry, which is just the reverse side of laughing) is a property always present in normal humans. *Actually laughing*, however, comes and goes; so it is an accident.

Let's take another example: Water is

(a) made of hydrogen and oxygen;
(b) in this glass;
(c) in this fountain;
(d) wet;
(e) freezes at 0 degrees C, 32 degrees F.

(a) describes the *essence* of water; (b) and (c) are predicable *accidents* of water, while (d) and (e) are *properties* of water. These examples show that properties are important for coming to understanding things, especially things in the physical world. The task of knowing things in nature is first to separate a thing's permanent properties from the accidents it has, attributes that come and go. Then sometimes we can go further and uncover features of the essence of a kind of thing by studying its properties. Properties, in short, reveal the essences of things.

A Deeper Look

Identifying Genus, Species, and Difference:
Plato's Example of Division

To see how using differences helps us divide concepts, consider the following passage taken from Plato's *Sophist*. Here the two characters (a "Stranger," who is like a stand-in for Socrates, and a young man named Theatetus) are dividing "art" (*techne*; *ars*) or "skill" in a way that will define the "art of the angler"—that is, the fisherman's skill.

> **Stranger:** Let us begin by asking whether an angler is a man having an art (a developed skill) or not having an art, but some other power.
>
> **Theatetus:** He is clearly a man having an art.

Stranger: And of arts are there two kinds?

Theatetus: What are they?

Stranger: All arts are either acquisitive or creative, in which class shall we place the *art of the angler*?

Theatetus: Clearly in the *acquisitive* class.

Stranger: And the acquisitive may be subdivided into two parts: there is *exchange*, which is voluntary, and is produced by gifts, hire, or purchase; and the other part of the acquisitive, which takes by force of word or deed, may be termed *conquest*?

Theatetus: That is implied in what has been said.

Stranger: And may not conquest again be subdivided?

Theatetus: How?

Stranger: Open force may be called *fighting*, and secret force may have the general name of *hunting*?

Theatetus: Yes.

Stranger: And there is no reason why the art of hunting should not be further divided.

Theatetus: How would you make the division?

Stranger: Into the hunting of *living* and *lifeless prey*.[2]

In the dialogue, they go on to further divisions, but already we can see that the art of the angler is defined as: (1) an art, that is (2) acquisitive, (3) a kind of conquest, (4) taking the form of hunting, (5) of living prey. In this definition there are two important things to notice.

First, the higher and lower terms, the genera and species, all fall into the same category. The divisions of Locke and Porphyry all fall into the category of substance. Humans are substances, and so too are "rational animals," "living things," and "bodies." And in Plato's division that defines "fishing," acquisitive arts and arts of conquest are both arts; they are different examples of the kind of quality we learned to call a "habit." And "exchange" and "conquest" are both kinds of "acquisitive arts."

Second, we can see that for each division, there is some criterion used for making that division. This means that for each division, there is some difference. Sometimes the difference is stated explicitly (such as the difference between using "open" and "secret" force), but at other times it is only implicit. While the species generated by division all fall under the same category—"an-

2. Plato, *Sophist* 218e–20b.

imals" and "humans" are both substances—the differences or criteria to divide the higher genus into species need not fall into the same category. So "rational" and "irrational" are not substances but qualities. And while "skill at hunting prey" is a quality, the prey hunted are substances, and the difference between living and lifeless is a distinct kind of quality.

Two Kinds of Accident: Predicamental and Predicable

You will probably have noticed that we have followed Aristotle in using the term "accident" twice, once in describing the nine categories other than substance and here, as one of the five predicables. The two uses of the term are not exactly the same, but they are analogous. The nine categories are called "accidents" because they do not have to belong to a given substance. This is because they fall outside the nature of the substance. They are called "predicamental" or "categorical" accidents. Being a categorical accident means that the accidental attribute is different from the substance of the thing, but must "exist in" that thing; it does not exist independently on its own. The color green is like this in relation to the leaves of the substance tree.

A predicable accident is similar in that it is not essentially connected with its subject term, but it is different in that the subject term does not have to be a substance; it could be anything. In "the man is white," therefore, "white" is a categorical accident because skin color is a feature of a human that is different from his humanity, and it has to exist in a subject substance, like a human. There is no white color floating free around the universe. White is also a predicable accident because there is no essential connection between human nature and the skin color white. But this relation is true, as well, for other subjects, for other substances, as in "the flower is white," but also for categorical accidents, like "the large area is white." Here "large area" and "white" describe two different categorical accidents of some unnamed substance, the first a quantity of it, the second a quality of it. Here the quality "white" is an accident of the quantity "large," because the quality has no intrinsic and necessary connection to the quantity.

An Example from Contemporary Science

As knowledge of the plant and animal worlds expanded over the centuries, especially after the scientific revolution of the seventeenth century, scientists did not abandon Aristotle's predicables, but concentrated on using genus and species in order to describe the natures of the different species. As we have seen, genus and species in logic are relative terms. In order to avoid the ambiguities of reusing "genus" and "species" over and over again in scientific classifications, the Swedish biologist Linnaeus (d. 1778) popularized giving different names to the levels in the taxonomic ranks (from Greek "taxis," meaning "rank") of plants and animals. Here is a current list used in biology:

Taxonomic Ranks	Example: Humans
Life	living things
Domain	eukaryote = cells have nuclei
Kingdom	animalia
Phylum	chordata = with dorsal nerve chord
Subphylum	vertebrata
Class	mammalia
Order	primates = first among mammals
Family	hominidae = "human-like"
Genus	homo
Species	homo sapiens = "rational human"

CHART OF ARISTOTLE'S FIVE PREDICABLES

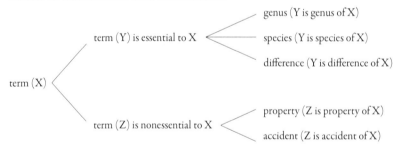

Primary Sources

Aristotle, *Posterior Analytics* 1.4, 6, 10.

Aristotle, *Topics* 1.1–9.

Aquinas, *Commentary on Aristotle's Posterior Analytics* 1, lesson 10, n. 2–7, lesson 33, n. 4–9.

Aquinas, *On Spiritual creatures*, art. 11c. On the difference between "accidental" categories and the predicable "accident," see *Summa Theologaie* I, q. 77, a. 1., ad 5.

Plato, *Sophist*.

Problem Set 10: Recognizing Essence, Property, and Accident

From Genus to Species

Instructions

The following are names for *genera*. Name *two* species under each genus:

1. fish
2. bird
3. triangle
4. rodent

5. number
6. metal
7. rectangle
8. acid

9. fruit
10. insect

From Species to Genus

Instructions

The following are names for species. Name two genera over each species.

1. monkey
2. maple
3. square
4. oxygen

5. tomato
6. skylark
7. gold
8. fifteen

9. wool
10. mosquito

Distinguishing Essence, Property, Accident

Instructions

In the following examples, state the relation between the *italicized* predicate and the *underlined* subject. Is the predicate (a) essential, (b) a property, or (c) an accident of the *subject*? (For essential predicates, see if you can distinguish genus, species, and difference.)

1. Water is *in the street*.
2. Water is *made up of hydrogen and oxygen*.
3. Water is a *liquid*.
4. Water is *necessary for life*.
5. Water *freezes at 32 degrees F, 0 degrees C*.
6. Hydrogen has an *affinity to combine with oxygen to form water*.
7. A triangle has *three sides*.
8. Some humans are *married*.

9. Humans are *animals*.

10. Humans are *substances*.

11. Humans are *risible* (they *can laugh*).

12. Humans are *laughing*.

13. Humans use *language*.

14. Humans are *political*.

15. Delicious apples are *red*.

16. The bobwhite *makes a noise that sounds like its name*.

17. Bobwhites are an *endangered species*.

18. Bears *have fur*.

19. Red is a *color*.

20. High C is a *musical note*.

21. America was *discovered by Europeans in 1492*.

22. American money does *not include any gold coins* (although it used to).

23. 2 times 2 = *four*.

Analyzing Prose Using the Predicables

Instructions

The following passages all concern the predicables. Read each passage and analyze it using the predicables. Determine what important truths (or what errors) about the predicables each passage contains.

1. "We can understand why a classification founded on any single character or organ—even an organ so wonderfully complex and important as the brain—or in the high development of mental faculties, is almost sure to prove unsatisfactory. This principle has indeed been tried with . . . insects, but when thus classed by their habits or instincts, the arrangement proved unsatisfactory. Classification may, of course, be based on any character whatever, as on size, color, or the element inhabited; but naturalists have long felt a profound conviction that there is a natural system. (Charles Darwin, 19th-cen. British evolutionary biologist, *The Descent of Man*, c. 6)

2. "Although man has many points of resemblance with the brutes, one trait is peculiar to himself—he improves: they are incapable of government." (Alexis de Tocqueville, 19th-cen. French writer, *Democracy in America*, bk. 1, c. 8)

3. "To say, then, that shape and color constitute the animal is an inade-

quate statement, and is much the same as if a woodcarver were to insist that the hand he had cut out was really a hand." (Aristotle, *On the Parts of Animals* I.I, 641a5–7)

4. "Next: how shall we define the whale, by his obvious externals, so as conspicuously to label him for all time to come? To be short, then, a whale is *a spouting fish with a horizontal tail.* There you have him. However contracted, that definition is the result of expanded meditation. A walrus spouts much like a whale. But the walrus is not a fish, because he is amphibious. But the last term of the definition is still more cogent, as coupled with the first. Almost any one must have noticed that all the fish familiar to landsmen have not a flat, but a vertical, or up and down tail. Whereas, among spouting fish the tail, though it may be similarly shaped, invariably assumes a horizontal position." (Herman Melville, 19th-cen. American novelist, *Moby-Dick*, c. 32)

5. "But finally here I am, having insensibly reverted to the point I desired, for, since it is now manifest to me that even bodies are not properly speaking known by the senses or by the faculty of imagination, but by the understanding only, and since they are not known from the fact that they are seen or touched, but only because they are understood, I see clearly that there is nothing which is easier for me to know than my mind." (Renee Descartes, 17th-cen. French philosopher, *Meditations on First Philosophy*, 1)

Describing Things Using the Predicables

Instructions

For the following terms, devise at least two other terms that describe (a) its essence; (b) its properties; (c) its accidents.

1. rabbit	10. walking
2. human (man)	11. being hit
3. oak	12. ten feet long
4. black widow spider	13. sweet
5. restaurant	14. Jesus (according to Christian
6. car	theology)
7. country	15. Angel Jibril / Gabriel
8. courage	(according to Islam)
9. fear	16. E = mc^2 (in physics)

Answering the "Why?" Question

Causes

The Essentials

The "Why?" Question—the Most Important Question—
Is a Search for Causes

Let's think back to Aristotle's four questions introduced in Lesson 5: (1) "Is it?" (Does X exist?), (2) "What is it?" (What is the essence or nature of X?), (3) "Whether?" (Is it a fact that X is Y?), and (4) "Why?" (What is the cause or reason why X is Y?). Now let's apply them to Aristotle's example of the child learning to identify her father and mother, who "begins by calling all men father, and all women mother, but later on distinguishes each of them."[1] The child learns about mother and father far earlier than learning names for them. She begins to learn about them by experiencing what they do for her. They clean her and hold her and comfort her. Her mother does this, but so too do her father and other people besides her mother. Assuming she is nursing, however, the most important thing in her young life comes only from one person, her mom who feeds her. At this point, our baby has begun to answer Aristotle's first three questions, even though it is long before she begins to acquire language, still longer before she can formulate what she

---

1. Aristotle, *Physics* 1.1, 184b11–13.

knows into grammatical discourse, and yet still longer before she can know reflectively what she is sure of and what not. She knows people who do things for her (q. 3). She then discerns that they are different from each other and that there is one who is special, who provides the food that comes from her breasts. This distinct person, her mother, exists (q. 1). And this person is her mother (q. 2). So in this way, she has a preliminary—but insufficient—answer to the question "What is mother?" It will take her many years to learn the true answer to this question. But in the meantime, she will make progress in answering it—that is, in developing a definition of "mother," by asking the fourth question: "Why?" Why does this person clean her and hold her and comfort her, and above all, feed her?

The question "Why?" begins the search for the reasons or causes why something happens, or why something is as it is. The tradition that acquiring the best knowledge involves searching for and finding causes goes back even before Socrates, Plato, and Aristotle. Thales (ca. 585 B.C.) of Miletus (a Greek city in what is now Turkey) is often accounted the first scientist and first philosopher, because he was the first man recorded in the Greek tradition to ask the question "Why?" and look carefully and deeply for an answer. He seemed to recognize that knowing the facts (which answer the question "Whether?"), while absolutely required to know anything, only gives us second-level knowledge. First-level knowledge comes from knowing the *reasons for the facts*. Aristotle records a story about Thales on just this point:

> The story goes that when they found fault with him for his poverty, supposing that philosophy is useless, he learned from his study of astronomy that there would be a large crop of olives. Then, while it was still winter, he obtained a little money and made deposits on all the olive presses, both in Miletus and in Chios. Since no one bid against him, he rented them cheaply. When the right time came, suddenly many people tried to get the presses all at once, and he rented them out on whatever terms he wished, and so made a great deal of money. In this way he proved that philosophers can easily be wealthy, if they desire to, but this is not what interests them.[2]

Thales observed the facts about the weather patterns during the winter and then deduced that such weather would cause a large olive crop. Knowing the causes is what made him rich. But asking the question "Why?" did not begin with Thales; it seems to be as old as the human race. The evidence is

2. Aristotle, *Politics* 1259a9–18.

that very early on in life, pretty soon after they begin to learn the differences among things, children begin to ask the question "Why?" Our little girl, too, will ask the question "Why?" She will apply it to her mother, and this will open up for her a better definition of "mother," one that can distinguish her own mother from wet nurses and her father.

Identifying the Four Causes through Examples
Taken from Human Artifacts

Causes are reasons why some event happens or something is as it is. With the advent of modern philosophy and science in the sixteenth century, the causes of *events* took predominance over causes of *things*. In the older view, the causes of some thing—why it exists and why it is as it is in the first place—took predominance. Both are important: the causes of both events and things help us understand the world. To understand that there are different kinds of causes and just what those causes are, let's consider some everyday examples. We'll follow Aristotle's lead and begin with the causes of "artifacts" or man-made things. They are often easier for us to understand than things in nature, because we have made them.[3]

After our little girl has grown up a bit, her parents may well give her that classic American toy—a little red wagon. First she'll be put in the wagon and taken for rides, then she'll stand using the wagon to lift herself up; afterward she'll put her toys and dolls in the wagon, and finally, when she is walking well, she'll take the position of mom or dad and pull things behind her in the wagon, as they pulled her in the wagon. Once she learns to some degree what her wagon is, she well may ask, "Why?" What has caused her wagon? Not what has caused the wagon to be here or there, not what has caused the wagon to be hers, but what has caused the wagon to be a wagon in the first place. A wagon, after all, is not a tricycle or a play car or a play kitchen.

Agent Cause

There are several quite different answers to the question "What caused the wagon?" In an earlier age, when more things were handmade, we might have been inclined to answer that her father or brother or uncle, or perhaps a

---

3. Aristotle, *Physics* 2.3, 194b16–195a2; Aristotle, *Metaphysics* 5.2, 1013a24–1014a26. Aquinas, *Commentary on Aristotle's Physics*, bk. 2, lessons 5–6; Aquinas, *Commentary on Aristotle's Metaphysics*, bk. 5, lessons 2–3.

clever friend, caused the wagon, because he made it. At present, such things are bought at a toy store. But even children realize the clerk there didn't make it; someone somewhere else, perhaps working in a factory, made it. This kind of cause goes by several names: the *agent* (from Latin *agere*, to do, and *agens*, the one who does), because he performed some actions to make it; or the *efficient* cause (from Latin, *facere*, "to make," and *effectus*, "what is made" or the effect), because his actions produced the wagon as an effect; or the *mover* (from Latin *movere*, "to move," and *movens*, "mover"), because the action of making a wagon involves motion on the part of the cause, as well as on the part of the thing being made. What all these names point to is a craftsman, who is a separate reality from the wagon (and therefore called an "extrinsic cause"), who causes the wagon by making it. They also point to the tools and implements such a craftsman must employ. And above all, they point to the actual activities the craftsman performs to produce the wagon: sawing and sanding. But just because you have an agent doesn't mean you automatically have a wagon.

Material Cause

In order to have a wagon, it must be made out of materials. When we think of materials, the first thing that comes into our mind is the "stuff" out of which something is made. And if asked for a definition of this "stuff," we note that it is extended in space in three *dimensions* (or four, if we are scientifically sophisticated and want to add time), it has density and weight, and two different pieces of material can't be in the same place at the same time. The reason why we use the term "materials" of these things is because Aristotle called this second kind of cause *hyle*, which originally meant wood, because many artifacts were then made out of wood, though he expanded the word to mean any physical stuff out of which something is made. *Hyle* was then translated using one of the Latin words for wood, *materia*, which in English became "matter," the stuff out of which something is made, its "material cause." And another, very important feature of matter that Aristotle noticed, in addition to it being the stuff out of which something is made, is that a pile of wood on the floor of the craftsman's shop is not a wagon, though it *can* be. It can be a wagon, but only if the wagon maker does something with the wood—namely, puts it together. Consequently, the wood is a wagon, but only *potentially*; by itself, it isn't yet a wagon, really or actually.

Other materials, like cloth or sand or leaves from the tree, can never become a wagon. Their kind of matter doesn't have the potential to become a wagon. In earlier eras, a little red wagon would have been made of wood, perhaps with wooden wheels and a few metal nails or screws. Later on, more sturdy wagons were made of metal, and the making of them normally took place in factories rather than backyards. Nowadays, most wagons are made of plastic, a kind of matter so complicated that most of us could not explain where the plastic for the wagon comes from. (Look it up online and you may be surprised at the answer.) In order to have a wagon we need the kind of materials that have a potential to be a wagon; in other words, "no matter, no wagon."

Formal Cause

The wagon maker must arrange the materials in the right way. A child's little red wagon must be the right size for a child, it must have wheels that allow it to roll, the wagon itself normally must be longer than it is wide, it must have sides in order to hold things, including children, and it must have a handle—preferably connected with the front wheels—by which it can be pulled. The materials must be put into this configuration or shape. If the materials have not yet assumed that shape, they are not yet *actually* a real wagon. It is the arranging of the materials into this wagon shape that produces a real and true wagon. And, of course, it's not a little red wagon until painted the right color. Greek had several terms for "figure" or "shape." They include *schema*, which focuses on something having a shape, and *morphe*, which focuses on the outline or shape a physical thing has. But the most important words for shape came from the word *eidon* ("to see"): *eidos*, which originally meant what is seen with your eyes and then was transferred to mean what is known with your mind, along with *idea*, which means the kind or sort of thing that is seen or known. The Latin word "to see" is *specere*, and *species* originally meant what is seen, the physical shape of something. But the most common Latin term for physical shape is *forma*, which became "form" in English. Following the Latin philosophers, English thinkers called this kind of cause the "form" or "formal cause."

In comparing the material and formal causes of things, Aristotle realized that the matter out of which something is made gives it the potential to be what it is: wood or metal or plastic can become a little red wagon. But it is the form of something that makes it actually or really to be what it is, in this case, really a little red wagon. Until the wood is given the shape of a wagon by the wagon maker, there is no actual or real little red wagon. The reason why is because the matter out of which an artifact is made gives it the potential to be what it is; but it is the form of the artifact that gives it the actuality of being what it is. The wood of the wagon gives it the *potential* to be a wagon, but its wagon shape makes it *actually* a wagon. The consideration of matter as potential and form as actual in human artifacts helped Aristotle to deepen his conception of matter and form; he found a more fundamental sense of each. The new senses of form and matter are particularly helpful to understand things in nature—flowers and bees and, above all, humans. Since natural things are more complicated than artifacts—yes, even including computers—Aristotle's causal explanations had to become more complicated, as well. It would take a whole philosophy course to go into all those complications, but using artifacts as a model, we can begin to identify the causes of some natural things, as we'll do in the next section.

Final Cause

But before we turn to natural things, we need to consider the fourth kind of cause, the "end" or "final cause." Thus far, we have identified three kinds of causes for the wagon: (1) It requires an agent to bring the potentiality found in the matter into the actuality of being a real wagon; (2) It is made from matter, which gives it the potential to be a wagon; and (3) It is given a certain form (Plato might call it "wagon-ness"), which makes it an actual or real wagon. But one more cause is required. The reason why the wagon has the configuration or form that it has is because of its *purpose*. What is that purpose? It is to provide a simple vehicle for transportation, by helping little boys and girls to have playful fun. Now this "transportation and playful fun" is the purpose or goal of the little red wagon, put into it by the craftsmen who made it. The Greeks called it the *telos*, the "end" of a thing. They did not mean "end" in the sense of the destruction of a thing, but in the sense of the fulfillment or perfection of a thing, because they recognized that most things in the world go through a process of development before they reach their full potential. Since the Latin word for "end" is *finis*, this fourth kind of cause is also called the final cause. But "final" doesn't mean "last in time." In fact, for artifacts, the final cause comes first: the wagon maker has to have an idea of the purpose of the wagon he will make before he determines its form and picks its materials. In this respect, then, the final cause is the first cause. In sum, form follows function.

The wagon is being used as intended when little girls and boys use it for playful transport. If they can't do so because it was poorly made, we call it a poor or bad or defective wagon. Now there is a second sense of final cause, built upon the first. If the little girl who owns the wagon can't get into the house, she could step up on the wagon to reach the doorbell, using the wagon as a stool. This is a goal she decides upon when she uses it for a purpose beyond its normal one, but based upon its normal purpose. If some terrorists or gang members steal the wagon in order to use it to transport hand grenades or IEDs, they are misusing it. This case would be more complicated still. They would be using it as transportation, to be sure. This is a misuse of the wagon. It is not in accord with the purpose put in it by the craftsman. It would be like someone defacing a statue or an artwork; in addition, it would be morally bad, as well, both because killing innocent people is morally bad and because teaching our little girl to transport hand grenades in her wagon is bad for the little girl. She might draw the lesson that she can do anything she wants with her wagon, just because it is hers, even destroy it, which would undercut her appreciation for the utility and beauty of things humans make, and of natural things, as well.

A Deeper Look

Matter and Form: Similar and Different

Working from examples like our little red wagon helped Aristotle understand a number of things about the four causes and especially about matter and form, considered more broadly. For instance, we don't have a "little red wagon" unless all four causes contribute to its reality. And it must be made out of the right kind of matter. You can make a sand castle out of sand, but not a real castle. It must be given the right form, by the right agent, and for the right purpose. Otherwise, no wagon. The matter and form of such things are *intrinsic* or internal causes of the thing. They must both be present in it for the thing to exist; without wood or metal or plastic, or without the form or configuration of a wagon, we can't have a real little red wagon. And form and matter can't be separated from each other except at the cost of destroying the wagon. But, while they both need to be present in something like the little red wagon for it to exist, they each contribute something different to the effect. Three important pairs of features of the wagon are due to its matter and form.

First, as we have already seen, the matter it is made from—the wood or metal or plastic—gives it the potential to be a little red wagon, but only the potential. It is the form that makes it actually a little red wagon.

Second, the little red wagon can change. It can be moved to a different place; it can be given to another little girl; and it can change so much that it is destroyed. Matter is the cause of it being changeable and destructible. By contrast, as long as the materials of the wagon have the form of a wagon, the wagon will remain a wagon. Form, then, is the cause of whatever relative permanence and perfection the thing has as a wagon.

The third pair of features Aristotle pondered for a long time. The little red wagon is both *this* little red wagon, a singular thing distinct from everything else in the universe, and a *little red wagon*, sharing a set of features, an "essence," in common with all other little red wagons. What causes its distinct individuality and its common essence? The causes of these two attributes must be *intrinsic* to the wagon, because once the wagon maker has done his work, these two features remain part of the wagon.

What makes the little red wagon a distinct individual thing, different from everything else? You might be inclined to say that it is distinct because it occupies a different place, perhaps at a different time from all the rest, because being in a place is how we know it is an individual different from other things. Now it is true that this wagon does occupy a different place from all the others at a given moment in time and can exist at a different time from other wagons. But is it a distinct individual wagon *because* it occupies a certain place, or does it occupy a certain place *because* it is already a distinct individual wagon? The second choice has to be the right one. It's already a distinct individual thing; this is why it occupies a certain place. The place where it is, because it is *extrinsic* to the wagon, can't be the cause making it an individual thing. Rather, being in that place already assumes it is a distinct individual thing. But being at that particular place does cause our knowing that this wagon is different from that one. So what makes it an individual wagon? Here we must look for something intrinsic to the wagon. What makes it a distinct individual thing is the materials it is made of. While it has the same *kind* of materials as other little red wagons, the actual, real matter in it is different from the matter that makes up anything else in the world. In short, the reason why it is *this* little red wagon, not *that* one, is because of the materials out of which it was made.

On the other hand, what in it makes it *similar in kind* to other things of the same sort—to other little red wagons? We can understand the cause that makes it *similar* once we see that this cause is the same one that makes it the kind of thing it is in the first place. And this is its form. All little red wagons have the same kind of form: they look, feel, sound, and ride in basically the same way.

In short, Aristotle found that for artifacts, matter is the cause of potentiality, destructibility, and individuality, while form is the cause of three opposite features of things—actuality, relative permanence, and the essences such things have in common with each other.

The Causes in Nature

It was at this point that Aristotle widened his conception of the four causes—matter, form, agent, and end—and used them to try to understand natural things, first of all, and then human institutions, human actions, human knowledge, and even human nature itself. Since natural things have forms not given to them by humans, these forms are more intrinsic to the things and less knowable to us than the forms of artifacts. Aristotle's causal explanations had to become more complicated to describe these more fundamental kinds of form. The full story of how he did so would take us too far into philosophy, well beyond logic. But in logic we need to see *how* we can use these four causes to understand such things. Since our task in logic is first to be able to recognize what other authors are saying and then develop and use the same skills that produced those ideas, Problem Set 10 starts with causal analysis of artifacts. Then it moves beyond them, into the realms of other, even more important things.

It is helpful to recognize the distinction Aristotle made between form and matter that is perceived on the sensible level and form and matter functioning on the intelligible level. In understanding the formal cause, it is important to recognize that the first kind of form philosophers recognized was physical shape or form. Because such forms can be perceived with our senses, we can call them "sensible forms." Colors, shapes, sizes, odors, sounds: all these can be sensed. The same thing holds true for the kind of matter out of which the wagon is constructed. The wood is "sensible matter." It takes up space by having length and width and depth, it is brown in color, it is hard to the touch, and one plank of wood can be placed next to another, but they can't both be in exactly the same place.

While we begin with sensible traits, we eventually turn our minds to features we can know with our minds, but cannot perceive with our senses. We can see this if we look a little more closely at our little red wagon and recognize that its sensible form involves much more than shape; it also includes smooth texture, size, weight, ease of pulling, not tipping over too easily. It is impossible to make up a list of the exact physical forms a wagon must have; but we do recognize with our mind, not with our senses, if an individual physical thing is or is not a wagon. When doing so, we have used our minds to move from sensible causes to intelligible causes. For our wagon, this matter includes whatever kind of matter can be made into a wagon, even if we don't understand much about that kind of matter yet; and the form we can understand includes whatever makes the wagon actually and really a wagon, what gives it the essence it shares with all other wagons.

When Aristotle applied to understanding nature these conceptions of matter and form that are understood by the intellect, he drew three philosophical conclusions that we should know for logical purposes, even if we can't pursue them as far as Aristotle did in his philosophical studies. Let's begin with intelligible form. We saw earlier that Aristotle had noted the difference between the category of substance and the nine accidental categories. Now if the actual traits of things fall into these ten categories, there must be a cause of those traits; and such a cause must be a form, since matter and form are the intrinsic causes of things, remaining in them after the efficient cause has done its work. So Aristotle distinguished between "substantial form," which gives a thing its fundamental nature or essence—like *dog* or *petunia* or *human*—and "accidental form," which gives a thing an accidental attribute—like *two feet long* or *hard* or *courageous*. What is important to note is that, while we can perceive directly with our senses accidental traits and in a way perceive the sensible forms that cause them, we can never perceive with our senses the substantial nature of something or the substantial form that causes that substantial nature. We come to know the substantial forms of things, which is how we come to know their substance, only by using our intellect and reasoning our way to the substantial nature or form of a thing. So the substantial form of something, whether an artifact or a natural thing, is an intelligible form, which we can understand only with our mind. This is the basic reason why other animals, even though they can know and learn many things, cannot understand things as deeply as humans can. Animals are limited to the level of the sensible, while humans can dig deeper, all the way to the intelligible level.

The final point concerns matter. Humans come to know matter by using their minds to proceed from the surface inward, reasoning analytically. Over and over, scientists and philosophers have discovered deeper and deeper kinds or levels of matter; often they have become convinced that they have found the deepest level of matter. The ancient Greeks called this level of matter an "atom," which means "unable to be cut" or "indivisible," and some Greek philosophers said it was the most basic kind of matter, from which all other matter and all other things are composed. This idea later was resurrected in the scientific revolution and has been a staple part of modern physics, as can be found on the Periodic Table of the Elements. But a funny thing has happened; every time philosophers or scientists think they have discovered the real atom, it turns out that later research shows it can be "cut" into smaller particles. Aristotle perceptively rejected the atomic theory on the grounds that any actual body can be cut into smaller and smaller bodies, at least theoretically. He concluded that there is a "first" or "prime matter," but it cannot be a body of definite size, shape, and weight. Rather, prime matter is a principle of physical things and is understood as *pure potentiality*, lacking all actuality, in comparison with substantial and accidental forms, which are intrinsic principles of actuality. The wood of our wagon is matter, a kind of matter that contains potentiality for change and destruction, but it also has certain actual traits. It is a second level of matter, more developed and actual than "prime matter," the most basic kind of matter, which in a way we can understand with our minds, but never see with our eyes.

Since we all have been raised in a scientific culture imbued with atomism, we might be tempted to think of the matter and form that make up things as two different "atoms" that can unite or be separated from each other, or like bricks in a wall, which can be pulled out of the wall. But that would be wrong. Atoms and bricks can be separated from each other and exist on their own, without themselves being changed intrinsically. Matter and form cannot, because they are intrinsic causes or principles of things, not things in themselves. The shape of the wagon cannot be separated from the wagon. If you turn it into a table, it is still made of the same matter, but it is no longer a wagon. The wagon is destroyed. And neither can the matter of the wagon be separated from the wagon. If you take the materials of the wagon and separate them, say, into a pile of wood and screws, you no longer have a wagon, even though you still have the materials. And if you burn the wood, you no longer even have the materials out of which it was made.

Primary Sources

Aristotle, *Physics* 2.3

Having made these distinctions, we now should proceed to consider the causes, their nature and number. The purpose of our inquiry is knowledge, and men do not think they know a thing until they have attained the *why* of it, which is to attain its primary *cause*. So it is clear that we, too, must do this concerning generation and destruction and every kind of physical change in order that, by knowing their principles, we can try to use these principles in solving each of our problems.

In one way, then, (1) *that out of which* a thing comes to be, and that persists, is called the cause—for example, the bronze of the statue, the silver of the bowl, and the genera of which bronze and silver are species [metal].

In another way, (2) the *form or the paradigm*—that is, the formula of the essence and its genera, are called causes. For example, the ratio of 2:1 of the octave, and its genus, number. And the parts of the definition.

Moreover, (3) the *primary principle of change* or of coming to rest. For example, the man giving advice is a cause, and the father is the cause of the child. And at the level of genus, what makes of what is made, and what causes change of what is changed.

Moreover, (4) in the sense of the *end or that for the sake of which* a thing is done. For example, health is the cause of walking about. "Why is he walking about?" We say, "in order to be healthy." And once we have said this, we think we have assigned the cause. The same thing holds concerning all the means which are taken, through the action of something else as means toward an end. For example, loss of weight, purging, drugs, or using surgical instruments are means toward health. All of these things are for the sake of the end, though they differ from one another in that some are actions, others are instruments.

Thomas Aquinas, *On the Principles of Nature*

C. 1, para. 7. Therefore, in order that there be generation, three things are required: being in potency, which is *matter*; non-existence in act, which is *privation*; and that through which something comes to be in act, which is *form*. For example, when from bronze a statue comes to be, the bronze which is in potency to the form of the statue is its matter; that which is shapeless or undisposed is the privation; and the shape from which it is called a statue is the form. But this is not a substantial form, because bronze, before the arrival of the form or shape, has existence in act, and its existence does not depend upon that shape, but it is said to be an accidental form. For all artificial forms are accidental. An art operates only on what is already constituted in existence perfected by nature.

C. 2, para. 16. And one should also understand that even though matter does not have in its nature any form or privation—just as in the definition of bronze there is neither shaped nor shapeless—nonetheless, matter is never denuded of form or privation, because sometimes it is under one form, sometimes under another. But through itself it can never exist, because, since in its own definition it does not have any form, it does not have existence in act, since existence in act is only from form, but it is only in potency. Therefore, whatever is in act cannot be called *prime matter*.

C. 3, para. 17. From what has been said, therefore, it is plain that there are three principles of nature; *matter*, *form*, and *privation*. But these are not sufficient for generation. What is in potency cannot reduce itself to act, as bronze which is in potency to being a statue cannot make itself a statue, but it needs an *agent* which draws the form of a statue from potency to act. But form could not draw itself from potency to act—I am speaking of the form of the thing generated, which we say is the term of generation—for the form is only in what has been made to exist. However, what is made is in the process of coming to be—that is, while the thing is coming to be. Therefore, it is necessary that besides matter and form there must be some principle that acts; and this is called the *efficient cause*, *mover*, or *agent*, or the principle from which there is motion.

C. 3, para. 18. And as Aristotle says in the second book of the *Metaphysics*, since everything which acts, acts only by intending something, it is necessary that there be another, fourth thing—namely, that which is intended by the agent; and this is called the *end*. And one should understand that every agent, both natural and voluntary, intends an end, but it does not follow that every agent knows its end or deliberates about its end. To know the end is necessary for those things whose actions are not determined but can order themselves to opposing ends, such as *voluntary agents*. Therefore, it is necessary that they know the end toward which they determine their actions. But in *natural agents* actions are determined; consequently, it is not necessary that they make choices about the means, which are for the sake of end.

Problem Set 11: The Four Causes

Identifying All Four Causes of a Thing

Instructions

Use Aristotle's doctrine of the four causes—material cause, formal cause, agent (or efficient) cause, and end (or final cause)—to identify all four causes of the following.

1. hammer
2. airplane
3. car
4. spider
5. hummingbird
6. human
7. a book review
8. slander
9. education
10. hydrogen
11. the American Revolution

12. the New Deal
13. NASA (National Aeronautics and Space Administration)
14. throwing a baseball
15. being hit in the arm by a bat
16. having an upset stomach
17. running to catch a bus
18. being the daughter of your mother
19. knowing geometry

Analyzing Prose Using the Causes

Instructions

In the following passages, most from the scriptures of some religions, first identify the *effect* produced, and then identify its four causes. Use the following model for your answers. There may be more than one example of cause-effect in some passages. Where there is more than one, analyze the two most important examples.

Effect produced: _____

Causes:

Type: Example in the passage:

_____   cause: _____

_____   cause: _____

_____   cause: _____

_____   cause: _____

1. "The Lord God said, 'It is not right that the man should be alone. I shall make him a helper.'...But no helper suitable for the man was found for him. Then the Lord God made the man fall into a deep sleep. And, while he was asleep, he took one of his ribs and closed the flesh up again forthwith. The Lord God fashioned the rib he had taken from the man into a woman, and brought her to the man. And the man said: 'This one at last is bone of my bones and flesh of my flesh. She is to be called woman, because she was

taken from man.' This is why a man leaves his father and mother and becomes attached to his wife, and they become one flesh." (*Genesis*, 2:18–24, New Jerusalem with emendations)

2. "When the people saw that Moses delayed to come down from the mountain, the people gathered themselves together to Aaron, and said to him, 'Up, make us gods, who shall go before us; as for the Moses, the man who brought us up out of the land of Egypt, we do not know what has become of him.' And Aaron said to them, 'Take off the rings of gold which are in the ears of your wives, and your sons, and your daughters, and bring them to me.' So all the people took off their rings of gold which were in their ears, and brought them to Aaron. And he received the gold at their hand, and fashioned it with a graving tool, and made a golden calf; and they said, 'These are your gods, O Israel, who brought you up out of the land of Egypt!'" (*Exodus*, 32:1–4 RSV)

3. When the angels said: O Mary, surely Allah give thee good news with a word from Him (of one) whose name is the Messiah, Jesus, son of Mary, worthy of regard in this world and the Hereafter, and of those who are drawn nigh (to Allah). And he will speak to the people when in the cradle and when of old age, and (he will be one of the good ones). She said: My Lord, how can I have a son and man has not yet touched me? He said: Even so; Allah creates what He pleases. When He decrees a matter, He only says to it Be, and it is. And He will teach him the Book and the Wisdom and the Torah and the Gospel. And (make him) a messenger to the Children of Israel (saying): I have come to you with a sign from your Lord, that I determine for you out of dust the form of a bird with Allah's permission, and I heal the blind and the leprous, and bring the dead to life with Allah's permission; and I inform you of what you should eat and what you should store in your houses. Surely there is a sign in this for you, if you are believers." (*Qur'an*, 3.41–48, trans. Maulana M. Ali)

4. "Jesus took Peter, James, and his brother, John, and led them up a high mountain by themselves. And he was transfigured before them; his face shone like the sun and his clothes became white as light. And behold, Moses and Elijah appeared to them, conversing with him. Then Peter said to Jesus in reply, 'Lord, it is good that we are here. If you wish, I will make three tents here, one for you, one for Moses, and one for Elijah.' While he was still speaking, behold, a bright cloud cast a shadow over them, then from the cloud came a voice that said, 'This is my beloved Son, with whom I am well pleased; listen to him.' When the disciples heard this, they fell prostrate and were very much afraid. But Jesus came and touched them, saying, 'Rise, and do not be afraid.'

And when the disciples raised their eyes, they saw no one else but Jesus alone. As they were coming down from the mountain, Jesus charged them, 'Do not tell the vision to anyone until the Son of Man has been raised from the dead.'" (*Matthew*, 1–9, RSV)

5. "Americans combine to give fêtes, found seminaries, build churches, distribute books, and send missionaries to the antipodes. Hospitals, prisons, and schools take shape in that way. Finally, if they want to proclaim a truth or propagate some feeling by the encouragement of a great example, they form an association. In every case, at the head of any new undertaking, where in France you would find the government or in England some territorial magnate, in the United States you are sure to find an association. I have come across several types of association in America of which, I confess, I had not previously the slightest conception, and I have often admired the extreme skill they show in proposing a common object for the exertions of very many and in inducing them voluntarily to pursue it." (Alexis de Tocqueville, *Democracy in America*, vol. 2, part 2, chapter 5)

6. "In certain remote corners of the Old World, you may still sometimes stumble upon a small district which seems to have been forgotten amidst the general tumult, and to have remained stationary while everything around it was in motion. The inhabitants are, for the most part, extremely ignorant and poor, they take no part in the business of the country, and are frequently oppressed by the government; yet their countenances are generally placid, and their spirits light.

"In America, I saw the freest and most enlightened men placed in the happiest circumstances which the world affords; yet it seemed to me as if a cloud habitually hung upon their brows, and I thought them serious, and almost sad, even in their pleasures.

"The chief reason for this contrast is, that the former do not think of the ills they endure, while the latter are forever brooding over advantages they do not possess. It is strange to see with what feverish ardor the Americans pursue their own welfare; and to watch the vague dread that constantly torments them lest they should not have chosen the shortest path which may lead to it.

"A native of the United States clings to this world's goods as if he were certain never to die; and he is so hasty in grasping at all within his reach, that one would suppose he was constantly afraid of not living long enough to enjoy them. He clutches everything, but he holds nothing fast, and soon loosens his grasp to pursue fresh gratifications...

"At first sight, there is something surprising in this strange unrest of so many happy men, restless in the midst of abundance. The spectacle itself is, however, as old as the world; the novelty is, to see a whole people furnish an exemplification of it....

"In democratic times, enjoyments are more intense than in the ages of aristocracy, and the number of those who partake in them is vastly larger: but on the other hand, it must be admitted that man's hopes and desires are oftener blasted, the soul is more stricken and perturbed, and care itself more keen." (Alexis de Tocqueville, *Democracy in America*, vol. 2, part 2, chap. 13)

7. "How was she created? I'm not sure if you realize this, but it was in God's image. How can anybody dare to speak ill of something which bears such a noble imprint?" (Christine de Pizan, d. 1430, French moralist, member of the court, author of "mirror of princes" works such as *The Book of the City of Ladies*)

8. "Having thus emptied and purged the virtues from the soul of the one they've possessed, and initiated in splendid rites, they proceed to return insolence, anarchy, extravagance, and shamelessness from exile, in a blaze of torchlight, wreathing them in garlands and accompanying them with a vast chorus of followers. They praise the returning exiles and give them fine names: calling insolence good breeding, calling anarchy freedom, calling extravagance magnificent generosity, and calling shamelessness courage." (Plato, *Republic* 560e, on the first step from extreme democracy to tyranny)

Different Kinds of Definitions

The Essentials

Terms and Definitions in Logic

In logic, we study the categories, predicables, and causes in order to use them in analyzing discourse and in creating our own discourse, whether written or spoken. What is primarily important about them, however, is that they are used to help us recognize, evaluate, and formulate *definitions of terms*. But what are definitions? Definitions are designed to sum up in a convenient and short formula the **essence** of what it is we are defining. They are not the same as that essence. They do not include everything we know about the thing defined. They do not even include everything we know about its essence. But they are a way of formulating—giving a particular and (we hope) insightful verbal formula to what we know about the essence of a thing. A definition, then, we might define as "a verbal formula uncovering the essence of the thing defined." Logic focuses on that formula, the structure definitions take. In philosophy and other disciplines, some of these same topics are studied, but with a different end in view. There the end is to arrive at a true definition and explanation of things, as opposed merely to understanding the kinds of definitions they are. This is because, as we have seen in Lesson 5, logic focuses on thinking in a correct manner—the *structure* of our reasoning—while the other subjects focus, or should focus, on the *content* of our thinking, on getting at the truth about things.

We all use terms that we only partially understand. I can distinguish deciduous from nondeciduous trees if I recognize that the leaves of deciduous trees change color and fall off the tree in the fall. This is the reason why we call that season "fall." But this is just the beginning. I do not know *why* deciduous trees lose their leaves—how losing its leaves might help the overall health of the tree, if it does. Nor do I understand the details of *how* the leaves change colors or the mechanism whereby the leaf falls off the tree's branch. Recognizing what we don't know should be a spur to producing better definitions of things. This is what Socrates tried to achieve in his dialectical questioning of men in Plato's dialogues (for instance, the conversation we saw in Lesson 9 in which Socrates divides the concept "the art of the angler" as an attempt to get to a definition of the art of the angler). A well-cast definition should give us important insight into the essence of what we are defining. But definitions have an important added benefit. Though definitions are formed through the first act of the mind, they play important roles in the two subsequent acts of the mind—judgment that produces propositions and reasoning that produces arguments. This is why logicians, beginning with Socrates, have spent a lot of effort on definitions.

Our purpose in this lesson is to learn the different *kinds* of definitions. This is important so we can recognize definitions in what we read. And it is also important in speaking and writing, because effective definitions can make for effective communication.

What All Definitions Have in Common — re read

There are no definitions of individuals in their individuality. While we often pride ourselves on our individuality, the only way to understand that individuality is to pile up terms that describe how we are different from other people; and the only way to do this is to include what we have in common with them. Those common characteristics—especially the fundamental ones—are more important, in the long run, than what is peculiar about us individually, when it comes to *understanding* things. Both understanding things and living with others requires us to focus on what is common. This is why definitions are designed to uncover the *universal* essences of things.

We arrive at definitions by first coming to understand the *extension* of terms: how widely they apply. Think of Aristotle's example of the baby: "A child begins by calling all men 'father' and all women 'mother,' but later on distinguishes each of them." This is why, when asked to define things, we often begin with examples, then widen our scope to include all members of that class. The first definition attempted in Plato's dialogues is invariably just an example. Examples are good, but they are only a start toward a universal definition. An accurate definition (*definiens*) has the same extension as the thing being defined (*definiendum*). This ensures that anytime we use one of these two terms in a sentence, we can correctly substitute one for the other. What the definition (*definiens*) is supposed to do is give an accurate description of the essence, one showing what every individual thing falling under that definition or term has in common. This is why all definitions are universals. When we get a definition that is too wide or too narrow, we adjust the definition to arrive at one with exactly the same extension and meaning as the thing defined. This ensures that the definition will apply to all individuals falling under the thing defined, but only to them.

How Definitions Are Different: Some Definitions of "Man" or "Human"

If we look at the definitions of "man" (or "human") in the first section of Problem Set 12, we can see how important for understanding definitions are the topics we have already studied in the logic of terms—universals, categories, predicables, and causes. These help us to understand the different kinds of definitions. Look over these definitions. Your first reaction may be that they are simply sentences all having the same subject, most or all of them being true. But when you look a second time you may notice that while the thing defined is the same ("man"), the definitions are different. They differ not merely in content, but also in structure. Try to see how the definitions—the predicates of these propositions—are structured. They are not all the same.

Let's look at a few examples. (7) is the kind of definition you might find in a not-so-good dictionary. It focuses on the term or word "man," telling us when we can use "man"—anytime we are talking about a member of the human race. Such a definition is one type of "nominal" definition, a term taken from the Latin word *nomen*, which means "word" or "noun." This kind tells us the extension of the term "man," but little about its meaning. Another type of nominal definition is one that gives us enough knowledge of the basic meaning of the word so that we can then search for a better or "real" definition, one that gives us knowledge of the kind of "thing" it is, so we then can move on to search for a better and deeper definition of the thing. Not all dictionary definitions are nominal definitions. But definitions that focus on the extension of the term, which is the first step in understanding its compre-hension or meaning, are nominal definitions. Neither Aristotle nor Aquinas recognized nominal definitions of this kind; they were distinguished from real definitions much later. But it is helpful for our study of logic to recognize these nominal definitions.

All the other definitions in the first section of Problem Set 12, are better than (7), because they are "real" definitions. "Real" is taken from the Latin word *res*, which means "thing." Logicians often used the term "nominal defi-nition" of the preliminary understanding of something we must have to in-vestigate that kind of thing, even if we aren't yet sure if it exists. For example, if you were to argue for the existence of the soul or of God or that individual things have a universal essence or nature, you would have to begin with some preliminary understanding of what the word "defined" means. This meaning of "nominal definition" is not exactly the same as the one just given, but we need to be aware of both senses of this term. While real definitions focus on the things defined, nominal definitions offer a preliminary idea of the mean-ing of a term, so we can search for better, real definitions.

Next, look at (3). Over the last two millennia this has become the classic definition of a human being. If you look at the definition "rational animal" you see that it falls into two parts, "rational" and "animal." This is not merely because there are two words in the definition. It has two parts because what is being defined is a species, the human species, which is a universal. The defini-tion is composed of the genus ("animal") immediately superior to the species being defined. Finding the genus often takes some amount of intellectual ef-fort. After you think you have identified the genus, then you can ask, "How do I divide the genus into two parts, one of which is "man"? To do so requires, as we have seen, finding the "difference" that distinguishes the two groups falling under the genus "animal"—men and what are normally called brute animals. We can see that this kind of definition is developed by using the technique of division that we first saw in Lesson 9 in order to come up with a definition that has this structure: species = genus + difference. Because these three terms are all logical notions, we'll call this kind of definition a **logical definition**. (Different logic books use different terms for this kind of defini-tion, but all recognize this kind of definition.) Because of the tremendous influence of Plato on Western thought, this kind of logical definition became the ideal kind of definition that other definitions imitate.

But coming up with the proper genus and the exact difference can be an exceedingly hard task. Other definitions often have the structure of defining a species by turning to something else besides genus and difference. This is why many of the other definitions of "man" include "animal" in the definition, but leave out "rational."

If you look at definition (1) you can see that "worrying" is used instead of the specific difference "rational." How does "worrying" compare with the logical definition? Do you worry because you are rational, or are you rational because you worry? Here we're not interested in which of these two traits—"rational" and "worrying"—we become aware of first. We're interested in how they compare as two real features of real human beings. Since "worrying" is a combination of "thinking about something troublesome" and "being anxious about that thing," an emotion, we can see that worrying is not the same as the human essence, nor is it a cause of the human essence. Rather, "worrying" is something we can do that follows upon being human; it flows out of the human essence as an effect follows from a cause. In short, described in terms of the predicables, the *ability* to worry is a *property* of humans, and the *act* of worrying is an *action* built upon this property, a predicable *accident*. Definition (1), then, works primarily through listing a *property* of humans. Definitions of this sort we'll call *descriptive* definitions. In a broad sense of the term "descriptive," every kind of definition describes the thing defined. But "descriptive" here is used as a technical term in logic. This kind of definition is called *descriptive* because it doesn't explain the essence as comprehensively as does a logical definition; nor does it uncover the causes of that thing or its essence. Rather, in terms of the predicables, a descriptive definition defines something using a property or accident of the thing. Good descriptive definitions define things through their properties, poor ones (15–18) do so through accidents.

Finally, consider definition (4). Here the genus "animal" is completely missing. Instead, the two parts of this definition give us two of the four causes of a human. First comes the human "body." This is the "matter" out of which a human is made. The second half of the definition adds on the form of a human—that is, the human form as understood by some philosophers (though not all), which is the soul. This definition is structured in a very different way from the two other definitions. It defines the human species, not by giving the essence outright or by giving a property flowing from the essence, but through one or another of the causes of the essence of the thing defined. The two causes found in definition (4) are the material cause and the formal cause of a human.

While logical, causal, and descriptive definitions are developed by looking at the essence using different logical notions, all three have the same goal: to move our mind from just knowing the extension of the thing defined, to achieve comprehension of the concept.

Different Kinds of Definitions

We can now generalize from the results of looking at examples of definitions of humans and set out the main kinds of definitions in a systematic way.

Nominal definitions: The term "nominal" comes from the Latin *nomen*, meaning "name" or "noun." For the ancient philosophers a nominal definition gives us enough preliminary knowledge of the meaning of a term to go further and study it in depth. But we also use "nominal definition" to point out the kind of definition that focuses merely on using the term or word correctly, without necessarily getting at the essence of the thing defined. Some dictionary definitions are nominal definitions in this sense.

Real definitions: They focus on the "reality" (*res*) defined. Properly speaking, there are no definitions of individuals. Individuals are defined by defining their species. All real definitions attempt to uncover the common essence of the thing defined.

Logical definitions: Logical definitions define the species of things by identifying the genus (or genera) under which the species fits and then adding the difference that distinguishes this species from other species falling under that same genus. This type of definition is the ideal kind of definition, but is very difficult to achieve. Many other definitions imitate logical definitions, often by identifying the genus (or something like it) but substituting something else for the specific "difference."

Causal definitions: Causal definitions identify the essence of the species defined, not directly, but by identifying one or more of its causes. Since normally the best knowledge of something is achieved through understanding it as an effect of its causes, causal definitions are quite useful.

Descriptive definitions: Descriptive definitions define the species of the thing defined by using one of its necessary properties. This amounts to defining a cause through its effects. Such definitions are widespread and very helpful. The reason why is that it is often difficult to come to understand the essence or the causes of something. The normal human approach to understanding things is to proceed from effect to cause, rather than cause to effect, because effects are normally much more evident to us. A thing can have numerous, correct descriptive definitions. This is why the same thing often is defined differently in different disciplines, and these different definitions don't have to be consistent with each other. Sometimes these definitions are consistent with each other, but sometimes they are not. Aristotle's definition "man is a political animal" is consistent with other definitions, such as "man is a rational animal." It is also more useful if you are studying political science. If you were studying communications or literature or linguistics, however, "man is an animal that uses and invents language" would be more helpful. But not all definitions are equally good or consistent with each other. Descartes's definition "man is a thinking thing" or "man is the composite of thinking thing and extended thing" is not consistent with other definitions given in the first section of Problem Set 12.

A Deeper Look

Looking at the extension that the definition and thing defined have in common and the essence the definition should reveal gives us some convenient rules for good definitions.

Rule 1: A definition should have the same extension as the term defined.

Rule 2: A definition should illuminate the universal essence of the thing defined.

Rule 3: The definition should be clearer than the thing defined.

Rule 4: The definition should have the same comprehension (or meaning) as the thing defined.

While it might seem that these rules lead to the conclusion that there is only one correct definition for each term, in fact they point in the opposite direction, as we can see by using the example of the "human" in Problem Set 12, in the section "Kinds of Definitions of Man—That Is, the Human." Good logical, causal, and descriptive definitions complement each other. But when one kind of definition conflicts with other definitions of the same thing, the lesson is that we still have a long way to go before the definitions are correct.

There are many other types of definitions identified by logicians and others who study definitions. Two others that are helpful for you to know about are intensional and stipulative definitions. Intensional definitions are easy to understand because the word "intensional" was invented to contrast with the "extension" or width of a term. Intensional definitions try to give the real meaning of terms. So "intensional definition" is usually just another way of saying "real definition."

Stipulative definitions are quite different. These are definitions that are stipulated—that is, laid down or simply assumed, without explanation or defense of their truth. There are at least three sorts of stipulative definitions. Stipulative definitions are sometimes merely asserted as a way of getting into a subject; when used this way they are not harmful. The definitions Euclid lays down at the very beginning of his *Elements of Geometry* are simply listed, with no further explanation or support. Stipulative definitions, however, are sometimes used in a second way by those who do not think it is possible for the human mind to achieve real definitions uncovering the real essences of things. Such definitions are arbitrary, a mask for ignorance, and betray an unwarranted skepticism about the human capacity to know things—all of which are bad because they undercut the enterprise of knowing. They lead us quite reasonably to ask, "Why should I accept your stipulation about the meaning of X, as opposed to someone else's?" Yet a third way of using stipulative definitions is when they function as preliminary opinions or hypotheses, subject to further refinement. This is an acceptable use of stipulative definitions. When used this way, stipulative definitions are a work in progress. We can see such work in the dialogues of Plato, where Socrates criticizes the definitions of his interlocutors, to see if they "come up to the mark," and also in many definitions used in politics and other of the so-called social sciences, especially those that use some variant of quantitative analysis and surveys of preferences. In order to test such stipulative definitions for soundness, it is helpful to be able to determine which of the more important types of definitions they are. This is one reason why learning how to identify the types of definitions is helpful for developing skill in logic.

Problem Set 12: Definitions

Kinds of Definitions of Man—That Is, the Human

Instructions

Identify what *kind* of definition the following definitions of "man" or "human" are. Are the following definitions of a human: (a) nominal or real? If real, are they (b) logical, (c) descriptive, or (d) causal? And if the definition is causal, which causes are contained in the definition: material, formal, efficient, or final cause?

1. Man is a worrying animal.
2. Man is an animal that can ask itself what it is.
3. Man is a rational animal.
4. Man is a composite of body and spiritual soul.
5. Man is a creature whose soul was especially created by God.
6. Man is a visible creature whose end is happiness.
7. Man is any member of the human race.
8. Man is a talking animal.
9. Man is a tool using animal.
10. Man is a religious animal.
11. Man is an argumentative animal.
12. Man is a political animal.
13. Man is an educated animal.
14. Man is an animal who can take care of himself.
15. Man is black.
16. Man is white.
17. Man is Hispanic.
18. Man is Asian.

Kinds of Definitions

Instructions

Analyze each of the following definitions taken from original sources. Note that all definitions here are real definitions; there are no nominal definitions. (a) Underline the thing defined (*definiendum*). (b) Circle the definition itself (*definiens*). (c) Indicate what kind of definition it is: nominal, logical, causal (which kind of cause), or descriptive. (d) If there is more than one definition in the passage, treat each definition separately.

1. "Rationalization may be defined as faulty thinking which serves to disguise or hide the unconscious motives of behavior and feeling." (Percival M. Symonds, 20th-cen. American psychologist, *The Dynamics of Human Adjustment*)

2. "Law is whatever is boldly asserted and plausibly maintained." (Aaron Burr, 18th-cen. American politician of dubious character, *Memoirs*, 2:14)

3. "All atoms consist of very small solid nuclei (diameter 10^{-12} cm) and extended outer shells (diameter 10^{-8} cm)." (C. F. von Weizsaecker, 20th-cen. German physicist)

4. The extremities of lines are points. (Euclid, ca. 300 b.c., *Elements of Geometry*)

5. "The basic idea that gives to the word 'democracy' its original and latent meaning is the idea of a social group organized and directed by all of its members for the benefit of all its members." (Ralph Barton Perry, 20th-cen. American philosopher)

6. "Accordingly, when a man is said to have the grace of God, there is signified something supernatural bestowed on man by God." (Aquinas, *Summa Theologiae* I-II, q. 110, a. 1.)

7. "The nucleus of the hydrogen atom is called a proton. This particle has a positive charge equal numerically to the negative electric charge of the electron and is so small that it takes 2.72×10^{26} to make a pound. The nuclei of atoms of other substances contain a number of protons equal to the atomic number of the element." (U.S. Atomic Energy Commission, ca. 1965)

8. "Love is nothing else but an insatiate thirst of enjoying a greedily desired object." (Michel de Montaigne, 17th-cen. French philosopher, *Essays*, vol. 3)

9. "A friend is a person with whom I may be sincere." (Ralph Waldo Emerson, 19th-cen. American author, *Essays: First Series*)

10. "The whole of government consists in the art of being honest." (Thomas Jefferson, *A Summary View of the Rights of British America*, 1774)

11. "Discovery consists of seeing what everybody has seen and thinking what nobody has thought." (Attributed to Albert Szent-Gyorgy, 20th-cen. Hungarian scientist, Nobel Prize)

12. "In science, the Apollonian tends to develop established lines to perfection, while the Dionysian rather relies on intuition and is more likely to open new, unexpected alleys for research.... The future of mankind depends on the progress of science, and the progress of science depends on the support it can find. Support mostly takes the form of grants, and the present methods of distributing grants unduly favor the Apollonian." (What Szent-Gyorgy actually said, *Science*, no. 176 [1972])

13. "Beauty is an emotional element, a pleasure of ours, which nevertheless we regard as a quality of things." (George Santayana, 20th-cen. Spanish philosopher, *The Sense of Beauty*)

14. "Compromise used to mean that half a loaf was better than no bread. Among modern statesmen it really seems to mean that half a loaf is better than a whole loaf." (G. K. Chesterton, *What's Wrong with the World*, 1910, chapter 3)

Analyzing More Sophisticated Definitions

Instructions

Consider the following, more difficult passages, which contain definitions. Pick out the definitions (there may be more than one). Then analyze them. If there is more than one definition in the passage, *treat each definition separately*. (a) Underline the thing defined (*definiendum*). (b) Circle the definition itself (*definiens*). (c) Indicate what kind of definition it is: nominal, logical, causal (be sure to indicate which kind of cause it is), descriptive.

1. "My friend George Bancroft defined democracy, in a lecture which I published in my *Boston Quarterly Review*, to be 'eternal justice ruling through the people.' I defined it in a series of resolutions adopted by a Democratic state convention, to be the 'supremacy of man over his accidents'—meaning thereby that democracy regards the man as more than his possessions, social position, or anything separable from his manhood—and got most unmercifully ridiculed for it. But the ridicule did not move me, and I held fast to the doctrine that the will of the people is that most direct and authentic expression of the divine will that can be had or desired." (Orestes Brownson, 19th-cen. American Catholic writer, in *Seeking the Truth*, ed. R. M. Reinsch)

2. "Democracy means government by the uneducated, while aristocracy means government by the badly educated." (G. K. Chesterton, 20th-cen. British author, *A Short History of England*)

3. "A democracy is a state which recognizes the subjecting of the minority to the majority." (V. I. Lenin, 20th-cen. Russian socialist)

4. "Democracy is only an experiment in government, and it has the obvious disadvantage of merely counting votes instead of weighing them." (Sir William Inge, 20th-cen. British Dean of St. Paul's Cathedral)

5. "Democracy is 'a charming form of government, full of variety and disorder, and dispensing a sort of equality to equals and unequals alike.'" (Plato, *Republic*, bk. 8, 558c)

6. "But in practice a citizen is defined to be one of whom both the parents

are citizens; others insist on going further back; say to two or three or more ancestors. This is a short and practical definition; but there are some who raise the further question: How did this third or fourth ancestor come to be a citizen? Gorgias of Leontini, partly because he was in a difficulty, partly in irony, said: 'Mortars are what is made by mortarmakers, and the citizens of Larissa are those who are made by magistrates: for it is their trade to make Larissaeans.' Yet the question is really simple, for, if according to the definition just given they shared in the government, they were citizens. This is a better definition than the other. For the words, 'born of a father or mother who is a citizen,' cannot possibly apply to the first inhabitants or founders of a state." (Aristotle, *Politics* 3.2, 175b23–33)

7. "When we talk of any particular sum of money, we sometimes mean nothing but the metal pieces of which it is composed; and sometimes we include in our meaning some obscure reference to the goods which can be had in exchange for it, or to the power of purchasing which the possession of it conveys." (Adam Smith, 18th-cen. Scots economist, *The Wealth of Nations*, bk. 2, c. 2)

8. "Art may be defined as a singleminded attempt to render the highest kind of justice to the visible universe, by bringing to light the truth, manifold and one, underlying its every aspect. It is an attempt to find in its forms, in its colors, in its light, in its shadows, in the aspects of matter and in the facts of life what of each is fundamental, what is enduring and essential—their one illuminating and convincing quality—the very truth of their existence. The artist, then, like the thinker or scientist, seeks the truth and makes his appeal." (Joseph Conrad, Polish-British novelist, *The Nigger of the Narcissus*, 1897, Preface)

9. "But children were allowed to leave school before that age to enter *beneficial* employment. Beneficial to whom, we should like to know. The children themselves? Or is it the parents, or the employer, or the community at large? It really does make a difference, does it not?

"So when we hear of a *beneficial or desirable* scheme, we should ask 'to whom?' When we hear of a movement called *subversive or revolutionary or destructive*, we are quite justified in inquiring what it is going to upset, or change, or destroy. If precise information is not forthcoming, we should probably not be far wrong if we suspected that all the speaker meant was that he personally approved of the scheme and disapproved of the movement." (R. W. Jepson, American psychologist, *Clear Thinking*, 1954)

10. "Plato having defined man to be a two-legged animal without feathers—a "featherless biped," Diogenes the Cynic plucked a cock and threw it over the wall of the Academy. Then he went in and said: 'This is Plato's man.' On which account, this addition was made to the definition, 'with broad flat nails.'" (Diogenes Laertius, 3rd cen. Greek philosopher, *Lives and Opinions of Eminent Philosophers*, "Diogenes")

Part 3

The Logic of Propositions

Statements and Propositions

The Essentials

Terms, Statements, and Propositions

In this lesson, we turn from the first to the second act of the mind, often called the act of "judgment," because in it we make mental judgments about the way things are. When what we think in our mind (or say or write) corresponds with the way things are, then we have attained truth, so our judgment is true. When what we think or say or write does not correspond, then we have not attained truth, so our judgment is false. If we say, "Socrates was a philosopher," and he really was, then our statement is true. If we say "Socrates was a great general," but in fact he was not, then our statement is false. The same need to correspond with reality is true of negative statements. So if we say that "water does not contain carbon," and it does not, then our statement is true. But if we say "water does not contain hydrogen," but it does, then our statement is false. The first act of the mind—apprehension of concepts—does *not* attain truth. Our concepts are true or false only when they are put into statements. Attaining truth distinguishes the second act of the mind from the first. We can even say that truth is the *end* or *purpose* of the second act of the mind and the statements we form using it.[1]

Both logic and grammar study statements, but they focus on different things. Grammar focuses on whether a statement, normally called by gram-

1. Thomas Aquinas, *Commentary on Aristotle's On Interpretation*, Prologue.

marians a "sentence," is grammatically correct—that is, the sentence follows the conventional rules of orderly speech of a particular language. When the grammarian studies the first act of the mind, he looks to see if the words are well-formed—spelled correctly and the right form of the word used at that point in a sentence. He asks questions like, "Should one use 'good' or 'well'?" And when he studies the second act of the mind, the grammarian is concerned with whether the statement as a whole makes an intelligible point and whether it does so following the rules of grammar and syntax—again, the rules of the particular language. As we saw earlier, **diagramming sentences is an excellent way to check our grammar.** The *logician* has different concerns, in great part because the primary focus of the logician is not on spoken or written languages—which are conventional signs and vary greatly—but on the mental thoughts that are the basis for spoken and written language and do not vary as much as languages do. The same mental thoughts—sometimes imprecisely called "mental language"—can be expressed in many spoken and written languages. When the logician studies the first act of the mind, he concentrates on terms and their definitions, as we have seen, in order to get to the unchanging intelligible content that the words we speak and write signify. And when he studies the second act of the mind, there is also a difference from the grammarian, for the logician focuses on the mental assertions we are making in order to obtain the truth, more than the written and spoken words we use to convey that truth. Consequently, while grammar concentrates on the written and spoken language we use to convey thought, logic uses written and spoken language as a vehicle or instrument to help us get to the mental content we try to express.

This focus on truth helps us **distinguish *terms* from *propositions*.** Propositions are more complex than terms—not that terms can't be complex as well, but in a different way. Consider the terms "dog" and "white." We can create a more complex term by adding together these two terms, as in "the white dog." Though this phrase is more complex than its component parts, adding them together in this way only produces another term, not a statement. We can see this because "the white dog" is neither true nor false. But truth and falsity enter the picture when we combine them in a different way, by forming the proposition "the dog is white." When said of a particular dog, this proposition *is* either true or false. What brings truth and falsity into the picture is the fact that the statement makes an assertion about the way things really are. By inserting the verb "is," we are not just piling one concept on top of another to form a more complex concept, but *asserting* that this is the way things really *are* in the world: "the dog *is* white." The issue of truth also allows us to distinguish *statements* or *sentences*, on the one side, from *propositions*, on the other. While all propositions are statements of some sort or other, not all statements are propositions. "Statement" is a wider class than "proposition," a wider genus, as it were. The reason why is that, while the vast majority of statements are true or false, there are a few that are neither true nor false. On the other hand, true and false apply to *all* propositions. Consequently, we can divide the wider class or genus "statement" into two sub-groups or species: statements that are *not* propositions and statements that *are* propositions. After considering a few kinds of nonpropositional statements—so we can learn to recognize them—we'll turn to the logically more important propositional statements.

Nonpropositional Statements

Let's consider a few statements that are not propositions because they are neither true nor false.

Questions

The first kind of nonpropositional statement is a question. In a way, questions are just "turned-around" propositions. Consider the question "Is it raining outside here today?" A positive answer would be, "Here it is raining outside today." The answer to a question is either true or false. But is the question itself either true or false? Well, no, not really. The reason why is that the answer makes an assertion about the way things really are. But the question makes no assertion. It merely prompts you to search for an assertive answer. The question is an intelligible sentence, more than a word or term and less than a paragraph or argument; but it is neither true nor false and so is not a proposition.

Commands

Commands or requests for someone to do something are also intelligible sentences. We understand them and follow the command—at least most of the time. Consider examples like these: "Please shut the door." "Don't touch

a hot stove!" "Stop!" Here we are telling someone how to act. If we then formulate a proposition describing what they have done, "he stopped" or "she
didn't stop," these propositions are either true or false. But the command itself
is not true, nor is it false. It is simply a way we have of ordering someone to
act in a certain way.

Performative Statements

A kind of statement related to commands is the "performative statement."
If a command tells us what to do, a performative statement is a kind of sentence we use actually to do something—to perform an action. Perhaps the
most well-known kind of performative statement is uttered at a wedding.
Consider the question, "Do you take this man for your lawful wedded husband?" and the response, "I do." The clergyman's question is really a kind of
command: Tell me whether or not you will to be married to this man. The
answer—"I do"—means a lot. It means more than "I want to marry him" or
"I promise to marry him" or "It is true that I want to marry him." In saying "I
do" we perform an act through language; we enter into the contract of marriage. This is why we call this use of language a marriage *vow*. With the vow
we enter into a new state of life. The same is true of religious vows. And it also
holds for oaths, like the oath of office government officials take, or the oath
members of the military take "to protect and defend the Constitution of the
United States," or the citizenship oath that all new citizens take. With such
statements we *perform* an action, one that puts us in a new state or condition,
one that may have many moral or legal consequences.

Different Kinds of Propositions

The vast majority of statements, however, are either true or false, which
means they are propositions. We can perhaps best define a proposition by
using Aristotle's four causes. We have already seen that the *purpose* or *final
cause* of a proposition is to attain the truth. This means a false proposition
doesn't live up to its very purpose as a proposition. This is why when we say
something we don't think is true, we usually spontaneously give off physical
indicators that undercut what we are saying and try to hide its falsity in a
"cloak of truth." It's embarrassing to say what is false, not just because we are
wrong, but also because humans possess thought and language in order to
know and state what is true, not what is false. This is also the main reason

why lying is wrong; it violates the very purpose of propositions. We all lie on occasion, to be sure, but that doesn't make it right. The *agent* or *efficient cause* of propositions is the human who composes them, using his mind. When we look for the *matter* of propositions, we are not looking for physical stuff, but for the component parts that make up propositions. These are concepts and terms: in the first instance mental concepts, in the second spoken and written words and terms. The *form* or structure of propositions is closely related to their end. Unlike complex concepts, like "flying fish," propositions like "those fish are flying" take the form of an assertion about the way things are. And assertions take the form of either affirmations—this *is* so—or denials—that *is not* so. We'll learn much more about such affirmative and negative propositions in subsequent lessons.

Categorical Propositions

Categorical propositions are the simplest kind of propositions. They are direct assertions—either affirmative or negative—about the way things are. Such propositions are the staple of human discourse and will form the focus of our study of the logic of propositions. Some examples are "Grass is green," "All dogs are animals," "Cats are not dogs," and "Some cats are not independent." You can see that each one of these statements is either true or false. The logic of categorical propositions is rather simpler than their grammar, for when analyzed logically a categorical proposition falls into three parts: the *subject* the proposition is about; the *predicate* said of or predicated of the subject, and the verb "is," called the *copula* because it "connects" the predicate with the subject, in order to make an assertion—whether affirmative or negative. Many categorical propositions do not have an explicit copula, because the verb "to be" is contained within all other verbs. Examples are "Grass grows," "Lucienne walks," and "The dog runs down the street." We could rewrite these three propositions as "Grass is growing," "Lucienne is walking," and "The dog is running down the street." We'll look at the structure of categorical propositions more carefully in Lesson 13. For now, we just need to realize there are two different kinds of categorical propositions.

The four examples in the previous paragraph are all **simple or regular categorical propositions**. Such statements are normally just called "categorical propositions," a practice we follow in this book. What makes these statements propositions is that they are assertions, taking the form of affirmations or negations; what makes them simple is that these propositions make definite affirmations or negations, with no further qualifications. We shall study these kinds of propositions in detail, because they are so important in their own right and for understanding arguments. The other kind, **modal propositions**, are covered under "A Deeper Look," later in this chapter.

Hypothetical Propositions

The term "hypothetical" is sometimes used as a synonym for "conditional"; but in fact conditional propositions are only one type of hypothetical proposition. Hypothetical propositions are either true or false, which is what makes them propositions. But they are more complicated than categorical propositions. They are generally formed by taking two (or more) categorical propositions and combining them, based on a certain logical connection between the two propositions. For this reason, the different types of hypothetical propositions are determined by the different types of logical connection between the two (or more) categorical propositions used to create a hypothetical proposition. The terms that express these logical relations are called "syncategorematic" terms because they take two (or more) categorical propositions and combine them. The three most important syncategorematic terms in English are "and" (for conjunctions), "or" (for disjunctions), and "if…then" (for conditions). Since categorical statements are the building blocks of hypothetical statements, in this book we shall study categorical statements first, then hypothetical statements. This order is the reverse of the order used in symbolic logic, and it is easier to learn.

Conjunctions: Perhaps the easiest kind of hypothetical proposition to understand is called a **conjunctive proposition** or, more often, a **conjunction**. In conjunctions, the two categorical propositions are combined. Consider the proposition "Ali is a Democrat, and Estella is a Republican." This proposition is made up of two categorical propositions added together to form one conjunction. For this proposition to be true, it is not enough that Ali is a Democrat; Estella must also be a Republican. Here is another example: "A university is an institution, and a person is an individual." If either of the two categorical propositions that make up the conjunction is false, then the whole conjunctive proposition is false. The normal English verbal sign of the logical relation of conjunction is the term "and" or "both…and."

Disjunctions: A second type of logical connection produces the second type of hypothetical proposition. If the two (or more) categorical propositions are presented as *alternatives*, the hypothetical proposition is called a

disjunctive proposition or **disjunction**. Some examples are, "Either you are coming to the lecture or your roommate is coming" and "Either you are for the war on terror or you are against it."

These examples point out one complication about disjunctions that should be mentioned at the outset. In the first example, it is possible that both you and your roommate will come to the lecture. This kind of disjunction, which includes the possibility of both categorical propositions being true, is called an "inclusive disjunction," because it "includes" the possibility that both propositions are true. The other example is what is called an "exclusive disjunction," because the proposition means that one or the other, *but not both*, alternatives can be true. For example, "either you are for conducting the war on terror or you are against it" *means* "either you are for conducting the war on terror or you are against it, *and* you cannot be both for the war and against it."

Conditions: Conditional propositions, or simply **conditions**, are the most important kind of hypothetical proposition, but also the most difficult. In a conditional proposition, the first categorical proposition sets out a "condition" that, if fulfilled, leads to the second categorical proposition. Consider this conditional proposition: "If you are in the room, then you came through the door." What it means is that on the condition that you are presently in the room, then it follows—that is, it must also be true—that you must have come into the room through the door. If we look at the structure of this proposition, the first categorical proposition, called the "antecedent" because logically it comes "before" (Latin *ante*) the second categorical proposition, which follows the word "if," then the second categorical proposition, called the "consequent" because logically it follows "after" (Latin *consequor*) the antecedent, is preceded by "then" to let us know that if the condition is fulfilled (or the antecedent is true), then the consequent must come about; it will also be true. The "before" and "after" here are logical, not temporal. In fact, in this case the antecedent—being in the room—actually happened after the consequent in time.

A Deeper Look

Modal Propositions

Modal propositions are more complicated than simple categorical propositions. They are important, but usually studied in an advanced logic course. "Modal" comes from the grammatical term "mood." Here the copula "is" changed, either by having its "mood" strengthened in the direction of necessity or weakened in the direction of possibility. When combined with the word "is," the copula becomes "is possible," or "is possibly," or "is necessary" or "is necessarily." But there are many other words that we use to express the modalities of possibility and necessity. Consider "He *may* be guilty" and "The earth *must* be round." The first sentence expresses possibility; it shies away from making a definite claim, in the way a simple or regular categorical proposition does, one like "He *is* guilty." One linguistic opposite of "possible" is "impossible," as in the proposition "He *cannot* be guilty." Another linguistic opposite of "possible" is "necessary," as in the proposition "He *must be* guilty." So here we have one regular categorical proposition—"he is guilty"—and three modal propositions— "he may be guilty," "he cannot be guilty," and "he must be guilty." The logic of such propositions turns out to be somewhat complicated, and we shall not take it up in detail. But we should learn to recognize modal propositions. One final point: logicians have noticed that impossibility is just necessity in a negative direction. "He cannot be guilty" is the same as "He must be innocent." Since "impossibility" can always be explained as "necessity of the opposite," there are really only two modal operators, not three: *possible* and *necessary*.

Symbolizing Hypothetical Propositions

Symbolic logicians have been helpful on another point in dealing with hypothetical propositions. Their fondness for mathematical-style symbols has led them to invent some symbols that help us see the different kinds of hypothetical propositions. First, let the lowercase letters p and q stand for *any* categorical proposition, while uppercase letters like P and Q stand for particular categorical propositions. For example, the categorical proposition "Socrates is a man" can be symbolized by one uppercase letter, say M. "Trees are green" could be symbolized by another uppercase letter, like G. Please remember, here the letter does *not* stand for the subject or predicate *term* of a categorical proposition, but it stands for the *whole categorical proposition*. In this system, the mathematical symbol for "not" (~) is used to indicate the negation of a proposition, such as ~p or ~M. The structure or logical relation or syncategorematic term between the two categorical propositions that are combined to create a hypothetical proposition can then be represented by a symbol that is *not* a letter of the alphabet.

Symbols for Conjunctions (p and q), (p & q)

The "and" relation is sometimes symbolized using the old-fashioned am-persand (&), though most logicians prefer a dot (·). We will use both. The symbolic form of a particular conjunction is (P & Q) or (P · Q), while the general type of this kind of proposition is symbolized by (p & q) or (p · q). The parentheses show that this is one proposition, a conjunctive proposition. Each of the three kinds of hypothetical propositions has its own logic, differ-ent from the other two, and so has its own symbol.

Symbols for Disjunctions (p or q), (p v q)

The normal English verbal sign of this kind of logical relation is the term "or" or "either…or." Since one of the Latin words for "or" is *vel*, disjunctions are symbolized using a small v. (P v Q) stands for some particular disjunctive proposition, while (p v q) stands for this type of proposition. Such proposi-tions are called *inclusive* disjunctions, because they "include" the possibility that both p and q are true. Such a disjunction is often symbolized using a small "v," as in (Y v R). For an *exclusive* disjunction, the proposition means that one alternative or the other, *but not both*, can be true. Logicians some-times use a capital "V" to symbolize such an exclusive disjunction, as in (W V ~W). In a way, however, the capital V is really unnecessary, because the capital V can be explained by combining the inclusive disjunction with a denial of the conjunction of the two propositions. For example, "either you are for conducting the war on terror or you are against it" *means* "either you are for conducting the war on terror or you are against it *and* you cannot be both for the war and against it." This proposition could be symbolized as follows (where ≡ means "is the same as" or "is identical with"): (W V ~W) ≡ [(W v ~W) · ~(W · ~W)]

Symbols for Conditions (If p, Then q) (p → q)

Since the normal verbal indicators of a conditional proposition are "if" and "then," we can say that conditional propositions always take the general form (if p then q). What symbolic logicians have done is invent a symbol for the "if…then…" relation that holds between the antecedent and consequent categorical propositions that make up the conditional proposition. In fact, they have invented a number of such symbols. We will use the arrow → because it shows clearly that in conditions there is a logical movement *from* the antecedent *to* the consequent. The "standard form" for any condition proposition will be (p → q), which is normally read "p implies q," because "implies" captures the "if…then…" relation. The particular conditional proposition we started with could be symbolized as (R → C). Such symbols help us to see at a glance the logical structure of conditional propositions.

In real-world thinking, however, we cannot ignore the *content* of such propositions, content normally contained in the verbal language used to utter or write them. That content helps us to understand when conditional propositions are true and when they are false. Consider the proposition "If something is human, then it is an animal," which we could symbolize as (H → A). It is pretty easy to understand about the truth or falsity of this whole proposition when the antecedent is true. The proposition means that if the antecedent is true, then the consequent must also be true. So, if the antecedent is true and the consequent also is true, then the whole proposition is true, as in this case. Now consider "If something is human, then it is a rock." When something is human, it cannot be a rock. In this case, the antecedent is true and the consequent is false. This kind of example helps us see that when the antecedent is true but the consequent is false, the whole conditional proposition is false.

But when the antecedent is false, it is harder to determine whether the whole proposition is true or false. This is a hard question that we won't try to answer here. But we should know how most symbolic logicians approach this point. They simply give a stipulative definition of the conditional relation in this case and say that any conditional proposition with a false antecedent is true, regardless of whether the consequent is true or false. This result may well seem counterintuitive to you. But one of the main reasons for saying this is so that the only time that a conditional proposition is false is when the condition is fulfilled, but the consequent does not follow. Another way of saying this is that the whole proposition is false only when the antecedent is true and the consequent is false. You might want to ponder this point; but it does make sense. Think of it this way. If the antecedent condition is not fulfilled, then you don't know what will be true of the consequent—it could be either true or false. Consider this example of a condition you might present to a child: "If you are good, then you'll get a lollipop." Consider if the child is not good. Well you won't give him a lollipop. But since there are other ways to get a lollipop, he might get one anyway. An overindulgent grandparent might give him one; or he might steal it from the pantry. So "you are *not* good" is consistent with both his getting and his not getting a lollipop.

Again, it is important to emphasize that these symbols for propositions are no substitute for thinking about the real content of what we think, say, and read; but they are very useful for concentrating for the moment of the logical form or structure of a given proposition.

Primary Sources

Aristotle, *On Interpretation*, c. 4–5.

Aquinas, *Commentary on Aristotle's On Interpretation*, Prologue. An excellent short presentation of the difference between the first and second acts of the mind.

The books Aristotle wrote in developing the logic of the second act of the mind are: *On Interpretation*, the primary text dealing with the second act of the mind and the statements and propositions it creates; *Prior Analytics*, which deals with reasoning, the third act of the mind especially the formal logic of arguments; it includes many examples that deal with the logic of propositions; and *Topics*, which deals with the logic of dialectical [probable] reasoning, which produces opinion, but not full knowledge. It is organized around the predicables, which Aristotle presents as a division of different kinds of propositions.

Problem Set 13: Statements and Propositions

Distinguishing Kinds of Propositions

Instructions

Classify the following statements as to *type*, using the following types of statements:

Types of statements
    Statement that is not a proposition
    Proposition
        Categorical
        Hypothetical
            Conditional
            Conjunctive
            Disjunctive

1. John made a mistake.
2. Dorothea did not make a mistake.
3. Zebras are like horses, they run.
4. Your solution to the math problem is inaccurate.
5. If Pedro takes the new job, he will make more money.
6. If Pedro doesn't take the new job, he won't make more money.
7. "All things are made of atoms." (Democritus, Greek philosopher [adapted], 5th-cen. b.c.)
8. There once was a woman who lived in a shoe.
9. She had so many children, she didn't know what to do.
10. If her children were bad, she whipped them all soundly.
11. She sent them to bed or occasionally let them stay up to watch television.
12. Either you will get an A on the exam or you will get a B.
13. "In war, resolution; in defeat, defiance; in victory, magnanimity; in peace, goodwill." (Winston Churchill, 20th-cen. British prime minister, *The Second World War*)
14. "We make a ladder of our vices if we trample those same vices underfoot." (St. Augustine, d. 430. Roman bishop, theologian, and philosopher)
15. "Either death is a state of nothingness and utter unconsciousness, or … there is a change and migration of the soul from this world to another." (Socrates, Greek philosopher, d. 39. b.c., from Plato, *Apology of Socrates*)
16. "Some books are to be tasted, others to be swallowed, and some few to be chewed and digested." (Francis Bacon, 17th-cen. English philosopher and politician, *Essays*, "On Studies," 1625)
17. "If God did not exist, it would be necessary to invent him." (Voltaire, 18th-cen. French, *philosophe*, letter)
18. "To thine own self be true; and it must follow as the night the day, thou canst not then be false to any man." (Shakespeare, d. 1616. *Hamlet*)
19. "Abandon hope all ye who enter here." (Dante, 14th-cen. Italian poet, *Inferno*)
20. "All power of fancy over reason is a degree of insanity." (Samuel Johnson, 18th-cen. British compiler of the first English dictionary, *Rasselas, Prince of Abyssinia: A Tale*)

21. "Cleopatra's nose: had it been shorter, the whole configuration of the world would have been altered." (Blaise Pascal, 17th-cen. French author, *Pensées*, no. 32)

22. "The Christian ideal has not been tried and found wanting; it has been found difficult and left untried." (G. K. Chesterton, 20th-cen. British author, *What's Wrong with the World*)

23. "The white man knows how to make everything, but he does not know how to distribute it." (Sitting Bull, 19th-cen. American Indian chief, in Bridger, *Buffalo Bill and Sitting Bull*, 320)

24. "No one could have questioned Labour's record in implementing socialism. Rather, it was the economic consequences of socialism—devaluation and a return of inflation—which were the obvious targets for attack. Very heavy public spending had kept the standard rate of income tax almost at wartime levels—nine shillings in the pound. Far from being dismantled, wartime controls had if anything been extended—for example rationing was extended to bread in 1946 and even potatoes a year later." (Margaret Thatcher, 20th-cen. British prime minister, *The Path to Power*)

Symbolizing Hypothetical Propositions

Instructions

For those statements in the previous sections that are hypothetical, go back to the statement, devise your own symbols for each statement, and then symbolize the statement.

Properties of Categorical Propositions

The Essentials

The Three Parts of Categorical Propositions

Before Aristotle, humans had used categorical propositions, and some had studied them fairly closely. But no one before Aristotle had noticed that in categorical propositions we can distinguish their *content* (the assertions they make about reality) from their *form* (the structure or arrangement the proposition takes). As we saw in Lesson 6, this distinction helped Aristotle invent logic; let's see how it works in categorical propositions. The first thing Aristotle noticed is that while the content of categorical propositions is virtually unlimited, the structure of all categorical propositions is quite uniform. He saw that each categorical proposition has the three parts we introduced in Lesson 12—subject, predicate, and copula. Let's now look more carefully at these parts and see what they reveal about the nature of categorical propositions.

Subject

The *subject* of the proposition is what the proposition is about—whether it comes at the beginning of the sentence, the end, or is stuck somewhere in the middle. Consider the first four examples in Problem Set 14.

1. All Texans are friendly.
2. Some Texans are friendly.
3. No Texans are friendly.
4. Some Texans are not friendly.

All four propositions have the same subject—"Texans." The subject—whether made up of one word or many—is one term, called the "subject term." Spotting the subject of a categorical proposition is the first step in understanding it. This is often easy, but occasionally difficult, in more complex sentences. The fact that these four propositions have the same subject—Texans—illustrates how logic focuses on the form or structure of propositions. This is the reason why many centuries ago, long before the invention of modern symbolic logic, logicians often resorted to symbols. The general symbol for the subject of a categorical proposition is S.

Predicate

The second part of a categorical proposition is called its *predicate*. It is also a term, the predicate term, so called because it is "predicated of" or "said of" the subject. Our four propositions all have the same predicate term—"friendly." In general, the predicate term is symbolized by P. Unlike conceiving a term using the first act of the mind, when we formulate a proposition, using the second act of the mind, we *assert* something. What is asserted is that the predicate "belongs to" or "applies to" or "is said of" or "is predicated of" the subject. The predicate can be "said of" the subject in two quite different ways, either affirmatively or negatively. With this point we come to the third part of a categorical proposition, which is quite different from the first two.

Copula

The third part of a categorical proposition is some form of the verb "to be" or "is." This is the part of the proposition that clearly separates complex terms from propositions. Complex terms, like "green grass," don't assert anything, so this phrase has no "linking verb" or *copula*. This is why such terms are neither true nor false by themselves. But if we link "grass" and "green" together, by adding "is," then we have produced a categorical proposition: "Grass is green." The copula linking directly together the subject and predicate of the proposition is what makes the proposition assert something. In "Grass *is* green," grass, a substance, is not exactly the same in nature as its color green, a quality. But *green* is united to *grass* in the sense that they are two aspects of one and the same thing—the green grass. So the predicate truly signifies an attribute of the subject.

The Logical Structure of Categorical Propositions: "Standard Form"

We have already noted that not every categorical proposition has an explicit copula because some form of the verb "is" is contained implicitly in every verb. This is what distinguishes nouns from verbs, "a walk" from "to walk" or "walks." But for the purposes of understanding the logic of propositions, we need to recognize that some form of "to be" is present implicitly in every verb; this is what makes it a verb. So in analyzing a categorical proposition we can always separate "is" from the verb in the predicate of the sentence in order to see the three parts of the proposition. If we focus on the *form or structure* of the first four problems in Problem Set 14 by substituting S for the subject and P for the predicate and connecting the subject and predicate by "is" or "is not," we can see their different structures, apart from their content:

1. All S is P.
2. Some S is P.

3. No S is P.
4. Some S is not P.

For the rest of the book, we will call these four structures the "Standard Forms" of categorical propositions. And often you will be asked to *reformulate* or restate categorical propositions in this Standard Form.

The way "is" unites S and P is determined by the ten categories. In "grass is green," grass and green form a kind of unity, but not an absolute identity, since substances are not the same kinds of things as colors. Since "is" is used implicitly or explicitly to unite all subjects and predicates in categorical propositions and the content found in the subject and predicate terms describes things using the categories, the concept of "is" or "being" is even broader or more universal than any of the ten categories, since it covers them all, though not in exactly the same way. This is the reason why we can say that the verb "is" is contained in or implicit in every verb and every verb can be expanded into a form that makes "is" explicit. So "The cat runs" can also be expressed as "The cat *is* running."

Finally, negative propositions, like "Some Texans are not friendly," add some form of the adverb "not" to the copula of the proposition in order to show that the predicate is *not* united to the subject, but the opposite happens: the predicate is *separated or denied* of the subject. This is the way the predicate is "said of" or "belongs to" the subject in a negative proposition, like "Grass *is not* a tree."

The Quality of Categorical Propositions

The fact that these four propositions all have the same subject and the same predicate helps us see how Aristotle saw that the differences among them are not based on their content—Texans and friendly people—but on their structure or form. These two structural features are called the proposition's *quantity* and *quality*.

The *quality* of a categorical proposition is not determined by its subject or predicate, but by its copula. All categorical propositions are either *affirmative* or *negative*. If the copula is some form of "is," the proposition is affirmative. This means the predicate is affirmed of the subject; the proposition asserts the predicate *is* true of the subject. The first two examples from Problem Set 14, (1) "All Texans *are* friendly" and (2) "Some Texans *are* friendly," affirm the fact that the trait *friendly* is true of Texans, of all of them in (1) and some of them in (2). When the copula is not stated explicitly, as in "Some Texans ride horses," you should remember that some form of "to be" is contained implicitly in the verb "ride." This is why this sentence can be reformulated as "Some Texans *are* riding horses," which shows that both "riding" and "horses" are part of the predicate and that the proposition is affirmative—the Texans *are* riding horses. Even if the content of the predicate contains a negative idea, if the predicate is affirmed of the subject, the proposition is affirmative, not negative. "Some Texans lie" is an affirmative proposition, even though *lying* has negative connotations. We can see this by expanding the proposition to make the copula explicit: "Some Texans *are* lying" or "Some Texans *are* liars."

The other two examples from Problem Set 13, (3) "No Texans are friendly" and (4) "Some Texans are not friendly," are *negative* propositions. Example (4) clearly connects the copula "is" with "not," showing that the term "not" in a negative proposition does not govern the subject or predicate but qualifies the copula "is," for *is not* is the opposite of *is*. So (4) clearly says that "Texans *are not* friendly," some of them, at least. Here the predicate "friendly" is *denied* or *removed* or *separated* from the subject *Texans*. This kind of separation of the predicate from the subject is characteristic of all negative propositions.

Example (3), "No Texans are friendly," is also a negative proposition. What makes it negative is the first word of the sentence: "No." Here "No" performs two functions. Even though "No" is separated from the copula by the term "Texans," in meaning "No" combines with the copula to mean "are not." So the proposition is saying "Texans *are not* friendly." But "No" has a second role. It also functions to determine the quantity of the proposition—which we'll learn about next. So don't be fooled; in this kind of sentence "are" does not function by itself, even if it is not standing right next to the negative term "No."

One might be inclined to reformulate this kind of proposition by using the term "all" and putting the negative term right next to "are," which produces the sentence "All Texans are not friendly." But for reasons we'll see in Lesson 15, this formulation is not a good one, because the sentence "All Texans are not friendly" is inherently ambiguous. In some contexts it may mean the same as "*No* Texans are friendly," but in other contexts, and most often, it means something quite different: "*Some* Texans are *not* friendly." But we'll consider this issue in the next lesson.

The Quantity of Categorical Propositions

Next let's consider the *quantity* of categorical propositions. Let's look again at our first two propositions:

1. All Texans are friendly.
2. Some Texans are friendly.

These two propositions have the same subject, the same predicate, and the same quality. But the subject of (1) is "*all* Texans," absolutely every one of them, while the subject of (2) is only "some Texans"—that is, some number of Texans less than all of them. Logicians call a proposition that is about *all* the members of the subject group or class a "universal proposition," because the proposition is asserting some attribute to be true about each and every instance of the subject term. The subject term being universal in quantity is what makes the proposition a universal proposition. This meaning of the term "universal" is similar to but slightly different from what it meant in Lessons 7 and 8. There we were contrasting individual things in the world, which we know through our senses, with general or universal concepts, which we know through our intellect. When such general concepts are used in categorical propositions, they can be applied either to all the things that fall under them, in a universal proposition like (1), or only to some of them, in a particular proposition, like (2).

The term "some" is not quite so precise. For the purposes of logic, we don't need to know for sure whether just one Texan is friendly, just a few are friendly, the vast majority are friendly, or all but one are friendly. All we are concerned to say is that some number of Texans—ranging from one to one less than all—are friendly; and we leave open the possibility that all of them are friendly. Logicians call this kind of proposition a "particular proposition," because the predicate is asserted of some particular part of the whole subject class. As before, the quantity of the subject term determines the quantity of the proposition. Here we need to be precise about terminology. Sometimes writers, especially philosophers, use the term "particular" as a synonym for "individual," meaning just one thing. But this is not what the term "particular" means here. We can see why if we remember that the word "particular" is formed from the word "part." So the subject of a particular proposition, then, includes some part of the whole subject class. We are following the long-established meaning of "universal" and "particular" as technical terms in logic—as technical as "energy" in physics or "integration" in calculus; we should be clear about what "particular" means.

As you would expect, one of the two other propositions among our four examples is universal and one is particular. Proposition (4), "Some Texans are not friendly," is easily recognized as a particular proposition because of the word "some."

Once again, Proposition (3), "No Texans are friendly," is a bit odd. As we saw, "no" means the proposition is negative in *quality*. But "no" also governs the *quantity* of the proposition. "No Texans are friendly" is quite the same as saying "None of the Texans are friendly." This second formulation shows clearly that we are talking about *all* the Texans, because the word "none" means "no one." So the proposition "No Texans are friendly" is universal. The proposition asserts something about the whole group or class of Texans: "not a single one of them is friendly," or we could say, "each and every one of them is not friendly."

In English, we usually express a universal affirmation by words like "all" or "every," and we express universal negatives by "no" or "none." Negative words like "no" and "none" perform two functions. They show the proposition is both *negative* in quality and *universal* in quantity. Such terms do double duty, as it were. This is not true of every language, but it is of English. As stated before, you might be tempted to state the universal negative by saying, for example, "All Texans are not friendly." But this kind of proposition is really ambiguous and in most contexts is *not* a universal proposition.

The Four Kinds of Categorical Propositions: A, I, E, O

Since these two formal or structural characteristics of propositions—quantity and quality—each include two possible types, when we look at their form or structure we can see there are four and only four *kinds* of categorical propositions: universal affirmative propositions, particular affirmative propositions, universal negative propositions, and particular negative propositions. The first four examples from Problem Set 13 cover all of these four possible types. Some clever logician, probably in the early medieval period, decided that he didn't want to repeat the full descriptions of these kinds of propositions, so he identified each of the four kinds with a letter. The Latin word *affirmo* means "I affirm," which is what you do in an affirmative proposition. So our medieval logician decided to use the first vowel in *affirmo*, which is A, as a marker for a *universal affirmative proposition*, and he used its second vowel, which is I, for a *particular affirmative proposition*. In Latin *nego* means "I deny," which is what you do in a negative categorical proposition. So E became the sign of a *universal negative proposition*, and O marked a *particular negative proposition*.

A: universal affirmative	All S is P	(*a*ffirmo)
I: particular affirmative	Some S is P	(aff*i*rmo)
E: universal negative	No S is P	(n*e*go)
O: particular negative	Some S is not P	(neg*o*)

A Deeper Look

Analyzing Categorical Propositions

In order to understand each categorical proposition according to its form, it is necessary to understand each of its formal features: its subject, predicate, quality, and quantity. Where should we start? A useful technique to use is to look at the proposition as a whole, recognize its grammatical parts in order to try to get the basic sense of the proposition. Then you can analyze it logically. The following order usually works pretty well:

1. Identify the *subject*, not worrying about whether the subject is universal or particular. Just think about the subject as a group or class. And don't leave anything out. The grammatical subject is often just one word, but the logical subject includes everything that modifies the grammatical subject. But don't

worry yet about words that determine the quantity of the subject, which is also the quantity of the proposition considered as a whole.

2. Use the same technique to identify the *predicate*. At this stage, leave out the copula. With normal verbs you will need to distinguish the *content* of the verb, say, "runs," from the form of the verb "is" that is implicit in such a verb. The *content* of the verb is part of the logical predicate, while the "is" part of the verb is the copula.

3. Determine whether the copula is affirmative or negative. This gives you the quality of the proposition. Usually some form of the words "no" and "not" indicate a negative copula and therefore a negative proposition; but sometimes other negative words are used to indicate a negative proposition.

4. Determine the quantity of the proposition—which is the same as the quantity of the subject term. Is it universal or particular? (We'll learn later that the predicate term also has a quantity, but don't worry about that now.) Using these four steps, you should be able to determine if a categorical proposition is A, I, E, or O. For many propositions, this question is easy to answer; but there are quite a number of propositions for which this question is rather more difficult.

5. For the final and most important step, *rewrite* the proposition as simply as you can. Simplifying is designed to make both its meaning and its logical type (A, I, E, or O) clear. You simplify its language in order to make sure you understand the meaning of the proposition you have read, in your own words, and that you understand its logical features: the subject group, predicate group, whether it is affirmative or negative, and whether it is universal or particular. In order to make the logical type clear, you should try to restate the proposition in **Standard Form**, making the quantity and quality of the proposition *explicit*. When we rewrite propositions we normally leave out some of the interesting nuances of a good author's prose, but rewriting and simplifying complicated discourse uncovers the logic of the author's reasoning, which is the purpose of logical analysis.

When I say "rewrite" the proposition, I mean literally that. Rewrite it to make sure you really understand it. You may not need to do too much rewriting for Problem Set 14, but try your hand at it here. You'll definitely need to rewrite many, if not all, of the propositions in Problem Sets 15 and 16 and for the rest of the book. Develop the habit now!

Problem Set 14: Basic Categorical Propositions

Four Kinds of Categorical Propositions

Instructions

Determine what *kind* of categorical proposition the following statements are (A, I, E, or O). For all propositions that are not already in Standard Form, rewrite them in standard form.

1. All Texans are friendly.
2. Some Texans are friendly.
3. No Texans are friendly.
4. Some Texans are not friendly.
5. None of the chimpanzees have been fed.
6. All airplanes are human artifacts.
7. Some citizens are uninvolved.
8. Most citizens vote in federal elections.
9. Some of our friends were not at the game.
10. All truck drivers have taken a special course.
11. No business is open on the holiday.
12. None of the vegetables at dinner tonight tasted like they should.
13. Nothing morally wrong is politically right.
14. Some of your books were lying open on the desk.
15. Some of the students at our table were not complaining about the food.
16. All of the parents of the new students were complaining about the costs.
17. Most of Maria's brothers and sisters were not complaining about her going off to college.
18. None of the union leaders in the negotiation are asking for increases in salary.
19. All the rabbits we saw are somewhere on that side of the road.
20. Nearly all of us liked the show.
21. "Ah, colonel, all's fair in love and war, you know." (Nathan Bedford Forrest, 19th-cen. Confederate General, to a Union officer he tricked into surrendering)
22. "All legislative Powers herein granted shall be vested in a Congress of the United States, which shall consist of a Senate and House of Representatives." (U.S. Constitution, Art. 1, Sec. 1.)

Recognizing the Kinds of Categorical Propositions

The Essentials

In Lesson and Problem Set 14, we covered basic or simpler categorical propositions. These propositions are straightforward because their subjects and predicates are clearly delineated, they have adjectives modifying the subject to determine its quantity, those adjectives are rather normal and easy to understand, and their predicates are not complicated. Make sure you understand the right answers in Problem Set 14 before moving on to Problem Set 15. In this lesson, we will look at several kinds of more advanced categorical propositions. Let us consider them one type at a time.

Propositions with Normal Verbs

As we have seen, implicit in every verb is some form of the verb "is." Consequently, we can always expand a normal verb into a verb with two parts, the first being a form of the verb "is" and the other some sort of participle of the verb expressed in the original sentence. Consider this proposition from Problem Set 15: "Some of the boys who skipped school ran across the railroad tracks." Here the subject is "some of the boys who skipped school." As it stands in the sentence, the predicate is "ran across the railroad tracks." In order to turn this proposition into what we can call **Standard Form**, with an explicit copula, we can change the verb from "ran" to "were running," which contains "were," the plural past tense form of the verb "is." This technique helps us clearly to identify the proposition as an I proposition. It also helps us see that when we split up the verb "ran," we divide it into the copula and into its content or meaning, which is part of the logical predicate of the proposition.

Nonstandard Word Order

Now let's consider the proposition "Blessed are the merciful." In this proposition the copula is explicit; we might at first think that "blessed" is the subject and "the merciful" is the predicate. But the subject is what the proposition is *about*; the predicate is what is *said* about or *attributed* to the subject. In this case, being *blessed* is attributed to those here called "the merciful," not the other way around. This proposition promises blessedness or happiness to those who are merciful. In this proposition, as it is stated, the predicate comes first and the subject second. To analyze this proposition correctly, you may wish to change the tense of the verb and, more importantly, the word order: *The merciful will be blessed.*

Quantity Not Explicit

"Blessed are the merciful" has another important trait. Once we see that "the merciful" is the subject of the proposition, not its predicate, then we have to wonder whether the subject is universal or particular, because there is no quantitative adjective like "all" or "some" that explicitly and obviously indicates the quantity of the proposition. Is it an A proposition or an I proposition? The answer ultimately resides in its meaning, which we are aware of in our mind. But there is also a verbal indicator that helps us, at least in English. This is the adjective **"the."** (Many other languages, however, will not have such a term in a proposition like this; some other languages do not even use an explicit copula, which makes them even harder to analyze.) In this case, we have to figure out what "the" tells us. In grammar, "the" is more precisely called the "definite" article, as opposed to the indefinite article "a." Sometimes "the" points to a definite individual, as in the proposition "The dog ran down the street." But this is not always true; and it is not true in this case. Here "the" points to the *whole* group or class of merciful people. Another example would be "The girls on the team were unhappy." Here "the" is used to tell us that it was *all* the girls on the team, not just some of them, who were unhappy. The same is true with "Blessed are the merciful." "The" tells us that *all* merciful people, not just *some* of them, are promised blessedness. So "Blessed are the merciful" is an A proposition, not an I proposition: "All the merciful will be blessed."

Subject Placeholder

It is especially popular in English to begin a sentence with a word that looks like the subject of the sentence, but really functions merely as a placeholder for the true subject, which is stated later in the sentence. Consider these two sentences from Problem Set 15: "There are some dogs coming down the street" and "It is sad to see your team lose." In these sentences, the words "there" and "it" might look at first glance to be the subjects of their sentences, because they come just before the verb. But they don't tell us *what* the subjects of these sentences actually are; they don't give us any content. What they do is "hold the place" for the subject that is stated later in the proposition. You can see this if you remember that the subject is what the proposition is *about*. The subject of the first proposition is "some dogs"; and the subject of the second proposition is "to see your team lose," which we can emend slightly to "seeing your team lose." So the first proposition is an I proposition: "some dogs are coming down the street." The other one says, "seeing your team lose is sad." But is it an A or an I proposition? There is no explicit quantity in the original sentence, so we have to make our best-informed judgment. The proposition predicates "sad" of a certain *kind* of outcome of a game: "seeing your team lose." The proposition, then, is an A proposition: *All seeing your team lose is sad*. Now this sentence is awkward. But sometimes it helps to revise a sentence into an awkward-sounding proposition in order to see its logic. We're trying to analyze normal discourse in order to understand its logic; but this doesn't mean that would should replace normal discourse with "logic-speak."

A Deeper Look

Singular Propositions

Aristotle himself recognized three kinds of propositions: universal and particular, but also singular propositions. Singular propositions have singular or individual things as their subject. Often the subject of a singular proposition is a proper noun: *John is a baseball player* or *Jane Austen is the greatest English novelist* or *London is the most famous city in the world*. But often we use an adjective that identifies the subject as a single thing: *This piece of pie is the best I have ever tasted* or *That possum is the ugliest animal I have ever seen.* While he recognized singular propositions, Aristotle did not do a lot with them in developing his logic. But we do use singular propositions in our syllogistic reasoning. Consider the classic example: "All humans are mortal. Socrates is a man. Therefore, Socrates is mortal." Here we are drawing a conclusion about just one individual man. If we think of an individual, say, Socrates, as a *class*, he is an unusual class, having only one member. In the proposition *Socrates is brilliant*, we are referring to only one person, to be sure, but we are referring to *all of him*, not to part of him, say, his left hand. This is one way to see why we should treat singular propositions like *Socrates is brilliant* in the way we treat universal propositions, for the purposes of logic. Such a singular proposition is not exactly the same as a universal proposition, like "All men are mortal." But in this case, Socrates, considered as a whole man, is brilliant, because he has a brilliant mind. This is how logicians have concluded that, in logic, there are only two kinds of categorical propositions, universal and particular. A singular proposition is, so to speak, like an odd kind of universal proposition.

This seems to be what Aristotle meant when he drew a parallel between universal propositions and singular ones: "Of such corresponding positive and negative propositions as refer to universals and have a universal character," his examples were "Every man is white" and "No man is white," and "Every man is just" and "No man is just" (A and E propositions), "if one is true the other must be false. This is the case also when the reference is to individuals, as in the propositions 'Socrates is white' and 'Socrates is not white.'" Here Aristotle is drawing an explicit parallel between universal propositions (A and E) and singular propositions. He does not say singular propositions *are* A or E, but they are *like* A or E.

Tricky O Propositions

Now let's consider a proposition like (22) in Problem Set 15: "Not every Georgian is friendly." This kind of proposition is an O proposition, but it can be confusing because it doesn't have the standard word order and language of an O proposition. Consider the proposition *Some Georgians are not friendly.*

This is clearly an O proposition. The subject "Georgians" is made particular by "some." And the predicate "friendly" is denied of these Georgians by adding "not" to the copula "is." Next consider the A proposition *Every Georgian is friendly*. Here "every" makes the proposition universal and "is" makes it affirmative. But what happens if we add "not" to the beginning of this sentence? The meaning of the sentence is changed dramatically, and not in the way you might at first think. Your first guess might be that *Not every Georgian is friendly* is an I proposition, thinking that when "not" is combined with "every" we get "some." But "not" combines with the rest of the sentence in a very different way. Consider this proposition: *Not every American will get to ride to the planet Mars in a space ship*. This proposition does not guarantee that *some American* will get to Mars. It may be that *no American* will get there. And considering the ramping down of the American space program, this is probably what will happen.

The way to understand *Not every Georgian is friendly* and *Not every American will ride to Mars in a space ship* is to recognize that the term "not" does not affect only the one word "every" that immediately follows it, but it has a more interesting effect; it affects every word that comes after it in the sentence. *Not every Georgian is friendly* really means *It is not the case that every Georgian is friendly*. Now what do we mean when we say this? Here it is better to compare *Not every Georgian is friendly* with the universal negative proposition *No Georgian is friendly*. Both of these propositions are negative; this results from "No" and "Not" in each sentence. But *No Georgian is friendly* is a universal proposition, while *Not every Georgian is friendly* is also negative, but particular. If *It is not the case that every Georgian is friendly*, then it must be true that *Some Georgians are not friendly*. Comparing it with *Every Georgian is friendly* tells us *Not every Georgian is friendly* must be negative; and comparing it with *No Georgian is friendly* tells us *Not every Georgian is friendly* must be particular. And a particular negative proposition is an O proposition. So based on this analysis, we can correctly rewrite *Not every Georgian is friendly* in standard form as *Some Georgians are not friendly*.

A practical example helps to understand the point. Suppose you are flying from Europe to Houston. This is your first time in Texas, but you have heard stories that Texans wear cowboy hats and boots, have rough manners, smell of hard life on the range, carry guns, and use them, too. In short, as a sophisticated European you expect to find that *All Texans are barbarians*. After your ten-hour flight, you are weighed down by your carry-on baggage, trip as you exit the walkway into the terminal, and your bags go everywhere. Immediately two people wearing cowboy hats and shirts that say "Welcome to Houston" pick you off the ground, corral your bags, and help you on your way. At this point, you have enough information to know it is true that *Not every Texan is a barbarian*. You are not in a position to know *All Texans are barbarians*, though we will find in Lesson 20 that you are in position to know that this proposition is false, or to know that *No Texans are barbarians*. You don't even have the information to know that *Some Texans are barbarians*. But you do know enough to say *Not every Texan is a barbarian*, because you can say that at least *Some Texans are not barbarians*. In short, you know the O proposition is true, but you don't yet know the I, E, or A propositions are true.

All S Is Not P

When introducing the universal negative proposition we used the form *No S is P*, we learned that there are some modifying adjectives, like "no," which affect both the quantity and the quality of the proposition. Consider the E proposition *No oranges are apples*. Here "no" tells us two things: First, the proposition is universal; it is about *all* oranges. Second, it is negative; "no" means the oranges are *not* apples. Another formulation you might use is *All S is not P*; in this case *All the oranges are not apples*. This formulation might seem advantageous, since "all" seems to make the subject "oranges" universal, and putting "not" next to the copula seems to make the proposition *negative*. And sometimes a proposition of this form is intended to be a universal negative proposition, as in this case. But consider the previous cases. What if we moved the "not" from being the first word in the sentence to placing it next to "are"? *Every Texan is not a barbarian* or *Every Georgian is not friendly*. Based on the previous analysis, you probably can see that these two propositions are not universal negative but particular negative, O propositions. Propositions of the form *All (or every) S is not P* will vary in meaning, depending upon context. Sometimes a proposition with this structure will be an E proposition, as is true of *All the oranges are not apples*. But at other times, a proposition with this structure will be an O proposition, as is true of *Every Texan is not a barbarian*.

So be careful! There is no substitute for your intelligent thought and judgment about the meaning of propositions. And there is no verbal formula you can memorize to give you the right answer 100 percent of the time about the meaning of a proposition or about logical reasoning generally. The underlying reason why is that logic is primarily about thought in your mind, only secondarily about the words you speak or write.

Negative Modifiers

Some languages allow double negatives, but English does not. One result of this grammatical rule affects the logic of a small number of negative modifiers, the most important being the word "few." Now "few" means some number, but a small number, smaller than "many." To express an affirmative proposition about some small number of things, in English we add on a demonstrative adjective to "few": normally "a few," but sometimes "the few." Consider *A few of the explorers were saved* or *The few who were saved gave thanks to their rescuers and to God.* The first proposition is affirmative and particular (I); the second proposition is affirmative and universal (A), for all of the few who were saved did give thanks.

Things are different, however, when "few" is used *by itself* to modify a subject. Consider propositions like *Few of Marco Polo's band of explorers made it to China and back to Italy* or *Few of those who take the GRE score 800 on the verbal or math sections of the test.* In these two cases, the negativity of the term "few" does two things. First and foremost, it affects the copula, making these negative propositions. Second, it reduces drastically the number of the subject class who actually achieve the predicate, so that it increases the number of the subject class who did *not* achieve the predicate. What the first proposition actually means is that *Most of Marco Polo's band of explorers did* not *make it to China and back to Italy*, a particular and negative proposition (O). Likewise, the second proposition means that *Most of those who take the GRE do* not *score 800 on the verbal or math sections of the test.* Once again, this is a particular and negative proposition (O). In both of these propositions, it is reasonable to assume the correlative I is true. Marco Polo himself, for instance, wrote his book about the expedition after he returned. But are you sure that somebody scored 800 on the GRE? Probably not, if 800 means answering all the questions correctly.

The general result of this look at more advanced categorical propositions is that we should realize that the meaning of the spoken or written proposition is determined by the mental proposition in our mind. And sometimes we mean one thing and say another. So one goal of logic is to bring into harmony what we think and what we say. Of course, sometimes what we think is also wrong. But it is the intellectual disciplines or subjects that have primary responsibility in this area. Here, a very old bit of wisdom is relevant: *Mean what you say and say what you mean.*

Finally, you should try to rewrite in Standard form most of the propositions in Problem Set 15. You want to get to the point where you can do so easily.

Problem Set 15: Advanced Categorical Propositions

Recognizing More Difficult Categorical Propositions

Instructions

Please identfy the following categorical propositions as A, I, E, or O. Simplify and rewrite all propositions in Standard Form.

1. Some of the boys who skipped class ran across the railroad tracks.
2. Most of the boys did not run across the tracks.
3. All elephants love dust baths.
4. Most Democrats follow the liberal political philosophy.
5. Dear to us are all the people who love us.
6. Foolhardy is the man who riots without cause.
7. Blessed are the merciful.
8. There are some dogs coming down the street.
9. It is sad to see your team lose.
10. There are five hundred thirty-two parts in this washing machine.
11. Blue jays are birds.
12. The animals in that part of the zoo have not been fed.
13. Socrates was a philosopher.
14. Alcibiades was a charming man.
15. Bananas contain a considerable amount of potassium.
16. Cavalier King Charles spaniels are beautiful dogs.
17. Pit bulls are not.
18. He who is not with me is against me.
19. None of the potatoes have been peeled.
20. Many revolutionaries have perished in their revolutions.
21. No Georgian is friendly.
22. Not every Georgian is friendly.

23. Not all of us are fools.

24. Snakes are not all harmful.

25. Not all that glitters is gold.

26. A few of the explorers were saved.

27. Very few people say all they mean.

28. Few if any politicians say what they mean.

29. Margaret came home late last night.

30. Irving is not unfriendly.

31. Not all the tires on my car are worn.

32. Poets are not all wise.

33. It is not polite to blow your nose at the table.

34. He will perish by the sword who lives by the sword.

35. Few mobsters live on to the age of retirement.

36. Many are called, but few are chosen. (Treat this as one proposition.)

37. Whoever laughs last laughs best.

38. No good tree bears evil fruit.

39. He that is his own lawyer has a fool for a client.

40. "That woman is a woman!" (*Shakespeare in Love* [movie])

41. "Beauty draws more than oxen." (George Herbert, 17th-cen. English author, *English Poems of George Herbert*, 244)

42. "The only biography that is really possible is autobiography." (G. K. Chesterton, 20th-cen. English author, *The Autobiography*)

43. "Time is the moving image of eternity." (Plato, d. 349 B.C., Greek philosopher, *Timaeus*, 37d)

44. "Some people will never learn anything for this reason that they learn everything too soon." (Alexander Pope, 18th-cen. British author, *Miscellanies in Prose and Verse*)

45. "All the gold in California is in a bank in the middle of Beverly Hills / In somebody else's name...." (Larry Gatlin, 20th-cen. American songwriter)

46. "All the gold in California is not in a bank in the middle of Beverly Hills / In somebody else's name...." (Gatlin [altered])

47. "There are three kinds of lies: lies, damned lies, and statistics." (Attributed to Benjamin Disraeli, 19th-cen. British prime minister, by Mark Twain, in *Chapters from My Autobiography*)

48. "*The web of our life is of a mingled yarn, good and ill together. Our virtues would be proud, if our faults whipped them not; and our crimes*

would despair, if they were not cherished by our virtues." Analyze the
first sentence. (Shakespeare, d. 1616, *All's Well That Ends Well*)

49. "God is dead; but considering the state the species Man is in, there
    will perhaps be caves, for ages yet, in which his shadow will be shown."
    (Friederich Nietzsche, 19th-cen. German philosopher, *Joyful Wisdom*,
    section 108)

50. "In our country the lie has become not just a moral category, but a
    pillar of the State." (Aleksandr Solzhenitsyn, 20th-cen. Russian novel-
    ist, Nobel Prize, reported by *New York Times*, January 22, 1974)

51. "How was she created? I'm not sure if you realize this, but it was in
    God's image. How can anybody dare to speak ill of something which
    bears such a noble imprint?" (Christine de Pizan, d. 1430, French
    moralist, member of the court, author of "mirror of princes" works
    such as *The Book of the City of Ladies*)

Categorical Propositions in Context

The Essentials

Context Is Important

Outside of the classroom, the normal context for statements and propositions is more extended discourse—for instance, in your personal conversations, reading, writing, and thinking. Considered grammatically, sentences are made up of words, and in normal prose they fall into paragraphs that themselves become parts of larger pieces of our discourse. As you know, there are more kinds of propositions than categorical propositions. So most extended discourse consists in several kinds of propositions. For the purposes of learning logic, we are concentrating first on the categorical propositions found in extended discourse; then we will consider hypothetical propositions. We'll do the same thing for arguments, treating first those using categorical propositions and then those consisting in hypothetical propositions. But our goal (or final cause) is improving our skill in understanding all the logical components of extended discourse. We will finish this book by putting together all the topics we have learned in analyzing extended arguments that contain different kinds of propositions and arguments. For the purposes of improving our logical skills, we will concentrate on mastering each of these different topics, one at a time, before we put them all together.

The context in which a sentence or proposition is placed has a definite impact on the meaning of the sentence or proposition. In addition, every human language is flexible enough so that the *categorical propositions* contained in, say, a paragraph, sometimes can be read straight off the sentences that make up the paragraph. But at other times, the most important categorical propositions a paragraph contains are found in the *point* or *thesis* of the paragraph. And this thesis, along with other important categorical propositions, may not be identical with one or another of the sentences in the paragraph. Important categorical propositions can make up just part of a sentence. However, sometimes an important categorical proposition extends into two or three sentences. This phenomenon happens more frequently the better the writer or speaker is.

Analysis Uncovers Propositions

The following plan can be used to analyze a passage of moderate length, say, a paragraph, in order to find the categorical propositions in it:

1. Read through the whole passage, trying to understand each sentence as it stands.

2. Identify those *sentences* that explicitly are categorical propositions.

3. Identify those *parts* of sentences that explicitly are categorical propositions.

4. Identify those categorical propositions that are contained in *more than one* of the sentences in the passage.

5. Identify the categorical proposition that is the basic point, "bottom line," or thesis of the passage.

6. Create a list of the categorical propositions contained in the passage, following the order in which they occur in the passage, numbering them from first to last.

7. Rewrite as you write out the propositions. This will help simplify the propositions, making their meaning clear and their type easier to identify.

A Deeper Look

Existential Import

For Aristotle, logic was a tool to help us understand real things by forming propositions about them. Since propositions are about real things, he thought a necessary aspect of all propositions—both universal propositions and particular propositions—was that each proposition asserts the existence of individual members of the subject class. "All apples are fruit" asserts that there really are apples, in addition to stating that those existing apples are fruit. Likewise, "Some apples are green" asserts there really are apples in addition to saying that they are green—but only some of them. Centuries later, the English mathematician and logician George Boole (1815–64) had some second thoughts on this point, which has come to be called "existential import." Concentrating on counterfactuals and imaginary figures, Boole thought, contrary to Aristotle, that universal propositions like "All unicorns have one horn" and "No unicorns have wings" do not assert the existence of anything at all, since unicorns don't really exist. He reduced the categorical proposition "all unicorns have one horn" to the conditional proposition "If something is a unicorn, then it will have one horn," or "if something is a unicorn, then it will have no wings." He then did something very important, but illogical. He generalized from understanding of propositions about counterfactuals to apply it to all A and E propositions. In other words, he reduced universal categorical propositions to conditional propositions. In Boole's interpretation, "All apples are fruit" does not assert the existence of any apples; it merely means that "if something is an apple, then it must also be a fruit." This innovation has the consequence that it denies the similarity between universal and particular propositions, as far as existential import is concerned. In Boole's interpretation, while I and O propositions have existential import, A and E propositions do *not*. If you have studied modern symbolic logic, you will know that this innovation was carried over into symbolic logic.

Boole's interpretation of categorical propositions has had a great influence on modern symbolic logic and on the teaching of logic. It is no accident that this interpretation was created by a mathematician. Ever since Plato said the objects of mathematics exist, but among the realm of the separate forms, while Aristotle said the objects of mathematics are taken by abstracting them from real things, but only exist as mathematical objects in the mind, mathematicians have had trouble figuring out the nature of the things they study and their relation to the world of our experience. The problem with Boole's interpretation is that in ordinary or "natural" language and thought about the real world, we do normally assert the existence of the subject of every categorical proposition, including A and E propositions. All too many contemporary logicians are inclined to support Boole by saying that on this point the very meaning of ordinary or "natural" language is, or should be, decided by the dictates of symbolic logic. The **problem** with this reasoning, however, is that **it is backward**. Logic comes from the logical character of "natural" language, not the other way around; and logic captures only a part of the richness of "natural" language. The same is true for grammar and rhetoric. To say otherwise would be like saying that, when we compare things in the real world with some theory about them, the real things must follow the theory. But this is backward; we judge theories by the things they are designed to explain, not the other way around. Human knowledge captures only a small part of the amazingly rich reality of the world. The same is true when we compare the subtleties of "natural" language with any kind of logic, symbolic, mathematical, or the kind of verbal, Aristotelian logic we are studying here.

There are **two ways to get out of the conundrum posed by Boole and to agree that Aristotle was correct** to say that A and E propositions do have "existential import." "All roses are flowers" assumes that roses exist; "No kangaroos are dogs" assumes that kangaroos exist. The first way is to split the difference and say that some universal propositions do have existential import—those about the real world—while universal propositions about imaginary or unreal things do not have existential import. While initially attractive, logicians have by and large rejected this answer because it would require two different logics for universal propositions—one for propositions about real things, the other about unreal or imaginary things.

A second and better answer to Boole is to remember that *existence* doesn't always mean the same thing. When we say our dog exists, we mean that it exists as a real thing in the natural world. But when we think or talk about Achilles or Hamlet—who said, "To be or not to be, that is the question"—we recognize that we are talking about something that exists in a manner of speaking, but not in the way our dog does. These characters exist in the way literary characters or folk heroes exist, in our imagination—whether individual or collective—when we read or hear or think about them. "Harry Potter goes to Hogwarts," is not true of the physical world, but Harry exists in the way literary characters exist. And judging from the tremendous role Harry has had in shaping for the better the minds of millions, this kind of existence can have a tremendous impact on our day-to-day reality. This answer means that universal propositions always assert the existence of their subjects—but that not all things exist in the same way: some exist in reality, some exist in the imagination, some in our thought, and some only in the mind of God. But we couldn't at all think about something, or be influenced by it, if it did not exist in some manner, for then it would be absolutely nothing.

While at first glance it might seem like this dispute among logicians doesn't involve much, in later lessons we will see that there is a lot involved. Look for more about "existential import" in the following three lessons. And remember that logic is just "codified common sense"; so don't leave your common sense at the door when you walk into logic class.

Problem Set 16: Propositions in Context

Identifying Categorical Propositions in Prose

Instructions

(a) Pick out at least five *categorical propositions* from each of the following passages. (b) Create a list of the categorical propositions found in each passage. (c) Rewrite each categorical proposition in Standard Form, cutting out all extraneous material. (d) Indicate whether each categorical proposition is A, I, E, or O.

1. In short, "I say that as a city we are the school of Hellas; while I doubt if the world can produce a man, who where he has only himself to depend upon, is equal to so many emergencies and graced by so happy a versatility as the Athenian.... For Athens alone of her contemporaries is found when tested to be greater than her reputation, and alone gives no occasion to her assailants to blush at the antagonist by whom they have been worsted, or to her subjects to question her title to rule by merit. Rather, the admiration of the present and succeeding ages will be ours, since we have not left our power without witness, but have shown it by mighty proofs. And far from needing a Homer for our eulogist, or others of his craft whose verses might charm for the moment only for the impression which they gave, to melt at the touch of fact, we have forced every sea and land to be the highway of our daring, and everywhere, whether for evil or for good, have left imperishable monuments behind us. Such is the Athens for which these men, in the assertion of their resolve not to lose her, nobly fought and died; and well may every one of their survivors be ready to suffer in her cause." (Thucydides, *The Peloponnesian War* 2.35–46, from Pericles's "Funeral Oration" to the Athenians)

2. "Sing, O Muse, of the anger of the son of Peleus, Achilles, and the destruction that brought pains by the thousands upon the Achaeans [Greeks].

It threw many strong souls of heroes down into the underworld of Hades, and gave their bodies to the feasting of dogs and birds. But the will of Zeus was achieved, accomplished since the time of the first conflict between the son of Atreus, the lord of men Agamemnon, and brilliant Achilles. So what god was it who brought them into bitter conflict? It was Apollo, son of Zeus and Leto, whose anger at the king [Agamemnon] drove terrible damage among the host of warriors; and men perished because the son of Atreus dishonored Chryses, priest of Apollo, when he walked on the seashore by the beached ships of the Achaeans, wanting to ransom back his daughter,...

"And he said: 'Sons of Atreus [Agamemnon and Menelaus], and you other strong-greaved Achaeans, the gods who live on Olympus grant you plunder in the city of Priam [Troy]; and after that, an easy journey home. But please return my own daughter [Chryseis] to me. And take this ransom offering, which gives honor to the son of Zeus, Apollo, who strikes from afar.'" (Homer, 9th-cen. b.c. Greek poet, *Iliad*, bk. I, 1–21)

3. "When the people saw that Moses delayed to come down from the mountain, the people gathered themselves together to Aaron, and said to him, 'Up, make us gods, who shall go before us; as for this Moses, the man who brought us up out of the land of Egypt, we do not know what has become of him.' And Aaron said to them, 'Take off the rings of gold which are in the ears of your wives, your sons, and your daughters, and bring them to me.' So all the people took off the rings of gold which were in their ears, and brought them to Aaron. And he received the gold at their hand, and fashioned it with a graving tool, and made a molten calf; and they said, 'These are your gods, O Israel, who brought you up out of the land of Egypt!' When Aaron saw this, he built an altar before it; and Aaron made proclamation and said, 'Tomorrow shall be a feast to the Lord.' And they rose up early on the morrow, and offered burnt offerings and brought peace offerings; and the people sat down to eat and drink, and rose up to play." (*Exodus* 32:1–6, trans. RSV)

4. "Four-score and seven years ago, our fathers brought forth upon this continent a new nation, conceived in liberty and dedicated to the proposition that all men are created equal.

"Now we are engaged in a great civil war, testing whether that nation—or any nation, so conceived and so dedicated—can long endure. We are met on a great battlefield of that war. We have come to dedicate a portion of that field as a final resting place for those who here gave their lives that that nation might live. It is altogether fitting and proper that we should do this.

"But, in a larger sense, we cannot dedicate, we cannot consecrate, we cannot hallow this ground. The brave men, living and dead, who struggled here have consecrated it far above our poor power to add or detract.

"The world will little note, nor long remember what we say here; but it can never forget what they did here.

"It is for us, the living, rather, to be dedicated here to the unfinished work which they who fought here have thus far so nobly advanced. It is rather for us to be here dedicated to the great task remaining before us; that from these honored dead we take increased devotion to that cause for which they gave the last full measure of devotion; that we here highly resolve that these dead shall not have died in vain; that this nation, under God, shall have a new birth of freedom, and that government of the people, by the people, and for the people, shall not perish from the earth." (Abraham Lincoln, 19th-cen. American president, *Gettysburg Address*)

5. "To suppose that the eye with all its inimitable contrivances for adjusting the focus to different distances, for admitting different amounts of light, and for the correction of spherical and chromatic aberration, could have been formed by natural selection, seems, I confess, absurd in the highest degree.... The difficulty of believing that a perfect and complex eye could be formed by natural selection, though insuperable by our imagination, should not be considered subversive of the theory." (Charles Darwin, 19th-cen. English scientist, *On the Origin of Species*)

6. "How came the bodies of animals to be contrived with so much art, and for what ends were their several parts? Was the eye contrived without skill in Opticks, and the ear without knowledge of sounds?...and these things being rightly dispatch'd, does it not appear from phaenomena that there is a Being incorporeal, living, intelligent...?" (Isaac Newton, 17th-cen. English physicist, *Opticks*)

7. "With savages, the weak in body or mind are soon eliminated; and those that survive commonly exhibit a vigorous state of health. We civilised men, on the other hand, do our utmost to check the process of elimination; we build asylums for the imbecile, the maimed, and the sick; we institute poor-laws; and our medical men exert their utmost skill to save the life of every one to the last moment. There is reason to believe that vaccination has preserved thousands, who from a weak constitution would formerly have succumbed to small-pox. Thus the weak members of civilised societies propagate their kind. No one who has attended to the breeding of domestic animals will

doubt that this must be highly injurious to the race of man. It is surprising how soon a want of care, or care wrongly directed, leads to the degeneration of a domestic race; but excepting in the case of man himself, hardly any one is so ignorant as to allow his worst animals to breed." (Charles Darwin, 19th-cen. English biologist, *The Descent of Man*)

Euler and Venn Diagrams of Propositions

The Essentials

Over the centuries logicians have developed symbols and diagrams as ways of representing logical points. They began to do so long before the invention of modern symbolic logic in the late nineteenth century. We have already seen some of the kinds of symbols devised to represent different kinds of propositions, such as *All S is P* and (p → q). In the eighteenth century, however, the Swiss mathematician Leonard Euler (1707–83), who spent most of his career in Russia and Germany because he failed to obtain the teaching post he wanted in his native Switzerland, took another approach to representing propositions. Rather than use letters to stand for terms or propositions, he represented terms and propositions by *diagrams*. In this lesson, we will look first at Euler's diagrams and then at the way the British logician John Venn (1834–1923) adapted them to make them more useful for representing both propositions and arguments.

Using Circles

Using symbols like S for the subject of a categorical proposition or p for a whole categorical proposition originally was simply a convenient way of abbreviating a longer word or sentence and generalizing it to signify any term or proposition. This practice goes back as far as Aristotle himself. In later centuries, and especially in modern symbolic logic, using such symbols shows the influence of mathematics on the practice of teaching logic. Algebra, for example, uses letters to stand in for any of a range of numbers. It is no wonder that this practice was mainly developed by mathematicians. Using diagrams to represent terms and propositions (and arguments, as we shall see) is a bit different, for it shows the influence of geometry.

The secret to the success of Euler and Venn diagrams is that they represent what in mathematics is often called a "set" of items by a circle or other curved two-dimensional figure. A set is the totality of a group of items included under the set, say, baseball bats. Bats can also be thought of as a "class" of things, a number of things that fit into the class because they all have the same characteristics. "Set" and "class" are primarily mathematical concepts, but since they represent a group of things, it was quite natural for logicians to think of a circle as a visual way to represent a term.

A circle represents a set or class or term, say, the term "Texan," to go back to our earlier example. Spatially, if the circle represents the "class" of Texans, then what is the inside of the circle represents Texans, while what is outside the circle represents non-Texans.

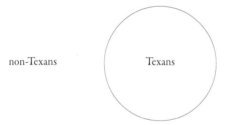

This particular example can then be generalized, so we can let the circle represent any class or term **P**. If so, the area outside the circle represents **non-P**:

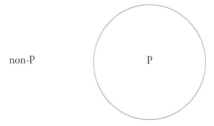

Euler Diagrams

Universal Affirmative Proposition

What Euler recognized is that you can use *two* circles, one for each term in a categorical proposition. Then you can visually represent the four kinds of categorical propositions with diagrams composed of two circles. Consider a universal affirmative proposition (A), such as "All Texans are friendly," or the general form of A propositions, "All S is P," using S for the subject term and P for the predicate term. When you assert "All Texans are friendly," what you are saying is that the whole class of *Texans* falls within the class of *friendly people*. This proposition can be visually represented by placing the circle of *Texans* wholly within the circle of *friendly people*. To generalize, the circle that represents the subject term (S) must lie wholly within the circle that represents the predicate term (P).

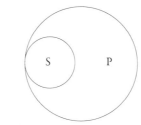

A Proposition

Universal Negative Proposition

A universal negative proposition (E) does the opposite. Consider "No Texans are friendly." Rather than including all the Texans under the term "friendly," it denies that any Texan falls under the description "friendly." Since the E proposition *separates* the predicate from the subject, this mental separation can be represented diagrammatically by separating the two circles. This geometrical separation represents the claim that none of the *Texans* are included within the class or term "friendly." Such an example can be generalized to symbolize all E propositions, which takes the form "No S is P."

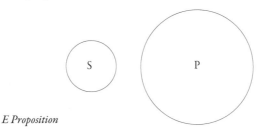

E Proposition

Particular Affirmative and Particular Negative Propositions

The two particular propositions (I and O) work quite differently. When we say "Some Texans are friendly" (I), we are saying there are some things that are both *Texans* and *friendly*. But when we say "Some Texans are not friendly" (O), we are saying there are some things that are *Texans*, but they are not *friendly*. We could also put the negation in the predicate term and say "Some Texans are non-friendly" (I). When we get to Lesson 20 and study Obversion, we'll see that "Some Texans are non-friendly" (I) and "Some Texans are not friendly" (O) have the same truth value. Euler recognized that an elegant way to represent the group of Texans who are friendly is to overlap the two circles. The common area represents things that are both *Texans* and *friendly*, or, to generalize, they are both S and P. The trick is to figure out how to distinguish I from O propositions in a diagram, since the basic figure—overlapping circles—is the same for both. Euler himself did this by setting the interlocking circles *side by side* for a particular affirmative proposition (I) and setting the interlocking S circle *over* the P circle for particular negative propositions (O). Another way is to place the name for the subject term *inside* the common area for particular affirmative propositions (I), to indicate that "some S *is* P"; and to diagram a particular negative proposition by placing the name of the subject term within the S circle but *outside* the common area, to indicate that "some S *is not* P." The following diagram follows the latter convention.

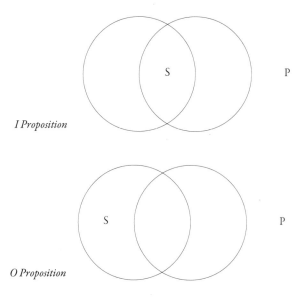

I Proposition

O Proposition

Whichever way you draw the diagram, Euler's was not a very happy way to distinguish I from O propositions, since the basic geometrical figure—interlocking circles—is the same in both cases. Another and more difficult problem is that the way Euler distinguished propositions diagrammatically required him to *change the diagram*. He used three different diagrams. This problem becomes important when we try to diagram not a single proposition, but an argument. As we shall see, the most basic kind of argument is a categorical syllogism, which involves three different propositions. Since he was a brilliant mathematician, Euler did manage to solve this problem; but to do so his diagrams became too complicated. About one hundred years later John Venn came to the rescue.

Venn Diagrams

If Euler's life was typical of the international career of the eighteenth-century European intellectual, John Venn's was typical of the British intellectual in the nineteenth century. The son of an Anglican clergyman who had been educated at Cambridge University, Venn went to Cambridge as well and stayed on there, first on the faculty of and then as president of Gonville and Caius College, in whose chapel the stained glass commemorating his life contains the Venn diagram of a categorical syllogism.

Venn simplified the Euler diagrams, thereby making them both more elegant and easier to use. His first change was to use the same geometrical figure to diagram all four categorical propositions. He used the two intersecting circles found in Euler's diagrams of particular propositions. If we say the two intersecting circles each represent some class or term, say, *Texans* and *friendly*, then a diagram with two intersecting circles includes four areas, each representing a different class. Note that to describe any area you have to describe it in relation to *both* terms found in the proposition. Consider the four areas in a diagram using the terms "Texan" and "friendly":

Area 1 = Non-Texan, nonfriendly.   Area 3 = both Texan and friendly
Area 2 = Texan, but nonfriendly   Area 4 = non-Texan but friendly

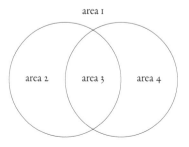

In order to distinguish the four kinds of categorical propositions from each other, Venn needed to invent some new devices to put in these areas of his diagrams. What he did was to invent a way of recording what was true about the class or term signified by a particular area. He said that for each area there are three possibilities:

1. If an area is left blank, this signifies possibility, not reality or existence. There may exist some members of that class or term, or there may not.
2. If an area has either an X or shading, this signifies either existence or the denial of existence, that is, non-existence:

   a. If an area has an X in it, this signifies that the type of thing represented by that particular area does exist.
   b. If an area is shaded or colored, this signifies that no such kind of thing represented by that area exists.

Thinking about a proposition in terms of the existence or nonexistence of certain kinds or classes of things—as determined by the subject and predicate of the proposition—helped Venn to symbolize diagrammatically what a categorical proposition means.

A Proposition

Let's consider a universal affirmative proposition (A), such as "All Texans are friendly," or the general type of an A proposition, "All S is P." Here is its Venn diagram:

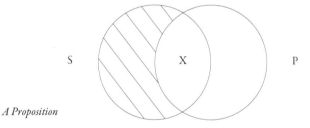

A Proposition

The two symbols added to the diagram illustrate the meaning of a proposition like "All Texans are friendly" by making two points. First, this diagram shades or colors area (2), which represents things that are S, because inside the

S circle, but are not P, because they are outside the P circle. In our example, then, area (2) represents things that are *Texans* but not *friendly*. The diagram shows visually that there do not exist any *Texans* who are not *friendly*, which is part of what "All Texans are friendly" means. Second, putting an X in area (3) represents things that are both S and P, because this area falls within both circles. The X in area (3) means that there do exist *Texans* who also are *friendly*. The combined effect of these two symbols is to say that there exist things that are Texans, and every one of the Texans is also friendly or "all Texans are friendly."

In this diagram, you can see visualized the issue of "existential import." The existence of *Texans* is represented by the X in area (3). A logician who does *not* assume the existential import of an A proposition would leave the X out of the diagram. The problem with leaving out X, of course, is that a proposition like "All Texans are friendly" is talking about real, existing Texans, not some purely imaginary Star Wars type of thing.

In addition, the diagram makes two other points about A propositions. By leaving open area (4), which signifies things that are *not Texans but are friendly* (non-S but P), the diagram leaves open the possibility—but only the possibility—that there are things that are *friendly* but are *not Texans*, like people from New York (where I used to live), or perhaps dogs. It does not say there really are such things, but neither does it say there are not such things. This point helps us see what we are claiming to know for sure in any given proposition and what we are not claiming to be sure about.

Finally, the diagram lets us see that "All Texans are friendly" makes no claim whatsoever about things that are neither Texans nor friendly, which is what area (1) represents.

There are other points one can see in the diagram, if one looks closely. In a couple of lessons, we will study conversion, which is reversing the subject and predicate of a proposition. Using the diagram, you can see that the *converse* of "All Texans are friendly" cannot be a *universal* affirmative proposition, but is limited to a particular affirmative proposition: "Some friendly people are Texans." The reason why is visible in the proposition, because area (3) has an X in it, but area (4) is left open. This means there *can* be people who are *friendly* but not *Texans*.

I Proposition

Now let's turn to a particular affirmative proposition (I). Here is the Venn diagram of the general type of I proposition: "Some S is P."

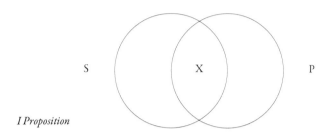

I Proposition

This diagram includes the X of the diagram of an A proposition, which means there are *Texans* who are *friendly*. But it leaves off the hatching out or coloring out of area (2), the part of S that is not also P, in our example, a *Texan* who is *not* also *friendly*. The result is that the diagram shows that at least "some Texans are friendly," which is the proposition being diagrammed. But the diagram leaves open two important possibilities. Unlike the A proposition, the I proposition fails to exclude from existence Texans who are not friendly, because area (2) is left open. "Non-friendly Texans" *may* exist, but they may not. Also, like the A proposition, it leaves open the possibility that there are friendly people who are not Texans.

E Proposition

Let's turn now to the universal negative proposition (E), such as "No Texans are friendly" or, in general form, "No S is P."

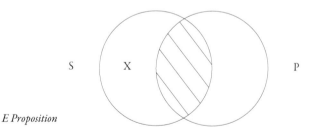

E Proposition

Like the A proposition, the E proposition has an X in one area and shading or coloring in another area; but in contrast with A, the areas are reversed.

First, it asserts the existence of Texans who are not friendly (S is not P). But from this assertion alone we don't know the quantity of the proposition—whether it is saying *all* Texans are not friendly or *some* Texans are not friendly. In order to exclude even the possibility of any Texan also being friendly, area (3) is shaded or colored. There cannot exist things that are *both* Texans *and* friendly people. The E proposition, however, does leave open the possibility of friendly people who are not Texans, in area (4). The fact that Texans are not friendly does not exclude Iowans, for example, from being friendly.

O Proposition

Finally, let's turn to the O proposition. An example is, "Some Texans are not friendly," which has the general form "Some S is not P."

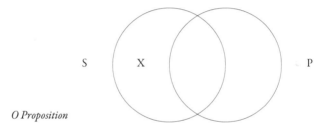

O Proposition

If we compare the O with the E proposition, the difference is nicely captured in their two diagrams. The E proposition excludes any possibility of finding Texans who are also friendly. The O proposition is different on this point. Area (3) is blank, so it is *possible* that there exist Texans who are friendly. The other feature of the E proposition is retained. The X in area (2) means that there do exist Texans who are not friendly. Finally, like the E proposition, the O leaves open the possibility that there can be friendly people who are not Texans, for area (4) lies wholly outside the circle of Texans.

Primary Sources

John Venn (1834–1923), *Symbolic Logic* (1881), reprinted 1971.

Problem Set 17: Euler and Venn Diagrams of Propositions

EULER DIAGRAMS

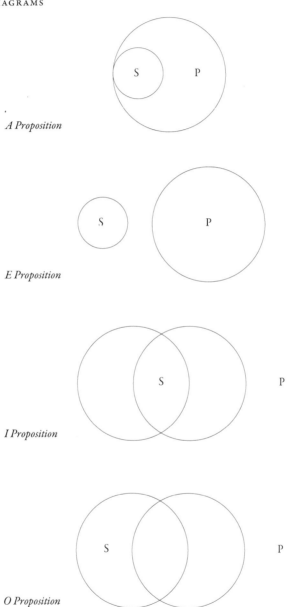

A Proposition

E Proposition

I Proposition

O Proposition

VENN DIAGRAMS

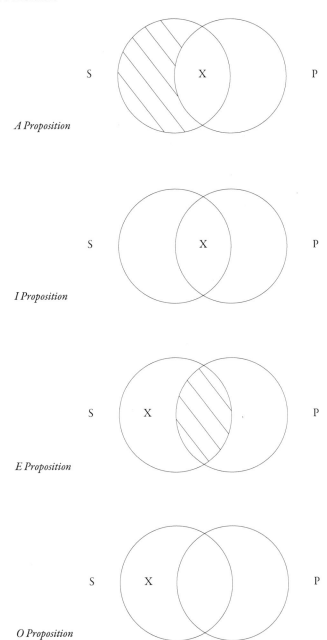

Learning to Draw Diagrams of Propositions

Instructions

Create Euler *and* Venn diagrams of the following propositions:

1. All Texans are friendly.
2. Some Texans are friendly.
3. No Texans are friendly.
4. Some Texans are not friendly.
5. None of the chimpanzees have been fed.
6. All airplanes are human artifacts.
7. Some citizens are uninvolved.
8. Most citizens vote in federal elections.
9. Some friends of ours were not at the game.
10. All truck drivers have taken a special course.
11. The animals in that part of the zoo have not been fed.
12. Socrates was a philosopher.
13. Not all the tires on my car are worn.
14. It is not polite to blow your nose at the table.
15. He will perish by the sword who lives by the sword.
16. Cavalier King Charles spaniels are beautiful dogs.

Opposition

The Essentials

Opposing Concepts and Opposing Propositions

Consider this ethical proposition: "All just people are honest." What is its opposite? Now opposites are not just different from each other; they are directly set off against each other based on some criterion. If you concentrate on the *content* of this proposition, you probably will focus on the two terms of the proposition: "just people" and "honest people." And the reason for doing so is that, like many ideas in ethics, both terms have concepts that oppose them: "unjust" is opposed to "just" and "dishonest" to "honest. The opposition between these two pairs of terms is an opposition between *concepts* that are incompatible with each other, like *large* vs. *small*, or *loud* vs. *quiet*, or *black* vs. *white*, up to and including the most universal and fundamental opposing concepts, *is* vs. *is not*. We saw in Lesson 12 that every categorical proposition includes *content*, as found in its two terms or concepts, which is sometimes called its "matter," but also has *structure,* as found in how the terms are related to each other, as an A, I, E, or O proposition, which is sometimes called the proposition's "form." What is the opposite of our proposition, when we concentrate on its content or matter? If we take the opposing terms in "All just people are honest" and put them together, the opposing proposition might be "*All* unjust people are dishonest," a very strong claim. Or perhaps the opposite is "*Some* unjust people are dishonest." Which of these two plausible answers is correct? Or is there another answer we haven't even thought of yet? There is a definite answer, but we'll have to wait until Lesson 20 to find out. The reason is that there is a difference between opposing *concepts* or terms, which we covered a bit when treating conceptualization, the first act of the mind, and opposing *propositions*, which is our concern here in considering the second act of the mind. *The first kind of opposition is that of opposing concepts or terms.* Unfortunately, focusing only on the terms involved does not give us a direct answer to our question about opposing propositions.

Here, however, we are concerned with this second kind of opposition, opposing *propositions*, as distinct from opposing terms; and here we need to focus on the *structure or form* of the proposition, rather than just on the content of its terms. What is the *proposition* opposing our A proposition: "All just people are honest"? The answer most people give is the E proposition "No just people are honest," because if our original proposition is true, this one must be false, and truth is the opposite of falsity. But if "*All* just people are honest" is true, doesn't the O proposition also have to be false: "*Some* just people are not honest"? Yes! Now we have two opposites of our initial A proposition. Which one is really the opposite proposition? The answer to this question is that both are opposites, but different *kinds* of opposites. In fact, if we focus on the structure of the propositions, there aren't just two; there are three opposites of our original A proposition. Once Aristotle followed his intuition that logic concentrates on the form or structure of a proposition, he realized that structurally speaking there are three opposites to *any* categorical proposition.

Opposing Propositions: The Square of Opposition

The reason each categorical proposition has to have three kinds of opposites is that, when we look at their structure or form, there are only four kinds of propositions, which are determined by their two structural features, their quantity and quality, as we saw in Lesson 14. To illustrate these relations, logicians devised the "Square of Opposition." In order to understand it, we can start with the four kinds of categorical propositions and then move to the three propositions that are opposed to each one of these four types. Since there are several kinds of opposing propositions, in order to avoid confusion Aristotle and his followers gave each of them a different name.

The Four Kinds of Categorical Propositions

A: All just people are honest.

I: Some just people are honest.

E: No just people are honest.

O: Some just people are not honest.

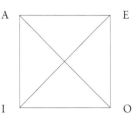

Square of Opposition

The Names of the Five Kinds of Opposite Propositions

Contradictories: A vs. O; E vs. I.

Contraries: A vs. E

Subcontraries: I vs. O.

Subalternates: A to I; E to O.

Subimplicants: I to A; O to E.

Five Different Kinds of Opposition

Let's now look at each of the five kinds of formally opposed propositions in more detail, based on being opposed in quality, in quantity, or in both. For each kind, let's start with an example.

Contradiction and Contradictory Propositions

Consider these two examples:

A vs. O: "All just people are honest" vs. "Some just people are not honest."

E vs. I: "No just people are honest" vs. "Some just people are honest."

Both of these pairs of propositions are contradictories. Ask yourself these two questions: For each pair, if one of the propositions is *true*, what must the other one be: true, false, or you can't be sure? Then ask: If one of the propositions is false, what about the other one: true or false or you can't be sure? Contradictory propositions are found at the ends of the two diagonals of the square. They are opposites of each other to the *maximum degree possible*. This means they cannot both be true, and they cannot both be false. Therefore, if one proposition is true the other *must* be false; and if one proposition is false the other *must* be true. There is no middle ground between contradictories.

The reason contradictory propositions are so strongly opposed can be seen by looking at the square. All the kinds of opposing propositions have the same subject term and the same predicate term. Contradictories differ as much as two propositions with the same subject and predicate can differ: they are opposed to each other in *both* quantity and quality. This is the reason we can know for sure that if one contradictory is true, the other must be false. And we can proceed in the opposite direction: if one is false, the other must be true. To make sure you understand this kind of opposition and the others to follow and don't just memorize the point, it is a good idea to take several examples and think about them.

In sum, *contradictory propositions are opposed in both quantity and quality. This is why they are incompatible in truth (they cannot both be true), and they are also incompatible in falsity (they cannot both be false).*

Contrariety and Contrary Propositions

Ask yourself the same question about these two contrary propositions: If one proposition is *true*, what happens with the other proposition? And if one is *false*, what about the other one?

A vs. E: "All just people are honest" vs. "No just people are honest."

Contrary propositions are found along the top of the square. They strongly oppose each other, but not to the maximum degree. If "All just people are honest" is *true*, it is impossible that "No just people are honest," because we started with the assumption that all of them *are* honest. The contrary E proposition must be false.

But what if "All just people are honest" is *false*? Is "No just people are honest" true or false or undetermined (you just don't know)? The answer is *undetermined*. Why? All it takes for the A proposition to be false is *one* counterexample, one just person who is not honest. But it is a long way from "some just person is not honest" (O) to "No just people are honest" (E). In fact, if

"All just people are honest" is false, there are two possibilities for its opposite. The first is that "No just people are honest" (E); but it is equally possible that "Some just people are honest" (I) and "Some just people are not honest" (O). Based *solely* on the falsity of the A proposition, we can't know which of these two alternatives is correct. So here we must admit our ignorance and say, based on the falsity of A, that the truth or falsity of E is *undetermined*.

Looking at the square of opposition helps us see the reason. Contrary propositions are opposed to each other *only* in quality—affirmative vs. negative—*not* in quantity. Opposition in quality—affirmative vs. negative—is the reason they cannot both be true. But since they have the same quantity—both A and E are universal—they can both be false. If "All just people are honest" is false, however, the only thing we know *for sure* is that the contradictory, the particular O proposition "Some just people are not honest," *must* be true, because this is what *makes* the A proposition false. To go beyond *some just people* to *all just people* (the subject of the E proposition) would be to go beyond the information we know for sure, based on the A proposition being false.

In sum, *contrary propositions are opposed in quality, but not in quantity. This is why they are incompatible in truth (they cannot both be true) but they are compatible in falsity (they can both be false).*

Subcontrariety, Subcontrary Propositions

Consider the following two subcontrary propositions. Ask yourself the same two questions: If one is *true*, what about the other; and if one is *false*, what about the other? Here you have to be careful. The question is not what *can* the truth status of the other proposition be, but what *must* its truth status be?

> I vs. O: "Some just people are honest" vs. "Some just people are not honest."

Subcontraries are found along the bottom of the square. Like contraries, these propositions are opposed in quality and the same in quantity. But since their quantity is *particular*, their relation to each other is different from contraries. Subcontraries can both be true, but they cannot both be false. You cannot draw a definite conclusion about one subcontrary based on the *truth* of the other; but if one is *false* you know for sure the other must be true.

Looking at the square helps to see why. Let's first consider the consequences of an I proposition being *true*. If "Some just people are honest" is true, it is easy to see that "Some just people are *not* honest" also *might* be true. And quite often, when we say "some are" we are also thinking "and some are not." But we only think this way because we have *independent evidence* for both propositions being true. But this is not the issue here. What we are concerned with is whether, based *only* on the truth of the I proposition, you can be *sure* that "Some just people are *not* honest." And we cannot be sure. Might be so, might not be so. Here the issue is whether we must draw a necessary inference that, because the I proposition is true, and based solely on this point, the O proposition must be true. But the answer is that this conclusion isn't necessary; this inference in invalid.

One way to see this point is to ask yourself how you come to know that "Some just people are honest." You determine their honesty by coming to know them, one by one, and making the judgment that each is honest. Just because they are just doesn't mean they also are honest; we have to determine whether a person has both of these two good traits or virtues—justice and honesty—independently of each other.

Having looked at what happens if the I proposition is true, now let's look at the consequences of the I proposition being *false*. What if "Some just people are honest" is *false*? Here we need to ask ourselves what set of facts would make the proposition "some just people are honest" false. This proposition would be true if just one just person were honest. So the only way "Some just people are honest" could be *false* is if its contradictory, "No just people are honest," (E) were true. But if an E proposition is true, then the particular O proposition lying under it also must also be true, since the particular proposition is just a special case falling under the universal proposition. The result: if it is *false* that "Some just people are honest" it must be *true* that "some just people are not honest."

In sum, *subcontraries are opposed in quality, but not in quantity. This is why they are compatible in truth (they can both be true) but they are incompatible in falsity (they cannot both be false).*

4. Subalternation, Subalternate Propositions

Now let's consider the two sides of the square. For contradictories, contraries, and subcontraries, it didn't matter which proposition we start with; but for subalternates and subimplicants, the direction we're going does matter. Are we going from top to bottom or bottom to top on the square? In sub-alternation, we are going down, from universal to particular. For the following two examples, ask yourself the same two questions as before: If the universal is *true*, what must the particular proposition be like; and if the universal is *false*, what must the particular be like?

> A to I: Moving from "All just people are honest" to "Some just people are honest."
>
> E to O: Moving from "No just people are honest" to "Some just people are not honest."

Subalternates and subimplicants are found along the sides of the square. Some logic textbooks do not have separate words for subalternates and su-bimplicants, but it is helpful to use different terms because their logical relations are quite different from each other. And some logic textbooks deny subalternation and subimplication to be oppositions, because they limit "opposition" strictly to one proposition being true and the other being false. But if we base ourselves on the square, we can see that these two relations are found on the square and do differ based on whether one goes up or down the sides of the square. For the first three kinds of opposites, the order in which you compare them does not matter; but with subalternates and subimplicants the *order in which you consider them* does affect the truth value of the opposing proposition. In subalternate propositions you move from universal to particular in quantity, while the two propositions have the same quality. In subimplicant propositions, you move in the opposite direction, from particular to universal.

For subalternates, if the universal proposition it *true*, then the particular proposition that lies under it on the square must also be true. This is easy to see, because the particular proposition is just a special case falling under the wider, universal proposition. If "All just people are honest" is true, then it clearly must be true that "Some just people are honest," since *some just people* is just part of the larger group of *all just people*.

On the other hand, if the universal is *false*, no conclusion can be drawn about its subalternate. For example, if "All just people are honest" were false, we don't know just from its being false whether "Some just people are honest" is true or not. Once again, one of two alternatives must be true, but we don't know which one: either some just people are honest and some are not (the most likely scenario); or it could be true that "No just people are honest."

Based on the falsity of the A proposition and on that alone, we are not be in a position to know for sure which of these two alternatives is true. The same logic applies to negative subalternates (E to O), though they are sometimes harder to analyze simply because they are negative.

In sum, *for subalternates, if the universal proposition is true, the particular under it must be true; but if the universal is false, the universal is undetermined.*

5. Subimplication, Subimplicant Propositions

Finally, let's move up the side of the square, from particular to universal; and we'll ask the same question as before. Consider these two pairs.

> I to A: Moving from "Some just people are honest" to "All just people are honest."
>
> O to E: Moving from "Some just people are not honest" to "No just people are honest."

Here again, the *order* in which one moves is absolutely important. *Subimplicants* are the reverse of subalternates. While in *subordination* we went *downward* from the universal to the particular proposition lying under it in the Square of Opposition, in *subimplication* we move *upward* from a particular proposition to the universal proposition standing over it, proceeding up the side of the square.

If the particular proposition is *true*, the universal proposition above it is undetermined, because such reasoning moves beyond the information we started with, since a particular proposition covers only one or some instances of the universal. If it is true that "Some just people are honest," we cannot know for sure, just from that statement, that "All just people are honest." The universal proposition *might* be true; but then again it might not be.

On the other hand, if we already know that the particular proposition is *false*, then the universal proposition standing over it also must be *false*. We can understand the reason if we ask ourselves what falsifies a universal proposition. The answer is this: just one counter-example. And the false particular proposition provides that counterexample. If it is false that "Some just people are honest," then we already would have enough information to know that it is also false that "All just people are honest," because we already have the counterexample. This example, however, is counterfactual, because there are just people who are also honest. Let's turn to a more realistic example. Suppose

"Some of the people in the room are over sixty-five years old" is false because all of them are under sixty-five. Then what about the universal subimplicant "All the people in the room are over sixty-five years old."? Here it is easy to see that the falsity of the particular (I) proposition is enough to falsify the universal (A) proposition, because just one person under sixty-five is enough to falsify the A proposition.

In sum, *for subimplicants, if the particular proposition is true, the universal proposition is undetermined; but if the particular proposition is false, the universal must be false.*

Helpful Tools for Everyday Thinking

Using Counterexamples

If you suspect a universal proposition (A or E) is wrong because it is an exaggeration, you don't have to go all the way to establish that the contrary universal proposition (E or A) is right. To show the universal proposition is false, all you have to do is show the contradictory particular proposition is true. This is called *finding a counter-example*, since just one case is enough to establish the truth of a particular proposition. For example, to show that "All just people are honest" is false, you only need to find one just person who is not honest. And the same thing is true for the E proposition.

Using the Truth Values in the Table of Opposites

TRUTH VALUES IN THE TABLE OF OPPOSITES

Type of Opposition	If first proposition is	Then the second proposition is
Contradictories:	T	F
	F	T
Contraries:	T	F
	F	U
Subcontraries:	T	U
	F	T
Subalternation:	T	T
	F	U
Subimplication:	T	U
	F	F

T = true proposition; F = false proposition; U = undetermined proposition, may be T or F.

Problem Set 18: Opposition

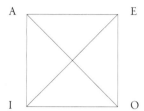

Classical Square of Opposition

Definitions

Contradictories: A vs. O; E vs. I.
Contraries: A vs. E
Subcontraries: I vs. O.
Subalternates: A to I; E to O.
Subimplicants: I to A; O to E.

Learning to Recognize Different Kinds of Opposition

Instructions

(a) Name the kind of opposition between the first and second propositions.

(b) Assume the first proposition is true or false as indicated. Is the second true, false, or undetermined?

1. (T) Some tools are saws. Some tools are not saws.
2. (T) All saws are tools. Some saws are not tools.
3. (F) No saws are tools. Some saws are tools.
4. (T) No tools are worthless. All tools are worthless.
5. (F) No lawyers are dishonest. All lawyers are dishonest.
6. (T) Some axes are sharp. Some axes are not sharp.
7. (F) Some elephants can fly. Some elephants cannot fly.
8. (T) Some mosquitoes carry malaria. All mosquitoes carry malaria.
9. (F) All mosquitoes carry malaria. Some mosquitoes carry malaria.
10. (T) Some of the Roman emperors were wise. None of the Roman emperors were wise.

11. (T) Some of the Roman emperors were wise. Some of the Roman emperors were not wise.

12. (T) Some of the Roman emperors were wise. All the Roman emperors were wise.

13. (F) None of the Roman emperors were wise. All the Roman emperors were wise.

14. (T) All scouts know how to tie knots. Some scouts do not know how to tie knots.

15. (F) Some scouts know how to tie knots. Some scouts do not know how to tie knots.

16. (T) Some of her scarves have been cleaned. All of her scarves have been cleaned.

17. (T) Some of her scarves have been cleaned. Some of her scarves have not been cleaned.

18. (F) Some of her scarves have not been cleaned. All of her scarves have been cleaned.

19. (T) Some bluebonnets are pretty. All bluebonnets are pretty.

20. (F) Some fish are warm blooded. All fish are warm blooded.

Creating Opposites

Instructions

(a) For the following propositions, create the kind of opposites indicated.

(b) Given that the first proposition is true or false, as indicated, is each of the opposites T, F, or U?

1. (T) No hummingbird is slow.	Contradictory:
	Contrary:
2. (F) Some hummingbirds are large.	Subimplicant:
	Subcontrary:
3. (T) Some saws have fine teeth.	Contradictory:
	Subimplicant:
4. (T) Some songs are beautiful.	Subcontrary:
	Contradictory:
	Subimplicant:

5. (T) Some politicians are dishonest.   Subimplicant:
                                              Subcontrary:

6. (F) All apples are red.   Contradictory:
                                              Contrary:

7. (T) No giraffes are insects.   Contradictory:
                                              Subalternate:

8. (F) No computers are outdated.   Contrary:
                                              Contradictory:

9. (T) Some economies are changeable.   Subimplicant:
                                              Contradictory:
                                              Subalternate:

10. (T) All apples are fruit.   Contrary:
                                              Subalternate:

Inferences Using Opposition

Instructions

The following passages contain inferences you can analyze using the Square of Opposition. Consider valid those inferences that follow, based on the Square of Opposition; all the rest are invalid.

(a) Identify the propositions, in order. Circle and number them, or write them out and number them.

(b) Identify each inference—that is, each reasoning from one proposition to another. Number each inference.

(c) Determine whether the inferences are valid; that is, does the truth status given in the passage for the consequent proposition *follow from* the truth status given for the antecedent?

1. If it is true that all plants are living things, then it is false that some plants are not living things.

2. If it is true that no neutrons are charged subatomic particles, then it is false that some neutrons are charged subatomic particles, and it is also false that all neutrons are charged subatomic particles.

3. If it is true that all hydrochloric acid is composed of hydrogen and chlo-rine, then it is false that no hydrochloric acid is composed of hydrogen and chlorine. And from the latter statement it also follows that it is true that some hydrochloric acid is composed of hydrogen and chlorine. And further, if it is true that some hydrochloric acid is composed of hydrogen and chlorine, then it follows that it is true that all hydrochloric acid is composed of hydrogen and chlorine, which is where we started.

4. If it is false that some water is made up of hydrogen and chlorine, then it is false that all water is made up of hydrogen and chlorine, and it also fol-lows from the first statement that it is true that no water is made up of hydro-gen and chlorine. This conclusion also follows from the second statement.

5. If it is true that all disposable contact lenses allow for natural tear flow, then it is false that some disposable contact lenses do not allow for natural tear flow. From the first statement, it also follows that it is false that some dis-posable contact lenses allow for natural tear flow. And from the second state-ment it is true that some disposable contact lenses allow for natural tear flow.

Conversion

Preliminaries

It may look like the exercises in Problem Set 18 are the kind of problems of interest only in a logic classroom, with no application to the wider world of practical or intellectual life. And the same criticism could be made of Problem Sets 19 and 20. But consider two points. First, while we have found several kinds of opposing propositions for our original proposition: "All just people are honest," we haven't solved the question of whether "All unjust people are dishonest" is its opposite, or whether its opposite is "Some unjust people are dishonest," or some other proposition. Second, we all recognize that quite often we don't understand the full meaning of what we are reading or saying or writing. Opposition helps us understand a proposition by seeing other concepts or other propositions that are opposed to it. Conversion and obversion, by contrast, help us uncover that full meaning of a proposition by seeing its *implications*, seeing other propositions that are consistent with the original proposition, and other propositions that are inconsistent with the original one.

For example, in Lesson 18 we saw that it is wrong to think that "some college students are moral" (I) necessarily implies that "some college students are not moral" (O), even though some people might think this inference is correct. And this is just one example among many. Lessons 19 and 20 are designed primarily to help us understand what we are saying, what others are saying, and what we are reading. It is helpful to test the truth of the propositions and arguments we (and others) say by looking forward to the consequences of those claims and backward to their presuppositions. Opposition, conversion, and obversion help us to look in both directions. These techniques go all the way back to Socrates as he is presented in Plato's early dialogues.

There is a second benefit in becoming proficient in solving these kinds of problems, which will become more apparent when we get to the logic of the third act of the mind, beginning with Lesson 23. When we argue—that is, when we reason—sometimes it is necessary to change the *form or structure* of the propositions used as premises or conclusions of an argument, even when we keep the same terms. We need to do so in order to make sure the arguments we use are valid, because invalid arguments never can insure that our conclusions are true. Studying the square of opposition, conversion, and obversion is designed to develop our skills at changing around propositions to formulate correctly the premises we need for arguments, premises that produce valid arguments and true conclusions.

Inferences: Valid and Invalid

The primary focus of logic is on the third act of the mind, the act of reasoning, when we use our mind to move from one point to another, especially when drawing a new conclusion based on information we already have. This process is also called "inferring" or "inference," which comes from the Latin verb *inferre*, which originally meant to carry or bring something to or into or against something, as when Roman soldiers would bring their legion's standard against an enemy when attacking them. Then Roman lawyers and philosophers (like Cicero) used "infer" to describe carrying a point in law or philosophy further, in order to draw a new conclusion. So logical inference means a movement of the mind in drawing a conclusion based on evidence. Now sometimes such conclusions are logical, when the conclusion follows from the premises or evidence. This is called a "valid" inference. But sometimes the conclusion does *not* follow from the premises, and to say it does is a mistake in reasoning. This is called an "invalid" inference.

Sometimes we use the terms "valid" and "invalid" as synonyms for "true" and "false," especially when we're not quite sure the statement is true, but we think it is. We say, "That's a valid point," when what we mean is "I think it might be true, but I'm not sure," or "I'll consider the point." But this is not the precise meaning "valid" has in logic, and can be misleading. "Valid" and "invalid," as well as "true" and "false," are technical terms with precise meanings. "True" and "false" concern propositions, and mean "the proposition does (or does not) comport with reality. But "valid" concerns reasoning and argument, and it means the conclusion we draw follows logically from the evidence or premises we have presented, while "invalid" means it does not.

Our study of the third act of the mind, the logic of reasoning, will concentrate on distinguishing valid from invalid arguments. We will devote a lot of space to that subject later. The reason for bringing up the topics of inference and validity now is that in considering the square of opposition we have already begun to make inferences and to judge their validity. There are two kinds of inference. Logicians call them "immediate inference" and "mediate inference." The term "mediate" comes from the Latin word *medium*, which means "middle," which you already know from sizes—small, medium, large. A mediate inference is one that needs a middle or linking term in order to draw the conclusion. Most inferences are like this, and our study of the logic of the third act of the mind will concentrate on mediate inferences. An example is this argument: all dogs are animals; and all animals are living things; so all dogs are living things. In this case, the common term "animals" is in the middle between "dogs" and "living things," linking them together. If we don't have such a middle term, we cannot draw the conclusion—at least, we cannot do so using this kind of reasoning.

In studying the Square of Opposition, we have encountered a different kind of reasoning or inference, an *immediate inference*, one we can make, and make validly, *without* having to use a middle term. When using the square of opposites, our reasoning went directly from one proposition to another; no third proposition was involved, and no middle term was involved. The subject and predicate terms in the proposition with which we started were the same two terms found in the conclusion. We saw that sometimes we could not determine whether the *opposite* proposition had to be true or had to be false, so in these cases no inference could be drawn. But sometimes we could. We saw that, if an A proposition is true, such as "all horses are living things," then its contrary E proposition, "no horses are living things," has to be false. This inference is valid, and it is an immediate inference, broadly speaking, one that proceeds directly from one proposition to another.

While a *true* A proposition, however, implies that its contrary E proposition must be *false*, this inference is not valid in the technical and precise meaning of the term "inference" in logic. Speaking precisely, a valid inference is one in which a *true* conclusion is derived from a *true* premise. The reason logicians use this narrow definition of "inference" is that inferences have a purpose: to draw new, true conclusions, since the whole purpose of logic is to increase our store of true conclusions, not false or undetermined ones. A valid inference, strictly defined, is reasoning in which, if the premises are *true*, then it follows that the conclusion must necessarily be *true*. On the square most of our "inferences" did not go from one true proposition to anther true proposition.

But there was one case on the square of opposition where we do infer a new, *true* proposition directly from another *true* proposition. Do you know which one it is? It is subalternation, which moves from a true A proposition to a true I proposition, or from a true E proposition to a true O proposition. See if you can figure out why.

The Essentials

Conversion

In this lesson, we'll look at *conversion*, another kind of immediate inference, then in Lesson 20 *obversion*. Both involve starting with a *single* categorical proposition and manipulating it to derive a second proposition validly from the first one. If the initial proposition (the premise) is true, the conclusion will have to be true.

Conversion is interchanging the subject and predicate terms of a proposition in order to form a new proposition. But there is an important proviso we must add. The new proposition (we can call it the "conclusion" or the "converse") must follow *validly* from the first one (we'll call it the "premise"). To convert the premise validly, as we'll see, we have to take care to get the *quantity* of the converse correct, which means that we need to be careful not to claim to know more in the converse than we knew in the premise. For if we *overstep the bounds* of the information contained in the premise, our inference will be invalid.

Since there are four kinds of categorical propositions, we will consider the converse of each of them in turn, as we did when beginning our study of categorical propositions, in Lesson 13. Let's look at the first four problems in Problem Set 18:

1. All Texans are Americans. (A)
2. Some Texans are friendly. (I)
3. No Texan is a New Yorker. (E)
4. Some animals are not air-breathing. (O)

Converting A Propositions

The task of finding the converse of "All Texans are Americans" requires us to keep the same two terms, but interchange them. In the converse, *Americans* will become the subject and *Texans* will become the predicate. In conversion, we are not allowed to change either of the two terms. This also means we can't change the *quality* of the proposition from affirmative to negative, because the new proposition—"No Americans are Texans"—would be false, an invalid inference. The converse must be an affirmative proposition.

Our first try at conversion might well produce this result: "All Americans are Texans." But we can see immediately that this is false, because there are Americans in the other forty-nine states. But to be valid, the converse of a true proposition must be true. But if we reduce the quantity to "*Some* Americans are Texans," we get the right answer. But *why* it is right?

To understand the reason the converse must be "*Some* Americans are Texans," let's focus on *quantity*. The quantity of "*All* Texans are Americans" is universal, because the subject *Texans* is universal. But how many *Americans* does the proposition include? You might be inclined to say the proposition should include *all* Americans, just like it includes all Texans. But let's think this over carefully. In "All Texans *are* Americans," the copula "are" means that the Texans referred to are the same as, or identical with the Americans we are referring to. They are the very same people, but with two distinct traits—*Texan* and *American*. But the Texans who are the same people as Americans do not exhaust the number of Americans; there are many more Americans than Texans. In "all Texans are Americans," the *Americans* must be only *some* Americans. Since we started off asserting something only about some Americans, when we produce the converse, *Americans* in the subject must only be "some" of them, particular, not universal. Otherwise, we would have stepped beyond the limit of our knowledge, since in the original A proposition we only made an assertion about *some* Americans, not all of them. The valid converse of an A proposition, then, must be an I proposition.

You can see visually why an A converts to an I if you look at the Venn diagram of an A proposition. There is an X only in part of the P circle. This means the A proposition asserts that only *some* P's exist. So when you reverse S and P in the converse proposition, you can see from the X still being in only part of the P circle, that the converse can only be about *some* P's.

Conclusion: "All S is P" (A) *converts to* "some P is S" (I).

We have learned something else that is very important. Not only does the *subject term* of a categorical proposition have a quantity (which is the quantity of the proposition); but *the predicate term has a quantity*, as well. So in converting any categorical proposition, we will have to take care not to over-extend the quantity of either of the terms, subject or predicate.

Converting I Propositions

Converting I propositions is easier. In the proposition "Some Texans are friendly," the subject term is explicitly particular, and our reasoning about the quantity of the predicate of an A proposition also applies to I propositions. "Some Texans are friendly" identifies *some Texans* with *some friendly* people; but only with some of the friendly people, since there are many more *friendly* people than *Texans*. The predicate of an I proposition, then, like that of an A proposition, must be particular. The I proposition "Some Texans are friendly" converts into another I proposition: "Some friendly people are Texans."

Conclusion: "Some S is P" (I) *converts to* "some P is S" (I).

We should also take note of the following consequence, which will be important when we take up categorical syllogisms: *Every* affirmative categorical proposition has a predicate that is *particular* in quantity.

Converting E Propositions

In addressing the conversion of negative propositions, we should begin by pausing to think about what a negative proposition is asserting. If affirmative propositions bring together to unify or identify their subject and predicate terms (there are many ways to describe this connection), negative propositions, like "no Texan is a New Yorker," do the opposite. They take apart or distinguish or divide off or separate *all Texans* from *New Yorkers*. But from how many New Yorkers? The answer is: from all of them. The predicate of such a negative proposition must be universal in quantity, otherwise we haven't really asserted a negative proposition at all.

While we can see from examples like this one that the converse of an E proposition must be another E proposition, we can also see this if we look at the *form* of an E proposition. Let's look in particular at how the *quality* of the proposition affects the *quantity of the predicate* of our E proposition: "No Texan is a New Yorker." We can see that the predicate must be *universal*, since we see that Texans and New Yorkers are two completely separate groups. If this proposition *didn't* separate *all* the Texans from *all* New Yorkers, that would mean that the Texans are separate only from some New Yorkers, but not from other New Yorkers. But consider these *other* New Yorkers. If the Texans are not separate from them, then you can't really say, "*No* Texans are New Yorkers," because the Texans might be the same as these *other* New Yorkers. This result simply denies the meaning of "No Texans are New Yorkers." The one and only way truly to separate the Texans from the New Yorkers is to separate them from *all* New Yorkers. The negative quality of an E proposition simply requires that its predicate must be universal.

When we convert any E proposition, then, like "No Texans are New Yorkers," the converse must be negative in quality, because we don't have any information *connecting* any Texans with any New Yorkers. The universal subject "Texans" must remain universal, and the universal predicate "New Yorkers" also must remain universal. The *converse* must be an E proposition: "No New Yorkers are Texans."

And we can find additional support if we remember the Euler diagram or the Venn diagram of an E proposition: all of S is separated from all of P.

Conclusion: "No S is P" (E) *converts into* "No P is S." (E)

One final word. In seeing why an E proposition converts into another E proposition, we can conclude that *every negative* proposition must have a *universal* predicate. The only way any negative proposition can mean what it says is for it to separate absolutely all of the predicate class from the subject class, whether that subject is particular or universal. In short, the predicate of all negative propositions, both I and O propositions, must be universal.

Converting O Propositions

Problem Set 19 has two problems we can consider when trying to convert O propositions, one that looks easy, but isn't, and the other that looks hard, but helps us see the reason for the correct answer. The examples are: "Some Texans are not friendly" and "Some animals are not air-breathing."

Let's begin with "Some Texans are not friendly." This is a negative proposition, so the converse will have to be negative. When we reverse subject and predicate, an easy answer for the converse would be, "Some friendly people are not Texans." The reason this answer looks easy and correct is that this proposition is negative, like the first; we have reversed the subject and predicate, as we must in conversion; it is a particular proposition, like the premise; and, above all, it is true, like the premise. We have gone from a true O proposition to another true O proposition. What could be wrong? The problem is that coming up with a new, true O proposition is not enough. Conversion is a form of *inference*; so the converse must follow validly from the premise. The problem is that from "some Texans are not friendly," and from this proposition only, you *cannot* validly derive "Some friendly people are not Texans." Why not?

There are two answers to this question. The first comes from looking at the formal structure of O propositions, remembering that the predicate of a negative proposition must be universal. When we apply this principle, the problem becomes clear. In "Some Texans are not friendly," "Texans" is particular and "friendly people" is universal, because all of the predicate *friendly people* have to be separated from or denied of the subject, *some Texans*. The predicate of *any* negative proposition must be universal in order for the proposition to be negative at all. When we reverse the subject and predicate of "some Texans are not friendly," "*friendly* people" becomes particular. This is fine, because if we know something about *all* friendly people, then we can draw a conclusion about *some* friendly people. But what about the other term, "Texans"? In the original proposition (or premise), we began knowing about *some Texans*, but when we reverse the subject and predicate terms in the converse, we claim to know something about *all Texans*. Why? Because "Texans" has become the predicate of a *negative proposition*. This inference is impossible, because we have overstepped the bounds of our knowledge. We started with a particular term, "some Texan," but tried to draw a conclusion about *all Texans*. Our conclusion is *invalid*.

The first answer to the question is based upon using the logical principle that the predicate of a negative proposition must be universal. The reason for turning to the second example, "Some animals are not air-breathing," is because we can see that this O proposition cannot be converted without making use of this logical principle, though it still holds for this proposition as well as the previous one. Here we need to clarify what the proposition "Some animals are not air-breathing" *means*. "Animals" means things that have natural bodies, are alive, have senses that make them aware of the world around them, and can move from place to place, such as birds and cats, eels, and spiders. By "air-breathing" is meant literally, a thing that breathes air directly, which requires lungs. With this clarification, you will quickly recognize the original proposition, "Some animals are not air-breathing," is true. Fish are like this. They have gills that allow them to take in oxygen from the water, not from air. Now what happens when you try to convert "Some animals are not air-breathing"? The only possible answer would be "Some air-breathing things are not animals." But this is clearly false, because everything that breathes air, where breathing means doing so with lungs, is an animal. The *content* of "Some animals are not air-breathing" shows that this proposition cannot be converted.

Looking at the Venn diagram also shows that an O proposition cannot be converted. The diagram has an X in the part of the S circle outside the P circle. In the premise of this example, the only things that one knows exist are animals that do not breathe air. Now look at the P circle. The premise says nothing at all about things in the P circle—in this case, things that breathe air. But any converse we might try would have to have an X somewhere in the P circle, otherwise we would have made no assertion about the subject of the converse, P, in this case, things that breathe air. In short, since the premise does not assert that any things that breathe air exist, at all, we cannot arbitrarily invent air-breathers that exist for the conclusion. About things that breathe air, in sum, "nothing in, so nothing out."

Conclusion: "Some S is not P" cannot be converted validly.

Quantity of Subject and Predicate Terms of Categorical Propositions

Type of proposition	Subject	Predicate
A	universal	particular
I	particular	particular
E	universal	universal
O	particular	universal

This chart will become extremely important when we take up categorical syllogisms.

Problem Set 19: Conversion

Converting Categorical Propositions

Instructions

Convert the following propositions by *validly* exchanging the subject and predicate terms, if possible.

1. All Texans are Americans.
2. Some Texans are friendly.
3. No Texan is a New Yorker.
4. Some Texans are not friendly.
5. Some animals are not air-breathing.
6. No man dies twice.
7. Some cats are pretty.
8. Some dogs are not pretty.
9. No prudent person is reckless.
10. Mesquites are slow-growing trees.
11. All snow is white.
12. Most snow is not sticky.
13. Some of the plates are broken.
14. Some parents are not nice to their kids.
15. Gemstones are often used in jewelry.
16. Not all sophists are recognized for what they are.
17. Frogs have powerful hind legs.
18. Flatterers will get nowhere with me.
19. "All science is organized knowledge." (Attributed to Herbert Spencer, 19th-cen. American philosopher, proponent of "Social Darwinism")
20. "No gifted eye can exhaust the significance of any object." (Thomas Carlyle, 19th-cen. British essayist, *On Heroes*, "Lecture 3: The Hero as Poet")
21. "All good things which exist are the fruits of originality." (John Stuart Mill, 19th-cen. British philosopher, *On Liberty*, chapter 3)
22. "What is fitting is honorable, and what is honorable is fitting." (Cicero, 1st-cen. b.c. Roman lawyer and philosopher, *On Duties*)
23. "Beauty is truth, and truth beauty." (John Keats, 19th-cen. British poet, "Ode on a Grecian Urn")
24. "All you can say of [an idea] then, either that 'it is useful because it is

true,' or that 'it is true because it is useful.' Both these phrases mean exactly the same thing, namely that here is an idea that gets fulfilled and can be verified." (William James, 19th-cen. American philosopher, *Pragmatism*, Lecture 6) Hint: To understand this argument, rewrite the two propositions in quotation marks, removing "because" and making each into a categorical proposition. Then ask if James has converted the first proposition successfully in producing the second.

25. "He [Edmund Burke] referred habitually to principles. He was a scientific statesman; and therefore a seer. For <u>every principle contains in itself the germs of a prophecy</u>. And, as the prophetic power is the essential privilege of science, so the fulfillment of its oracles supplies the outward, and (to men in general) the only test of its claim to the title." [Convert the underlined sentence.] (Samuel Taylor Coleridge, 19th-cen. English poet, *Biographia Literaria*, chapter 10)

26. "God helps those who help themselves." (Mistakenly attributed to the Bible, this idea has been expressed by several, including Algernon Sydney, d. 1683, English politician; Ben Franklin, American patriot, from *Poor Richard's Almanac* (1757); Sophocles and Aesop, Greek writers [its oldest sources].)

Obversion

The Essentials

What Is Obversion?

In Lesson 18, we saw how to *convert* a proposition validly so that, when reversing subject and predicate, the new proposition must be true if the old proposition is true. We saw that, in conversion, the quality of the proposition remains the same: affirmative propositions convert to affirmative ones, negative propositions convert to negative ones. But sometimes, when trying to understand or develop arguments, we need to *change the quality* of a proposition in order to get another proposition that is more useful to the argument we are trying to develop. We may need to switch between affirmative and negative propositions. This kind of immediate inference is called "obversion."

In obversion, changing the quality of a proposition must be done *validly*. If an obversion is invalid, then the truth of the original proposition cannot ensure that the obverse is true. And when that happens, if we use the invalid obverse in a syllogism, we can't be sure the conclusion will be true.

Since the purpose of obversion is to change the quality of a proposition validly, obversion involves three things: (a) We need to keep the *subject* of the proposition the same. An obverted proposition (also called the obverse) is about the same subject as the original proposition. (b) We need to change the *quality* of the proposition to its opposite, from affirmative to negative or from negative to affirmative. (c) Since the subject must remain the same while the quality changes, we need to change the predicate to its opposite, from P to ~P, to obvert a proposition validly.

Keeping the subject the same is not a problem. And changing the quality to its opposite is normally straightforward, since we move from "is" to "is not" or the reverse. But in changing P to non-P sometimes we need to be careful. The easiest way would be simply to add the prefix "non-" to a positive predicate (P to non-P) or the reverse. For example, "mortal" would become "non-mortal" or "immortal." But quite often such a mechanical procedure is not accurate. Suppose we are choosing paint colors and decide we don't want the wall in the room to be "white." There is a wide range of options open to us, since black, yellow, and blue are all "non-white." We need to think about what the *appropriate* and realistic opposite predicate might be. If you are painting the living room, you probably don't want the walls black. The context of the proposition often helps to determine the appropriate opposite of the original predicate term.

Since there are four kinds of categorical propositions, we should consider each kind, as we did when converting propositions. Let's consider the following:

1. All sports are strenuous. (A)
2. No human is perfect. (E)
3. Some Texans are honest. (I)
4. Some Texans are not honest. (O)

Obverting A Propositions

In considering "All sports are strenuous," the first term we might think of is "non-strenuous." Technically this answer would not be an error; but it would not be the most accurate answer, because in standard English, the normal opposite of "strenuous," when we just want to negate the word, is "*un-strenuous*." But there is a much better term, one that is expressed positively: "easy." By definition, the obverse must keep the same subject and must be a negative proposition, since the original was affirmative. Will the obverse also be a universal proposition? Yes. We are looking for a universal, negative proposition, one whose subject is *sports*. We learned earlier that the standard form for universal negative propositions is *No S is P*. So the first part of the obverse should be, "No sports are...." To find the predicate, we need to remember that we are trying to reason *validly*. If we simply were to keep the predicate term as it is, then the new proposition would be, "No sports are strenuous," which can't be correct, since it is the contrary of the original, and therefore false, if the original is true. So, we need to change "strenuous" to its opposite. We might first think of "No sports are non-strenuous," but this is not normal English, and "non-strenuous" isn't precise. "No sports are easy" (E) is accurate and meaningful, the best answer.

Conclusion: "All S is P" (A) obverts to "No S is ~P" (E).

Obverting E Propositions

Next let's consider obverting an E proposition, like "No human is perfect." By definition, the obverse has the *same subject* and must be *affirmative*: "All humans are...." The predicate can't be "perfect," since that would produce a contrary proposition, which would have to be false. Since "imperfect" is the opposite of "perfect," the obverse must be "All humans are *im*perfect."

Conclusion: "No S is P" (E) obverts to "All S is ~P" (A).

Obverting I Propositions

Now let's look for the obverse of an I proposition, such as "Some Texans are honest." Again, by definition, the subject is "Texans," and the quality must be negative: "Some Texans are not...." The predicate term must be the opposite of the original; it must be *dis*honest. The obverse, then, is "Some Texans are not dishonest."

It is true that the sentence "Some Texans are not dishonest" has a weaker connotation than "Some Texans are honest," but the logical force of the two propositions is the same. You can see this visually by comparing the Venn diagrams of the two propositions.

Conclusion: "Some S is P" converts to "Some S is not ~P" (O).

Obverting O Propositions

Finally, consider an O proposition, like "Some Texans are not kind." The obverse must have "Texans" as its subject and be a particular affirmative proposition, taking the form "Some Texans are...." Now the opposite of "kind" is "*un*kind"; the obverse of the original proposition will be "Some Texans are unkind." This proposition means exactly the same thing as the original proposition, "Some Texans are not kind." The only difference is the negative feature of the original proposition in the copula ("is not"), but in the obverse it is in the predicate ("unkind").

Conclusion: "Some S is not P" converts to "Some S is ~P" (I).

Summary: Valid Obversions

1. A proposition obverts to an E proposition.
2. E proposition obverts to an A proposition.
3. I proposition obverts to an O proposition.
4. O proposition obverts to an I proposition.

A Deeper Look

Finding the Right ~P

As we have seen, the original predicate term may very well have more than one opposite. In this case, we will have to think carefully and choose the most appropriate opposite. Consider "All religious people are theists." Let's focus on its predicate and subject. Now "theist," found in the predicate, is a word favored by philosophers and theologians (and logicians). It comes from the Greek word *theos*, which means "god." A theist is a person who says that some sort of god actually exists. Nowadays, most theists are also *monotheists*, because they say only one God exists, but there are several other kinds of theists (including *polytheists*, who say that many gods exist). Let's simplify the problem by sticking to the contemporary options: one God or no God.

The subject of the original proposition is "religious people." To get a true proposition for the obverse we have to change the predicate term, "theist," to its opposite. We might think of "non-theist," but just adding "non-" to the original predicate is usually not the best choice, because it's not precise. In this case there are two realistic choices for the opposite of "theist." The stronger option is claiming there is no God; God does not exist. A person who thinks this way is an *atheist*. This word is formed by adding the Greek privative prefix "a" to the Greek word for a god (*theos*). The weaker option is claiming not to say either there is or is not a God. Such a person fundamentally says, "I don't know" or "I don't think." One general Greek word for knowing or thinking is *gnosis*; the English term for someone who doesn't know is "agnostic," literally "not knowing" or "not thinking." Since the term "theist" concerns the *object* of our thought, not the *thinking* about that object, the better obverse of "All religious people are theists" seems to be "No religious person is an atheist." This is especially true if the way the agnostic lives his life is no different from the way an atheist does—that is, without reference to God.

For a famous argument about these three options—theism, agnosticism, atheism—and how you live your life, look at the quotation from Blaise Pascal in PS 20, which is known as "Pascal's Wager."

Advanced Manipulations

The kinds of immediate inferences do not have to end with one conversion or obversion. These two manipulations can be combined in sequence with each other by alternating conversion and obversion. This produces three more kinds of results, called "partial contraposition," "full contraposition," and "inversion." While you don't need to become fully adept at these more advanced manipulations, you should know about them. And if you like word games, you probably will enjoy playing around with them.

While you can follow any sequence you want, in order to get all the way to what is called the "inverse" of a proposition, you need to alternate obverting and converting. The sequence varies, depending on whether your initial proposition is affirmative or negative. The abbreviations used in the following text are: o = obverse and c = converse.

1. For universal affirmative propositions, the sequence is "ococ," and the inferences to the inverse are valid.

   Original proposition:
   Obverse: Obvert the original proposition. [o]
   Partial Contraposition: Next, convert the result. [oc]
   Full Contraposition: Next, obvert the result again. [oco]
   Inversion: Next, convert the result again [ococ].

2. For universal negative propositions, the sequence is "coco," and the inferences to the inverse are valid.

   Original proposition:
   Converse: Convert the original proposition. [c]
   Partial Contraposition: Next, obvert the result. [co]

Full Contraposition: Next, convert the result again. [coc]
Inversion: Finally, obvert the results. [coco]

Example 1. Starting with a universal affirmative proposition:

Original proposition: All sports cars are troublesome. (A)
Obverse: No sport cars are untroublesome. (E) [o]
Partial contrapositive: No untroublesome things are sport cars.
    (E) [oc]
Full contrapositive: All untroublesome things are non-sport
    cars. (A) [oco]
Inverse: Some non-sport cars are untroublesome. (I) [ococ]

Example 2. Starting with a universal negative proposition:

Original proposition: No good people are vicious. (E)
Converse: No vicious people are good people. (E) [c]
Partial contrapositive: All vicious people are bad people.
    (A) [co]
Full contrapositive: Some bad people are vicious people.
    (I) [coc]
Inverse: Some bad people are not virtuous people. (O) [coco]

Every multi-step manipulation must produce a valid immediate inference. As you can probably guess, for many propositions you can't go through the whole sequence.

Example 3. Starting with a particular affirmative proposition:

Original proposition: Some trees are beautiful. (I)
Obverse: Some trees are not ugly. (O) [o]
Partial contrapositive: Can't be done; there is no valid converse
    of an O proposition. [oc]

Example 4. Starting with a particular negative proposition.

Original proposition: Some trees are not beautiful. (O)
Obverse: Some trees are ugly. (I) [o]
Partial contrapositive: Some ugly things are trees. (I) [oc]
Full contrapositive: Some ugly things are not non-trees.
    (O) [oco]
Inverse: Can't be done; there is no valid converse of an
    O proposition. [ococ]

We can see, therefore, there are no valid inverses for particular propositions, whether affirmative or negative. But you can go part of the way down this sequence.

The Opposite of "All Just People Are Honest"

We began Lesson 18 by considering the opposite of "All just people are honest." We have seen that there are three *propositions* that oppose this proposition, since opposing propositions have the same subject term and predicate term as the original. The contrary ("No just people are honest") and contradictory ("Some just people are not honest") of this proposition must be false. But its subalternate ("Some just people are honest") must be true.

We also can derive a new proposition whose *terms* are the opposites of the terms contained in the original proposition, one that is consistent with our original proposition, because it is derived from it by using conversion and obversion. We derive this kind of opposite proposition through devising its *inverse*, in which each term is the opposite of the original term that corresponds to it: "just" changing to "unjust" and "honest" changing to "dishonest."

> *Original Proposition*: All just people are honest. (A)
> *Obverse*: No just people are dishonest. (E), by o.
> *Partial Contrapositive*: No dishonest people are just. (E) by oc.
> *Full Contrapositive*: All dishonest people are unjust. (A) by oco.
> *Inverse*: *Some* unjust people are dishonest. (I) by ococ.

Of course, *All* unjust people are dishonest (A), would be an *invalid* inference from the full contrapositive.

Problem Set 20: Obversion and Advanced Manipulations

Obversion

Instructions

Obvert the following propositions by changing them to the opposite quality, while keeping the same subject term.

1. All sports are strenuous.
2. No human is perfect.
3. Some Texans are honest.

4. Some Texans are not honest.

5. Some legends are not credible.

6. Some caves are habitable.

7. Most solids are not crystals.

8. All games are organized.

9. No humans are immortal.

10. Every tulip is planted.

11. All blue jays are loud.

12. Some hawks are quick.

13. Every iguana is harmless.

14. Some ants are wingless.

15. All religious people are theists.

16. Purple is a darker color than yellow.

17. Giraffes are taller than humans.

18. Socrates was wise.

19. All the battlements of the castle are manned.

20. None of the wagons are non-horse-drawn.

21. "No man is a hero to his valet." (Madame de Cornuel, 17th-cen. French hostess of a famous salon)

22. "All men are weak." (W. S. Landor, 19th-cen. English poet)

23. "All necessary truths come from clear and distinct ideas." (After Descartes)

24. "All science is organized knowledge." (Attributed to Herbert Spencer, 19th-cen. American philosopher, proponent of "Social Darwinism")

25. "Let us examine this point of view and declare: 'Either God exists, or He does not.' To which view shall we incline? Reason cannot decide for us one way or the other: we are separated by an infinite gulf. At the extremity of this infinite distance a game is in progress, where either heads or tails may turn up. What will you wager? According to reason you cannot bet either way; according to reason you can defend neither proposition.

"So do not attribute error to those who have made a choice; for you know nothing about it.

"'No; I will not blame them for having made this choice, but for having made one at all; for since he who calls heads and he who calls tails are equally at fault, both are in the wrong. The right thing is not to wager at all.'

"Yes; but a bet must be laid. There is no option: you have joined the game.... Let us weigh the gain and the loss involved in wagering that God exists. Let us estimate these two probabilities; if you win, you win all; if you lose, you lose nothing. Wager then, without hesitation, that He does exist.

"'That is all very fine. Yes, I must wager, but maybe I am wagering too much.'

"Let us see. Since there is an equal risk of winning and of losing, if you had only two lives to win you might still wager; but if there were three lives to win, you would still have to play (since you are under the necessity of playing); and being thus obliged to play, you would be imprudent not to risk your life to win three in a game where there is an equal chance of winning and losing. But there is an eternity of life and happiness." (Blaise Pascal, 17th-cen. French mathematician and religious thinker, *Pensees*)

Advanced Manipulations

Instructions

See if you can produce the *inverse* of some of the previous propositions.

Hypothetical Propositions

The Essentials

We have already met hypothetical propositions in Lesson 11. Since then we have looked rather carefully at *categorical* propositions; now let's return to *hypothetical* propositions and look carefully at them. The purpose of this lesson is to become skilled at recognizing the different kinds of hypothetical propositions used in normal verbal language—what contemporary logicians call, somewhat oddly, "natural language." (The oddity is because all written and spoken languages are conventional signs, not natural signs, as we learned in Lesson 7. All language is conventional, a human invention; it is not natural. But we will use the phrase "natural language" because it is convenient.) Later in Lesson 29, we will take up hypothetical *arguments*.

Definitions of Logical Symbols

In Lesson 11, we met some of the symbols modern logicians have devised in order to symbolize hypothetical propositions. Here is a reminder of what was introduced there.

Propositions: Small case letters, like p, q, or r, stand for *any* categorical proposition.

Particular propositions: Large case letters, like A, B, or C, stand for *some definite* categorical proposition, such as "the economy is growing" or "you'll have a lollipop."

Negation: To express the negation of a proposition, modern logicians do not worry about exactly what kind of opposite the negative is. Rather, they simply put a mathematical symbol for negation, such as (~), before the symbol for the proposition negated. The symbol ~p means the denial or negation of the proposition p, and ~A means the denial of proposition A.

> Example: If L is "you'll have a lollipop," then ~L is "you won't have a lollipop."

Parentheses: To clarify where propositions begin and end, you can put parentheses (…) or brackets […] around propositions.

> Example: (~L) points out the proposition "you won't have a lollipop."

Disjunctions: Disjunctions take the general form (p v q), which means the disjunctive proposition "p or q." The v is used because one Latin word for "or" was *vel*. A specific disjunction takes the form (A v B). Logicians sometimes distinguish the symbol for inclusive or weak disjunctions, where both alternatives can be true (p v q), from the symbol for exclusive or strong disjunctions, where only one alternative can be true (p V q). However, the symbol for strong disjunction is really not needed, since a strong disjunction can also be expressed by the conjunction of a weak disjunctive proposition with a proposition denying the conjunction of the two terms. In symbols, (p V q) is the same as $[(p \lor q) \cdot \sim(p \cdot q)]$.

It is *important* to remember here that A and B signify categorical *propositions*; they do not signify *terms*, which is what S and P signified in the symbolization of a categorical proposition: "S is P."

> Example: "Either Augustine was a bishop or Marx was an atheist" can be symbolized as (A v M).

Conjunctions: Conjunctions often include the word *and*; logicians sometimes use the ampersand (&), a typesetter's symbol, for "and." They also use a dot (·) for conjunction.

Example: "Socrates was a philosopher, and Aeschylus was a
playwright" can be symbolized as (S & A) or as (S · A), where S
signifies "Socrates was a philosopher" and A signifies "Aeschylus
was a playwright."

Conditions: For conjunctions and disjunctions, it does not matter which of
the two propositions comes first. Conditions are a different story. The order
of the propositions makes *all* the difference, so logicians have given them different names. The *if* clause is called the *antecedent*, from the Latin word that
means it *goes before* the other clause, or if you prefer a word derived from
Greek, the *protasis*. The *then* clause is called the *consequent*, from the Latin
word meaning *follow along*, or *apodasis* in Greek. *Before* and *after* here refer to
their *logical* relation, not a chronological sequence. The antecedent lays down
a condition that, when fulfilled, will *ensure* that the consequent follows. The
antecedent is like a "promissory note" that guarantees the consequent will
come about as long as the antecedent condition is realized. To describe the
relation of moving from antecedent to consequent, logicians often use the
word "implies," as in "p implies q." They also have resorted to symbols that
move from the antecedent to the consequent, such as an arrow pointing to
the right (p → q). This proposition can be read "if p, then q" or "p implies q."

Example: "If the economy grows, then tax revenue will also grow,"
is (E → R), where E means "the economy grows" and R is "tax
revenue grows."

Three Kinds of Hypothetical Propositions

Hypothetical propositions are formed by combining two or more categorical propositions into one longer proposition, related to each other using
"syncategorematic" terms. There are three types of hypothetical propositions:
conditions, disjunctions, and conjunctions.

Conjunctions

Conjunctions are formed when we combine two categorical propositions,
often using the word "and" to do so.

Example: "Socrates was a philosopher, *and* Aeschylus was a
playwright."

This conjunction can be symbolized (S • A), where S means "Socrates was a philosopher" and A means "Aeschylus was a playwright."

However, a proposition can be a conjunction using other words than "and." At the end of this lesson there is a list of other words that can be used to create a conjunction.

> Example: "Augustus was a Roman Emperor, *but* Virgil was a Roman poet."

This conjunction can be symbolized (A • V), where A means "Augustus was a Roman emperor" and V means "Virgil was a Roman poet."

Sometimes a conjunction is formed without using a word at all.

> Example: "Winston Churchill was a great speaker, Davey Crockett was not."

This conjunction can be symbolized by (W • D), where W means "Winston Churchill was a great speaker" and D means "Davy Crockett was not a great speaker."

These examples show that, even though different words are used, the logical notion of conjunction in our mind is the same if we ignore subtle nuances in emphasis conveyed by different syncategorematic terms. All three examples also show that for a conjunction to be true, *both* of the categorical propositions that make it up must be true. If both Churchill and Davey Crockett were great speakers, the last example would be false—that is, not true.

Disjunctions

Disjunctions are formed when we put two categorical propositions into the same statement, but we set them out as alternatives rather than combining them. The most normal way to indicate a disjunction is by using the words *or . . .* or *either . . . or. . . .*

> Example: "Either Augustine was a bishop or Anselm was an atheist."

This proposition can be symbolized by (Ag v An), where Ag means "Augustine was a bishop" and An means "Anselm was an atheist." This particular example illustrates the fact that for a disjunctive proposition to be true, one or the other of the categorical propositions that make it up must be true, but they don't both have to be true.

There are other examples, however, of disjunctive propositions where both the disjuncts are true.

> Example: "Either Augustine was a bishop or Marx was an atheist."

This proposition can be symbolized by (Ag v M), where Ag means "Augustine was a bishop" and M means "Marx was an atheist." This disjunction is true because *one* of the disjuncts is true; but as a matter of fact, both of the disjuncts are true. Many disjunctions are like this, where both disjuncts *can* be true. These are called "inclusive" disjunctions.

There are still other disjunctions that are *exclusive*, because only one of the disjuncts can be true, they cannot both be true.

> Example: "Either Louis XIV of France was called 'the Sun King,' or he was not."

Only one of these two alternatives can be true; and in fact, it is the first one. One can sometimes have fun with the difference between these two kinds of disjunctions. If the waiter asks you whether you want the soup or the salad, you can simply say "yes," meaning you want both. A waiter who knows logic will inform you, however, that he was setting out an exclusive rather than an inclusive disjunction; you must choose one or the other.

Conditions

Conditional propositions are the most important and the most difficult. A sign of their importance is the fact that sometimes logicians use the term "hypothetical proposition" to mean "conditional proposition." But in fact, conjunctions and disjunctions are also hypothetical propositions.

As the name says, conditional propositions are formed by making the antecedent the condition for the consequent. The most normal way of relating the two categorical propositions together in English is by using the terms "if" or "if…then," where "if" introduces the condition or antecedent and "then" introduces the consequent.

> Examples: "If the economy grows, then tax revenue will also grow."
> "If you are over ten years old, you are also over two years old."
> "If you are good, then you'll get a lollipop."

These propositions can be symbolized, as follows:

> $(E \rightarrow R)$, where E means "the economy grows," and R means "tax revenue grows."

(10 → 2), where 10 means "you are over ten years old," and 2 means "you are over two years old."

(G → L), where G means "you are good," and L means "you get a lollipop."

A Deeper Look

What Logical Symbols Mean

One of the important achievements of contemporary symbolic logic has been to develop logical symbols that help us see the structure of a hypothetical proposition and so make it easier to distinguish different kinds of hypothetical propositions, especially the many different kinds of conditional propositions.

We should note, however, that there are two quite different ways to understand the relation between these logical symbols and the normal or "natural" language we speak and write.

(1) The Aristotelian approach, which we are following, holds that symbols (especially the symbols &, v, and →) are signs capturing part, but only part, of the rich meaning of normal written and spoken language (especially their correlative words: *and*, *or*, and *if... then*). Normal or "natural" language consists in signs capturing part, but only part, of the meaning included in thoughts in our minds. (All of us have experienced the difficulty of putting exactly what we are thinking into words.) Finally, our thoughts are themselves signs, capturing part, but only part, of the inexhaustible complexity of reality itself. (You can refer back to Lesson 7 on this point.)

(2) The opposite approach, which is taken in most textbooks of symbolic logic, is called the "truth-functional" approach. On this approach, the meaning of the logical symbols, for hypothetical propositions especially, is not determined by their *meaning* in "natural" language, but the meaning of the symbols as determined by their *truth conditions*. This is why the approach is called "truth functional." By and large, there are not many important differences in results when following these two approaches, except when we get to *conditional* propositions, where the differences will be noted.

Please remember, then, that the main reason for using logical symbols *in this book* is that they help us to focus on the *form or structure* of hypothetical propositions, which can become quite complicated in "natural" language.

Once we see that structure, it becomes easier to evaluate the logical coherence of arguments in "natural" language.

Counterfactual Conditions and Material Implication

In comparison with conjunction and disjunction, the truth status of a conditional proposition is rather more difficult to pin down and has been a subject of debate by logicians, both medieval logicians and contemporary symbolic logicians. There are four possible combinations of true and false for the antecedent and consequent.

1. Antecedent is true and consequent is true.
2. Antecedent is true, but consequent is false.
3. Antecedent is false, but consequent is true.
4. Antecedent is false and consequent is false.

The first two combinations are straightforward. Let's take the proposition "If the economy grows, then tax revenue also will grow" (E → R).

1. If it is true that the economy grows, and it is also true that the tax revenue grows, then the conditional statement, considered as a whole, will be true.

2. On the other hand, if it is true that the economy grows, but it is false that tax revenue grows, then the conditional statement is false. Why? Because what the conditional proposition means is that the antecedent or condition *the economy grows* was supposed somehow to *ensure* that the consequent *tax revenue increases* also will be true. But the consequent is false, so the conditional statement, considered as a whole, is *false*, because the economy growing *did not ensure* that tax revenues would increase.

We should note that the logic of the proposition does not consider *how* the economy growing would increase tax revenues; that is a matter for the science of economics to establish. But logic is concerned with the fact that the conditional proposition states that the consequent will in fact happen if the antecedent is fulfilled, without getting into the exact reasons.

The third and fourth combinations are more difficult because they are counterfactual: they both assume the antecedent is false. In this case, the economy is *not* growing, so the antecedent is not fulfilled. Two possibilities are open for the consequent: tax revenue still grows or tax revenue does not grow—that is, the consequence is true or the consequence is false. Combinations (3) and (4) capture these two consequences. But this is not the whole story. The issue is not just the combinations of truth and falsity in the antecedent and consequent; even more important is this: What does the syncategorematic connective *if... then* (as stated in natural language, or →, as stated in symbols), *mean* when the antecedent is *not* true? Here, the two approaches to understanding conditional propositions part company.

On the Aristotelian approach, the meaning of *if... then*, remains the same—namely, that p *ensures* q, but it no longer applies to the real situation—namely, the situation where the economy is not growing, to which we have applied it. In short, there is no p, so it cannot influence q in any way. The result is that q may be true or false—that is, tax revenues may go up or go down. This is how to understand what combination (3) and (4) mean in this approach. Said otherwise, in these two cases the economy growing cannot *ensure* that tax revenues will increase for the simple reason that the economy is not growing in the first place; so it can't ensure anything.

The "truth-functional" understanding of the meaning of → is based solely on the truth conditions of (p → q). It applies in the same way to all four combinations of truth conditions and is therefore called "material implication," because what "implication" *means* is determined by the matter—that is, the four truth conditions—of the proposition (p → q). In this approach, the *meaning* of combinations (1) and (2) are determined by the truth conditions of combinations (1) and (2). Since p is true in both, the meaning of the implication—namely, (p → q) follows the "natural language" meaning. On (1), p is true and q is true, so (p → q) must be true. On condition (2), p is true and q is false, so (p → q) must be false. In our example, the economy grows but tax revenues do not increase, so to say a growing economy ensures increasing tax revenues is false.

An alternative way to describe combination (2), however, is to say: it cannot be the case that there is a growing economy but no increase in tax revenue, or, in general symbols: (~p v q). On the "truth-functional" approach, this disjunction is understood to describe the very *meaning* of the inference →. Then what happens in the four combinations listed above? Not only is the conditional statement true in combination (1), it is also true in combinations (3) and (4); the only case in which (p → q) is false is combination (2).

Unfortunately, this way of understanding what *if... then* and → mean leads to certain *paradoxes of material implication*, which are well-recognized by symbolic logicians.

Concerning combination (1): In this scenario, p is true, q is true, and (p → q), understood to be equivalent to (~p v q), is also true. Now, if these truth conditions determine the very meaning of →, then they will hold for *any* two true propositions. What about propositions *totally unrelated* to each other? Consider this example: "If zebras are animals, then water is H_2O" (Z → W). On the "truth-functional" approach, not only would Z be true, and W would be true, but the *implication* would be true, as well. That means that Z would *really and actually imply* W. But it is more accurate to the real or "natural" language meaning of *if… then,* to say that Z does *not* imply W, because implication just doesn't apply in this situation, since the realities signified by the two propositions simply have nothing to do with one another.

Concerning combinations (3 and (4): In both these cases, p is taken to be false. But this makes ~p true. And a further consequence is that (~p v q) will be true, no matter whether q is true or false, since a disjunction is true if only *one* of the disjuncts is true. When p is false, then (~p v q) is true, and so (p → q) is also true, no matter whether q is true or false and no matter whether p and q are in reality related to each other. When we then apply material implication back to "natural" language, more paradoxes ensue. For example, consider a case where p and q are not related to each other: "If donkeys are goats, then the U.S. is a country." Here the implication from p to q is true; the false proposition "donkeys are goats" actually and really implies that "the U.S. is a country." In addition, "donkeys are goats" actually and really implies the opposite, that "the U.S. is not a country." And what about the case where there is an intrinsic connection between p and q? Consider "If you are outside in the rain, then you'll be wet." Now suppose ~p—namely, "you are not outside in the rain." This false proposition truly implies both the true proposition "you'll be wet" and the false proposition "you won't be wet."

Contemporary logicians have tried to deal with such paradoxes in a variety of clever ways, which we do not have the time or the need to cover. But the paradoxes show that for our purposes in studying the logic of normal and "natural" language, we will do two things. First, we will use logical symbols *only* for the purpose of understanding the meaning of "natural" language propositions, for they do capture much of that meaning. But we will *not* limit the very meaning of "natural" language propositions within the constraints of "material implication."

Second, we will make use of the aid symbolic logic provides in understanding combinations (1) and (2), as presented previously, without worrying about (3) and (4). And we will interpret combinations (3) and (4) to mean simply that when the antecedent of a conditional proposition is false, no inference or implication need be drawn, because the antecedent *cannot ensure* that the consequent is either true or false. The false antecedent is consistent with the consequent being *either* true or false. The advantage of this interpretation of combinations (3) and (4) is that it is fully in accord with the meaning of *if… then* in "natural" language.

Practical Advice: Some Verbal Hypotheticals and their Symbols

By this point it should be clear that there are normally many ways to express a certain kind of hypothetical proposition. The number of logical relations here is much less than the number of ways to express those logical relations in English (or any other language). This is another reason logicians have so taken to expressing hypothetical propositions and hypothetical arguments using symbols. The symbols help us understand what it is we are saying. Since the number of expressions in what logicians call "natural language" (in this case, English) far surpasses the number of logical relations or types of hypothetical propositions, let's end this chapter by correlating, in summary form, different expressions in English with their logical meaning and symbolization.

VERBAL HYPOTHETICALS AND THEIR SYMBOLS

English Expression	English Used with p and q	Symbolic Expression
and	p and q	$(p \cdot q)$
both	both p and q	$(p \cdot q)$
but	p but q	$(p \cdot q)$
although	although p, q	$(p \cdot q)$
	p although q	$(p \cdot q)$
however	p, however q	$(p \cdot q)$
nevertheless	p, nevertheless q	$(p \cdot q)$
yet	p, yet q	$(p \cdot q)$
or	p or q	$(p \vee q)$
either…or	either p or q	$(p \vee q)$
neither…nor	neither p nor q	$\sim(p \vee q)$ or $(\sim p \cdot \sim q)$
if…then	if p, then q	$(p \to q)$
if	if p, q	$(p \to q)$
if	q, if p	$(p \to q)$
implies	p implies q	$(p \to q)$
is implied by	q is implied by p	$(p \to q)$
entails	p entails q	$(p \to q)$
is entailed by	q is entailed by p	$(p \to q)$
in case	in case p, then q	$(p \to q)$
in the event that	in the event that p, then q	$(p \to q)$
provided that	provided that p, then q	$(p \to q)$
provided that	q, provided that p	$(p \to q)$

Problem Set 21: Hypothetical Propositions

Learning to Symbolize Hypothetical Propositions

Instructions

Use these letters as symbols to symbolize the propositions that follow.

S_p = "Socrates was a philosopher."
S_k = "Socrates knew a lot."
P_p = "Plato was a philosopher."
P_k = "Plato knew a lot."
A_p = "Aristotle was a philosopher."
A_k = "Aristotle knew a lot."
P_S = "Plato was the student of Socrates."
A_P = "Aristotle was the student of Plato."

1. Socrates was a philosopher.
2. Plato was the student of Socrates.
3. Aristotle was the student of Plato.
4. Socrates was a philosopher and Plato was a philosopher.
5. Socrates was a philosopher and Plato was, too.
6. If Socrates was a philosopher, then Socrates knew a lot.
7. If Socrates was a philosopher, then Socrates did not know a lot.
8. Either Socrates was a philosopher or Socrates was not a philosopher.
9. Either Socrates knew a lot or Socrates did not know a lot.
10. If Plato was the student of Socrates, then Plato did not know a lot.
12. Plato knew a lot, and so did Aristotle, but Socrates did not.
13. If Socrates did not know a lot and Plato was the student of Socrates, then Plato did not know a lot.
14. If Socrates did not know a lot, but Plato did know a lot, then Plato was not the student of Socrates.
15. Aristotle knew a lot, and so did Plato, so Plato was not the student of Socrates, but Aristotle was the student of Plato.

Symbolizing with Your Own Symbols

Instructions

Make up your own specific symbols (S, M, F, L, etc.), and symbolize the following propositions:

1. If you are good, you will get a lollipop.
2. But if you are not good, you will not get a lollipop.
3. Either you are good or you are not good.
4. Either you will get a lollipop or you will not get a lollipop.
5. If you are good, then you will get a lollipop; but if you are not good, you won't get a lollipop.
6. Socrates was a philosopher, but Aeschylus was not a philosopher.
7. Thomas Aquinas was a philosopher, but he was also a theologian.
8. Thomas Aquinas could not be both a philosopher and a theologian.
9. If flowers bloom in the spring but not in winter, then May is colorful but December is drab.
10. Assuming flowers bloom in the spring but not in winter, May will be colorful, December drab.
11. If flowers bloom either in the spring or in the summer, in the spring the young will turn their thoughts to love.
12. If Ramon went swimming, then Maria went dancing.
13. Ramon went swimming, but Maria went dancing.
14. Ivan does drive a Toyota and Amy does drive a Subaru.
15. Winston Churchill was a great speaker.
16. Winston Churchill was a great writer.
17. Winston Churchill was a great writer and Churchill was a great speaker.
18. Winston Churchill was a great writer and a great speaker.
19. If Winston Churchill was a great speaker, then he was not a great writer; no one can be great at both.
20. "The Times, Places and Manner of holding Elections for Senators and Representatives, shall be prescribed in each State by the Legislature thereof; but the Congress may at any time by Law make or alter such Regulations, except as to the Place of Chusing Senators." (U.S. Constitution, Art. 1, Sec. 4)
21. "If any Bill shall not be returned by the President within ten Days (Sundays excepted) after it shall have been presented to him, the Same shall be a Law, in like Manner as if he had signed it...." (U.S. Constitution, Art. 1, Sec. 7)

Advanced Conditional Propositions

A Deeper Look

In comparison with Lesson 21, this whole chapter is really "a deeper look." Here we take up some more advanced conditional propositions by comparing how we express them in English and using symbols. Here we will see that symbols can help us to understand the meaning and the logical consequences of more advanced conditional propositions. One way they do so is to help us to see when different verbal formulations mean the logical relations are different, and when the language is different but the logical relations are the same.

Negative Conditions

Often we want to set out a negative condition. The normal way we do this in English is by using the word "unless" or by negating the antecedent.

"Unless you come through the door, you can't get into the room."
"If you don't come through the door, you can't get into the room."

These two examples show the logical force of "unless" is the same as "if not." This equivalency can also be seen when we try to symbolize negative conditions. The second sentence is symbolized ($\sim D \to \sim R$), where D stands for "you come through the door" and R stand for "you can get into the room."

And the first sentence is symbolized in exactly the same way, as ($\sim$D $\rightarrow$ $\sim$R), for "unless p" means "if not-p."

Contraposition

Seeing how to symbolize a negative condition gives us a clue that contraposition is a valid inference. Contraposition literally means "reversing the positions" of the antecedent and consequent of a conditional proposition. This "turning around" p and q in a conditional proposition is somewhat similar to conversion of the subject and predicate terms of a categorical proposition. When we say "if you don't come through the door, you can't get into the room," we can ask ourselves what would follow logically if we tried to turn around the antecedent and consequent. Since affirming the antecedent of a conditional proposition ensures the predicate will come about, "not coming through the door" guarantees you will never "get into the room." In this example, we are assuming that coming through the door is the only way to get into the room. If we suppose "you did get into the room," then based on the original negative conditional proposition, what would follow is the opposite of the original antecedent—namely, "you came through the door." In short, from "if you don't come through the door, you can't get into the room," it would follow that "if you did get into the room, then you must have come through the door." Using the same symbols as before, then, we now see that if we suppose ($\sim$D $\rightarrow$ $\sim$R), then it follows that (R $\rightarrow$ D). The same relation works in the opposite way, as well. Contraposition is a useful way to check on the meaning of conditional propositions, and it can be generalized in the following definition.

Definition of contraposition: $(p \rightarrow q) \equiv (\sim q \rightarrow \sim p)$.

Sufficient Condition

Symbolic notation allows us to distinguish sharply *three kinds of conditions*: "sufficient conditions," "necessary conditions," and "necessary and sufficient conditions." In a way, we have already met the first two kinds of conditions, in considering the basic meaning of conditional propositions and in looking at contraposition. Let's begin with the easiest of these three to understand—sufficient conditions.

Think back to the basic meaning of a conditional proposition (p → q). The "if clause" or antecedent means that if it is realized (or is true), then that is enough to *guarantee* that the consequent will also be realized (or true). In short, the antecedent is *sufficient*, by itself, to ensure the consequent. For this reason, another name for a *regular* conditional proposition is a "sufficient condition."

> **Example:** "If you are good, then I'll give you a lollipop."

If you say this to a child (G → L), she will rightly think you are *guaranteeing* her a lollipop, on the *condition* that she behaves well ("is good"). And she will be upset and rightly feel mistreated if she does behave well, but you don't give her the lollipop. For, as children usually say, you have *promised* her the lollipop as a reward, on the condition that she is a good little girl.

Definition of Sufficient Condition: p is a sufficient condition of q when (p → q).

Necessary Condition

There are other conditional propositions that mean something quite different from regular or sufficient conditions. They involve a different logic. These propositions set *necessary* conditions—that is, conditions that must be met before you are even eligible for the reward set out in the consequent. Students are very familiar with prerequisites that must be met in order to be accepted at a high school or college or graduate or professional school or for enrolling in a certain course.

> **Example:** "A high school diploma is required for being accepted at a university."

Here the logical relation between attaining the high school diploma and being accepted at a university is *not* that the high school diploma guarantees your being accepted to the university, which would be symbolized (D → U), where D means "you have attained a high school diploma" and U means "you have been accepted at university." Quite the contrary; the logical relation is one of fulfilling a necessary prerequisite that clears the way for your acceptance at the university, but does not guarantee it. There are two ways of expressing necessary conditions, one negative and the other positive.

Negative Statement of Necessary Condition

Often the most intuitively obvious way to express a necessary condition, such as the one mentioned, is to express it negatively: "If you are not a high school graduate, then you will not be accepted to the university." The negative antecedent ("you are not a high school graduate") expresses clearly that having a high school diploma does not guarantee acceptance to university. But there is a guarantee here. Not having a high school diploma guarantees that you will *not* be accepted at the university. This negative way of setting up a necessary condition can be expressed as $(\sim D \rightarrow \sim U)$.

Definition: *negative* statement that p is a necessary condition of q: $(\sim p \rightarrow \sim q)$.

Teenagers are very familiar with necessary conditions of this sort.

> **Example:** "If you don't clean up your room, you won't get the car tonight."

This necessary condition can be symbolized negatively as $(\sim R \rightarrow \sim C)$, where R means "You clean your room" and C means "You get the car tonight." While children might not understand that such necessary conditions do not guarantee use of the car, teenagers understand this all too well. For there may be other factors at work, such as, "Your homework must be done," or "You can't drive Phyllis in the car, because she'll want to go to the medical marijuana store," or the all-time favorite, "If you are nasty to mom or dad sometime between cleaning the room and the time for you to use the car, you still won't get use of the car."

Positive Statement of Necessary Condition

There is a second, positive way to express a necessary condition. We can see this way by starting with the negative way of expressing a necessary condition. Take the statement "If you are not good, then I won't give you a lollipop," symbolized as $(\sim G \rightarrow \sim L)$. This proposition is a guarantee that if you do not behave well, you will not get a lollipop from me. But if this statement and its guarantee are true, then what do we know, if we see you with a lollipop given by me? We know you were good, because if you had not been good, you would not have the lollipop. We can also express this necessary condition—namely, that your being good is a necessary condition of you getting a lollipop from me—in this positive way: "If you got a lollipop, then you were good."

This conditional proposition is expressed symbolically as (L → G). Since being good was a *necessary* condition of getting a lollipop, then if you got the lollipop, you *must* have been good. At this point, you can see how helpful the logical relation of contraposition is, because (L → G) and (~G → ~L) are the contrapositives of each other.

Definition: *positive* statement that p is a necessary condition of q: (q → p).

Necessary and Sufficient Condition

If you combine a necessary condition with a sufficient condition, then what results is a "necessary and sufficient condition." Logicians often express this relation with the phrase "if and only if" or "iff," where the first "if" sets out a sufficient condition, while the "only if" expresses a necessary condition.

> **Example:** "If and only if you are good, you will get a lollipop from me."

While we don't normally speak this way, the awkward expression "if and only if" does describe quite precisely what we mean, which is "If you are good, you will get a lollipop from me; and also, if you get a lollipop from me, then you were good." You can see that the "necessary and sufficient condition" is simply the conjunction of two conditions, one necessary and the other sufficient. In this case, the one and only way to get a lollipop from me is to be good. This proposition is different from the sufficient condition alone, "If you are good, you'll get a lollipop from me," which does not rule out your getting a lollipop in some other way—making one, stealing one, finding one on the floor. The necessary and sufficient condition does rule out other ways of getting the lollipop. Since there are two ways to express a necessary condition, there are two ways to express a necessary and sufficient condition.

Definitions:

1. *Negative* way to express that p is a necessary and sufficient condition of q:

$$(p → q) • (~p → ~q)$$

2. *Positive* way to express that p is a necessary and sufficient condition of q:

$$(p → q) • (q → p)$$

The positive way of expressing the necessary condition in (2) shows that the arrow of inference runs in *both* directions. Logicians have invented two other symbols to express the "necessary and sufficient condition": (a) what is called the bi-conditional (p ↔ q), with an arrow that runs in both directions; and (b) logical equivalence, with an equal sign that has three rather than two lines (p ≡ q). Both expressions mean the same thing.

"Only If" Propositions

In our normal conversation and writing, we do not use the expression "if and only if." So how do we express "necessary and sufficient conditions" in normal language? In English, the "necessary and sufficient condition" is usually expressed by the phrase "only if.…"

Here are some examples: "*Only if* you are good will I give you a lollipop." Alternatively, holding out the possible reward first, a parent would more likely say: "I will give you a lollipop, *only if* you are good."

Both of these sentences express the necessary and sufficient condition: $(L \to G) \cdot (G \to L)$. But there is a problem with the expression "only if." Sometimes we use it to express not a "necessary *and* sufficient condition" but merely a "necessary condition."

> **Example:** "*Only if* you train hard will you run the mile in four minutes."

Many people know that there have been very few humans in track history to have run the mile in four minutes or less. It is impossible that training hard by itself could ever ensure that a runner could do the mile in four minutes. So this proposition cannot possibly have as part of its meaning "if you train hard then you will run the mile in four minutes" $(T \to 4)$. Here "only if" is used to state a *necessary condition*, expressed negatively: "If you do not train hard, you will not run the mile in four minutes" $(\sim T \to \sim 4)$; and this is all it means. You can also express this necessary condition by contraposing this proposition: "If you ran the mile in four minutes, you must have trained hard" $(4 \to T)$.

Consequently, when dealing with "only if" expressions you will have to *make a judgment about the true meaning of the proposition*. It is impossible to employ some sort of *mechanical rule* to interpret "only if" statements, since the expression "only if" is inherently ambiguous; and symbolizing such statements helps us see the ambiguity they involve.

Combined Propositions

As you have no doubt guessed by now, it is not necessary that a proposition stop at one hypothetical expression. More complicated hypothetical propositions can be formed by combining two or more hypothetical expressions. We shall see that such *combined* statements become much more important when we turn to hypothetical arguments. And they are a favorite of educators who create standardized tests like the LSAT and the GRE. Here we should note their existence and be able to recognize them.

> **Example:** "If Gloria learns English well, then she will get a good job and make lots of money."

This sentence is fundamentally a conditional proposition, "if p, then q." What makes it slightly more complicated is that q is itself a hypothetical proposition, a conjunction. The full proposition should be symbolized as $[G \to (J \cdot M)]$, where G is "Gloria learns English well," J is "Gloria will get a good job," and M is "Gloria will earn a lot of money."

Problem Set 22: Advanced Hypothetical Propositions

Advanced Conditional Propositions

Instructions

Create your own symbols and symbolize the propositions for the following statements.

1. Joe goes to the game if and only if Jamal plays quarterback; and Andrew kicks field goals.
2. Melinda goes to the game, if and only if Jamal plays quarterback and Andrew kicks field goals.
3. Virginia will run for class president only if Claudio does too.
4. Virginia won't run unless Claudio does.
5. Only if Claudio runs will Virginia run.
6. Unless Virginia runs, Claudio won't run.
7. Unless you're good, you won't get a lollipop.
8. Being good is a sufficient condition for getting a lollipop.
9. Being good is a necessary condition for getting a lollipop.
10. Pleasure will increase only if pain doesn't increase.

11. Pleasure will increase unless pain increases.

12. Unless pleasure increases or pain decreases we'll fail to reduce mental depression.

13. If Gloria learns to read and write well, she will get a good job and make lots of money.

14. If Gloria learns to read and write well, she will get a good job and make lots of money, providing she doesn't waste her time watching the Astros in the World Series.

15. Unless Gloria learns to read and write well, she won't get a good job and make lots of money.

16. If Luis plays violin, then Manuel plays viola, unless Carlos plays trumpet.

17. Nguyen is waiting patiently and Jaime is a nervous wreck, provided that either Sandra said she'd be late or Imelda does not plan to come.

18. If Shawna does not write poetry, then Howard writes music; but it is not the case that if Shawna writes poetry, then Howard does not write music.

19. If the fact that Sarah is a lawyer implies that Clarence cares for computers, then it is not the case that either Mary Therese bakes pies for Thanksgiving or Jon builds boats.

20. If Stephanie catches crickets, then if Baldemar builds beds, then if Kyley herds hogs, then Matthew writes for the student newspaper.

21. The fact that Ian works for MI6 or Darrell works for MI5 is a necessary condition for Daniel to call them in from the cold, in case Philip was not part of the plot or Kurt was not caught.

Advanced Conditional Propositions in Prose

Instructions

Create your own symbols and then symbolize these propositions.

1. "None but the brave deserves the fair." (John Dryden, 17th-cen. British poet, "Alexander's Feast; or, The Power of Music An Ode, in Honour of St. Cecilia's Day")

2. "If ideas are modes of thought, ideas are not images of anything, nor do they consist of words." (Spinoza, 17th-cen. Dutch philosopher, *Ethics*, simplified)

3. "If a President shall not have been chosen before the time fixed for the beginning of his term, or if the President elect shall have failed to qualify, then the Vice President elect shall act as President until a President shall have qualified." (U.S. Constitution, 20th Amendment, Sec. 3, ratified 1933)

4. "If he rode across the river with a hard bunch like the Suggses, he would be an outlaw, whereas if he stayed, the nesters might try to hang him or at least try to jail him in Fort Worth. If that happened, he'd soon be on trial for one accident or another." (Larry McMurtry, 20th-cen. American writer, *Lonesome Dove*)

5. "Israel will not have long-term security without the full recognition of a viable and proper Palestinian state and a peace accord with all Arab nations." (Jacques Chirac, 20th-cen. president of France)

6. "There are only three possibilities: either your sister is mad, or she is telling lies, or she is telling the truth. You know she does not tell lies, and she is obviously not mad, so we must conclude she is telling the truth." (C. S. Lewis, 20th-cen. English writer, *The Lion, the Witch, and the Wardrobe*)

7. "When in Rome, live as the Romans do; when elsewhere, live as they live elsewhere." (Attributed to St. Ambrose, as advice to St. Augustine, 4th-cen. philosopher) [What Augustine actually wrote, in *Letter* 36, c. 14, about the advice Ambrose gave to Augustine for his mother, St. Monica, about fasting was: "'When I am here [in Milan] I do not fast on Saturday; but when I am at Rome I do; whatever church you may come to, conform to its custom, if you would avoid either receiving or giving offence.' This reply I reported to my mother, and it satisfied her, so that she scrupled not to comply with it; and I have myself followed the same rule."]

8. "You can only find truth with logic if you have already found truth without it." (Attributed to G. K. Chesterton, 20th-cen. British writer, but not by him)

9. "So long as men worship the Caesars and Napoleons, Caesars and Napoleons will arise to make them miserable." (Aldous Huxley, 20th-cen. British author, *Ends and Means*, 1937)

10. "A man with wings large enough and duly attached might learn to overcome the resistance of the air, and conquering it, succeed in subjugating it and raise himself upon it." (Leonardo da Vinci, 15th-cen. Italian polymath, from *The Flight of Birds*, 1505)

11. "No Person shall be a Representative who shall not have attained to the Age of twenty-five Years, and been seven Years a Citizen of the United States, and who shall not, when elected, be an Inhabitant of that State in which he shall be chosen." (U.S. Constitution, Art. 1, Sec. 2)

12. "Hitler knows that he will have to break us in this island or lose the war. If we can stand up to him, all Europe may be free, and the life of the world may move forward into broad, sunlit uplands. But if we fail, then the whole world, including the United States, and all that we have known and cared for, will sink into the abyss of a new dark age made more sinister, and perhaps more prolonged, by the lights of a perverted science. Let us therefore brace ourselves to our duty and so bear ourselves that if the British Commonwealth and Europe lasts for a thousand years men will still say: This was their finest hour." (Winston Churchill, British prime minister, June 18, 1940, Speech in the House of Commons) [There are several hypothetical propositions here. Symbolize the hypothetical proposition contained in each sentence in the quotation.]

13. "But if there is no resurrection of the dead, then Christ has not been raised; if Christ has not been raised, then our preaching is in vain and your faith is in vain." (1 Cor 15:13–14 RSV)

14. "You must not build upon foundations of prayer and contemplation alone, for, unless you strive after the virtues and practice them, you will never grow to be more than dwarfs." (Teresa of Ávila, d. 1582, Spanish mystic, reformer of the Carmelite Orders of both women and men, mentor of St. John of the Cross, from *Interior Castle*)

Part 4

The Logic of Arguments

Lesson 23

Two Kinds of Reasoning

The Essentials

In Lesson 6, we saw that reasoning was one of the three acts our mind performs when we are thinking. In the act of *reasoning*, our mind moves from one point to another in order to get to yet a third point. In doing so, our mind produces within itself an argument. And arguments are important because that is how we use our mind to discover *truths we did not know before*.[1] If we couldn't reason, we would either be like God—who is so intelligent that he knows everything already—or we would be like the other animals, who don't reason at all, at least not in the intellectual way we do, using abstract or universal concepts that extend far beyond our own sense experience. This is why, since the time of the Greeks, philosophers have said that humans "live on the horizon between the gods and the beasts."

Taken very broadly, there are two kinds of reasoning. You may already be familiar with their names: *deductive* reasoning and *inductive* reasoning. Let's turn to the classic example of deductive reasoning that logicians have been using since the time of Aristotle, the one we used in Lesson 6:

All men are mortal.
Socrates is a man.
Therefore, Socrates is mortal.

1. Aquinas, *Commentary on the Posterior Analytics of Aristotle*, Prologue.

This kind of argument is called a *categorical syllogism* because its three parts are categorical propositions. The way it works is that when the two premises—the first two sentences—are *taken together*, they lead necessarily to the conclusion—the third sentence. The term "man" (or "human") is what links together the terms "Socrates" and "mortal" in the conclusion. There is more than one type of deductive argument, but all deductive arguments have this in common: they draw a conclusion by means of a *middle term* or a series of middle terms.

You might ask, "How do we know the two premises are true?" The answer is that we use the other type of reasoning—*induction*. We use induction in the first act of the mind in order to develop universal concepts like *man* by *abstracting* or drawing out the universal man *from* our experience of particular men. In the second or *minor* premise here, we are saying the individual we call Socrates fits under the universal concept *man*. If we already have the universal concept *man* in our mind, then it is easy to establish the truth of the minor premise by comparing Socrates with other men and with the content of the concept *man*. We might informally call this using the "duck test": if it looks, acts, and sounds like a duck, then it's a duck. Here we are seeing if the individual we call Socrates fits under a description of *man* that we have already developed by studying other men and abstracting the universal concept *man* from them by focusing on the *essence* the men we have analyzed have in common with each other. And how do we develop that universal concept in the first place? We start by comparing individual men, seeing what they have in common and how they are different. There is a difference between inductive reasoning itself and intuition of the concept of the essence—which is where inductive reasoning leads; but we'll take up that issue when we treat induction. We can see here that the kind of inductive reasoning that produces universal concepts is the foundation for all subsequent acts of the mind.

The major premise of our argument works a bit differently, though, because it is not limited to one universal concept but involves two concepts, put together in the proposition "all men are mortal." We weren't born with that proposition already in our minds, yet we somehow came to have it. It's a proposition that we refine over the course of our lives; but once we first attain it, we never abandon it completely. We are perfectly willing to use it as the basis for applying it to new people we meet, to people long since dead, like Socrates himself, and to people we shall never meet, say, our great-great grandchildren. If we developed the *concepts* of *men* and *mortal* through abstraction, which is a process of inductive generalization, then we should use a similar process to derive the *proposition* "all men are mortal." The main difference is that we don't merely arrive at concepts, but at a universal *proposition* formed from concepts.

Consequently, you can see that we need *both* deductive and inductive reasoning. The most important difference between these two types of reasoning is that deductive reasoning proceeds by means of a universal middle term, but inductive reasoning does not. *In inductive reasoning there is no middle term.* Our mind proceeds directly from *examples* of a universal conclusion to that conclusion. These two kinds of reasoning complement each other. So it is imperative that we learn what they are like, learn to recognize how different they are, then see how they can work together.

We will begin our study of the third act of the mind with deductive reasoning, because its structure is the focal point of formal logic. Then we will take up inductive reasoning as the necessary companion to deduction. Finally, we will look at how the two types of reasoning work together.

Primary Sources

Thomas Aquinas, *Commentary on the Posterior Analytics of Aristotle*, Prologue. Here Aquinas sets reasoning and argument in relation to the first two acts of the mind and then explains the different levels of knowledge we can attain using syllogistic reasoning. An excellent short overview that helps us see the full range of and importance of reasoning our way to true conclusions.

Problem Set 23: Distinguishing Deductive from Inductive Reasoning

Drawing *Conclusions* Deductively or Inductively

Instructions

Consider the following *propositions*. How would you establish whether or not they are true? Would you use deduction, induction, or could you do it either way?

1. No one in the U.S. Senate is over 100 years old.
2. Salt is made up of NaCl.
3. Humans have an immortal soul.
4. The earth is a sphere.

5. Cheetahs run faster than humans
6. Most college graduates succeed in business.
7. The universe had a beginning.
8. Water boils at 180 degrees F ($=$ 75 degrees C).
9. When equals are added to equals the results are equal.
10. Euthanasia is morally wrong.
11. The blood in the human body circulates.
12. All the U.S. presidents been native born.

Distinguishing Deductive from Inductive *Arguments*

Instructions

Consider the following *arguments*: (a) What is the main conclusion? (b) Is there one or more than one argument for this conclusion? (c) For each argument in the passage, is the argument deductive or inductive?

1. Travelers to the tropics have often remarked that this climate is very hard on machinery. In fact, someone touring by car is amazed at the danger from rust. Then the natives only smile and wonder why the tourists do not notice the amount of moisture in the air.

2. "The history of all hitherto existing society is the history of class struggles. Freeman and slave, patrician and plebeian, lord and serf, guild-master and journeyman, in a word, oppressor and oppressed, stood in constant opposition to each other, carried on an uninterrupted, now hidden, now open fight." (Karl Marx and Friedrich Engels, 19th-cen. revolutionaries, *Communist Manifesto*, 1848)

3. "The cow, the goat, and the deer are ruminants. The cow, the goat, and the deer are horned animals. Therefore, all horned animals are ruminants." (Adapted from Aristotle)

4. Do you know why a stack of magazines tied in a bundle will be very difficult to burn up in a trash pile? If you understand about a fire's need of oxygen, you have the answer. As you can see, the magazines have very little air, except on the outer surface. That is the reason they are so difficult to burn.

5. Now it is scarcely possible to conceive how the aggregates of dissimilar particles should be so uniformly the same. If some of the particles of water were heavier than others; if a parcel of the liquid on any occasion were constituted principally of these heavier particles, it must be supposed to affect the

specific gravity of the mass, a circumstance not known. Similar observations may be made on other substances. Therefore, we may conclude that the ultimate particles of all homogeneous bodies are perfectly alike in weight, figure, etc. In other words, every particle of water is like every other particle of water; every particle of hydrogen is like every other particle of hydrogen, etc. (John Dalton, d. 1844, English chemist, propounded the modern atomic theory)

6. "The chromosomes in our germ cells are not affected by any change that takes place within our body cells. What this means is that no change...made in us in our lifetimes...can be passed on to our children through the process of biological heredity." (Amram Scheinfeld, 1939, American journalist, author of popular science books, *Your Heredity and Environment*, 1964)

7. "As the species of the same genus usually have, though by no means invariably, much similarity in habits and constitution, and always in structure, the struggle will generally be more severe between them, if they come into competition with each other, than between the species of distinct genera. We see this in the recent extension over parts of the United States of one species of swallow, having caused the decrease of another species. The recent increase of the missel-thrush in parts of Scotland has caused the decrease of the song-thrush. How frequently we hear of one species of rat taking the place of another species under the most different climates!" (Charles Darwin, 19th-cen. English evolutionist, *On the Origin of Species*, chap. 3, sec. 6)

The Categorical Syllogism

The Essentials

There are two kinds of deductive arguments: those based on categorical propositions and those based on hypothetical propositions. We will begin with categorical arguments, and with the most elementary of them, the *categorical syllogism*. From this base we will move on to more complicated categorical arguments, those that have more than one middle term. These can be thought of as a series of connected categorical syllogisms. After that, we will take up deductive arguments that use hypothetical propositions, and therefore are called hypothetical arguments. This is the most natural way to learn about the logic of the third act of the mind, as it mimics the way we gradually learned to argue as children.

Modern symbolic logic, however, follows the reverse order. It starts with hypothetical arguments (included in what is called "propositional calculus") and then moves to categorical statements and arguments (in "predicate calculus"). This order is helpful in mathematical applications of logic, which concentrate on proving one symbolic logical proposition from another, rather than using symbols to understand the logic of "natural" language, as we have been doing. This approach to logic puts off treatment of the most natural form of argument—categorical syllogisms—very much to the end of the study of logic; but we shall begin our consideration of arguments with categorical syllogisms.

Arguments: Truth, Validity, Soundness

The categorical syllogism consists in three categorical propositions, two of which are used to deduce the third as a conclusion. Thinkers before Aristotle certainly used deductive arguments like categorical syllogisms, and they also used hypothetical syllogisms. One of the reasons Plato so opposed the sophists was because he thought they had plausible arguments for some erroneous ideas. Their chief mistake was that they thought—quite like contemporary relativists—that humans cannot attain true and certain knowledge; the best we can do is plausible or probable opinions. The sophist Protagoras, for example, had famously said, "Of all things the measure is man—of the things that are, that they are, and of the things that are not, that they are not." Plato thought the exact opposite is true; humans are not the "measure" for deciding whether our knowledge of things is true, but rather things are the "measure" for deciding whether our ideas are true. Our ideas are true when they conform to things and false when they do not. So Plato, then, concluded that the sophists were wrong and dismissed their conclusions, but he also rejected their ways of arguing.

When Aristotle came to weigh the claims of the sophists against those of his beloved teacher Plato, he tried to give each side its due. He found that Plato had better conclusions (though he did not agree with Plato about everything); but when it came to arguments, he found that the sophists were not as bad as Plato had thought. The reason was that in studying arguments, Aristotle came to realize that there is a difference between the *content* of an argument—which is contained in the terms that make it up—and the style, structure, or *form* the argument takes. He realized that what makes the conclusion "flow necessarily" from the premises of an argument is *not* what it is about—its content—but the *form* or *structure* of the argument. In short, there is a difference between the *truth* of the conclusion—which is determined by whether it corresponds to reality—and whether the conclusion follows necessarily from the premises of the argument—what is called its *validity*.[1] One can have a perfectly valid argument that leads to a false conclusion. Consider this silly argument:

All animals with long necks are elephants.
All giraffes have long necks.
Therefore, all giraffes are elephants.

1. Aristotle, *Prior Analytics* 1.4–6; Aquinas, *Commentary on Aristotle's Posterior Analytics*, bk. 1, lesson 13, no. 3, lesson 36, no. 7.

What makes this argument silly is not its structure or form; in fact, the argument is valid. If both premises were true, since the conclusion does follow from the premises, the conclusion also would be true. The reason the conclusion is false is because the first premise is false. The only time we can be sure that the conclusion *must* be true is when the argument is not just valid but *sound*. A sound deductive argument is an argument that is (1) valid—its premises lead necessarily to its conclusion, and (2) its premises are true. Only this combination of truth and validity can ensure a conclusion that must be true.

Let's repeat this important point. Only *propositions* are *true* or *false*. This is so, even though in ordinary speech we sometimes use the term "valid" about propositions when we really mean they "might be true" or are "likely to be true, but I'm not sure." And only *arguments* are *valid* or *invalid*. The conclusion of a valid argument follows necessarily from its premises; the conclusion of an invalid argument does not. Finally, arguments are *sound* (its opposite is unsound) when the argument is valid *and* the premises are true, because it is the truth of the premises that *ensures* the truth of the conclusion.

You probably can see, then, that deductive arguments are a good way to expand our knowledge, to discover new truths. Based on what we already know, we can draw conclusions that are new truths, ones we didn't know before. Sometimes we do this by starting with the premises and discovering in the conclusion a truth we did not previously know. This is called arguing "synthetically," by synthesizing or bringing together the premises. However, quite often what we do is proceed from the conclusion back to the premises. If we think the conclusion is true, we look around for an argument that will prove the conclusion. If we find such an argument, and its premises also are true, then we have proven that the conclusion must be true, as well. This is how we transform opinions into knowledge. This way of arguing deductively is called arguing "analytically," because we analyze the conclusion into its subject and predicate and then look for a "middle term" that shows they must be linked together. Since this way of using syllogisms is so important, Aristotle used the term "analytics" as the title of his most important logic book, which was subsequently divided into the *Prior Analytics* (which contained his formal logic) and the *Posterior Analytics* (which set out his theory of demonstrative arguments, the strongest kind of deductive arguments).

The Structure of the Categorical Syllogism

Here is a categorical syllogism, already set up in what we'll call "standard logical form." For example:

All mammals are animals.
All lions are mammals.
Therefore, all lions are animals.

The third sentence is the conclusion that is derived from the first two sentences, called premises. Since each categorical proposition has two terms—its subject term and its predicate term—the maximum number of terms in three categorical propositions is six. But you will notice that these three propositions do not contain six terms, or five, or four; they contain only three terms. Each term is used twice. The reason why a categorical syllogism must have three and only three terms is because each term must be repeated in order to produce the *connections* among the terms that ensure that the conclusion follows logically from the two premises.

Since the *validity* of a syllogism depends upon its structure, not its content, at this point we need to set out some terminology in order to identify different formal features of the syllogism. We'll begin with the conclusion, since deriving a conclusion is the goal of a syllogistic argument. Like all categorical propositions, this conclusion has a subject term (*lions*) and a predicate term (*animals*). By convention, the subject term *of the conclusion* is called the "subject term of the syllogism." Likewise, the predicate term of the conclusion is called the "predicate term of the syllogism." These terms can be symbolized by S and P, respectively, as we did for categorical propositions. But remember, S and P here are S and P for the *whole syllogism*, not just the conclusion. In our syllogism, "lions" has less extension than "animals," and "animals" has more extension than "lions." In Latin, the word *minor* means "less" and the word *major* means "more," so the S term is called the "minor" term and the P term is called the "major" term. (Remember, these are the S and P terms when we are dealing with propositions *in a syllogism*; they don't apply when we are considering a proposition by itself.) You will notice that the minor and major terms are found in the conclusion, and each one is found in one of the premises. We can use the S and P terms to distinguish the two premises. The *major premise* is the one that includes the *major term*, while the *minor premise* is the one that includes the *minor term*. In real arguments, the two premises and conclusion can occur in any order. Indeed, some logic books follow a different order, beginning with the minor premise, rather than the major premise. To show that we recognize the *logical* order of an argument, when we analyze an argument in prose, we will put the three propositions in the following traditional and standard order:

Major premise
Minor premise
Conclusion

There is one other term in our sample syllogism: "mammals." This term is *not* part of the conclusion, though it is the reason for the conclusion; it is found *only in the premises*. In this particular syllogism, the extension of "mammals" falls *midway* between "lions," which is narrower, and "animals," which is wider. It is no surprise that it is called the "middle term." However, there is a much more important reason why it is called the middle term. Quite often in deductive arguments we are first aware of the conclusion; we think it is true, but don't know for sure. (We do know in this simple example; but ignore that for the time being.) If we think the conclusion is true, then the S and P terms in the conclusion need to be *linked directly together, in order* to show they are connected. This is the function of the *middle term*—to connect the S and P terms to one another. A traditional image for this connection is to think of the S and P terms as links, like links in a chain. Separate links don't make a chain. The only way to produce a small chain is to "link" the S and P terms by means of the *middle term*, which is called "middle" because it provides a connection, like a link in a chain.

If we ignore the content of our syllogism, we can see its structure:

Major premise: All M is P.
Minor premise: All S is M.
Conclusion: Therefore, all S is P.

Aristotle's main insight, then, was that the validity of the categorical syllogism is determined not by the content of the S, M, and P terms, but by the form or structure of the syllogism. However, there is more to the form of the syllogism than the basic configuration of its S, M, and P terms. The validity of a syllogism depends on two precise features of its form—the *figure* and *mood* of the syllogism.

Figures of the Categorical Syllogism

Once Aristotle realized that the structure of a syllogism determines its validity, he noticed that the M and P terms in the major premise can be in the order of our example (M is P) or the reverse (P is M). And this is true, as well, for the S and M terms in the minor premise. But the conclusion is different. *By definition*, we call the subject of the conclusion the "S term" and the predicate of the conclusion the "P term." If we temporarily leave aside the quantity and quality of each proposition, we can determine the *figure* or basic structural configuration of a syllogism. Since the conclusion always takes the form "S is/is not P," there are only four figures. (Aristotle himself only recognized the first three, because all valid syllogisms in the fourth figure can be "reduced" or rewritten as valid syllogisms in one of the first three figures.) The figure of a syllogism depends upon whether the S, M, and P terms are the subject or predicate in the premises where they occur. In a way, the numbers assigned to the figures are arbitrary; but the first figure was called "first" by Aristotle, because it is the only figure in which we can draw universal affirmative conclusions, as in our sample syllogism earlier. Such syllogisms are the heart of deductive reasoning.

Figure:	*Names*		Subject and predicate of each proposition	
Figure I:	Major premise:		M	P
	Minor premise:		S	M
	Conclusion:	Therefore,	S	P
Figure II:	Major premise:		P	M
	Minor premise:		S	M
	Conclusion:	Therefore,	S	P
Figure III:	Major premise:		M	P
	Minor premise:		M	S
	Conclusion:	Therefore,	S	P
Figure IV:	Major premise:		P	M
	Minor premise:		M	S
	Conclusion:	Therefore,	S	P

In this presentation of the four figures, you should notice that the copula ("is" or "is not") has been omitted. We'll come back to the copula, which determines the *quality* of the proposition, when we turn to the "mood" of the syllogism. For the time being, we are just looking at the relative positions of M and P in the major premise and S and M in the minor premise.

A good way to remember the numbers of the figures is to start with the most obvious kind of syllogism, which is the first figure. "All men are mortal. Socrates is a man. Therefore, Socrates is mortal." In the second figure, the middle term is the *predicate* of both premises. The third figure is just the reverse of the second; in the third, the middle term is the *subject* of both premises. In the fourth figure, the order of the terms in both premises is the reverse of the first figure.

Moods of the Syllogism

The second structural feature that determines whether a categorical syllogism is valid or invalid is its "mood." (Sometimes logicians use the term "mode," because the original Latin word was *modus*.) To the structure as determined by the *figure* of the syllogism, the *mood* adds the *quantity* and *quality* of the premises and conclusion. As you will remember, when taken together, the quantity and quality of any categorical proposition determine its structure: A (universal affirmative), I (particular affirmative), E (universal negative), or O (particular negative). Consequently, the mood consists in three letters: the first for the kind of proposition the major premise is, the second for the kind of proposition the minor premise is, and the third for the kind of proposition the conclusion is.

Example: our syllogism showing that "all lions are animals" has the mood AAA, because each of three propositions in the syllogism is A. That argument is also a first-figure syllogism. Its complete structural description, which determines whether or not the syllogism is valid, is "First figure, AAA."

The figure is determined by the arrangement of the S, M, and P terms in the three propositions that make up the syllogism, while the mood is determined by the kind of propositions in the syllogism. And since validity or invalidity are determined purely by the form or structure of the syllogism, not by its content, all first-figure AAA syllogisms are valid, no matter what their content. When treating arguments in logic, we concentrate on the validity of the argument. We should remember, however, that acquiring knowledge requires arguments to be *sound*, not just valid. But the truth of the premises is not determined by logic; it is studied in all the other disciplines. This is why Aristotle called logic the primary "tool" (*organon*) we use to acquire knowledge in any area.

A Deeper Look

Valid Arguments

In order to determine which forms of syllogism are valid and which are invalid, Aristotle seems to have taken an empirical approach, investigating each kind of argument structure. Now there are eight possibilities for the major premise—four affirmative propositions and four negative propositions. This is because the M and P terms can be either the subject or predicate of the major premise, a premise can be universal or particular, and a premise can be affirmative or negative ($2 \times 2 \times 2$). The same is true of the minor premise. The conclusion, however, must have the S term as its subject and the P term as its predicate, which means there are only four possibilities there. Now $8 \times 8 \times 4 = 256$; so there are 256 possible arrangements of figure and mood. Fortunately, most of them are invalid, there are only 24 valid combinations of figure and mood.

Since mood is determined by the kinds of propositions involved—A, I, E, or O—some clever (but now unknown) medieval logician had the idea that he would add some consonants to these vowels in order to come up with a name for each of the valid types of syllogism. Then he put them into a mnemonic verse that students over the centuries have memorized, as a way of remembering nineteen of the valid syllogistic forms.

> Barbara, Celarent, Darii, Ferio*que prioris;*
> Cesare, Camestres, Festino, Baroco *secundae;*
> *Tertia,* Darapti, Disamis, Datisi, Felapton,
> Bocardo, Ferison, *habet; Quarta in super addit*
> Bramantip, Camenes, Dimaris, Fesapo, Fresison.

The way to use this verse is to see that there are four valid forms of syllogism in the first figure, four in the second, six in the third, and five in the fourth. Also, all the valid syllogisms in the second figure draw a *negative* conclusion, while all the valid syllogisms in the third figure draw a *particular* conclusion. Look at *Barbara,* the first one. The three vowels in her name are AAA, so "Barbara" stands for a first-figure AAA syllogism. *Celarent*, by contrast, stands for a first-figure EAE syllogism. This system continues down to *Fresison*, which stands for a fourth-figure EIO syllogism. These names actually contain more information. Names that begin with the same consonant stand for syllogisms closely related to each other, in this way: a syllogism in the second, third, or fourth figures that begins with the letter C, for example, can be "reduced" to Celarent in the first figure by manipulating the three propositions in it. This reduction shows that a valid first-figure syllogism, like Celarent, more basically and more obviously is valid than Cesare, Camestres, or Camenes. And some of the other consonants tell us how to perform such reductions. The letter "s" tells us to *simply convert* the proposition it follows. If you convert the major E premise of Cesare in the second figure, you will get a syllogism in Celarent in the first figure. The letter "p" indicates "accidental" (*per accidens*) conversion of the preceding proposition, and the letter "m," standing for "mutation," tells you to switch the order of the premises. Finally, the letter "c" indicates you must perform a more complicated change called "contradiction."

This mnemonic verse, however, leaves out six other valid types of syllogisms. For example, an I proposition follows validly from an A formed out of the same two terms (which we saw is Subalternation in the Square of Opposites). Since Barbara is valid, Barbari also is valid. Five valid syllogisms are derived through subordination: first-figure AAI and EAO; second-figure EAO and AEO; and fourth-figure AEO. Finally, there is one oddity: Baroco is reduced to Barbara by contradiction or "reduction to absurdity."

Memorizing these names is not the only way to see if a categorical syllogism is valid. After all, Aristotle himself had no verse to consult; he had to look at each possible combination, all 256. Over the centuries, many logicians have taken a different approach. They have tried to devise *rules* for determining whether a syllogism is valid. Logic books vary greatly in the number of rules they offer. Part of the fun in logic, as in mathematics, is trying to devise a system with the fewest rules. In Lesson 25, I'll set out my own four rules for valid syllogisms. (This is the fewest number of rules I could devise, fewer than the number found in other logic textbooks.) We'll meet them after doing Problem Set 24 here, which is designed to give you practice in spotting the structure of a categorical syllogism. As is often the case in logic, distinguishing the *form* of a syllogism from its *content* is an art or skill we have to learn, easier for some people, harder for others. Take as much time as you need to become proficient at separating the matter from the form of the syllogisms in Problem Set 24. Then try to decide if you think each syllogism is valid or invalid. You can use the medieval mnemonic to check your work.

Problem Set 24: Identifying Categorical Syllogisms

Syllogisms in Standard Form

Instructions

For each syllogism, identify (a) minor term and minor premise; (b) major term and major premise; (c) middle term; (d) conclusion; (e) figure; and (f) mood.

Then try to figure out *intuitively* whether the syllogism is valid or invalid.

1. All animals are living things.
   All cheetahs are animals.
   Therefore, all cheetahs are living things.
2. All carpenters are industrious.
   All swindlers are industrious.
   Therefore, all swindlers are carpenters.
3. Every circle is a geometrical figure.
   Every circle is round.
   Therefore, some round things are geometrical figures.
4. No stones are soft.
   Every pillow is soft.
   Therefore, no pillow is a stone.
5. All gang members are rude.
   No Boy Scout is a gang member.
   Therefore, no Boy Scout is rude.
6. All Frenchmen are wine drinkers.
   Some beer drinkers are not wine drinkers.
   Therefore, some beer drinkers are not Frenchmen.
7. All NASA engineers have graduate degrees.
   But no one with a graduate degree left school at the age of ten.
   Therefore, no one who left school at the age of ten is a NASA engineer.

Syllogisms in Normal Prose

Instructions

For each of the following categorical syllogisms, identify: (a) minor term and minor premise; (b) major term and major premise; (c) middle term; (d) conclusion; (e) figure; (f) mood. Then try to figure out *intuitively* whether each syllogism is valid or invalid.

1. Socrates was a man. And all men have souls. So Socrates had a soul.

2. No Roman legionnaires survived the battle of Adrianople. But all the Roman heavy cavalry survived that battle. So none of the Roman heavy cavalry were Roman legionnaires.

3. Frenchmen are very logical and since Houstonians are not Frenchmen, we can conclude that Houstonians are not very logical.

4. All subatomic particles are invisible to the human eye. We know this because all subatomic particles have to be seen with electronic microscopes, and most things invisible to the human eye have to be seen with electron microscopes.

5. Since some Democrats are socialists, and some socialists are friendly guys, we can conclude that some friendly guys are Democrats.

6. All Republicans are capitalists. And no capitalists are friendly guys. So it follows that no friendly guys are Republicans.

7. All patriots are voters. And some citizens are not voters. So some citizens are not patriots.

8. No philosopher is a mathematician. But mathematicians know what mathematics is. So no philosopher knows what mathematics is.

Validity of Categorical Syllogisms

The Essentials

The Usefulness of Rules to Show Validity

As the initial explorer of the terrain of formal logic, Aristotle contented himself with discovering which kinds of categorical syllogisms are valid and indicating how each valid type of syllogism worked. At least, he did so for the first three figures of the categorical syllogism. He did not recognize the fourth as a distinct figure, not because the fourth was completely unknown to him, but because it is the inverse of the first figure and therefore can be "reduced" to the first figure. Later logicians disagreed and gave the fourth figure its own rightful place. As schoolmasters, logicians saw the need to simplify and standardize Aristotle's account of what makes syllogisms valid or invalid. One way they did this was to invent devices like the poem we saw in Lesson 24. But such a mnemonic device cannot explain to curious students *why* a syllogism is valid or invalid. So later, many schoolmaster logicians turned to the technique of devising rules for determining the validity of syllogisms. Students could memorize the rules, learn to apply them, and perhaps come to see why the rules are good ones—how they work to separate the "wheat from the chaff" among categorical syllogisms.

As I write this chapter I have before me five different texts in Aristotelian logic, all written in the twentieth century. It is surprising how different are their accounts of the rules for validity. All agree that to be valid a syllogism must follow *all* the rules; violating any rule is enough to cast a syllogism into the outer darkness of invalid arguments, where there is "the weeping and gnashing of (logical) teeth." But about the number, content, and explanation of the rules, they differ widely. One book has eight rules. A second book follows Aristotle in denying the fourth figure and then goes on to list five "general rules," to which it adds six "particular rules for each figure," for a total of eleven rules for only three figures. And three of the books give no rules at all, but substitute instructions for how to use Venn diagrams to determine validity.

In order to simplify them as much as I can, I have reduced the rules to four. And in order for you to see that these rules are by no means arbitrary, I have attempted to show how they *flow from the very nature of a syllogism*. In fact, the rules are just convenient ways of codifying certain formal features of a valid syllogism. The first rule concerns the *basic structure* of the syllogism; the three propositions must contain only three terms, no more and no less. The second rule concerns the *quantity* of the *middle term*. The third rule concerns the *quantity* of the *minor* and *major* terms. And the fourth rule concerns the *quality* of the three propositions in the syllogism. A good way of understanding any rules is to look at the violations of the rules, along with the rules themselves. In fact, that most classic of all lists of rules—the Ten Commandments—lists mainly the violations of the rules, even though each negative commandment implies certain positive injunctions. Violation of a logical rule is called a "fallacy" (from the Latin word for deceit), and reasoning that violates a logical rule is called "fallacious." We'll first look at the four rules themselves, then after that, in "A Deeper Look," we'll cover the fallacies, as well.

To help us understand the rules, we'll look at all four rules using a syllogism that we can see easily is valid, because the kind of reasoning is already familiar to us. Consider this First Figure, AAA syllogism:

All animals (M) are living things (P).
All leopards (S) are animals (M).
Therefore, all leopards (S) are living things (P).

Rule One: A Valid Syllogism Must Have Three and Only Three Terms

The description of a syllogism in Lesson 23 actually covers this rule. The reason why a basic categorical syllogism must have exactly three terms comes from the fact that the syllogism is a way of reasoning from what we already know—the two premises—to what we do not yet know—the conclusion. In order to move from the premises to the conclusion, each of the two terms in the conclusion—the S and P terms—must occur in one of the two premises. If this were not true, our conclusion would just be a "stab in the dark"; we wouldn't have a basis in knowledge for drawing a conclusion about S and P. At the other extreme, neither of the premises can contain both the S and P terms as stated in the conclusion, because then we wouldn't be gaining any new knowledge at all. We would just be saying "because S is P, it follows that S is P." Now this is not an inference that gives us any new knowledge. There must be a middle term (M) that justifies our linking together S and P in the conclusion.

In our example, "leopards" is the minor term (S); "living things" is the major term (P); and "animals" is the middle term (M) that links together S and P.

A helpful way to think of the need for a middle term is actually to start with the conclusion and ask yourself: what is it that helps us understand that S is linked to P? Or why is P "predicated of" or "said of" S, as Aristotle would put it? What helps us and justifies us in linking S with P is the middle term. But if the middle term occurred only in one premise, then it couldn't link together the S and P terms in the conclusion. The only way to attain this linkage is for the middle term to be repeated, that is, for it to be found in both premises. Then it can serve as a link that connects S and P. You can represent how the middle term does this diagrammatically.

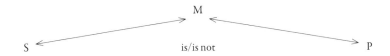

Here are a few examples that illustrate how the middle term helps answer a question:

1. Question: Why are all insects (S) living creatures (P)? Answer: because insects are a type of animal (M).

2. Question: Why does a stack of magazines tied up in a bundle (S) not burn up very easily (P)? Answer: because it is hard for oxygen to get to the paper sheets when they are compacted tightly (M).

3. Question: Why do snowshoes or skis (S) help you to walk on snow better than using just your feet (P)? Answer: they distribute your weight over a wider surface area, so there is not as much pressure on each part of the surface of the snow (M).

Rule One simply stated: S and P must be "linked" together through M.

Rule Two: the Middle Term of a Valid Syllogism Must Be Distributed at Least Once

In our example, "animals" is the middle term (M) that links together "leopards" (S) and "animals" (P). Rule Two states that the middle term, which only occurs in the two premises, must be *distributed* in at least one of them. "Distributed" is simply a traditional synonym for "universal," while its opposite, "undistributed," is a synonym for "particular." The word "distributed" was used to indicate that the term is applied or "distributed" all the way across its full extension, including everything it signifies. Why does the middle term have to be universal at least once? The reason is because it is the middle term that links the S and P terms in the conclusion. But to have a valid syllogism, we must be certain that the linkage between S and P is *tight* or *secure*. The problem of a *loose* or undistributed middle term can arise in cases where the middle term, when used in the major premise, is particular and so can refer only to *one part* of the class of things it signifies, while when that same middle term is used in the minor premise, it is also particular but refers only to *another part* of the class of things signified by the middle term. In our example, "animals" in the major premise ("All animals are living things") is universal; it covers all animals. So the syllogism is in accord with Rule Two. In the minor premise, however, it is not universal, because only some of the animals in existence are leopards. But Rule Two is still followed, in the major premise. The only way to ensure that the middle term will actually connect the S and P terms in the conclusion is for the middle term to be *universal* in at least one premise. It can be universal in both; that would just make the linkage between S and P *extra secure* or *double tight*.

Rule Two simply stated: M must "securely link" S and P.

Rule Three: The Minor and Major Terms of a Valid syllogism
Must Be Properly Extended

In Rule Two we compared the way the middle term was used in the two premises. In Rule Three we are looking at the minor term (S), "leopards" in our example, and the major term (P), "living things." In Rule Three we compare the two usages of the minor term, in the minor premise and the conclusion, and the two usages of the major term, in the major premise and the conclusion. The point to remember in these comparisons is that in a syllogism we are proving something new—the conclusion—not out of thin air, but based on what we already know—the two premises. We can draw a new conclusion validly, but not one that goes completely beyond the information with which we started. For example, if we start our reasoning by knowing about Oedipus and Jocasta and Thebes, we have no basis for drawing a conclusion about George Washington and Virginia and cherry trees. The same thing holds true for the *quantity* of the terms we are using in a syllogism. If we start out knowing about *some* of the students in our class, say, that they are women, we cannot deduce a conclusion about *all* the students in the class, say, that they are all women; at least, we can't draw the conclusion just from knowing about only *some of the students*. Rule Three tells us that, for the minor and major terms, we cannot expand our conclusion beyond the information base we had in our premises. If the term is particular in a premise, it must be particular in the conclusion; we cannot expand it to a universal term in the conclusion. That would be like going from knowing about some of the people in class to drawing a conclusion about all the people in class. On the other hand, if the major or minor term is universal in its premise, then it can be either universal or particular in the conclusion. If we know, for example, that *all* the students in class are under thirty years old, we can easily deduce that *some* of them must be under thirty years old.

In our example, the minor term "leopards" is universal in the minor premiss, and it is universal in the conclusion. And the major term "living things" is particular in the major premiss, and particular in the conclusion. So this syllogism follows Rule Three.

There are really two ways to state Rule Three, a positive formulation and a negative one.

Rule Three (stated positively): a term that is universal in the conclusion must be universal in its premise; but a term that is particular in the conclusion can be either particular or universal in its premise.

Rule Three (stated negatively): you cannot go from a particular term in a premise to a universal term in the conclusion.

Rule Three simply stated: don't go "beyond your information base" about S and P.

Rule Four: The Quality of the Conclusion of a Valid Syllogism Follows the Quality of the *Weaker* Premise

Rule One concerned the basic structure of a syllogism: an argument with three propositions but only three terms. Rules Two and Three concerned the quantity of the three terms in the syllogism. Rule Four concerns the quality of the three propositions that make up the syllogism. The rule is stated using the concepts of "weaker" and "stronger" premise. To know things we use both negative and affirmative propositions: "humans are animals"; "humans are not toads." These two simple examples show that affirmative propositions are inherently "stronger" in giving us knowledge of things because they tell us something positive and real about things. Negative propositions only tell us about what something is not, not what it is. We could multiply negative propositions about the subject *human* indefinitely, and, while we would know something in knowing what humans *are not*, these propositions would not amount to nearly as true a knowledge of humans as the one sentence "humans are rational animals." In general, negative propositions are weaker than affirmative propositions.

Once we see the relative strength of negative and affirmative propositions, it becomes easier to understand Rule Four. Consider the possibilities.

(1) If *both* the premises are *affirmative* and a conclusion follows validly, it must be affirmative. The reason why is that two affirmative premises don't open up the possibility of saying anything negative unless we add on a third, negative premise. But they can authorize an affirmative conclusion: "If Socrates is a man, and all men are animals," then this leads to the affirmative conclusion that "Socrates is an animal," but it doesn't lead the mind to any negative conclusions, like "Socrates is not a god." In our example, both the premises are affirmative, and so is the conclusion. So our example follows Rule Four.

(2) If *one* premise is *affirmative* and the other premise is negative, any conclusion validly drawn must be negative. The reason why is that a negative proposition separates its subject from its conclusion: "Humans are *not* centipedes." If one premise separates the middle term from the S or P term, then the only kind of conclusion we can draw will separate S and P. If "humans

aren't centipedes," we *might be* able to use "centipedes" to draw a negative conclusion about humans; but we are not in any position to draw a positive conclusion about humans.

(3) What about two negative premises? Here no conclusion can be drawn. Consider these premises: "No murderers are friendly people" and "No friendly people are drunks." Can we use the middle term "friendly people" to draw any *definite* conclusion relating *murderers* and *drunks*? Definitely not. There *might* be some murderers who are also drunks; but then again they might be two completely separate groups. These two negative premises don't give us enough information to be sure even about a negative conclusion.

We can sum up these three possibilities:

Rule Four: the quality of the conclusion follows the weaker premise.

1. From two affirmative premises, only an affirmative conclusion can be drawn.
2. From one affirmative premise and one negative premise, only a negative conclusion can be drawn.
3. From two negative premises, no conclusion can be drawn.

A Deeper Look

Violating Rule One: The Fallacy of Equivocation

It is generally easy to determine if a syllogism follows Rule One. Just make sure there are three and only three terms in the syllogism: S, M, and P.

There are, however, two ways that Rule One can be violated. For easier syllogisms, sometimes one of the three terms—while repeating the same language—means something different. When the same term is used in different sentences, but means something different, this is called "equivocation." And when this happens in a syllogism, the connections that particular term should ensure are not made.

I have an example from raising my children. When she was about eleven, one of my daughters and I were walking along South Braeswood Ave., from Chimney Rock Blvd. to Hillcroft St., in Houston, where we stopped at our favorite donut shop. Upon leaving the shop we split up, but agreed that we would "meet at the bank" in thirty minutes. As you might expect, I went into the bank building across Hillcroft, while my daughter went to the riverbank of Braes Bayou, across South Braeswood Ave.

For other syllogisms, something similar but more difficult can happen. Sometimes we think we are reading (or hearing) a categorical syllogism, but we are having a hard time finding the three terms. For writers and speakers seldom are as careful with the terms they use as they might be. (This is actually a good thing, since completely logical language is usually boring. Read British philosophers of the fourteenth or the twentieth centuries for evidence.) The solution here is to analyze carefully what the author is saying. Remember to look *through the words* to the *concepts* he or she is trying to express. Here the trick is to simplify without distorting, by putting the author's meaning *in your own words*. This is why learning to put an argument into your own, simplified language is absolutely necessary for understanding what you read and for increasing your logical proficiency.

Violating Rule Two: The Fallacy of the "Undistributed" Middle Term

The fallacy that violates Rule Two is called the fallacy of the "undistributed middle term," where the middle term is *particular* in both premises. A classic case of an undistributed middle is a second-figure AAA syllogism, as in no. 2 in Problem Set 24:

All dogs are living creatures.
All cats are living creatures.
Therefore, all cats are dogs.

We already know independently from this syllogism that the conclusion is false. But remember that we can have a valid syllogism and still derive a false conclusion if one of the premises is false. Since both premises are true, on first inspection we strongly suspect that this syllogism is invalid. And we can see pretty easily that the problem is with the middle term. But what exactly is the problem? It comes to light if we systematically go through all the terms and determine the quantity for each. Since the major premise, minor premise, and conclusion are all A propositions, their subjects are universal, but their predicates are particular. Think about the middle term this way. The major premise unites *all dogs* with only *some* of the *living creatures*, because the premise leaves open at least the possibility that there are other living creatures besides dogs. And the same is true of the minor premise: *all cats* are identical with only *some* of the *living creatures*. Now are we assured that there is any overlap or identity between *the living creatures that are dogs* and *the living creatures that are cats*? No, we are not. They are like two quite separate slices of the big pie of *living creatures*. The only way to ensure *secure linkage* between the S and P terms in the predicate, therefore, is when the M term refers to the *whole* M class at least once—that is, when it universal at least once.

Violating Rule Three: The Fallacy of the Overextended Term

"Overextension" of a term means extending the quantity from particular to universal. There are two kinds of "overextended" terms. If the *minor* term is overextended, the fallacy is called "Illicit Minor." The term "licit" comes from the Latin word *lex*, which means "law" or "rule." So an *illicit* term is one that is *illegal* or *unlawful*, according to the rules of logic, because it breaks those rules. If the *major* term is overextended, the fallacy is called "Illicit Major." No. 3 in Problem Set 25 is an example of an overextended term.

> All cops are well-trained.
> No firemen are cops.
> Therefore, no firemen are well-trained.

As was true for the middle term, the way to determine this argument is fallacious is to compare the extension or quantity between the two usages of the minor term and between the two usages of the major term. First determine the quantity for all six usages of the terms in the syllogism.

> All cops (universal) are well-trained (particular).
> No firemen (universal) are cops (universal).
> Therefore, no firemen (universal) are well-trained (universal).

The minor term "firemen" obeys Rule Three, because it goes from universal in the minor premise to universal in the conclusion. We have *not* illicitly overextended the number of firemen we are talking about, when we move from premise to conclusion. But the major term is a different case. Here "well-trained" is a *particular* term in the premise, but "well-trained" is a *universal* term in the conclusion. We have gone well beyond the bounds of our information base in moving from the major premise to the conclusion. The problem is this: we don't start off knowing about *all* the *well-trained* people, we only know about *some* of them (cops); and we never learn information about the other *well-trained* people outside the group we started off knowing about (firemen). We have extended our conclusion beyond our information base.

Violating Rule Four: Not Following the "Weaker" Premise

Over the centuries, logicians have never devised a name for violations of Rule Four. This is undoubtedly because this rule is the easiest to understand intuitively, so that very seldom do we violate it.

Rule Four stated simply:

a. "affirmative" plus "affirmative" = "affirmative."
b. "affirmative" plus "negative" = "negative."
c. "negative" plus "negative" = nothing.

Using the Rules

The problems in Problem Set 25 are already set up for you. The first sentence is the major premise; the second sentence is the minor premise; and the third sentence is the conclusion. To use the rules, the best technique is to go through the rules in order:

a. Find the three terms: minor term, major term, middle term.
b. Determine the figure of the syllogism.
c. Determine the mood of the syllogism. (Remember that validity is determined by the combination of figure and mood; however, you can use the rules even if you don't recognize the figure and mood.)
d. Check the syllogism using Rule 1.
e. Determine the quantity for each of the six terms in the syllogism.
f. Check the middle term using Rule 2.
g. Check the minor term using Rule 3.
h. Check the major term using Rule 3.
i. Check the quality of the conclusion using Rule 4.

Some people will find the syllogisms in Problem Set 25 to be quite easy, while others will find some of them more difficult. Even if you find them to be easier, master this systematic technique for checking validity. If you don't need it for a particular syllogism, fine; but everyone will have to rely on it at some point in the course. Everyone should master the technique of using the rules *now*. Please notice that using the rules depends upon your mastering material from the logic of terms and from the logic of propositions. Throughout our treatment of the logic of arguments, we will depend upon the two earlier parts of logic. If there is something you now need but that you didn't quite master earlier (say, distinguishing the four different kinds of categorical propositions), go back to the earlier lesson and problem set and *practice* until you *perfect* your logical habits on *that point* we covered earlier. Then come back to Problem Set 25.

Problem Set 25: Validity of Categorical Syllogisms

Using the Rules to Determine Validity

RULES FOR VALIDITY, BRIEFLY STATED

Rule	*Fallacy*
1. Three terms (= link)	Equivocation
2. Universal middle term (= secure link)	Undistributed middle
3. Proper extension of major & minor (= limit the extension)	Overextension Illicit minor term Illicit major term

4. Correct quality, quality follows the
   weaker premise

   (-) & (-) = no conclusion
   (+) & (-) = (-) conclusion
   (+) & (+) = (+) conclusion

Instructions

Determine whether the following syllogisms are valid or invalid, using the four rules. First, identify: major term, minor term, middle term, figure, mood, *and* validity, using the following schema for your answer:

Major premise:
Minor premise:
Conclusion:
Figure:
Mood:
V/I:
Rule violated:

Try to rewrite the propositions, putting them into **standard form.** This will make it easier to test for validity.

The Logic of Arguments

A: All S is P.
I: Some S is P.
E: No S is P.
O: Some S is not P.

1. All humans are rational.
   None of the people who failed the test were rational
   Therefore, none of the people who failed the test are humans.
2. All dogs are living creatures.
   All cats are living creatures.
   Therefore, all cats are dogs.
3. All cops are well-trained.
   No firemen are cops.
   Therefore, no firemen are well-trained.
4. No carpenter is a professor of history.
   All professors of history love the study of history.
   Therefore, no one who loves the study of history is a carpenter.
5. Every fisherman loves the sea.
   No drug dealer is a fisherman
   Therefore, no drug dealer loves the sea.
6. Every fisherman loves the sea.
   Some Texans love the sea.
   Therefore, some Texans are fishermen.
7. Every fisherman loves the sea.
   Some Houstonians are fishermen.
   Therefore, some Houstonians love the sea.
8. Every circle is round.
   Every circle is a geometrical figure.
   Therefore, some geometrical figures are round.
9. No squares are circles.
   All circles are geometrical figures.
   Therefore, some geometrical figures are not squares.
10. All waves obey wave equations.
    All matter obeys wave equations.
    Therefore, all matter is waves.
11. All patriots are voters.
    Some citizens are not voters.
    Therefore, some citizens are not patriots.

12. Everything good is pleasant.
    All eating is pleasant.
    Therefore, all eating is good.
13. All the dishes were used.
    Some of the dishes were also washed.
    Therefore, some of the things washed were also used.
14. All rodents have four incisor teeth.
    All rats are rodents.
    Therefore, all rats have four incisor teeth.
15. Some rodents are rats.
    All rodents have four incisor teeth.
    Therefore, some animals with four incisor teeth are rats.
16. All rats are rodents.
    Every animal with four incisors is a rodent.
    Therefore, some animals with four incisors are rats.
17. Every crustacean has a hard outer shell.
    Every lobster is a crustacean.
    Therefore, every lobster has a hard outer shell.
18. No lobsters are good to eat.
    Every lobster is a crustacean.
    Therefore, no crustaceans are good to eat.
19. All Italians are Europeans.
    Some artists are Europeans.
    Therefore, some artists are Italians.

Categorical Syllogisms in Prose

The Essentials

In this lesson we take one more step toward the kinds of syllogisms you encounter in everyday speech, in more formal and serious speech, in writing, and in published works. The main difference between Problem Set 25 and Problem Set 26 is that here the problems are set out as prose passages.

Analyzing Arguments in Prose

The very first thing you have to do here is to determine whether or not there is an argument in the passage. The way to do that is first to look for a possible conclusion. Quite often there are telltale words that mark a conclusion, just as we learned that there are a variety of words that point out different kinds of hypothetical statements. Once you have spotted what you think is the conclusion, then search around for premises. In a categorical syllogism, the conclusion will be a categorical proposition. And the conclusion will contain two terms—the minor and major terms. Once you have spotted them, the search for premises becomes easier, because each of the two premises will contain either the minor or major term. In this way you can uncover the middle term. At this point, you can arrange the syllogism into the order we have called its standard form.

major premise
minor premise
conclusion

Now look carefully at the three terms. It is usually very helpful to *simplify* each of the three propositions that make up the argument. To clarify the terms and what kinds of propositions make up the syllogism, it is usually best to try to *restate each of the propositions in your own way*, to paraphrase the argument in a way that makes the terms and propositions more precise. Then try to put your formulation of each proposition in standard form. It helps to *simplify* without distorting the *subject, predicate,* and *middle terms.* It also helps to make *explicit* the *quantity* of each proposition. And be sure you are clear about whether each proposition is affirmative or negative—the *quality* of the proposition. These points will help you to determine if the proposition is A, I, E, or O. Be especially careful about the *logical* subjects and predicates, which need not be the same as grammatical subjects and verbs. In everyday arguments we often change back and forth between terms and their opposites—even in the same arguments. Be sure you express the terms of the syllogism consistently. And always remember that the copula is *hidden* within each verb.

Once you have simplified and clarified the three propositions that make up the categorical syllogism, it's time to test it for validity. You can go immediately to the four rules, or you can determine its figure and mood to help decide whether it is valid or invalid. Until you have mastered the rules and can use them easily, it is best to rewrite the argument in standard form *before* you test it for validity.

By the end of this process, in which you are analyzing the argument in prose, you should know major term, minor term, middle term, major premise, minor premise, conclusion, figure, mood, and validity (and if it is invalid, which rule is violated). These are the points upon which you will be quizzed and tested.

A Deeper Look

Steps in Analyzing Categorical Syllogisms in Prose

1. Determine if there is an argument at all. If so, make a preliminary guess about whether it is valid.

2. In your analysis, look first for the conclusion.
3. Identify the S and P terms in the conclusion.
4. If the conclusion is a categorical proposition, look for premises to see if the argument is a categorical syllogism.
5. Use the S and P terms to find premises that contain them.
6. The premises will help you discover the M term.
7. Put the *argument* into *standard logical order*: major premise; minor premise; conclusion.
8. Clarify the argument by restating the two premises and the conclusion as simply as you can, putting all three *propositions* into *standard logical form.*
9. Apply the four rules in order.
10. A syllogism is valid only if it obeys *all* four rules.

Verbal Indicators of Premises and Conclusions

Words That Often *Precede Premises*

if
since
because
for
as, inasmuch as
the reason is
inferred from
derived from
proven by

Words That Often *Precede a Conclusion*

therefore
then
hence
so
accordingly
consequently
proves
as a result

thus

for this reason, [conclusion then stated]

it follows

shows

implies

There are, of course, syllogisms that do not have verbal indicators for premises or conclusions. But most arguments do give some kind of verbal hint. Another kind of verbal indicator often used is to introduce the language of necessity into the conclusion. For example, "X and Y being so, Socrates *must* have been a pious man." The language of necessity points out the conclusion.

Problem Set 26: Categorical Syllogisms in Prose

Using the Rules to Determine Validity

Instructions

Determine whether the following syllogisms are valid or invalid, using the four rules. Identify: major term, minor term, middle term, figure, mood, *and* validity, using **standard logical order**, as follows:

Major premise:
Minor premise:
Conclusion:
Figure:
Mood:
V/I:
Rule violated:

Rewrite the propositions, putting them into **standard form**. The reason for doing this is to make sure you understand the logical form of the syllogism—its figure and mood—in order to determine whether it is valid.

A: All S is P.
I: Some S is P.
E: No S is P.
O: Some S is not P.

1. My mother wears army shoes. And everyone who wears army shoes was in the army. So can't you see that my mother was in the army? (from W. R. Houser, my father, a World War II veteran)

2. Now you know, John, that raccoons shed their fur at the end of May. Since the South American mirana also sheds its fur in May, the mirana must be a raccoon.

3. Georgette will learn logic easily because she is interested in it, and interest makes for easy learning.

4. Frenchmen are very logical and, in view of the fact that Texans are not Frenchmen, we may conclude that they are not very logical.

5. You can't call a baby a rational animal, for a rational animal is able to reason and a baby is not able to reason.

6. Granted that no provident person wastes money, and that some provident persons are generous, it is also true that some generous persons do not waste money.

7. Assuming that he is over forty and that baseball players are too old at forty for the major leagues, he will have to be dropped from the roster.

8. Seeing that stocks have been falling in price for several months this year, and that a decline in stock prices invariably heralds a recession, we may infer that we are in for a lag in the economy.

9. Every religious person goes to church every Sunday. I see that Fr. Miller goes to church every Sunday, so I am quite confident that Fr. Miller is a religious man.

10. We know that whatever has long claws can be very harmful. We also know that black bears have long claws. It is clear, then, that black bears can be very harmful.

11. Every poor mechanic is a menace to society, for every poor mechanic fails in his responsibilities to society. And everyone knows that those who are a menace to society fail in their responsibilities to society.

12. Since some burrowing mammals are carnivores, and not every raccoon is a burrowing mammal, some raccoons are not carnivores.

13. I tell you that fossils are the hardened remains of plant or animal life from a previous geological era. The reason is that fossils are preserved in rock formations. And some of the things preserved in rock forma-

tions are the hardened remains of plant or animal life from a previous geological period.

14. Since every parrot has a brightly colored triangular beak and the pelican is not a parrot, we can conclude that the pelican does not have a brightly colored triangular beak.

15. Apes are never angels; and philosophers are never apes; therefore philosophers are never angels.

Venn Diagrams of Categorical Syllogisms

The Essentials

Before beginning this lesson, it would be helpful to go back and reread Lesson 16. This will refresh your knowledge of how to use Venn diagrams for categorical *propositions*. What you have learned subsequently is that a categorical syllogism has three parts—major premise, minor premise, and conclusion. You will remember that what makes a valid categorical syllogism work is the combined effect of both premises. When taken together, they necessitate the conclusion. What is helpful about Venn diagrams of categorical *syllogisms* is that they show how the conclusion follows from the premises in a very interesting way. What you do is diagram both premises on the same geometrical figure, this time one made of three, not two, interlocking circles. If the argument is valid and you diagram the premises correctly, the conclusion will already be found in the diagram. You don't diagram the conclusion, but you *see* the conclusion in the diagram of the two premises. The fact that the conclusion is already there is the sign that the argument is valid. If the conclusion is not already there, then the syllogism is invalid. You can see visually why an invalid argument is invalid—where it falls down.

The Basic Venn Diagram of a Syllogism

A good way to begin diagramming categorical syllogisms is to diagram each of the two premises by itself. Then transfer the diagram of each premise onto the three-circle figure. Putting both premises into the same figure shows the combined impact of the premises. But you do have to be careful. In the Venn diagram of a syllogism there are three circles, one standing for the subject term of the conclusion (the minor term), the second standing for the predicate term of the conclusion (the major term), and one standing for the middle term that provides the *bridge* linking the minor and major terms. Consider the basic figure for Venn diagrams of syllogisms, before we have drawn either premise into it.

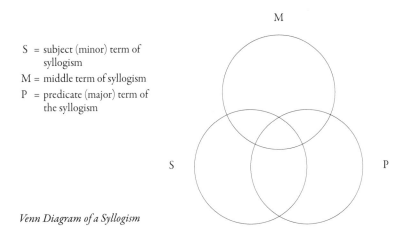

S = subject (minor) term of syllogism
M = middle term of syllogism
P = predicate (major) term of the syllogism

Venn Diagram of a Syllogism

This is the standard and easiest configuration of the Venn diagram of a categorical syllogism. The S or minor term is in the lower left circle, the P or major term is in the lower right circle, and the M or middle term is in the upper circle. When we look for the conclusion we will be looking at the two lower circles, in an order that runs from S to P in looking from left to right. If your geometrical imagination is good enough, however, you can take any circle for any of the three terms.

You will probably have noticed that, since there are three circles instead of two, each circle is divided into four parts, not just two, as happened when we diagramed categorical propositions. This means you will have to be careful when hatching out or shading areas and also when putting an X in an area.

Quite often you must put an X on the line that divides a common area into two parts, because the proposition you are diagramming cannot, by itself, determine on which side of this dividing line the X falls. This will become clear as we go through examples. First, let's divide up the diagram for a syllogism into numbered parts, as we did for the Venn diagrams of propositions.

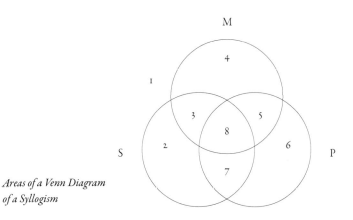

Areas of a Venn Diagram
of a Syllogism

Be sure you understand what each numbered area represents. You need to describe each area in relation to *all three circles*.

Area 1 = nonhuman, nonanimal, nonliving, or non-S, non-M, non-P.
Area 2 = human, nonanimal, nonliving, or S, non-M, non-P.
Area 3 = human, animal, nonliving, or S, M, non-P.
Area 4 = nonhuman, animal, nonliving, or non-S, M, non-P.
Area 5 = nonhuman, animal, living, or non-S, M, P.
Area 6 = nonhuman, nonanimal, living, or non-S, non-M, P.
Area 7 = human, nonanimal, living, or S, non-M, P.
Area 8 = human, animal, living, or S, M, P

Venn Diagram of a First-Figure AAA Syllogism

Now let's diagram a first-figure AAA syllogism.

Major premise:	All animals are living things.	All M is P.
Minor premise:	All humans are animals.	All S is M.
Conclusion:	Therefore, all humans are living things.	So, all S is P.

The S circle (human) is made up of areas 2, 3, 7, and 8. The M circle (animal) is made up of areas 3, 4, 5, and 8. And the P circle (living thing) is made up of 5, 6, 7, and 8.

When we diagram the major premise, we will hatch or shade both areas 3 and 4, since they fall outside the circle of *living things*. And we will have to put an X somewhere in the area made up of 5 and 8, since they represent things that are both animals and living things. But the proposition "All animals are living things," *considered just by itself*, does not say whether the animals we are talking about are human (area 8) or nonhuman (area 5). So we will have to put the X *on the line* between areas 5 and 8.

When we diagram the minor premise, something similar happens. We have to hatch or shade areas 2 and 7, which signify things that would be human but not animals. We have to put an X into the common area, somewhere in area 3 or 8. If we had not already diagrammed the major premise, we would put the X on the line between 3 and 8. But we have already diagrammed the major premise, and in doing so we hatched or shaded out area 3. The only place for the X to go is in area 8.

Can we see the conclusion—"All humans are living things"—already in the Venn diagram of the two premises? Yes, we can. What we need to see are two things. First, areas 2 and 3 need to be hatched or shaded out; and they are. Second, we need to find an X somewhere in the common area between "human" and "living thing." That common area is made up of areas 7 and 8. And there is an X in area 8. The two requirements for the conclusion already being in the diagram are met, so the syllogism is valid.

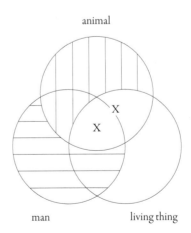

animal

*Diagram of a Valid
Affirmative Syllogism*   man   living thing

A Deeper Look

Venn Diagram of a Valid Negative Syllogism

Let's take one more example of a valid syllogism, this time one with a negative conclusion. Syllogisms of the first figure EAE are valid. Consider the following syllogism:

Major premise:	No mammal with a trunk is a kangaroo.	No M is P.
Minor premise:	All elephants are mammals with trunks.	All S is M.
Conclusion:	So, no elephants are kangaroos.	No S is P.

Again, we will make use of the areas of the diagram as numbered, divided into eight areas. We'll diagram the major premise first.

The major premise is a universal negative proposition, so areas 5 and 8 must be hatched or shaded. An X needs to be put somewhere in areas 3 and 4. From the major premise alone, we don't yet know whether the *mammals with a trunk* are elephants (area 3) or not (area 4), so we'll put the X on the line between areas 3 and 4. At this point we know there are some mammals with trunks that are not kangaroos, but that is all we know.

Now let's add the minor premise to our diagram. This is a universal affirmative proposition (A), whose subject is elephants. We know that we need to hatch or shade out everything in the S circle that is outside the M circle. These are areas 2 and 7. We also know that there exist elephants with trunks, areas 3 and 8 in the diagram. But area 8 has already been hatched or shaded out when we diagrammed the major premise. The only place where the X that is part of the minor premise can fall is in area 3.

Can we see the conclusion "No elephant is a kangaroo" already in the diagram? Yes, for two reasons. First, areas 7 and 8 must be hatched or shaded out, in this way separating the elephants from the kangaroos; and they are. Second, there must be an X somewhere in the elephant circle. Again, there is; the X is in area 3. You can see in the diagram that this syllogism is valid (and so too are all first-figure EAE syllogisms).

mammal with a trunk

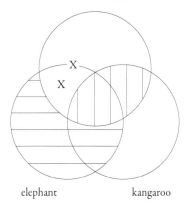

elephant   kangaroo

Finally, let's consider an invalid syllogism. Here is a second-figure AAA syllogism.

Major premise:	All cats are animals.	All P is M.
Minor premise:	All dogs are animals.	All S is M.
Conclusion:	Therefore, all dogs are cats.	All S is P.

For this kind of syllogism, diagramming will help us see the undistributed middle term. But we have to be very careful where we place our X's. In diagramming the major premise we also have to remember that "dogs" is its subject, not its predicate. So we'll diagram the major premise moving from P to M, not from M to P (see p. 304).

As with every A proposition, we have to hatch or shade out things that would be cats but not animals, outside the circle of animals—that is, hatch or shade areas 6 and 7. We also have to put an X somewhere in the area common to "cats" and "animals"—that is, areas 5 and 8. But as before, we don't know just from "all dogs are animals" by itself whether the dogs we are talking about are inside the cat circle (area 8) or outside the cat circle (area 5). (Remember, this is an easy example. Of course, we know *from independent information* that cats are not dogs; but we're trying to figure out what we can know *from these two premises alone*.) So what we'll do, as before, is put the X "on the line" between areas 5 and 8. When diagramming the minor premise the same thing happens. We have to hatch or shade out areas 2 and 7 and put an X on the line between areas 3 and 8.

What is the result? If the argument were valid we would have to see two things. First, areas 2 and 3 would both have to be hatched or shaded. But they are not; only area 2 is hatched or shaded out. Since area 3 is still open, there can be a cat that is not a dog. This is one reason the argument is invalid.

Second, some part of the area common to "cats" and "dogs" (areas 7 and 8) would have to have an X in it, in order to show that there really are cats that are dogs. But this is not true either. Area 7 is shaded; there cannot exist any cats that are also dogs in this area. Both the X's are *on the line* adjoining area 8; but this is not enough. There would have to be an X *inside* area 8 in order to know for sure that there exist *cats* that also are *dogs*. The argument is invalid. This is a typical example of an argument with an *undistributed middle term*.

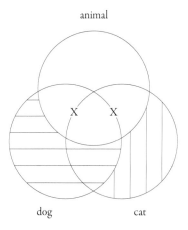

animal

dog   cat

If you are having trouble putting both propositions into the diagram with three interlocking circles, it sometimes helps to begin by diagramming each premise independently. First diagram each premise by itself, using only *two* interlocking circles located outside the final diagram with three circles. Then you can *transfer* the diagram of each premise to the three-circle diagram. When you do this, however, make sure you are careful about where to put X's, since often they go on lines.

The problems in Problem Set 26 are taken from Problem Sets 24 and 25. So go back to them if you need to remind yourself what you decided about the validity of a particular syllogism, when you used the four rules of validity. Your answers using the rules and using diagrams should be the same. Use the method that you find easier to check the results you get using the method that is harder for you. Diagrams are an excellent *backup plan*, but it is easy to make mistakes with them.

Problem Set 27: Venn Diagrams of Categorical Syllogisms

Determining Validity Using Venn Diagrams

Instructions

Draw Venn diagrams for each of the following syllogisms. Using your Venn diagram, determine whether the syllogism is valid. Check your work using the four rules for validity.

1. Every fisherman loves the sea.
   Some Houstonians are fishermen.
   Therefore, some Houstonians love the sea.
2. Every fisherman loves the sea.
   No drug dealer is a fisherman
   Therefore, no drug dealer loves the sea.
3. Every fisherman loves the sea.
   Some Texans love the sea.
   Therefore, some Texans are fishermen.
4. No squares are circles.
   All circles are geometrical figures.
   Therefore, some geometrical figures are not squares.
5. All patriots are voters.
   Some citizens are not voters.
   Therefore, some citizens are not patriots.
6. Everything good is pleasant.
   All eating is pleasant.
   Therefore, all eating is good.
7. All Italians are Europeans.
   Some artists are Europeans.
   Therefore, some artists are Italians.
8. Frenchmen are very logical and, in view of the fact the Texans are not Frenchmen, we may conclude that they are not very logical.
9. Every religious person goes to church every Sunday. I see that Fr. Miller goes to church every Sunday, so I am quite confident that Fr. Miller is a religious man.
10. Since some burrowing mammals are carnivores, and not every raccoon is a burrowing mammal, some raccoons are not carnivores.

Enthymemes and Epicheiremas

The Essentials

What Are Enthymemes and Epicheiremas?

In this lesson we arrive at two kinds of argument we use and encounter in everyday discourse, as well as in what we read and write. What we have called the "standard categorical syllogism" consists of three propositions (two premises and one conclusion) and three terms. Humans being what we are, though, we often leave out parts of our reasoning process. Sometimes this happens because we think the argument so easy to follow that we don't need to put in all three propositions. At other times, we are not quite bright enough to figure out an appropriate premise, but we are confident that the premise we do know is enough to lead to the conclusion. At still other times, we think we have supplied all the premises required, but we have not.

An argument with a missing premise is called an "enthymeme." This Greek word comes from the two words that make it up. An enthymeme leaves part of the argument *en*, or *inside*, our *thymos*, one of many Greek words for the soul or one of its parts. An enthymeme is a syllogism with a missing part. That part may be in our mind, but it is not down on the page or spoken to our audience. In English, we might call an enthymeme a "limping" syllogism, because it misses a leg and so just "limps" along.

An *epicheirema* is the opposite kind of argument. This term has a strange history. Aristotle used it to describe an argument where one tries very hard to give a demonstrative proof of something, but fails. Much later in the history of logic, when in the eighteenth century English logicians were first writing their logic books in the English language as opposed to Latin, they tried to use a lot of Greek terms, as had become popular during the humanist period. "Epicheirema" was one of them, but they changed the meaning of this term from what it had meant for Aristotle. The term comes from the Greek words *epi*, which means *on* or *to*, and *cheir*, which means *hand*, so for these later logicians an *epicheirema* was an argument in which we *really put our hand to the task of proof*, and (unlike what Aristotle himself had said), we often succeed. We will follow this later understanding of the term "epicheirema." An epicheirema contains the basic syllogism, but offers additional argumentative support for one or both of its premises. In English, we might call an epicheirema an "extended argument," though we will see there are other kinds of extended arguments.

Definitions: In short, we can think of an enthymeme as a categorical syllogism with a basic part missing and an epicheirema as a categorical syllogism with an extra part—some sort of evidence supporting one or both of its premises.

Recognizing and Using Enthymemes

Aristotle recognized that we frequently use enthymemes in oral discourse, in speeches and everyday conversation. This is partly because we are lazy, but more because deductive arguments set up in an explicit manner, with all their parts and premises, are often uninteresting and boring because they spend too much time on points that are too easy and too little time on parts that are harder for us. In his *Rhetoric,* Aristotle gave the name "enthymeme" to *any* rhetorical syllogism. We, however, will follow the technical meaning of "enthymeme," as used in *logic,* where it means any deductive argument with part of the basic argument missing. Since there are three primary parts to a categorical syllogism—major premise, minor premise, and conclusion—logicians distinguish the *first-order enthymeme* (which lacks its major premise), from a *second-order enthymeme* (which lacks its minor premise), and from a *third-order enthymeme* (which lacks its conclusion).

In analyzing enthymemes, the first thing to do is recognize that the argument *is* an enthymeme. This is done by first looking for the conclusion—which gives you the minor and major terms—and then using these two terms to search for the two premises. When you have searched hard but can't come up with the missing premise (or missing conclusion), you should suspect the argument is an enthymeme.

But in fairness to the author, you can't stop here and say the argument is invalid just because it misses an important piece. A fair-minded and sympathetic reader will go back to the two propositions that are present and try to *reconstruct* the missing premise. To reconstruct a premise, you determine what the two terms are that make up the missing proposition. You get these terms from the two propositions you do have. Normally you will know the S and P terms from the conclusion, and you will know either S or P, along with the M term, from the one premise you have. Your job as "reconstructor" or "sympathetic reader" is to create the missing premise based on the terms you do have. Most often you will be confronted with two alternative reconstructions, say, "All M is P" or "All P is M." Here you will have to make a *judgment* about what you think the author's intention was. Normally the author had in mind the more obviously true of the possible reconstructed premises, or the one you have more reason to believe he was mentally inserting into the argument, based on other things the author has said. Once you have reconstructed the missing proposition, you need to put together the whole (now reconstructed) syllogism. At this point you can test for validity. If the argument turns out to be invalid, you may want to go back and try the other formulation of the missing premise. However, here is where you need to be careful. It is wrong automatically to assume the author meant the premise that makes the syllogism valid; and it is equally wrong always to use the premise that makes the syllogism invalid.

Some Examples

As usual, let's start off with an example from our problem set.

EXAMPLE 1: Suicide and Wealth

Problem Set 28, number 3: "One can be rich without being happy. The proof is the number of rich people who commit suicide."

This is a good enthymeme on which to practice, since it involves a number of steps. The phrase "The proof is" shows us that the second sentence is a premise. The first sentence should be the conclusion. But when we look carefully at the first sentence, we quickly see that, while "one" is the *grammatical* subject, it is *not* the *logical subject*. "One" is just standing in for the logical subject. The proposition is really about *rich people*; this is its logical subject. So set out in standard form, the conclusion is "Some rich people are not happy." (We could use "unhappy" as the P term, but the syllogism is easier to understand this way, since "happy" actually is used in the conclusion.) The second sentence must be a premise, because it is introduced by "the proof is." But which one? Since its subject is *rich people*, the S term, it must be the minor premise. Once again, this proposition is not stated in standard form; we need to interpret what "the number of" means. It means some number less than all, which makes the minor premise particular. "Some rich people commit suicide." So thus far we have:

Major premise:
Minor premise: Some rich people (S) commit suicide (M).
Conclusion: Some rich people (S) are not happy (P).

From the minor premise and the conclusion we can see that the M term is "people who commit suicide" or "suicides"; while the P term is "happy" or "happy people." At this point we have two possible major premises to try out. We know the Major premise must be a negative proposition, because the conclusion is negative, and we know it must contain the M and P terms.

Possible Major 1: "No people who commit suicide are happy."
Possible Major 2: "No happy people commit suicide."

In this case, the choice between the two possible major premises is easy. Both mean basically the same thing, and the one converts into the other. The argument is valid, whatever premise is chosen. The reconstructed syllogism can be:

Major premise: [No people who commit suicide are happy.]
Minor premise: Some rich people commit suicide.
Conclusion: Some rich people are not happy.

A Deeper Look

A Second Enthymeme

EXAMPLE 2: Islam and Jihad

You should realize, however, that often the possible choices for a missing proposition are *not* equally likely, nor will both be valid. To see this, let's consider Problem Set 28, no. 2: "All the 9/11 attackers were Jihadists. I know this because they all were Muslims." Here we can go through the same process.

The phrase "I know this because" introduces a premise. It looks like "All the 9/11 attackers were Jihadists" is the conclusion, and "all the 9/11 attackers were Muslims" is the stated premise. If so, then S is "9/11 attackers," M is "Muslims," and P is "Jihadists." If you don't know much about Islamic religion and culture, you might think that "Jihadists" is just another name for "Muslims." The only way around this mistake is to learn more about Islam. Once you see that "Muslim" and "Jihadist" do *not* mean the same thing, you can see that there are two possibilities for the Major premise, the two universal affirmative propositions we can form from the M and P terms:

Possible Major 1:   "All Muslims are Jihadists."
Possible Major 2:   "All Jihadists are Muslims."

In this case, it is more difficult to choose the Major premise. No. 1, "All Muslims are Jihadists," would certainly make the syllogism valid. But the proposition isn't actually true. Even if it is true that Islam, as traditionally understood, includes belief in "jihad" or holy war, at least in some circumstances, that would not be enough to make all Muslims "Jihadists"—that is, people who advocate jihad or "religious war" against other Muslims or the Western world, or the United States in particular. (There are plenty of Muslims who understand "jihad" to mean not military war against someone else, but an inner struggle with yourself to improve yourself morally.) On the other hand, the second possibility ("All Jihadists are Muslims"), which is true, produces an *invalid* syllogism.

Choosing between the two possibilities is more difficult in this case without other information about the speaker or writer. Let's look at both options. If Major premise 1 is chosen, then the argument would be valid but unsound, because the Major premise would be false, even if, as the proponents of Islamism say, "all Muslims *should be* Jihadists." If we take possible Major premise 2, then, while this proposition is true, the argument would be invalid. The overall result is that the argument is unsound, because either the Major premise is untrue or the argument is invalid.

Recognizing and Using Epicheiremas

EXAMPLE 3: Bill Jones

If you look at No. 4 in Problem Set 28, you will see the opposite kind of argument. Here there is more to the argument than just the basic syllogism.

> Bill Jones is a local contractor who should not be allowed to stay in business. I know a lot of people, including myself, who were swindled by this contractor. In my own case, I paid him for the cost of both labor and materials for an addition to my home, and as it turned out, later received from the lumber company a bill for the cost of the materials. Talk about cheating! No contractor who is in the habit of swindling people should be allowed to stay in business. So again, I say, let's get rid of people like Bill Jones.

This paragraph begins and ends with what is essentially the same proposition: the conclusion, which is repeated for emphasis. Here we have to state the terms of the conclusion precisely in order to find the two premises. A fair restatement of the conclusion is, "Bill Jones is not a contractor who should be in business." "Bill Jones" is the S term, and "a contractor who should be in business" is the P term. Once we have seen these two terms, then we can see that the second sentence states the minor premise. But we can restate it in simplified form: "Bill Jones is a swindler." This lets us see that "swindler" is M. Reading down the passage, we see that the third and fourth sentences do not give us the major premise, which must be a proposition containing both M and P. But the fifth sentence does contain those two terms; it looks like the major premise. We can set out the basic syllogism in standard form.

Major premise: No swindler is a contractor who should be in business.

Minor premise: Bill Jones is a swindler.

Conclusion: Bill Jones is not a contractor who should be in business.

This basic syllogism is a valid argument—first-figure EAE (or "Celarent"). But what about the third sentence? It is not irrelevant to the basic syllogism, even though it is not one of its two premises or its conclusion. What the third sentence does is offer support for the truth of the Minor premise. To show that "Bill Jones is a swindler," the author offers us his own case. He paid Jones for the cost of the materials, but Jones did not use that money to pay the lumber company for the materials, as he should. He pocketed the money designed to cover both the cost of the labor (and profit) and the cost of the materials. The lumber company gave the materials to Jones in the good-faith expectation he would pay them when he received payment for the job by the author. This is a classic swindle: charging the homeowner for the materials but not paying the lumber company. Because such information gives evidence supporting the truth of the premise, it's called the "proof" of the premise, in this case, the minor premise. In this example, there is no "proof of the Major premise," because the author thinks it obvious that swindling contractors should not be allowed to stay in business.

In addition to the basic syllogism that draws the overall conclusion, then, an epicheirema has either "proof of the major premise" or "proof of the minor premise," or both. In analyzing an epicheirema, you should begin with the basic categorical syllogism. Then look to see if there is additional relevant information. If it takes the form of a proof of one of the premises, then the argument is an epicheirema. Please remember that such proof can take many forms: it might be another categorical syllogism, with the major (or minor) premise of the basic syllogism as its conclusion. But such proof might just as well be some personal experience, recitation of a set of facts, an inductive argument, or simply citing some kind of authority. We'll not worry at this stage about determining the exact form of argument the proof might be; it is enough to understand that the evidence supports one of the two premises.

Legal Arguments

A dispute like the one involving Bill Jones might well end up in court. And this example can give us insight into how legal arguments work. In its basic outline, the legal argument for a case (both for prosecution and defense) has one premise (the major premise) that states the relevant law and a second premise (the minor premise) that states the facts of the case. To prove his case, a lawyer combines the legal premise with the factual premise to produce a conclusion—either guilty or not guilty. Looking at legal arguments this way shows that in order to arrive at a conclusion of guilty or not guilty, a lawyer must address both the facts of this particular case and the law that covers this sort of case. This is why lawyers must be prepared to address both matters of law and matters of fact in their legal arguments. Their arguments about the law that covers the case are like proofs of the major premise. And their arguments about the facts of the case are like proofs of the minor premise. In short, legal cases cannot be won by addressing merely the law or by addressing merely the facts. Both law and facts have to be brought together to argue persuasively and logically in court.

From this brief look at legal arguments, we can learn something important about other arguments over human behavior. Quite often, people try to resolve such disputes by only looking at the facts: "Just give me the facts, ma'am." But by themselves, the "facts" never resolve an argument about human behavior, arguments where we are evaluating the behavior of others or of ourselves. Such arguments always need to address matters of law in a wider sense than statutory law or Constitutional law or precedent, the kinds of law lawyers treat. These arguments need to address a more fundamental and more important kind of law, "moral law," which is the final court of appeal for all moral disputes over how humans behave.

Summary

In analyzing enthymemes and epicheiremas, we employ the techniques for analyzing a regular categorical syllogism in order to see if it is valid. What makes these arguments a bit harder is figuring out how to deal with the missing part or the extra parts of the argument. Mastering these techniques is essential to dealing with more difficult deductive arguments.

Problem Set 28: Enthymemes and Epicheiremas

Identifying and Evaluating Enthymemes and Epicheiremas

Instructions

Determine whether the following arguments are enthymemes, epicheiremas, or use both forms of argument. Then test for validity. Set out your work using the following schema:

Type of syllogism: (1) regular, (2) enthymeme, (3) epicheirema, (4) both enthymeme and epicheirema
Major premise:
Minor premise:
Conclusion:
Figure:
Mood:
Proof of Major Premise (if present):
Proof of Minor Premise (if present):

V/I (Valid or Invalid):
Rule violated:

1. All gentlemen hold open car doors for ladies. I'm presuming that you are a gentleman, Edward. And since you know logic, I'll let you draw your own conclusion. (In memory of my grandmother, Mrs. Josie B. Houser, who taught me this lesson)

2. All the 9/11 attackers were Jihadists. I know this because they all were Muslims.

3. One can be rich without being happy. The proof is the number of rich people who commit suicide.

4. Bill Jones is a local contractor who should not be allowed to stay in business. I know a lot people, including myself, who were swindled by this contractor. In my own case, I paid him for the cost of both labor and materials for an addition to my home, and as it turned out, later received from the lumber company a bill for the cost of the materials. Talk about cheating! No contractor who is in the habit of swindling people should be allowed to stay in business. So again, I say, let's get rid of people like Bill Jones.

5. An economy based on excessive taxation is fundamentally an unsound economy. Every government has, of course, the right to tax both individuals and corporations, inasmuch as taxation is the only means that a government has of maintaining itself in existence. When, however, the costs of taxation are so high that they are prejudicial to a free economy, a situation has developed in which the government is no longer serving the interests of the citizenry at large. Is there any doubt about the fact that the economy of our government, based as it is on a system of excessive taxation, is fundamentally an unsound economy?

6. "It is the party leaders who must be got rid of. For you see, a party leader is just like a wolf—like a starving wolf; if he is to exist at all he needs so many small beasts a year." (Henrik Ibsen, 19th-cen. Swedish dramatist, *An Enemy of the People*)

7. "Consequently, as God is supremely immutable, it belongs to him to be eternal." (Thomas Aquinas, 13th-cen. theologian, *Summa Theologiae* I, q. 10, a. 2)

8. "No man whatever believes, or can believe, exactly what his grandfather believed; he enlarges somewhat, by fresh discovery, his view of the universe, and consequently his theorem of the universe." (Thomas Carlyle, 19th-cen. author, *On Heroes*, chapter 4, "Hero as Priest")

9. "Men act by a rational judgment, for they deliberate about what is to be done." (Thomas Aquinas, *Commentary on Aristotle's Metaphysics*, bk. 1, lesson 1, n. 11)

10. "Man is the only animal that laughs and weeps, for he is the only animal that is struck by the difference between what things are and what things ought to be." (William Hazlitt, 19th-cen. British essayist, "On Wit and Humor")

11. "A machine can handle information; it can calculate, conclude and choose; it can perform reasonable operations with information. A machine, therefore, can think." (Edmund C. Berkeley, 20th-cen. American pioneering computer scientist, *Giant Brains or Machines That Think*)

12. "As I view the matter, theology in relation to the theistic hypothesis swings like a pendulum between two opposite extremes, each of them impossible of acceptance. There is too much evil in Nature for Theism in its traditional form to be true; and there is too much good in the world for Theism in some form not to be true." (W. P. Montague, mid-20th-cen. prominent American philosopher, *The Ways of Things*, 112–13)

13. In his history *The Second World War*, vol. 1, entitled *The Gathering Storm*, Winston Churchill recorded the following conversation in 1935, between M. Pierre Laval, French premier and defense minister, and Russian dictator Josef Stalin:

"M. Laval now went on a three days' visit to Moscow, where he was welcomed by Stalin. There were lengthy discussions, of which a fragment not hitherto published may be recorded. Stalin and Molotov were, of course, anxious to know above all else what was to be the strength of the French Army on the Western Front: how many divisions? What period of service? After this field had been explored, Laval said: 'Can't you do something to encourage religion and the Catholic Church in Russia? It would help me so much with the Pope.' 'Oho!' said Stalin. 'The Pope! How many divisions has *he* got?'"

Stalin's rhetorical question is really an argument. Can you put it into standard logical form?

14. "The value of any commodity...to the person...who wants...to exchange it for other commodities is equal to the quantity of labor which it enables him to purchase or command. Labor, therefore, is the real measure of the exchangeable value of all commodities." (Adam Smith, 18th-cen. Scots economist, *The Wealth of Nations*, bk. 1, chap. 5)

15. "Because Babylon is vile, it does not follow that Jerusalem is vile." (Eric Gill, 20th-cen. English artist, *Autobiography*, 244)

16. "A nation without a conscience is a nation without a soul. A nation without a soul is a nation that cannot live." (Winston Churchill, 20th-cen. British prime minister)

17. "Who controls the past controls the future. Who controls the present controls the past." (George Orwell, 20th-cen. British writer, from his novel *1984*)

18. "Logic is a matter of profound human importance precisely because it is empirically founded and experimentally applied." (John Dewey, American philosopher, "progressive" educator, *Reconstruction in Philosophy*, 1920)

19. "Of those who see the essence of God, one sees him more perfectly than another. This does not take place as if one had a more perfect likeness of God than another, since that vision will not be through any likeness. But it will take place because one intellect will have a greater power or faculty to see God than another. The faculty of seeing God does not belong to the created intellect naturally, but through the light of glory.... Hence the intellect which has more of the light of glory will see God more perfectly." (Thomas Aquinas, *Summa Theologaie* I-II, q. 5, a.2)

20. "No subject other than heat has more extensive relations with the progress of industry and the natural sciences; for the action of heat is always present, it penetrates all bodies and spaces, it influences the processes of the arts, and occurs in all the phenomena of the universe." (Joseph Fourier, French physicist and revolutionary, *The Analytical Theory of Heat*, 1822)

21. "All living things again including ourselves work according to regular laws, in just the same way as do non-living things, except that living things are much more complicated.... Looked at objectively and scientifically, a man is an exceedingly complex piece of chemical machinery." (Attributed to Julian Huxley, 20th-cen. British evolutionary biologist)

22. "Solid bodies are related, with respect to their possible dispositions, as are bodies in Euclidian geometry of three dimensions. Then the propositions of Euclid contain affirmations as to the relations of practically rigid bodies." (Albert Einstein, 20th-cen. German physicist, "Geometry and Experience," January 27, 1921)

23. "A miracle is a violation of the laws of nature; and as a firm and unalterable experience has established these laws, the proof against a miracle, from the very nature of the fact, is as entire as any argument from experience can possibly be imagined." (David Hume, 18th-cen. Scots philosopher, *An Enquiry Concerning Human Understanding*)

24. "Metaphysical propositions are neither true nor false because they assert nothing." (Simplified version of Rudolf Carnap, founder of logical positivism, *The Logical Syntax of Language* [Full quote: "According to this view, the sentences of metaphysics are pseudo-sentences which on logical analysis are proved to be either empty phrases or phrases which violate the rules of syntax. Of the so-called philosophical problems, the only questions which have any meaning are those of the logic of science. To share this view is to substitute logical syntax for philosophy."])

25. "For we can explain nothing but what we can reduce to laws whose object can be given in some possible experience. But freedom is a mere idea, the objective reality of which can in no way be shown according to natural laws or in any possible experience." (Immanuel Kant, 18th-cen. German philosopher, *Prolegomena to Any Future Metaphysics*)

26. "The power of gravity is of a different nature from the power of magnetism; for the magnetic attraction is not as the matter attracted. Some bodies are attracted more by the magnet; others less; most bodies not at all. The power of magnetism in one and the same body may be increased and diminished; and is sometimes far stronger for the quantity of matter than for the power of gravity." (Isaac Newton, 17th-cen. English physicist, *Mathematical Principles of Natural Philosophy*, bk. 3, prop. 6, cor. 5)

27. "There is a certain moral failure, too, on the part of an educational institution that does not allow the student to make his own the treasure of the accumulated thoughts of the race. So the failure of the elective system was a moral failure. The official historian of Harvard said of President Eliot that he had defrauded the Harvard students of their cultural heritage." (Robert Hutchins, 20th-cen. president, University of Chicago, founder, "Great Books" program)

28. Not all is gold that glitters, for tin glitters sometimes.

29. "Wisdom is the principal thing; therefore, get wisdom." (Proverbs 4:7)

30. "Whoever disobeys us [the Laws of Athens] is, as we maintain, three times wrong: first, because in disobeying us he is disobeying his parents; secondly, because we are the authors of his education; thirdly, because he has made an agreement with us that he will duly obey our commands." (Plato, d. 348 B.C., Greek philosopher, *Crito*)

31. "Every man has a property in his own person. This nobody has any right to but himself. The labour of his body and the work of his hands, we may say, are properly his. Whatsoever, then, he removes out of the state that nature

hath provided and left it in, he hath mixed his labour with it, and joined to it something that is his own, and thereby makes it his property." (John Locke, 17th-cen. English philosopher, *Second Treatise on Government*)

32. "When all the prerogatives of birth and fortune are destroyed, when all the professions are open to everyone, and when you can reach the summit of each one of them on your own, an immense and easy career seems to open before the ambition of men, and they readily imagine that they are called to great destinies. But that is an erroneous view that experience corrects every day. The same equality that allows each citizen to conceive vast hopes makes all citizens individually weak. It limits their strengths on all sides, at the same time that it allows their desires to expand.

"Not only are they powerless by themselves, but also they find at each step immense obstacles that they had not at first noticed.

"They destroyed the annoying privileges of a few of their fellows; they encounter the competition of all. The boundary marker has changed form rather than place. When men are more or less similar and follow the same road, it is very difficult for any one of them to march quickly and cut through the uniform crowd that surrounds and crushes him.

"This constant opposition that reigns between the instincts given birth by equality and the means that equality provides to satisfy them torments and fatigues souls." (Alexis de Tocqueville, *Democracy in America*, vol. 2, part 2, chapter 13)

33. "Dogmatic beliefs are more or less numerous, depending on the times. They are born in different ways and can change form and object; but you cannot make it so that there are no dogmatic beliefs, that is to say, opinions that men receive on trust and without discussion. If each person undertook to form all his opinions himself and to pursue truth in isolation, along paths opened up by himself alone, it is improbable that a great number of men would ever unite together in any common belief.

"Now, it is easy to see that no society is able to prosper without similar beliefs, or rather none can continue to exist in such a way; for, without common ideas, there is no common action, and, without common action, there are still men, but not a social body. So for society to exist, and, with even more reason, for this society to prosper, all the minds of the citizens must always be brought and held together by some principal ideas; and that cannot happen without each one of them coming at times to draw his opinions from the same source and consenting to receive a certain number of ready-made beliefs." (Alexis de Tocqueville, *Democracy in America*, vol. 2, part 1, chapter 2)

Extended Categorical Arguments

The Essentials

In Lesson 28, we encountered the most classic type of longer categorical argument, the epicheirema. It contains the basic syllogism deducing the fundamental conclusion of the argument, and it adds support for one or both of the premises, what medieval logicians called "proof of the major premise" or "proof of the minor premise." Epicheiremas are not the only categorical arguments that extend beyond the basic syllogism. Most of what we might call "real-life" categorical syllogisms are longer arguments. In this chapter, we will meet a few more. Epicheiremas extend beyond the basic syllogism by moving *out to the side* of it, so to speak, in the sense that when we put them into *standard form* we usually set the *proofs* of major and minor premises to the side of those premises. The longer arguments we will consider in this chapter extend beyond the basic syllogism by moving *down* the page, incorporating more and more conclusions (we can call them "intermediate conclusions"), until we arrive at a *final conclusion*.

The most obvious among such longer arguments is called a *sorites*, from the Greek word for a "heap" (*soros*), because we heap up a long syllogism by throwing several syllogisms together. If a basic categorical syllogism is like a small chain made up of S—M—P, a *sorites* is a longer chain with more middle terms, such as: S—M1—M2—M3—P. There are many other—and more important—categorical and deductive arguments. These we construct by putting together smaller arguments. Such arguments can take many forms, so logicians have not developed names for most of them. We are not without resources, however, to help us understand them. We will cover two techniques for helping to understand such longer arguments: *outlining the argument* and *diagramming the argument*.

We should remember that once we analyze a longer argument into its parts, we can always consider each categorical syllogism that makes up the longer argument and determine whether that particular syllogism is valid and sound. Of course, the whole argument is *valid* only if all the parts are valid. And the same goes for it being *sound*.

Sorites

As you can tell from Problem Set 29, the seventeenth-century philosopher Leibniz loved the sorites or chain argument. This seems appropriate for the man who also invented calculus, which involves stringing together numbers in the process called "integration." (The physicist Isaac Newton independently invented calculus about the same time.) To analyze this kind of argument is to realize that it simply brings together all the premises of several categorical propositions, stating only the final conclusion and leaving out all the intermediate conclusions. Consider the section "Longer Arguments," in Problem Set 29:

> Since happiness consists in peace of mind, and since durable peace of mind depends on the confidence we have in the future, and since that confidence is based on the knowledge we should have of the nature of God and the soul, it follows that knowledge is necessary for true happiness.

The last proposition is the conclusion: happiness is knowledge of the nature of God and soul. And Leibniz presents the premises in a reasonable order, though not in what we have called "standard logical order." We can see this if we set out the argument in the order in which it is presented and simplify the terms.

Written Order	*Symbolized*
(1) Happiness is peace of mind.	H is P
(2) Peace of mind is confidence in the future.	P is C
(3) Confidence in the future is knowledge of God and the soul.	C is K
(4) Therefore, happiness is knowledge of God and the soul.	H is K

Premise (1) contains the minor term, *happiness*; and (3) contains the major term, *knowledge of God and the soul*; and (4) contains the conclusion. So we can reorder the premises to make the argument more like *standard logical order*:

Logical Order	*Symbolized*
(3) Confidence in the future is knowledge of God and the soul.	C is K
(2) Peace of mind is confidence in the future.	P is C
(1) Happiness is peace of mind.	H is P
(4) Therefore, happiness is knowledge of God and the soul.	H is K

The logical order of the argument, however, is so similar to the written order that we don't need to reorder it to see the *links* formed by the *two middle terms*, C and P. Following the written order in which Leibniz set out his argument leads pretty directly to the logical order of his argument. Leibniz's sorites is our first example of outlining an argument, to which we now turn.

Argument Outlines

Longer arguments can get so involved that it can become too difficult initially to set up, on its own, each syllogism or smaller argument they contain. This is where *argument outlines* and *diagramming arguments* become useful, especially as a *first step* in understanding an argument.

Argument outlines can take many forms, but it is best to keep the process as simple as you can. First read through the whole argument. Keep going until you get to what you think is the end of the author's argument, in its *written (or spoken) order*. Then try to locate the most important conclusion. After that, locate the intermediary conclusions that lead to that ultimate conclusion. Then bring in whatever premises you can find to support each of the intermediate arguments that lead to the ultimate conclusion. The purpose here is to identify the *logical order* of the author's argument. As you can probably tell, we already have our first example of an argument outline in the example from Leibniz. For a second example, let's turn to the section "Short Arguments," in Problem Set 29:

> There are many movie "remakes" of Dickens's *A Christmas Carol*. The one I saw on the Hallmark Channel last night was pretty bad. The plot didn't make sense unless you already knew the Dickens story; the script was terrible; the costumes were worse, and the acting was not very good.

Here is the *logical* order, as captured in an *outline*:

(1) The Hallmark show had a poor plot.
(2) The Hallmark show had a terrible script.
(3) The Hallmark show had worse costumes.
(4) The Hallmark show had inferior acting.
(5) Therefore, the Hallmark show was bad.

In the original passage, the conclusion is stated before the premises (which often happens). But it is pretty apparent that (5) is the overall conclusion, so in setting out the *logical order*, the conclusion (5) goes last. There is an important difference, however, between Leibniz's argument and the Hallmark argument. Leibniz's sorites is one continuous argument, because it proceeds step by step, adding new premises to arrive at the conclusion. These points function like the premises in a syllogism: they *work together* with each other.

But the Hallmark argument doesn't do that. Premises (1), (2), (3), and (4) work *independently* from each other to lead to the overall conclusion. Each of these premises, considered by itself, leads to the conclusion. The argument is stronger the more such premises we can find to support the conclusion. Each stated premises works on its own, alongside the other reasons for the conclusion, rather than needing the other reasons in order to get to the conclusion in the first place. The outline found in (1) through (5) doesn't really point out the structure or form set out in the argument. This deficiency points to the need to use an argument diagram.

A Deeper Look

Argument Diagrams

Argument diagrams are not designed to capture the details of an argument, or even its main content, but they are designed to let us see, in an informal way and as a first step, the *basic logical structure* of the argument. The idea is to take the symbol for a conditional implication, the arrow (which was used for this purpose long before the invention of contemporary symbolic logic) and plot the *logical path*, so to speak, found in more complicated reasoning. The Hallmark argument is a good example, so we'll compare the structure of the Leibniz argument and the Hallmark argument.

Leibniz argument   Hallmark argument

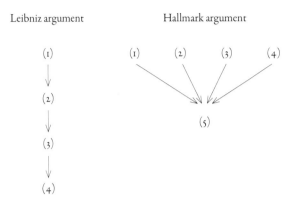

These diagrams show how different the reasoning is in the Leibniz and Hallmark arguments. Once you see the basic logical structure of such arguments, you then can turn to the details of each of the parts of the argument, such as the steps from (1) to (2) to (3) to (4) in the Leibniz article, or step (1) to (5), step (2) to (5), step (3) to (5), and step (4) to (5) in the Hallmark article.

The sections of Problem Set 29 are designed to move from easier to more difficult arguments. You should spend some time on problems from *each* of the three sections. Be sure you make it all the way to the *classic arguments*, because these are at once the most important and the most difficult, since they put you in touch with the reasoning of a few of the greatest thinkers. Though difficult, they are also the most interesting and most rewarding.

Problem Set 29: Longer Categorical Arguments

Diagramming Arguments

Instructions

For the following passages, number or alphabetize the propositions in the passage, and then develop a diagram showing the overall argument contained in the passage. These shorter passages are designed to give you practice in diagramming deductive arguments.

Succinct Arguments

1. There are many movie "remakes" of Dickens's *A Christmas Carol*. The one I saw on the Hallmark Channel last night was pretty bad. The plot didn't

make sense unless you already knew the Dickens story. The script was terrible. The costumes were worse, and the acting was not very good.

2. I don't think I'll take American Philosophy this semester, because it conflicts with a required course in English I need to take for my major, and taking a science course my schedule would cover more areas, which is good for a liberal arts education.

3. Business conditions will improve over the next year (how could they get worse!), and when they do then corporate profits will increase. Increasing profits will then drive up stock price. So it looks like investing in the stock market is a good idea.

4. Government regulation tends to delay the introduction of new drugs. When a harmful drug is introduced, the government regulators get blamed for approving it; but when a drug is beneficial, the regulators don't get a financial reward for approving it. So government regulators are inclined to be excessively cautious when it comes to approving new drugs.

5. It is very dangerous to carry a can of gas inside your car. Gas easily bursts into flame. And it has terrible explosive power. Just think, when your engine burns gas, it can move two thousand pounds of car at speeds up to 140 mph.

6. Welfare programs are intended to help the poor, but the existing ones don't help. Rather, they encourage the break-up of poor families and discourage poor people from seeking jobs. And perhaps the worst aspect of the current welfare system is that it creates a habit of dependence on government, which tends to trap those on welfare. So the current welfare programs should be reformed.

7. "Robbery had not been the object of the murder, for nothing was taken." (Arthur Conan Doyle, 19th-cen. British writer, *A Study in Scarlet*, 1887)

8. "How often have I said to you, Dr. Watson, that when you have eliminated the impossible, whatever remains, however improbable, must be the truth? We know that he did not come through the door, the window, or the chimney. We also know that he could not have been concealed in the room, as there is no concealment possible. Whence, then, did he come?'

"'He came through the roof.'

"'Of course he did. He must have done so.'" (Arthur Conan Doyle, 19th-cen. British writer, *The Sign of the Four*, 1890)

Instructions

Longer Arguments

For the following longer passages, you should do two things: (1) Produce an outline or diagram of the overall argument contained in the passage. Then try to determine if the overall argument of the passage is valid or invalid. (2) See if the passage contains one *primary* syllogism. If so, set that syllogism out in standard form and test it for validity.

1. "Put in its simplest form, this Theory of Vanishing Choice rests on a crude syllogism. Science and technology have fostered standardization. Science and technology will advance, making the future even more standardized than the present. *Ergo*: Man will progressively lose his freedom of choice." (Alvin Toffler, 20th-cen. American "futurist" writer, *Future Shock*, 1971)

2. "Since happiness consists in peace of mind, and since durable peace of mind depends on the confidence we have in the future, and since that confidence is based on the science we should have of the nature of God and the soul, it follows that science is necessary for true happiness." (Gottfried Wilhelm Leibniz, d. 1716, German philosopher and mathematician, *Felicity*, in *Leibniz: Political Writings*, 82–85)

3. "It is clearly evident that marijuana should be legalized and tobacco banned. On the one hand, tobacco is detrimental to a person's health. Look at all the evidence. Study after study has indicated a connection between tobacco and cancer. Moreover, the Surgeon Generals have repeatedly warned that tobacco is injurious to health. Marijuana, on the other hand, is not detrimental to health, producing only mild euphoria." (Barrie Wilson, *The Anatomy of Argument*, 1980)

4. "Nor is there anything smart about smoking. A woman who smokes is far more likely than her nonsmoking counterpart to suffer from a host of disabling conditions, any of which can interfere with her ability to perform at home or on the job…. Women who smoke have more spontaneous abortions, stillbirths, and premature babies than do nonsmokers, and their children's later health may be affected." (Jane E. Brody and Richard Engquist, "Women and Smoking," 1972)

5. "Man, being reasonable, must get drunk Man; The best of life is but intoxication." But whoever gets drunk, sleeps. Now those who sleep do not sin. But whoever does not sin goes to Heaven. Therefore, the man who gets drunk goes to heaven. (George Gordon, Lord Byron, d. 1824, English poet, "Don Juan" [first sentence only; the rest is added])

6. "Virtually all large, complex organizations in the U.S., for example, are best classified as bureaucracies, though the degree and forms of bureaucratization vary. Its 'ideal' form, however, is never realized for a variety of reasons. For one thing, it tries to do what must be (hopefully) forever impossible—to eliminate all unwanted extra-organizational influences upon the behavior of members. Ideally, members should act only in the organization's interests. The problem is that even if the interest of the organization is unambiguous, men do not exist just for organizations. They track all kinds of mud from the rest of their lives with them into the organization, and they have all kinds of interests that are independent of the organization. The ideal form also falls short of realization when rapid changes in some of the organizational tasks are required. Bureaucracies are set up to deal with stable, routine tasks; that is the basis of organizational efficiency. Without stable tasks there cannot be a stable division of labor, the acquisition of skill and experiences, planning and co-ordination, and so on. But when changes come along, organizations must alter their programs; when such changes are frequent and rapid, the form of organization becomes so temporary that the efficiencies of bureaucracy cannot be realized.... Finally, bureaucracy in its ideal form falls short of its expectations because men are only indifferently intelligent, prescient, all-knowing, and energetic. All organizations must be designed for the 'average' person one is likely to find in each position, not the superman." (Charles Perrow, *Complex Organizations*, 1972)

7. "Many a reader will raise the question whether findings won by the observation of individuals can be applied to the psychological understanding of groups. Our answer to this question is an emphatic affirmation. Any group consists of individuals and nothing but individuals, and psychological mechanisms which we find operating in a group can therefore only be mechanisms that operate in individuals. In studying individual psychology as a basis for the understanding of social psychology, we do something which might be compared with studying an object under the microscope. This enables us to discover the very details of psychological mechanisms which we find operating on a large scale in the social process. If our analysis of socio-psychological phenomena is not based on the detailed study of human behavior, it lacks empirical character and, therefore, validity." (Erich Fromm, 20th-cen. German psychologist, *Escape from Freedom*, 1941)

8. "The human soul is a thing whose activity is thinking. A thing whose activity is thinking is one whose activity is immediately apprehended, and

without any representation of parts therein. A thing whose activity is immediately apprehended without any representation of parts therein is a thing whose activity does not contain parts. A thing whose activity does not contain parts is one whose activity is not motion. A thing whose activity is not motion is not a body. What is not a body is not in space. What is not in space in insusceptible of motion. What is insusceptible of motion is indissoluble, for dissolution is a movement of parts. What is indissoluble is incorruptible. What is incorruptible is immortal. Therefore, the human soul is immortal." (Gottfried Wilhelm Leibniz, d. 1716, German philosopher and mathematician)

9. "It should be abundantly clear that New Testament Christianity rejects the immortality of the soul. For one thing, the various writings in the New Testament (e.g., 1 Cor 15:13, Rom 8:23, and many other passages) speak only of 'resurrection of the dead' or 'resurrection of the body,' not 'immortality of the soul.' For another thing, the notion of the dead being resurrected is a very different notion from the soul's being immortal, as can be readily discerned from the following considerations. First of all, if the soul were immortal, then it could never die, and the person would continue on forever. Yet, for New Testament Christianity, continuation of life is a conditional matter, conditional, that is, upon having entered the New Life made possible by Jesus Christ. Secondly it is important to notice that the New Testament never divides the nature of man into two distinct types of substances, e.g. soul and body. From the New Testament perspective (building upon its Judaic foundations), man is a complex unity of willing, thinking, feeling, and doing, and, as such, either stands apart from or is united with God as a whole person. Thirdly, notice the New Testament attitude towards death. Socrates, in the Greek tradition, believing in the immortality of the soul, confronts death calmly, almost as a friend. Jesus, on the other hand, confronts death as an enemy to be struggled with and finally to be defeated." (Oscar Cullman, *Immortality of the Soul or Resurrection of the Dead?*, 1958)

10. "By human standards the number of signals employed by each species of animal is severely limited. One of the most curious facts revealed by recent field studies is that even the most highly social vertebrates rarely have more than 30 or 35 separate displays in their entire repertory. Data compiled by Martin H. Moynihan of the Smithsonian Institute indicates that among most vertebrates the number of displays varies by a factor of only three or four from species to species. The number ranges from a minimum of 10 in certain fishes

to a maximum of 37 in the rhesus monkey, one of the primates closest to man in the complexity of their social organization.... In the extent of their signal diversity the vertebrates are closely approached by social insects, particularly honey bees and ants. Analyses by Charles G. Butler at the Rothamsted Experimental Station in England, by me at Harvard University, and by others, have brought the number of individual known signal categories within single species of these insects to between 10 and 20." (E. O. Wilson, 20th-cen. American biologist, "Animal Communication," 1972)

11. "The diet works because it specifically mobilizes fat, stimulates the release of ketones and fat mobilizers, thereby suppressing hunger; causes a disproportionately greater loss of fat; helps eliminate excess water; stabilizes blood sugar; lowers insulin levels and cortisol levels; and delivers a metabolic advantage." (Robert C. Atkins and Shirley Linde, *Dr. Atkins' Super-Energy Diet*, 1977)

12. "Samuel Butler's *The Authoress of the Odyssey* was first published in 1897 and is still available in a modern edition. Butler argues on behalf of two main theses: first, that the *Iliad* and *Odyssey* were composed by two different authors approximately two hundred years apart, the *Odyssey* being the later of the poems; second, that the *Odyssey* was written by a young woman living on Sicily. It is this notion that the *Odyssey* is the work of a woman which concerns the present issue. In order to make his case, Butler first tries to remove initial doubts on the part of the reader by showing that there were women poets at the time the epic was composed. He then goes on to examine closely internal evidence which the poem itself provides that could lead one to suppose that it was the work of a woman. The poet, for example, has made numerous errors which Butler tells us no man would make, such as describing a boat as having a rudder fore and aft. Much of the story is built around feminine interests of home and family life. In contrast to the foolish foibles of mankind, womankind in the *Odyssey* is portrayed as something to be taken very seriously. Men are consistently placed in the position of needing the support and wise counsel of women." (Denis Dutton, "Plausibility and Aesthetic Interpretation," 1977)

13. "For some years the suspicion had existed among the more inspired geneticists that viruses were a form of naked genes. If so, the best way to find out what a gene was and how it duplicated was to study the properties of viruses." (James Watson, 20th-cen. American biologist, co-discoverer of DNA in 1953 with Francis Crick, from *The Double Helix*, 1968)

14. "The existence of biological predispositions [toward crime] means that circumstances that activate criminal behavior in one person will not do so in another, that social forces cannot deter criminal behavior in 100 percent of a population, and that the distributions of crime within and across societies may, to some extent, reflect underlying distributions of constitutional factors." (James Q. Wilson and Richard Herrnstein, 20th-cen. American political scientists, from *Crime and Human Nature*, 1985)

15. "A foolish consistency is the hobgoblin of little minds, adored by little statesmen and philosophers and divines. With consistency a great soul has simply nothing to do. He may as well concern himself with his shadow on the wall. Speak what you think now in hard words and tomorrow speak what tomorrow thinks in hard words again, though it contradict everything you said today." (Ralph Waldo Emerson, 19th-cen. American writer, from "Self-Reliance," 1841)

16. "Neither parole nor probation are justifiable.... They are a demonstrable failure in reducing inmate recidivism. They undermine the deterrent impact of the law on criminals, while demoralizing crime victims with their outrageous leniency. Most important, they jeopardize public safety." (Robert James Bidinotto, *Criminal Justice: The Legal System vs. Individual Responsibility*)

17. "The U.S. Constitution, as amended, is the fundamental law of the land. Under it, the powers of the federal government in general and Congress in particular are delegated by the people, enumerated in the document, and thus limited. The Tenth Amendment, the final member of the Bill of Rights, makes that point perfectly clear when it states, 'The powers not delegated to the United States by the Constitution, nor prohibited by it to the States, are reserved to the States respectively, or to the people.'

"Congress may act in any given area or on any given subject, therefore, only if it has authority under the Constitution to do so. If not, that area must be addressed by state, local, or private action." (Roger Pilon, "Restoring Constitutional Government," Cato Institute, 1995)

18. "I'm a sick man...a mean man. There's nothing attractive about me. I think there's something wrong with my liver....

"I've been living like this for a long time, twenty years or so. I'm forty now. I used to be in government service, but I'm not any more. I was a nasty official. I was rude and enjoyed being rude.... When petitioners came up to my desk for information, I snarled at them and felt indescribably happy whenever I managed to make one of them feel miserable." (Fyodor Dostoyevsky, 19th-cen. Russian novelist, *Notes from Underground*, 1864)

Instructions

Classic Arguments

For these even more substantive arguments, take three steps for your analysis: (1) Identify the question asked and the author's final or overall answer. (2) Set out an argument diagram for the argument found in the passage. Here you usually will start with the author's *written* order, but your goal is to arrive at the author's *logical* order. These two orders *may or may not* be the same. (3) If the author's final answer depends on *points not found in the passage* quoted, add these points to the points made explicitly in the author's argument. If the passage includes points that you think are *extraneous* to the main line of the author's argument, leave these out. The main purpose of this step is to help you see the structure or form of the author's reasoning. In other words, here your task is *simplifying without falsifying* the author's fundamental argument. You can go back and look at details later.

1. "A question arises [for the Prince]: is it better to loved than feared, or feared than loved? One should wish to be both loved and feared, but because it is difficult to find them united in one citizen, it is much safer to be feared than loved, when of the two one must be dispensed with. Because this is to be asserted of all men: they are ungrateful, fickle, false, cowards, covetous.... The prince who, relying entirely on their promises, has neglected other precautions, is ruined. For friendships that are obtained with money may indeed be earned, but they are not secure, and in time of need cannot be relied upon. Men have less scruple in offending one who is loved than one who is feared, for love is preserved by the link of obligation, which, owing to the baseness of men, is broken at every opportunity for their own advantage. But fear preserves you [the prince] by a dread of punishment which never fails." (Niccolo Machiavelli, 16th-cen. Italian political writer, *The Prince*, 1532, chapter 17)

2. "All men by nature desire to know. And an indication of this is the delight we take in our senses; for even apart from their usefulness, they are loved for themselves, and above all the other senses the sense of sight. For not only with a concern for action, but even when we are not going to do anything, we prefer seeing, one might say, to everything else. The reason is this: most of all the senses, sight makes us know and bring to light many differences between things." (Aristotle, *Metaphysics* 1.1, 980a23–28)

3. "We must explain, then, that nature belongs to the class of causes which act for the sake of something.... A difficulty presents itself. Why should not nature work, not for the sake of something, nor because this is so, but just as the sky rains, not in order to make the corn grow, but of necessity? What is drawn upwards must cool, and what has been cooled must become water and descend, the result of this being that the corn grows. Likewise, if a man's crop is spoiled on the threshing-floor, the rain did not fall for the sake of this—in order that the crop might be spoiled—but this result just followed. Why then should it not be the same with the parts in nature, for example, that our teeth should come up of necessity—the front teeth sharp, fitting for tearing, the molars broad and useful for grinding down the food—since they did not arise for this end, but it was merely a coincident result; and so with all other parts in which we suppose that there is purpose? Wherever, then, all the parts came about just as they would have been if they had come to be for an end, such things survived, being organized fortuitously in a fitting way; whereas those which grew otherwise perished and continue to perish.... Such are the arguments, and others of this kind, which may cause difficulty on this point. Yet it is impossible that this should be the true view. For teeth and all other natural things either invariably or normally come about in a given way; but of not one of the results of chance or fortune is this true." (Aristotle, *Physics* 2.8, 198b10–37)

4. "We see things that lack intelligence, such as natural bodies, act for an end, and this is evident from their acting always, or nearly always, in the same way, so as to obtain the best result. Consequently, it is plain that not fortuitously, but by design, do they achieve their end. Now whatever lacks intelligence cannot move toward an end, unless it is directed by some being endowed with intelligence and knowledge, as an arrow is shot to the mark by the archer. Therefore, some intelligent being exists by whom all natural things are directed to their end; and this being we call God." (Thomas Aquinas, *Summa Theologaie* I, q. 2, a. 3)

5. "Happiness is the perfect good. But power is imperfect. For as Boethius says, 'The power of a man cannot relieve the gnawings of care, nor can it avoid the thorny path of anxiety'; and, further on, he says, 'Do you think a man is powerful who is surrounded by attendants whom he may inspire with fear even more than they fear him?' Therefore, happiness does not consist in power. Two reasons, in addition, show this is true. First, because power has the character of a beginning, but happiness has the nature of an end. Secondly, because power is open to either good or evil, while happiness is man's supreme and proper good." (Thomas Aquinas, *Summa Theologaie* I-II, q. 2, a. 4)

6. "It is emphatically the province and duty of the Judicial Department to say what the law is. Those who apply the rule to particular cases must, of necessity, expound and interpret that rule. If two laws conflict with each other, the Courts must decide on the operation of each.

"So, if a law be in opposition to the Constitution, if both the law and the Constitution apply to a particular case, so that the Court must either decide that case conformably to the law, disregarding the Constitution, or conformably to the Constitution, disregarding the law, the Court must determine which of these conflicting rules governs the case. This is of the very essence of judicial duty.

"If, then, the Courts are to regard the Constitution, and the Constitution is superior to any ordinary act of the Legislature, the Constitution, and no such ordinary act, must govern the case to which they both apply.

"Those, then, who controvert the principle that the Constitution is to be considered in court as a paramount law are reduced to the necessity of maintaining that courts must close their eyes on the Constitution, and see only the law.

"This doctrine would subvert the very foundation of all written Constitutions. It would declare that an act which, according to the principles and theory of our government, is entirely void, is yet, in practice, completely obligatory. It would declare that, if the Legislature shall do what is expressly forbidden, such act, notwithstanding the express prohibition, is in reality effectual. It would be giving to the Legislature a practical and real omnipotence with the same breath which professes to restrict their powers within narrow limits. It is prescribing limits, and declaring that those limits may be passed at pleasure.

"That it thus reduces to nothing what we have deemed the greatest improvement on political institutions—a written Constitution, would of itself be sufficient, in America where written Constitutions have been viewed with so much reverence, for rejecting the construction. But the peculiar expressions of the Constitution of the United States furnish additional arguments in favour of its rejection." (John Marshall, 19th-cen. Chief Justice, U.S. Supreme Court, *Marbury v. Madison*, 1803)

7. "Since, in centuries of equality, no one is obliged to lend his strength to his fellow, and no one has the right to expect great support from his fellow, each man is independent and weak at the very same time. These two states, which must not be either envisaged separately or confused, give the citizen of democracies very contradictory instincts. His independence fills him with

confidence and pride among his equals, and his debility makes him, from time to time, feel the need for outside help which he cannot expect from any of his equals, since they are all powerless and cold. In this extreme case, he turns his eyes naturally toward this immense being that alone rises up amidst the universal decline. His needs and, above all, his desires lead him constantly toward this being, and he ends by envisaging it as the sole and necessary support for individual weakness.

"Democratic centuries are times of experiments, of innovation and of adventures. A multitude of men is always engaged in a difficult or new enterprise that they are pursuing separately without being burdened by their fellows. The former very much accept, as a general principle, that the public power must not intervene in private affairs, but, by exception, each one of them desires that it helps him in the special matter that preoccupies him and seeks to draw the action of the government in his direction, all the while wanting to restrain it in all others.

"Since a multitude of men has this particular view at the same time on a host of different matters, the sphere of the central power expands imperceptibly in all directions, even though each one of them wishes to limit it. So a democratic government increases its attributions by the sole fact that it lasts. Time works for it; it profits from all accidents; individual passions help it even without their knowing, and you can say that a democratic government becomes that much more centralized the older the democratic society is." (Alexis de Tocqueville, *Democracy in America*, 1835, vol. 2, part 4, chap. 3)

8. "C. 9: That there is a circulation of the blood, is confirmed.

"Proposition 1: . . . Lest anyone should say the we give them words only, and make mere specious assertions without any foundation, and desire to innovate without sufficient cause, *three things* are presented for confirmation which, once they have been asserted, I conceive that the truth I contend for will flow from them necessarily and appear as a thing manifest to all. *First*, the blood is incessantly transmitted by the action of the heart from the vena cava to the arteries in such quantity that it cannot be supplied from the ingesta [digested food, the source of blood according to earlier scientists, like Galen, 2nd cen. A.D.], and in such a manner that the whole must very quickly pass through the organ [the heart]. *Second*, the blood under the influence of the arterial pulse enters and is impelled in a continuous, equable, and incessant stream through every part and member of the body, in much larger quantity than were sufficient for nutrition, or than the whole mass of fluids could supply. *Third*, the veins in like **manner** return this blood incessantly to the heart from parts and members of the body. Once these points have been proved, I think it will be manifest that the blood circulates, revolves, propelled and then returning, from the heart to the extremities, from the extremities to the heart, and thus that it performs a kind of circular motion....

"C. 14: Conclusion of the Demonstration of the Circulation

"And now I may be allowed to give in brief my view of the circulation of the blood, and to propose it for general adoption.

"Since all things, *both argument and visual proof,* show that the blood passes through the lungs and heart by the force of the ventricles, and is sent for distribution to all parts of the body, where it makes its way into the veins and porosities of the flesh, and then flows by the veins from the circumference on every side to the Centre, from the lesser to the greater veins, and is by them finally discharged into the vena cava and right auricle of the heart, and this in such quantity or in such a flux and reflux thither by the arteries, hither by the veins, as cannot possible be supplied by the ingesta [=food ingested], and is much greater than can be required for mere purposes of nutrition; it is absolutely necessary to conclude that the blood in the animal body is impelled in a circle, and is in a state of ceaseless motion; that this is the act or function which the heart performs by means of its pulse; and that it is the sole and only end of the motion and contraction of the heart." (William Harvey, English Physician, *On the Motion of the Heart and Blood in Animals,* 1628)

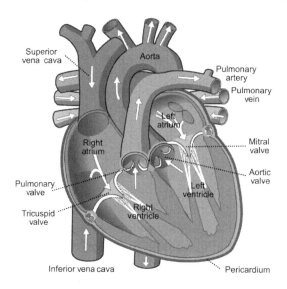

Hypothetical Arguments

The Essentials

In this lesson we will turn away from deductive arguments made up of categorical propositions and turn to the logic of deductive arguments whose parts are *hypothetical* propositions. You will remember from Lesson 19, when we studied hypothetical propositions, that there are three kinds of hypothetical propositions: conjunctions, disjunctions, and conditions. So it makes sense that there are three kinds of hypothetical arguments: conjunctive arguments, disjunctive arguments, and conditional arguments. Since conditional propositions are the most important kind of hypothetical *propositions*, it stands to reason that conditional arguments will be the most important kind of hypothetical *arguments*. We will look briefly at conjunctive and disjunctive arguments, but we will concentrate on conditional arguments.

Some conditional arguments, also called conditional syllogisms, are hypothetical all the way through; the propositions that make up the premises are themselves hypothetical propositions, and the conclusion is a hypothetical proposition. An example would be this pure conditional argument: "If tulips are plants, then they need water; and if plants need water, then they depend upon rain; so if tulips are plants, then they depend upon rain." But the more important hypothetical arguments include some hypothetical propositions, but also include categorical propositions. An example would be this classic conditional argument: "If Socrates is a human, then he is mortal; but Socrates is a human; therefore, he is mortal." This kind of hypothetical syllogism is more important, because it draws a categorical conclusion, not a hypothetical one. You can probably see that this kind of hypothetical argument is very close to the categorical syllogism: "All humans are mortal; and Socrates is a human; therefore, Socrates is mortal." Indeed, the interpretation of categorical propositions normally used in symbolic logic says that the meaning of the categorical syllogism *just is* this hypothetical syllogism. While this identification goes too far, it does show the close connection between conditional syllogisms and categorical syllogisms.

Review of Logical Symbols

In Lesson 19, we found that in order to understand hypothetical propositions, it is helpful to symbolize them. Our study of hypothetical *arguments* makes use of the same symbols we used earlier. It will help to remind ourselves of what some of those symbols mean. If you need a fuller explanation, please look back at Lesson 19.

Definitions of Symbols

p, q, r = any categorical proposition
A, B, C = some definite categorical proposition
Negative: $\sim$p = denial or negation of p
Conditional statement: $(p \rightarrow q)$ = "if p, then q."
Conjunction: $(p \cdot q)$ = "p and q" or $(p \& q)$ = "p and q."
Disjunction: $(p \vee q)$ = "p or q."
Strong disjunction: $(p \vee q)$ means [(p or q) and not (p and q)]; [(p v q) & $\sim$(p & q)]
Weak disjunction: $(p \vee q)$ means "p or q" and possibly "p and q"
Equivalence: $(p = q)$ means $[(p \rightarrow q) \cdot (q \rightarrow p)]$

Some Important Conditional Relations

Contraposition

"If you are good then you will get a lollipop" also means that "if you didn't get a lollipop then you were not good." $(p \rightarrow q) = (\sim q \rightarrow \sim p)$

Types of Conditions

Condition (also called *sufficient* condition): "if p then q," (p → q)

Necessary Condition: "if not p then not q"; or "if q then p." (~p → ~q) or (q → p)

Necessary and sufficient condition: "if and only if p, then q"; or "if p then q, and if q then p"; or "if p then q, and if not p then not q." [(p → q) • (q → p)] or [(p → q) • (~p ⊃ ~q)].

Examples:

Sufficient Condition: "If you are good you will get a lollipop." (p → q)

Necessary condition:

> "If you are not good you won't get a lollipop." (~p → ~q)
> Or "If you got a lollipop you were good." (q → p)

Necessary and sufficient condition:

> "If and only if you are good will you get a lollipop."
> Or "If you are good you will get a lollipop, and if you are not good you won't get a lollipop." [(p → q) • (q → p)]; or [(p → q) • (~p → ~q)].

"Only if" expressions are *ambiguous*, they can mean either a necessary condition or a necessary and sufficient condition, depending upon context:

Examples:

Necessary condition: "Only if you train hard will you run the mile in four minutes."

> (~T → ~F), or, by contraposition: (F → T)

Necessary and sufficient condition: "You will get a lollipop only if you are good."

> [(~G → ~L) • (G → L)] or (G ≡ L)

Conditional Syllogisms

In some conditional arguments, all the propositions that make them up—both premises and conclusion—are conditional propositions. You can probably see that the only way to draw a conditional conclusion is if all the premises leading to it are themselves conditional propositions. Arguments like this are called "pure conditional syllogisms."

Pure Conditional Syllogisms

Here is an example of a *pure* conditional syllogism, one that might be spoken by a fond aunt to her niece:

If you get a lollipop, then you will be happy.
If you are good, then you will get a lollipop.
Therefore, if you are good, then you will be happy.

This particular argument can be symbolized as:

$(L \rightarrow H)$
$(G \rightarrow L)$
Therefore, $(G \rightarrow H)$

The argument takes the following general form:

$(q \rightarrow r)$
$(p \rightarrow q)$
Therefore, $(p \rightarrow r)$

By symbolizing this conditional syllogism we can see intuitively that it is valid. And we can see that it is quite close to a first-figure AAA categorical syllogism, which we already know is valid. The main difference is that the conclusion here is only a conditional statement, not a categorical statement. (You can also probably see that this conditional syllogism is exactly how logicians who deny existential import to A statements interpret first-figure AAA categorical syllogisms. They say, erroneously, that such categorical syllogisms are in reality only conditional syllogisms.)

This argument is just one kind of pure conditional syllogism. Such arguments vary in form or structure, depending upon whether they are made up of affirmative conditional statements or negative conditional statements and how the categorical propositions that make up the conditional propositions are arranged. Not all pure conditional syllogisms are valid; but the invalid ones are pretty easy to spot. To do so, you can depend upon your mastery of categorical syllogisms.

(Regular) Conditional Syllogisms

Much more important are we might call "regular" conditional syllogisms, though they are normally called simply "conditional syllogisms." Such syllogisms have a definite structure. They have a *major premise* that is a conditional proposition. Their *minor premise* is a categorical proposition, one that either affirms or denies one of the two categorical propositions that make up the conditional statement in the major premise. Finally, their *conclusion* is also a categorical proposition, one that affirms or denies the other categorical proposition that makes up the conditional proposition that is the major premise. While this abstract statement of the structure of a conditional syllogism might seem at first glance to be rather hard to understand, when we look at the four possible kinds of conditional syllogisms, we can readily understand it. If we look at their content, there are innumerable possible conditional syllogisms, but when we look at their *form* or *structure*, there are only the following four kinds.

Their names are based on something you already know. For a conditional statement like *if p, then q* ($p \to q$), the categorical proposition p is called the "antecedent," and the categorical proposition q is called the "consequent." The four kinds of conditional syllogisms are called

(a) affirming (or positing) the antecedent (*modus ponens*);
(b) affirming (or positing) the consequent;
(c) denying the antecedent;
(d) denying the consequent (*modus tollens*).

The reason why the first and last types were given Latin names is that these two kinds are valid; but the other two are invalid. We can see this by returning to our example of the child and the lollipop.

Affirming the Antecedent (*modus ponens*)

Here is an example of *affirming the antecedent* or *modus ponens*. It is something an aunt or babysitter might well say to a small child:

Major premise	If you are good, then you will get a lollipop.	($p \to q$)
Minor premise	You were good.	p
Conclusion	Therefore, you get a lollipop.	Therefore, q

What the major premise does is promise the child that, if she is good, then the speaker guarantees she will get a lollipop. To put the point in logical terms, if the child fulfills the condition set out in the antecedent p, then the consequent q will also happen. This is basically what a conditional statement means, as we saw in Lesson 19. Then the minor premise adds that the child actually was good, or, in logical terms, the condition is actually fulfilled. The reason why the conclusion is *valid* is that the conditional major premise means that if the condition is fulfilled, the consequent will come about.

Conclusion: Affirming the Antecedent Is Valid

Affirming the Consequent

If we take the same antecedent and consequent, the same p and q, but now affirm the consequent (q), here is what the *affirming the consequent* syllogism would be:

Major premise	If you are good, then you will get a lollipop.	$(p \rightarrow q)$
Minor premise	You got a lollipop.	q
Conclusion	Therefore, you were good.	Therefore, p

There is a good reason why this argument is *invalid*. The major premise means that being good is *one* way to get a lollipop, the one the aunt is telling her to follow. But there are other ways to get the lollipop. The child might find one in her room, she might make one, she might buy one at the candy store, she might steal one from the same store, and it is just conceivable she might kill someone for the lollipop. Fulfilling *any* one of these conditions is enough to get a lollipop. So being good is *not* the only way to get a lollipop. Consequently, if you have the lollipop, we know you satisfied one of the conditions for getting the lollipop, one of the ways to get one. But we do *not* know for sure that you fulfilled *this* particular antecedent and that you got your lollipop by being good. So the argument is invalid. In short, "if you are good, then you get a lollipop" does not mean the same thing as "if you have a lollipop, then you were good."

Conclusion: *affirming the consequent is invalid.*

Denying the Antecedent

Again using the same p and q, here is what *denying the antecedent* looks like:

Major premise	If you are good, then you will get a lollipop.	$(p \to q)$
Minor premise	You were not good.	$\sim p$
Conclusion	Therefore, you did not get a lollipop.	Therefore, $\sim q$

The same reason why affirming the consequent is invalid also comes into play here. The major premise means that one, but only one, of the possible ways of getting a lollipop is to be good. "If you are good, then you get a lollipop" is very different in meaning from "only if you are good, then you will get a lollipop." Since there are other ways to get a lollipop besides being good, you might have followed one of those other ways to obtain your lollipop.

Conclusion: *denying the antecedent is invalid.*

Denying the Consequent (*modus tollens*)

Again using the same p and q, here is what the conditional syllogism *denying the consequent* looks like:

Major premise	If you are good, then you will get a lollipop.	$(p \to q)$
Minor premise	You did *not* get a lollipop.	$\sim q$
Conclusion	Therefore, you were not good.	Therefore, $\sim p$

To see why this kind of argument is *valid*, we need to concentrate first on the minor premise: "you did not get a lollipop." What this means is that, however many ways there are to get a lollipop—and we may not even be aware of all of them—you did not successfully pursue *any* of the many ways to get a lollipop. That's why you don't have one. But among those many ways is being good. Now the major premise guaranteed that if were good, in logical terms, if you fulfilled the condition, then would get a lollipop. Since you don't have one, we can conclude that you did *not* fulfill this one of the many ways of obtaining a lollipop.

Conclusion: *denying the consequent is valid.*

A Deeper Look

Disjunctive Syllogisms

A second kind of hypothetical syllogism uses a disjunctive proposition as its major premise instead of a conditional proposition. Here is an example of the kind of disjunctive syllogism you can find in Sherlock Holmes or other mystery stories:

Major premise	*Either* the killer wore red gloves *or* the red cat left a hair on the carpet.	(p v q)
Minor premise	The killer did not wear red gloves.	~p
Conclusion	Therefore, the red cat left a hair on the carpet.	Therefore, q

In this kind of argument, the minor premise states that one of the alternatives is false. So if one of them *must* be true, which is what the major premise means, then the other alternative, the one not denied in the minor premise, must be true. So a disjunctive syllogism like this is *valid*. On the other hand, since in an inclusive disjunction the alternatives can both be true, affirming one of them in the minor premise would not guarantee anything about the other alternative. It might be true or it might be false.

Conjunctive Syllogisms

The third kind of hypothetical syllogism starts not with a conditional proposition or a disjunctive one, but with a conjunctive proposition. The conjunctive major premise can take two forms, an affirmation of the conjunction or a denial of the conjunction.

Positive Conjunctive Syllogism

Here is an example of a positive conjunctive syllogism:

Major Premise	"Houstonians are good and Dallasites are bad sports fans."	(p • q)
Conclusion	"Therefore, Houstonians are good sports fans."	Therefore, p

Admittedly, this is an odd syllogism. The reason there is no need for a minor premise is because what a conjunctive proposition *means* is that both the propositions p and q are true, because this is the only way that the conjunction of the two can be true. So if the conjunction as a whole is true, then one part of it, considered on its own, also must be true. As you can imagine, this kind of argument is found mainly in logic textbooks, not in the real world.

Negative Conjunctive Syllogism

Negative conjunctive syllogisms are more important and are truly syllogisms. Here is a typical example:

Major premise	You can't be a citizen of Texas and of Oklahoma at the same time.	$\sim(p \cdot q)$
Minor premise	You are a citizen of Texas.	p
Conclusion	Therefore, you are not a citizen of Oklahoma.	Therefore, $\sim q$

The major premise denies that both p and q can be true. What it means is that the conjunction is not true; it does not mean that each of the conjuncts is not true. That statement would be $(\sim p \,\&\, \sim q)$. The minor premise then affirms p. Since p and q cannot both be true, according to the major premise, the conclusion that follows is that the other conjunction cannot be true; it must be false. If q were also true, then the major premise would be false; but it is laid down to be true.

DeMorgan's Theorem

DeMorgan's Theorem, named after a nineteenth-century British logician, Augustus de Morgan, lets us see the reason why negative conjunctive syllogisms are valid. This theorem shows we can move back and forth between disjunctive and conjunctive propositions as long as we are mindful about negations, as well as "our p's and q's." The theorem has two halves:

$$(a) \sim(p \cdot q) \equiv (\sim p \text{ v} \sim q)$$
$$(b) \sim(p \text{ v } q) \equiv (\sim p \cdot \sim q)$$

Remember that the identity sign ($\equiv$) means that inferences in both directions are valid. It's sometimes written as $\leftrightarrow$ (an arrow going in both directions).

In its expanded version, it means $[(p \to q) \cdot (q \to p)]$. So we can see what (a) means by expanding it:

$$\text{(a) } [\sim(p \cdot q) \to (\sim p \vee \sim q)] \cdot [(\sim p \vee \sim q) \to \sim(p \cdot q)]$$

Since either half of this conjunction can be separated from the other half, it follows that

$$\sim(p \cdot q) \to (\sim p \vee \sim q)$$

Now let's put this back into ordinary language, using the previous example: "If you can't be a citizen of both Texas and Oklahoma at the same time, then either you're not a citizen of Texas or you're not a citizen of Oklahoma."

It is also possible to develop arguments that combine features of conditional, disjunctive, and conjunctive syllogisms. We'll call these *complex hypothetical arguments* and cover a few of them in the next lesson.

Problem Set 30: Hypothetical Arguments

Conditional Arguments

Instructions

Indicate whether the following *conditional* arguments, already set up in standard form, are valid or invalid by (a) determining specific symbols for the two premises and conclusion by symbolizing the argument; and (b) determining the premises and conclusions' validity.

1. If a country is in debt then its citizenry will be dissatisfied.
   Now the citizenry of the United States are clearly dissatisfied.
   Therefore, the United States is in debt.
2. If George practices every day then he will make the team.
   Now George is practicing every day.
   Therefore, George will make the team.
3. If George does not practice every day, then he will not make the team.
   Now George does practice every day.
   Therefore, George will make the team.
4. If all the soldiers in this latest military incursion into another country are American, then the exercise will be successful.
   Now the exercise was a success.
   Therefore, all the soldiers must have been American.

5. If all the soldiers in this latest military incursion into another country are American, then the exercise will be successful.

But not all the soldiers in the present incursion are American.

Therefore, the exercise will not be successful.

6. If the bridge across the river is washed away, you will not be able to get to the other side.

Now the bridge is washed away.

Therefore, you cannot get to the other side.

7. If the bridge across the river is washed away, you will not be able to get to the other side.

Now you could not get to the other side.

Therefore, the bridge must not have washed away.

8. If the bridge across the river is washed away, you will not be able to get to the other side.

You could get to the other side.

Therefore, the bridge was not washed away.

Hypothetical Arguments in Prose

Instructions

Set up the following hypothetical arguments in standard form. Determine whether the arguments are conditional syllogisms, disjunctive arguments, or conjunctive arguments. Then test for validity.

1. If the theory of evolution is correct, then when it comes to geology, the fossils found in lower geological formations will be less complex than those found in higher geological formations. Now geologists have found that the fossils found in lower geological formations are in fact less complex than those found in higher formations. Therefore, the theory of evolution is correct.

2. The moon accompanies the earth in its yearly revolution around the sun, if it revolves around the earth once a month. But the moon does accompany the earth in its yearly revolution around the sun. Therefore, the moon revolves around the earth once a month.

3. The moon accompanies the earth in its yearly revolution around the sun. But the moon accompanies the earth around the sun only if the moon revolves around the earth. Therefore, the moon revolves around the earth.

4. If that dog is a poodle it will have the distinctive kind of hair cut poo-

dles have. Now you can see that the dog is not a poodle. Consequently, it will not have the distinctive poodle cut so adored by poodle lovers.

5. Money will not draw interest if it is not invested. Now you can see that Aunt Alberta's money was securely invested. So it will certainly make money for her.

6. If the mountain will not come to Muhammed, then Muhammed will come to the mountain. Now in point of fact Muhammed did go to the mountain. So the mountain must not have come to Muhammed.

7. "I am deceived. But if I am deceived, then I must exist. Therefore, I must exist." (Augustine, d. 430, Christian bishop, theologian, philosopher; adapted from *Confessions*)

8. Where there is no free choice there can be no morality. Since he is insane, he cannot be blamed.

9. "Mr. Macawber: 'Annual income: twenty pounds, annual expenditure: 19 pounds, 19 shillings, 6 pence; result: happiness.' Now Mr. Macawber actually spent less than he earned. Therefore, he must have been happy." (Charles Dickens, 19th-cen. writer, *David Copperfield*)

10. "Let us weigh gain and loss in calling heads that God is. Reckon these two chances: if you win, you win all; if you lose, you lose nothing. Then do not hesitate, wager that He is." (Blaise Pascal, 17th-cen. philosopher, *Pensées*)

11. "If the real nature of any creature leads him and is adopted to such and such purposes only, or more than to any other; this is reason to believe that the author of that nature intended it for those purposes. Thus, there is no doubt that the eye was intended for us to see with." (Joseph Butler, Anglican bishop, theologian, and philosopher, *The Analogy of Religion, Natural and Revealed, to the Constitution and Course of Nature*, 1736)

12. "If ideas, meanings, conceptions, notions, theories, systems are instrumental to an active reorganization of the given environment, to a removal of some specific trouble and perplexity, then the test of their validity and value lies in accomplishing this work. If they succeed in their office, they are reliable, sound, valid, good, true. If they fail to clear up confusion, to eliminate defects, if they increase confusion, uncertainty and evil when they are acted upon, they are false. Confirmation, corroboration, verification lie in works, consequences. Handsome is that handsome does. By their fruits, ye know them." (John Dewey, 20th-cen. American philosopher and progressive educator, *Reconstruction in Philosophy*)

13. "Now with this done, if one should next take up the earth's position,

the observed appearances with respect to it could be understood if we put it in the middle of the heavens...it is once for all clear from the very appearances that the earth is in the middle of the world." (Ptolemy, 2nd-cen. a.d., Greco-Egyptian astronomer, *Almagest*)

14. "Now if precisely the same effect follows whether the earth is made to move and the rest of the universe stay still, or the earth alone remains fixed while the whole universe shares one motion, who is going to believe that nature (which by general agreement does not act by means of many things when it can do so by means of few) has chosen to make an immense number of extremely large bodies move with inconceivable velocities, to achieve what could have been done by a moderate movement of one single body around its own center?" (Galileo, Italian astronomer and physicist, *Dialogue Concerning the Two Chief World Systems*, 1632)

15. "No man can serve two masters; for either he will hate the one, and love the other; or else he will hold to one, and despise the other." (Matthew 6:24, trans. RSV)

16. "All conservatism is based upon the idea that if you leave things alone you leave them as they are. But you do not. If you leave a thing alone you leave it to a torrent of change." (G. K. Chesterton, 20th-cen. British essayist, *Orthodoxy*, "The Eternal Revolution")

17. "First of all, we must note that the universe is spherical. The reason is that either, of all forms, the sphere is the most perfect, needing no joint and being a complete whole, which can be neither increased nor diminished; or that it is the most capacious of figures, best suited to enclose and retain all things; or also that all the separate parts of the universe, I mean the sun, moon, planets, and stars, are seen to be of this shape; or that wholes strive to be circumscribed by this boundary, as is apparent in drops of water and other fluid bodies when they seek to be self-contained. Consequently, no one will question the attribution of this form to the divine bodies." (Nicholas Copernicus, Polish astronomer, *On the Revolutions of the Heavenly Spheres* 1.1, 1543)

18. "Between these alternatives there is no middle ground. The constitution is either a superior paramount law, unchangeable by ordinary means, or it is on a level with ordinary legislative acts, and, like other acts, is alterable when the legislature shall please to alter it.

"If the former part of the alternative be true, then a legislative act contrary to the constitution is not law: if the latter part be true, then written constitutions are absurd attempts, on the part of the people, to limit a power in its own nature illimitable. (John Marshall, 19th-cen. Chief Justice, U.S. Supreme Court, *Marbury v. Madison* [1803])

19. "This is the way it is, men of Athens, in truth. Wherever someone positions himself, thinking it best, or wherever he is positioned by his commander, there he must stay and run the risk, it seems to me, and not take into account death or anything else compared to what [28d] is shameful. So I would have done terrible things, men of Athens, if, when the commanders whom you elected to order me had positioned me, at Potidaea, and Amphipolis, and Delium, they positioned me and I ran the risk of dying like anyone else, but when the god positioned me, as I have supposed and assumed, ordering me to live by philosophizing and examining myself and others, I had then left my position because I feared death, or any other thing [29a] whatever, this would be terrible. And truly then someone might justly bring me into court, saying that I do not believe there are gods, because I would be disobeying the divine, and fearing death, and thinking I am wise when I am not. For to fear death, men of Athens, is in fact nothing other than to seem to be wise, but not to be so. For it is to appear to know what one does not know. No one knows if death might not even turn out to be the greatest of all goods for a man; but men fear it, as though they knew full well it is the greatest of evils. And how is this not this objectionable ignorance: supposing you know what you do not know? But men of Athens, I am perhaps different also from many men here in this, that if I were to say that I am wiser than anyone in anything, it would be in this: that since I do not know enough about the things in Hades, so also I acknowledge that I do not know. [29b]

"But I do know this: that it is bad and shameful to do injustice and to disobey one's superior, whether god or human. So compared to the bad things which I know are bad, I will never fear or flee the things about which I do not know, as they might even happen to be good. So that not even if you let me go now and if you disobey Anytus—remember he said that either I should not have been brought in here at all, or, since I was brought in, that it is not possible not to kill me, for he said before you that if I am acquitted, soon your sons, pursuing what Socrates teaches, will all be completely corrupted [29c]—if you would say to me with regard to all this: 'Socrates, this time we will not obey Anytus; we will let you go, but on this condition: that you no longer spend time in these investigations, or in philosophizing; and if you are caught still doing this, you will die—if you would let me go then, as I said, on these conditions, I would say to you: "Men of Athens, I salute you, and I love you, but I will obey the god rather than you. And as long as I breathe and am able to do so, I will certainly not stop philosophizing; and I will exhort you; and I will explain this to any of you I happen to meet. And if I stayed then, I will speak about just the sorts of things it is my custom to speak about."'" (Plato, d. 348 B.C., *Apology of Socrates*, from Socrates's speech to the jury, Grube trans. emended)

Advanced Hypothetical Arguments

The Essentials

There are many ways to combine the kinds of hypothetical arguments we studied in Lesson 30 into longer arguments. Here we will look at two particularly interesting and important hypothetical arguments: *reductio ad absurdum* arguments and *dilemmas*, sometimes called *paradoxes*. After that, we will turn to the kinds of hypothetical arguments you find in standardized tests, like the GRE, LSAT, and MCAT. If you are planning on taking one of these standardized tests, it is good to get one of the many test preparation books on the market. These prep books can't improve your basic intelligence, but they can help improve your logical skills if you put in a lot of practice. Spending just a little time with one of them can help you in one important area. After using a prep book, you should be familiar with the *kinds of questions* you will encounter on the test, and you should be able to take less time to answer the test questions involving logic, or what is sometimes called "critical thinking," more quickly.

Reductio ad absurdum Arguments

The Latin phrase *reductio ad absurdum* means "reduction to absurdity." This kind of argument is quite different from what we might call the kind of positive arguments supporting a conclusion we have studied up until now. The way this argument works is that it assumes some proposition is true (p), then argues that if p is true, then another proposition q, which we think is false, or know is false, or is just nonsensical, must follow. In structure this kind of argument is a *modus tollens* syllogism, though it may take many steps to get all the way to a conclusion.

$(p \rightarrow q)$
~q (because q is absurd)
Therefore, ~p

There are many areas where *reductio* arguments come in handy. Sometimes it is difficult to come up with a syllogism or other deductive argument to prove a conclusion in a positive way. While it is natural to resort to inductive argument in such cases, sometimes an inductive argument is difficult to find or is unconvincing. Consider this proposition: "The whole is greater than the part." This statement is obvious, and it is exceedingly difficult, indeed impossible, to think of a prior statement we could use to prove it. On the other hand, we don't need a lot of evidence to see it is true. The reason is because it is an example of what philosophers call a "principle," one of those basic truths that you assume at the outset of your thinking. In this case, you assume this truth when you are thinking about geometry, and actually when you are thinking about almost anything. But it is possible to offer arguments for basic truths like this one. In such arguments, you begin by assuming the principle is false, then derive deductively an "absurd" consequence that follows from assuming the principle is false. Since the absurd consequence must be false, the negation of the principle must be false, as well. And this means the principle must be true.

Let's follow out this line of reasoning with our example:

If the whole is *not* greater than the part, then one slice of pie will be as large as the whole pie.

But one slice is *not* as large as the whole pie.
Therefore, the whole *is* greater than the part.

$(\sim W \rightarrow P)$
$\sim P$
W

Since the principles of a discipline are its basic starting points, which we must assume are true if we are to prove anything at all in that discipline (say, in geometry), philosophers often resort to this kind of argument, not to demonstrate but to support and defend the principles of a discipline.

Socrates was a great advocate of *reductio* arguments, though he used them in another way in his technique of asking people questions. When the Oracle at Delphi said "no one is wiser than Socrates," he didn't sit back in a self-satisfied way, but went around asking people questions. His questions were designed to test people's beliefs, because often we will profess two beliefs that are inconsistent with each other. In the early dialogues of Plato, we can see Socrates "putting to the test" the views of his interlocutors, especially about their ideas concerning good and bad, moral virtue and vice. He would typically "back you into a corner" by showing that your belief leads to absurd consequences. In the *Apology*, Socrates does this to Meletus when, in defending himself against the charge of "corrupting the youth," he got Meletus to say that everyone in Athens was a wise teacher of the youth except Socrates, who was the only man in the whole of Athens who was corrupting them—an absurdity. This kind of "absurdity" in the Socratic style was called an *elenchus* or "refutation." Socrates did this to refute bad ideas, but even more to make his interlocutor realize his own ignorance. This recognition, Socrates thought, is absolutely necessary for each of us to achieve, because recognizing our own ignorance is the necessary first step in becoming wise.

Philosophers and politicians and, in fact, almost everyone, recognize that when ideas clash in disagreement, we have to do two things. We need to argue for what we think is true. But we also need to argue against what seems to be false. This second half of the arguing process is where *reductio ad absurdum* arguments become useful.

Dilemma or Paradox

> There are two kinds of paradoxes. They are not so much the good and the bad, nor even the true and the false. Rather they are the fruitful and the barren; the paradoxes that produce life and the paradoxes that merely announce death. Nearly all modern paradoxes merely announce death. (G. K. Chesterton, *Illustrated London News*, March 11, 1911)

Another kind of argument that is often used in trying to argue against another position is the dilemma or paradox. This is where two alternatives are set before us, each of which has unhappy consequences. A dilemma is like a double *reductio* because both alternatives lead to a conclusion that is in a way "absurd," or at least something we don't like or don't believe. The two alternatives are called the "horns" of the dilemma.

Here is a kind of dilemma devised by the medieval logician Jean Buridan and called "Buridan's Ass": "Asses love hay, and when hungry will always move toward hay in order to eat. When more than one bale of hay is offered, since the ass is not an intelligent creature like a human, the ass will always go for the more delectable bale of hay. Now suppose the farmer sets before an ass two bales of hay, equally delectable in every way, and at an equal distance from the ass. What will the ass do? Well, he'll starve, because there is no reason for him to prefer one bale of hay over the other."

For another example, go back to the problem set in Lesson 4, number 6. In that passage from *Pride and Prejudice*, Elizabeth Bennett has received a very unflattering proposal of marriage from her cousin Mr. Collins, an officious Anglican clergyman. She has refused him. Then her mother insists on Elizabeth marrying Mr. Collins and brings her to her father. Mr. Bennett says, "An unhappy alternative lies before you, Elizabeth. From this day you must be a stranger to one of your parents. Your mother will never see you again, if you do *not* marry Mr. Collins, and I will never see you again, if you do."

Here is how the dilemma works:

If Elizabeth marries Mr. Collins, then her father will never see her again; and if she does not marry Mr. Collins, then her mother will never see her again.

Either Elizabeth marries Mr. Collins or she refuses to marry him.

Therefore, either she will never see her father again or she will never see her mother again.

Here is her argument:

Major premise: $(C \rightarrow {\sim}F)$ & $({\sim}C \rightarrow {\sim}M)$

Minor premise: $(C \lor {\sim}C)$

Conclusion: Therefore, $({\sim}F \lor {\sim}M)$

Putting a dilemma into symbols makes it easier to see what kind of dilemma it is. This is one of four kinds of dilemmas. A dilemma is called *constructive* when the minor premise affirms the antecedents of the two conditional statements in the major premise. In Mr. Bennett's dilemma, the argument is *modus ponens* or *affirming the antecedent*. A dilemma is called *destructive* when it denies the consequents of the two conditional statements in the major premise, making the argument *modus tollens* or denying the consequent. A dilemma is called *simple* when the conclusion is a categorical proposition; it is called *complex* when the conclusion is a hypothetical statement—namely, a disjunction.

Here are the four kinds of dilemmas, in symbolic form:

(1) Simple constructive dilemma:	$(p \rightarrow q) \, \& \, (r \rightarrow q)$ $(p \lor r)$	
Therefore,		q
(2) Complex constructive dilemma:	$(p \rightarrow q) \, \& \, (r \rightarrow s)$ $(p \lor r)$	
Therefore,		$(q \lor s)$
(3) Simple destructive dilemma:	$(p \rightarrow q) \, \& \, (p \rightarrow r)$	$(\sim q \lor \sim r)$
Therefore,	$\sim p$	
(4) Complex destructive dilemma:	$(p \rightarrow q) \, \& \, (r \rightarrow s)$	$(\sim q \lor \sim s)$
Therefore,	$(\sim p \lor \sim r)$	

Can you tell which kind of dilemma is the one put by Mr. Bennettt to Elizabeth?

A Deeper Look

Standardized Test Arguments

Hypothetical arguments have become a regular part of standardized tests such as the ACT, SAT, MCAT, LSAT, and GRE. On virtually all of these tests, the "critical thinking" (or "logic") sections use questions that involve hypothetical arguments. By far the best way to try to answer these questions is to become skilled at answering questions about hypothetical arguments by using symbolic logic. There are many kinds of questions that can be asked. The questions normally asked take the form of what currently are called "logic games," which are somewhat removed from hypothetical arguments in real-life situations or in published works, and they are usually more complicated. But they are designed to see if you can see the logical implications of groups of three or four hypothetical propositions. Problem Set 31 contains two sets of questions typical of these standardized tests. The questions about philosophy are followed by consideration of tactics you can follow to determine the answer to the question. If you will be taking one of these standardized tests, it is advisable to purchase one of the many practice books available. The other set of questions is based on tests given some years ago.

While there are many books available to help you to prepare for standardized tests, to prepare for the "critical thinking" part of a test, practice with the problems in such a book is quite helpful. I would give the following book the highest rating: David Killoran, *Power Score LSAT Logic Games Bible* (Charleston, S.C.: PowerScore, 2015).

Problem Set 31: Standardized Test–Style Arguments

Logic Games–Style Questions

Instructions

Read the scenario and the initial conditions set out, which I call "rules." Then try to answer each of the questions. After each question I have set out some suggestions, labeled "Tactics," for answering that question. The format follows standardized tests.

Scenario: **Plato examines some students in his Academy.**

There is a story in the ancient sources that about 380 B.C., Plato decided that he should examine the students in his new school, the Academy. The students he examined were Isocrates, Xenophon, Aristotle, Theatetus, Speusippus, and Eudoxus. In order to make it easier to use logical symbols, from now on, we will just use the first letter of each student's name: Isocrates = I, Xenophon = X, Aristotle = A, Theatetus = T, Speusippus = S, and Eudoxus = E. The examinations were rather strenuous. Plato would devote one whole day to examining each student, and all six students would be examined on six consecutive days, leaving one day of the week to rest. The schedule for the examination must be in accord with the following rules:

Rule 1. I is examined either on day 1 or day 6.
Rule 2. T is examined on some day earlier than S is examined.
Rule 3. S is examined on the day immediately before E is examined.
Rule 4. If X is examined on day 3, then S is examined on day 5.

Problem 1. Which of the following orders *could be* a list of the students, in the order of their scheduled examinations, moving from day 1 through day 6?

a. I, S, E, A, T, X.   d. X, T, S, E, I, A.
b. X, A, T, S, E, I.   e. T, A, X, S, E, I.
c. X, T, S, A, E, I.

Problem 2. Which of the following *must* be *false*?

a. The exam for X is scheduled for Day 4.
b. The exam for A is scheduled for Day 6.
c. The exam for T is scheduled for Day 4.
d. The exam for S is scheduled for Day 3.
e. The exam for E is scheduled for Day 2.

Problem 3. Which student of Plato *cannot* take his exam on Day 5?

a. E   d. T
b. X   e. S
c. A

Problem 4. The examinations for Day 3 and Day 5, in this order, could be those of

a. X and E   d. E and T
b. X and A   e. E and A
c. A and X

Tactics for Solving the Problems

Overall Strategy Before Reading the Questions

Note any facts or inferences that can be drawn directly from the scenario or rules.

a. List the 6 days in order:
   Day 1: ___ , Day 2: ___ , Day 3: ___ , Day 4: ___ , Day 5: ___ ,
   Day 6: ___ .
b. Note that A can take the exam on any day.
c. Write out the rules in a convenient notation.
   Rule 1. I takes exam on (Day 1 v. Day 6)
   Rule 2. T → (= precedes) S and
   Rule 3. S → (= precedes by 1 day) E
        Inference: T → S →$_1$ E
   Rule 4. (X is Day 3) → (S is Day 5)

Problem 1 Tactics: Look at the rules to see if their logical relations eliminate any of the five choices for the order of the exam.

Rule 1: Since I must be on Day 1 or Day 6, Answer D is immediately eliminated.

Rule 2: Since T must precede S (T → S), Answer A is eliminated.

Rule 3: Since S must precede E by only one day (S → E), Answer C is eliminated.

Rule 4: For answer E: Since X is examined on Day 3, Rule 4 says S must be examined on Day 5. But this is not true, so Answer E is eliminated.

Correct answer: B, the only answer left open.

Problem 2 Tactics: The question asks for what *must be false* or, since thinking in terms of truth is usually easier, it also asks for what *cannot be true*. The four rules do not tell us directly anything that cannot be true. But Rules 2 and 3 taken together mean S precedes E by one day, and T must precede E by at least two days. But if E takes the test on Day 2, there is no room for T to take it 2 days earlier. Conclusion: E cannot be true.

Correct answer: E.

Problem 3 Tactics: This question is asking what *cannot be true*. If you start with the possible answers, you can work through them until you find the correct one. But a quicker way is to start by looking at the implications of the rules. T must precede S and S must precede E by one day (T → S →₁ E). So the latest T could take the exam would be on Day 4. So T cannot take the exam on Day 5.

Correct answer: D.

Problem 4 Tactics: As before, look over the rules first. Rule 4 says that if X is examined on Day 3, then S must be examined on Day 5. This immediately eliminates (A) and (B). Next, (T → S →₁ E) means T cannot be examined on Day 5, which eliminates answer (D).

Choosing between answers (C) and (E) requires the opposite approach: examining the logical consequences of these answers. In answer (C), A is examined on Day 3 and X on Day 5, which is consistent with Rule 1, but there is no room for the three members of sequence (T → S → E). But on answer (E), there is room: (T → S → E) on days 1, 2, and 3. And A can be examined on Day 5.

Correct answer: E.

GRE/LSAT Hypothetical Arguments (without Comments)

Problem 1. Scenario: If Anita goes swimming, then Bill also goes swimming. If Carol and Desiree go swimming, then Ed also goes swimming. But Ed does not go swimming. Which of the following, if added to the statements above, will allow one properly to conclude that, *therefore*, Anita does *not* go swimming?

    I. If Bill goes swimming, then Carol goes swimming.
    II. Bill goes swimming only if either Carol or Desiree goes swimming.
    III. Bill goes swimming only if Carol and Desiree both go swimming.

    a. I only   d. II and III only
    b. II only   e. I, II, and III.
    c. III only

Scenario for Problems 2 and 3: A person who does not exercise will not be healthy, and a person who is not healthy will not lead a productive life. It follows logically that everyone _____.

Problem 2. The best completion of the sentence with the blank is:

    a. should exercise.
    b. who doesn't exercise won't lead a productive life.
    c. should lead a productive life.
    d. who exercises will lead a productive life.
    e. should be healthy.

Problem 3. Which of the following statements, if true, would greatly weaken the argument above?

    I. There are people who are healthy, although they don't exercise.
    II. There are people who lead productive lives, although they're not healthy.
    III. There are people who lead productive lives, although they don't exercise.

    a. I only   d. I and II only
    b. II only   e. I, II, and III.
    c. III only

Scenario for problems 4 to 8: A doctor has prescribed an exercise program for a patient. Choosing from exercises P, Q, R, S, T, U, V, and W, the person must perform a routine of exactly five different exercises each day. In any day's routine, except the first, exactly three of the exercises must be ones that were included in the routine done on the previous day, and any permissible routine must also satisfy the following conditions:

If P is in a routine, V cannot be done in that routine.

If Q is in a routine, T must be one of the exercises done after Q in that routine.

If R is in a routine, V must be one of the exercises done after R in that routine.

The fifth exercise of any routine must be either S or U.

Problem 4. Which of the following could be the routine for the first day of the program?

a. P, R, V, S, U   d. U, Q, S, T, W
b. Q, S, R, V, U   e. V, Q, R, T, S
c. T, U, R, V, S

Problem 5. If one day's routine is P, Q, W, T, U, each of the following could be the next day's routine *except*:

a. Q, R, V, T, U   d. W, T, U, V, S
b. Q, T, V, W, S   e. W, T, S, P, U
c. W, R, V, T, U

Problem 6. Which of the following is true of any permissible routine?

a. P cannot be done third.   d. R cannot be done fourth.
b. Q cannot be done third.   e. U cannot be done fourth.
c. T cannot be done third.

Problem 7. If the patient chooses R and W for the first day's routine, which of the following could be the other three exercises chosen?

a. P, T, U   d. T, S, U
b. Q, S, V   e. T, S, V
c. Q, T, V

Problem 8. If R is the third exercise in a routine, which of the following *cannot* be the second exercise in that routine?

a. Q   d. U
b. S   e. W
c. T

Lesson 32

Induction

The Essentials

Why Induction?

We have seen that the Freshman English definition of deduction—going from the universal to the particular—does not really capture the essence of deduction. For one thing, it is possible to deduce universal conclusions, not just particular ones. This definition leaves out the true nature of deductive reasoning: drawing a conclusion by using universal middle terms. By contrast, the Freshman English definition of induction—going from particular to universal—is better. But it is still not complete. The most important difference between these two types of reasoning is that deductive reasoning proceeds by means of a universal middle term, but inductive reasoning does not. *In inductive reasoning there is no middle term.* Our reason proceeds directly from examples that fall under the universal conclusion to that conclusion.

We have seen the need for induction while studying deductive syllogisms. Let's return to the classic example logicians love to use:

> All men are mortal.
> Socrates is a man.
> Therefore, Socrates is mortal.

The conclusion is *sound* only if the premises are true.

As we saw in Lessons 6 and 7, we use induction in the first act of the mind, in order to develop universal *concepts* like *man*, by "abstracting" the universal *man* from our experience of particular men. In the minor premise here we are saying that the individual Socrates fits under the universal concept *man*. If we already have the universal concept *man* in our mind, then it is easy to establish the truth of the minor premise by comparing Socrates with the content of the concept *man*. This is sometimes called using "the duck test": if it looks, acts, and sounds like a duck, then it's a duck. Here we are seeing if the individual we call Socrates fits under a description of *man* that we have already developed by studying other men and abstracting the universal concept *man* from them by focusing on the essence the men we have analyzed have in common with each other. We can see here that the kind of inductive reasoning that produces universal concepts is the foundation for all subsequent acts of the mind.

The major premise works a bit differently, because it involves two concepts, put together in the proposition "all men are mortal." We weren't born with that proposition already in our minds, yet we somehow came to have it. It's a proposition that we refine over the course of our lives; but once we first attain it, we never abandon it completely. We are perfectly willing to use it as the basis for applying it to new people we meet, to people long since dead—like Socrates himself—and to people we shall never meet, say, our great-great-grandchildren. If we developed the *concepts* of *men* and *mortal* through abstraction, which is a process of inductive generalization, then we should use a similar process to derive the *proposition* "all men are mortal." The main difference is that we don't arrive at mere concepts, but at a universal *proposition* formed from these concepts.

There are many ways of thinking about what nowadays is described by the term "induction." But let's start with the *core* or *essence* of induction. How do we come to know, for example, that "all men are mortal"? The way we do so is through experience—either direct or indirect—of individual humans dying. We see or hear about people dying, say, our great-grandparents or our grandparents; we hear or witness our relatives or the relatives of our friends dying; then we begin to read history and literature, where death is a universal theme. We aren't too old before we are in a position for our mind to move from the individual people we know who have died to a much larger group of people, and then quickly on to every human. In our reasoning, we generalize *beyond* the group of people we know have died to others we infer will die, and then infer beyond this to *all men are mortal*. The *essence* of inductive argument is starting with a limited factual base and *generalizing or universalizing beyond that base*. From knowing that "great-grandma died" and "grandfather died" and "Tia Maria died" and "my friend's brother died," we generalize to the universal proposition "all humans die."

Three Kinds of Induction

There are three kinds of inductive reasoning that we need to know about if we are to understand the nature of induction. Their names were not invented by Aristotle himself, but by later logicians in the Aristotelian tradition. They are: complete enumerative induction; partial enumerative induction; and abstractive induction. We'll consider each in turn. But before we do that, it is helpful to have a few examples in mind, since learning is usually facilitated by examples.

There is an ancient story about Plato's school, the Academy, which says that he put a sign over the entrance gate: "No one allowed who has not studied geometry." For an example from geometry, let's pick *triangle*. Here are some helpful propositions about triangles.

(T1) "The triangles she cut out of paper are white."

(T2) "The three interior angles of a triangle are equal to two right angles (180 degrees)."

(T3) "A triangle is a three-sided plane figure."

(T4) "Triangles do not make good wheels."

Aristotle studied in Plato's school for about twenty years, agreed with much his teacher said, but disagreed on one important point. Plato had said we can have true and certain knowledge only of things that are themselves certain, unchanging, and therefore immaterial, what Plato had called "forms." Aristotle agreed that we can have true knowledge of immaterial realities, but he added that we can have true and certain knowledge of physical or material things, as well, such as water. Here are some propositions about *water*:

(W1) "Water freezes at 0 degrees C/ 32 degrees F."

(W2) "There is water in those four buckets in the corner of the garage."

(W3) "Water is made up of H_2O."

(W4) "Water cools you off after exercise in hot weather."

Since logic and philosophy are no enemy of religion (though some people have said they are), let's pick one example from religion, the *Apostles of Jesus*. Here are some propositions about the Apostles:

(A1) "There were twelve Apostles of Jesus."
(A2) "All the Apostles were Jews."
(A3) "All the Apostles were males."
(A4) "All the Apostles died as Christian martyrs."
(A5) "The Apostles were the primary messengers of his evangelization, after Jesus' death."
(A6) "The Apostles were chosen personally by Jesus."

Complete Enumerative Induction

Perhaps the simplest kind of induction to understand is *complete enumerative induction*. This kind is called *enumerative* because we simply count up instances that fall under a universal concept or proposition. In *complete enumerative induction* we reason from particular things to a universal conclusion by counting up *all* the instances of the universal conclusion. Only a complete counting is *sufficient* to ensure that our induction is correct.

Our religious concept, *Apostle of Jesus*, provides a helpful example, A1: "There were twelve Apostles of Jesus." How do we come to know this is true? We start by counting the Apostles—hence, "enumeration." How many Apostles will we have to count? All twelve. Why? The reason here is important, since it distinguishes this kind of induction from the other two kinds. The reason is that there is no necessary and intrinsic connection between being an Apostle of Jesus and the fact that there were twelve of them.

If you think back to the doctrine of the predicables from Lesson 9, the reason becomes clearer. When we compare how the number *twelve* (in the predicate) is related to *Apostle of Jesus* (the subject) we can see that twelve does not describe the *essence* or definition of Apostle, nor does it describe a *property* of being an Apostle, but is a *predicable accident* of Apostle. The connection between *twelve* and *Apostle* is not necessary, but contingent; there could have been five or fifty-five, had Jesus so chosen (A6). To see this, it helps to understand the definition of the word "apostle." The word "apostle" is just a transliteration of the Greek word *apostolos*, which means "messenger," a man who is sent "out" (*apo*) on a "military journey" (*stolos*), as in the Trojan war. So A5 is a good definition of apostle: "Jesus's Apostles were the primary messengers of

364 The Logic of Arguments

his evangelization, after his death." You can see from this definition that there is no intrinsic and necessary connection between *Apostle of Jesus* and *twelve*.

A4 is another example requiring complete enumerative induction, because being an Apostle does not require that one die as a martyr, even though it is an ancient tradition of Catholic and Orthodox Christians that all the Apostles were martyred. That the twelve Apostles were Jewish males is an even stronger Christian tradition, based squarely on their names and activities, as recorded in the New Testament. Clearly one *can* establish this conclusion by a *complete* enumerative induction; and this way of doing so establishes *no* necessary connection between being an Apostle and being a Jewish male. What makes this proposition more difficult, however, is that Jesus personally chose the Apostles. Was being a Jewish male a requirement in Jesus' own mind? If so, this fact might open up another way to establish the proposition: "The twelve Apostles were Jewish males." (More of this point later.)

Far easier to decide are other examples of propositions established through complete enumerative induction. There is no intrinsic and necessary connection between being cut out of white paper and being a triangle (T1) or being contained in the four buckets in the corner of the garage and being water (W2). In both of these cases, the predicates are *predicable accidents* of their subjects, and only a full counting is *sufficient* to establish these inductive conclusions.

In one way, complete enumerative induction doesn't fulfill the central aspect of inductive argument, that generalization moves *beyond* the data with which we start, because the conclusion "all the twelve Apostles were Jewish males" is simply a convenient way of summarizing the results of our complete survey of the Apostles. We should end by noting that it is ironic that the main reason why some logicians and philosophers over the centuries have distrusted inductive arguments is because they believed—erroneously—that *all* valid inductions really should be inductions by complete enumeration, even though such a complete counting is impossible in most cases. If this kind were the only type of induction possible, we would all have to be skeptics. But we can reject skepticism, because this is not the only kind of induction; there are two more.

Partial Enumerative Induction

The second kind of inductive argument is the foundation for science, philosophy, and all the empirical disciplines. It is also enumerative; we proceed by counting up examples. "All men are mortal" and "All water is composed of hydrogen and oxygen" are examples of this kind of induction. In these cases, it is impossible to count up *all* the examples before drawing our inductive generalization. This is why it is called *partial* enumerative induction. The way we determine that "all water is H_2O" is to do electrolysis on some beakers of water. How many? Here is where judgment comes into the picture. We need a *sufficient* number to establish the conclusion. What is a sufficient number? We know it is less than *all* and more than *one*; but we can't come up with some magic rule stating exactly how many examples are always needed. Why not? Because the criterion for a *sufficient* number is whatever number it takes to establish a connection, an *intrinsic and necessary connection*, between the subject "water" and the predicate "H_2O."

The lack of a definite number drives some logicians, philosophers, and scientists crazy. But it shouldn't. For there is a real difference between the terms involved in complete and partial enumerative inductions. We just saw that the reason we have to "count up" *all* the Apostles is because there is *no* intrinsic and necessary connection between being a *Jewish male* and being an *Apostle of Jesus*. But there *is* an intrinsic and necessary connection between *water* and H_2O. It is the very essence or nature of water to be composed of two hydrogen atoms and one oxygen atom. Without precisely these two elements arranged in a certain physical structure, there is no water. So what we need are a sufficient number of examples to rule out other elements, to insure that all examples of water examined are made up of H_2O, and, most importantly, to determine there is an intrinsic and necessary connection between the subject and the predicate in the proposition "All water is H_2O." This is what authorizes us to take the step from *some* water to *all* water.

But how do we know there is such an intrinsic and necessary connection? We do *not* know it through inductive generalization; nor do we know it through some kind of deduction. We know it through the *intuitive intellectual insight* mentioned earlier. (Its name in Greek is *nous*; in Latin it is *intellectus*; in classical Arabic it is *'aql*.) Such thinking gives us *in-sight* where we *see into* the nature of water enough to know its components are hydrogen and oxygen. Such insight does not come easily; it comes only after long experimental results, and often not even then. The same is true for the syllogism with which we began this lesson. Inductive generalization produces the proposition *all men are mortal*; but it is only insight into the nature of men that lets us see the *intrinsic and necessary connection of humans with death*.

Now there is a difference between these two cases—complete and partial enumerative induction—which we can describe using the predicables we studied in Lesson 8. "All water is H$_2$O" tells us about the *essence* of water, but *all men are mortal* gives us a *property* of human animals; it does not describe the human essence. The same thing is true if we compare the proposition *a triangle is a three-sided plain figure* with the proposition *the three angles of a triangle equal two right angles* (or 180 degrees). The first statement describes the essence of a triangle; the second describes one of its properties, one you may have proven is true when you took geometry in secondary school.

Abstractive Induction

The role of intuitive insight in induction is even more prominent in *abstractive induction*. This kind of induction is absolutely required for any sort of human thought and knowledge. We have already seen it at work in producing, through the process of "abstraction," the universal concepts (first act of the mind) we need for all thought and knowledge. Without "abstractive induction" we couldn't know anything at all for sure. It is called "abstractive" because this is the kind of inductive reasoning we first use to develop universal *concepts* through abstraction from sense experience. We start by observing Socrates, Plato, and Aristotle and gradually develop the concept of *man* or *human being* that is so generalized and universal that it applies to all humans—past, present, and future. At this point we need to distinguish between the universal *concept* "human" and some particular *definition* of this concept, whether the familiar "rational animal," or Aristotle's favorite definitions "animal with speech" and "political animal" or the semiotic definition "semiotic animal." Now we may be mistaken about how to define humans correctly. But we are not mistaken that there is some universal concept covering all humans and that in older English the word signifying this concept is "man," in more recent English it is "human being," in Latin it is *homo*, in Greek *anthropos*, and in classical Arabic it is *insan*.

Thus far, we have not gone beyond what we learned about the abstractive induction of *concepts* in Lessons 6 and 7. What is new about "abstractive induction" is that we also use it in order to establish fundamental *propositions* about reality, truths that form a necessary foundation for all knowledge. Aristotle's three favorite examples of this kind of principle of knowledge—he called them *axioms*—are: (1) the principle of non-contradiction ("Something cannot both be and not be true of a subject at the same time, in the same place, and in the same respect"); (2) the law of the excluded middle ("An attribute either is or is not true of a subject; there is no middle ground between 'is' and 'is not'"); and (3) "When equals are subtracted from equals the results are equal." Later Aristotelians added a fourth favorite: (4) "The whole is greater than the part." These four principles are obviously true; at least they are obviously true once you understand the abstract language in which they are put.

We need experience to understand these four axioms. But we don't use experience in the way we do with partial enumerative induction. What experience does in knowing these axioms is inform us of the *meaning* of the words. Once we understand the meaning of the terms, we *see* at once (through intuitive intellectual insight) that, for example, any whole must be larger than any part of it, or between *is* and *is not* there is no third option, for something cannot both *be* and *not be* (for example, red) in the same respect and at the same time. In a way, the predicates of these propositions are already contained in their subjects. So what we need experience for, then, is to let us know the meaning of the subject and predicate terms; that is all. This is different from partial enumerative induction. In partial enumerative induction, we can know what the words "water" and "human being" mean without knowing that water has to be made up of H_2O or that *a human is a rational animal*. We have to experiment repeatedly to find examples of water being made up of H_2O; then from those examples we generalize inductively; and finally we see intuitively. For *a human is a rational animal* we also need a lot of experience of individual humans as a basis for our induction. And for more sophisticated definitions of a human, such as Aristotle's definition that a human is *a substance composed of intellectual soul and organic body*, we need much more experience and thought.

Partial enumerative inductions and abstractive inductions both live up to the definition of induction as *generalizing* beyond our experience and in this respect are quite different from complete enumerative induction. But they are also different from each other, because we use our experience in different ways. For some abstractive inductions, we can draw the inductive conclusion quickly and easily, because all we need experience for is to tell us the meaning of the words. This is why Aristotle said the common axioms of thought are known to *all* humans, at least implicitly. For other abstractive inductions, however, like the definitions of things, we need much more experience and often some experimentation. Partial enumerative induction, too, requires a lot of effort, because experience needs to provide more than just the meaning of the terms; it provides us with examples of the connection between the subject and predicate of the universal proposition we are trying to establish inductively. So we need many examples to analyze in order to determine whether there is a connection and whether the connection between subject and predicate is just happenstance (a predicable accident) or the predicate is connected with the subject intrinsically and necessarily (as its essence or a property).

A Deeper Look

What Is Induction?

Now that we know the three kinds of induction, we are in a better position than before to generalize inductively from these three types and try to come up with a more universal definition of induction. An inductive argument is a process of reasoning (third act of the mind), one that produces a conclusion that is a proposition (second act of the mind). This conclusion, say, "all animals are mortal," is the pay-off of inductive arguments. And this pay-off is huge, because without it we could never acquire the premises from which to begin deductive arguments. The two modes of argument—deduction and induction—work in harmony with each other, or they should. We need induction to arrive at many of the premises necessary for deductions; and we need deductions to lead us to new conclusions, which in turn lead us to search for more inductions, which will further widen the scope of our knowledge.

There are two main reasons why, over the centuries, some logicians and philosophers have had trouble accepting the results of inductive generalization. First, the *logicians* recognize that an inductive argument is formally invalid; that is to say, it is formally invalid *if we think of induction as a kind of deduction*. But it isn't. There are some fine logicians who have found it difficult to accept this simple fact. But the inventor of the theory of the syllogism—Aristotle—recognized that not everything can be proven through syllogisms. That would involve an infinite regress, since every syllogism starts with premises we get from prior knowledge of some sort. The only way out of this conundrum is to recognize that inductive reasoning is fundamentally different from deductive reasoning and that deductive reasoning *depends upon* inductive reasoning. In induction we *must* generalize beyond our data base; in deductive reasoning we *never* can.

The second reason some *philosophers* have trouble accepting induction is this: we sometimes make mistakes when reasoning inductively. But in reply we should say that we make mistakes in deductive reasoning, as well! That's no reason to "throw the baby out with the bathwater." The mistakes we make with inductions are to think we really know something through induction when we don't, because our base in experience is too narrow or we have not been successful in distinguishing what is essential from what is accidental about something. This is sometimes called the "black swan problem." For centuries, Europeans were convinced that "all swans are white," because all the swans they had seen were white. But then European explorers discovered black swans in Australia. So some philosophers thought the existence of black swans undermined inductive reasoning. But they were too hasty. The real answer is that "swan" is a *genus*, not a *species*. All the European species of swans are white, but some of the Southern Hemisphere species of swans are black. The color of a swan is not part of the essence of the swan when considered at the level of genus, even though color might be part of the essence of a swan considered at the level of species.

To better understand induction, it is important to add that, considered by itself, the process of inductive generalization is incomplete. This is true both for abstracting universal *concepts* and for induction of universal *propositions*. Inductive generalization allows us to reason from particulars to universals and from narrower to wider universals. We did this earlier when we studied the abstraction of universal concepts by considering Porphyry's Tree in Lesson 8. Moving up Porphyry's Tree, we proceeded from Socrates, Plato, and Aristotle to the species *human* that they all have in common, to the genus *animal* that is still wider or more universal, and beyond, all the way up to *substance*.

Moving up, however, to more universal concepts and propositions is different from *knowing* they are true. To *know* rather than just be of the *opinion* that humans are a natural species, and that *animal* is one of their genera, and that *all men are mortal* requires us to have *intuitive intellectual insight* into the very nature or essence of the human animal. Such *intellectual insight* is a mental act different from the inductive reasoning process and from deductive reasoning, for that matter. Intellectual insight "caps off" or completes the process of inductive generalization, both in the first act of the mind, when we achieve universal concepts, and in the second act of the mind, where we achieve universal propositions. Intellectual insight, however, is *not* automatic, precisely because it is a different kind of mental activity from reasoning—either inductive or deductive reasoning. So the highest form of mental activity is not reasoning—either inductive or deductive—but intellectual insight, the kind that happens when you have been struggling to see whether a concept is accurate or a proposition is true, and then, all of a sudden, you say what the great mathematician and physicist Archimedes said, "*Eureka !*", "I have found it!"

Archimedes's insight came when in the public bath. He realized his body displaced a volume of water greater than the volume displaced by stone or metal of the same weight, but smaller in volume because denser. This insight allowed him to answer a problem given him by King Hiero II of Syracuse (d. 215 B.C.). Hiero had given the royal goldsmith an amount, determined by its weight, of pure gold, in order to make a votive crown for the temple of one of the gods; but Hiero had been told the goldsmith had diluted the gold with silver and taken some of the gold for himself. Since silver is a less dense metal than gold, if the crown had been diluted with silver, it would be larger in volume than one made of the same weight of pure gold and therefore displace more water than the same weight of pure gold. Sure enough, the crown did displace more water than the same weight of pure gold, so it had been diluted with silver. There is no report of what the tyrannical Hiero did to the goldsmith, but we can guess.

Primary Sources

Aristotle and Aquinas focused more on deductive reasoning than on inductive. We need to look at several places in their works in order to understand their views on induction. After the scientific revolution of the seventeenth century, many philosophers devoted themselves to studying inductive reasoning, but most, like the British empiricists, such as Hume, thought of induction as a kind of incomplete deduction, which led them to skepticism.

Aristotle. *Prior Analytics* 2.23

———. *Posterior Analytics* 2.19.

———. *Metaphysics* 1.1.

———. *Topics* 1.12–18.

Thomas Aquinas, *Commentary on Aristotle's Posterior Analytics*, bk. 2, lesson 20.

———. *Commentary on Aristotle's Metaphysics*, bk. 1, lesson 1.

Problem Set 32: Induction

Distinguishing Inductive from Deductive Arguments

Instructions

Which of the following questions would be answered by induction alone? Which deductively? Which both ways?

1. Do humans have souls?
2. Do most college graduates succeed in business?
3. Did the world have a beginning?
4. Does water boil at 210 degrees F?
5. Is euthanasia morally wrong?
6. Must the blood circulate?
7. Have all the U.S. presidents been native born?

Different Kinds of Inductions

Instructions

What *kind* of induction is used to establish the following conclusions: (1) complete enumerative induction; (2) partial enumerative induction; (3) abstractive induction?

1. All snow is white.
2. Humans are rational.
3. All the Apostles were Jews.
4. Malaria is carried by mosquitoes.
5. All hydrogen is combustible.
6. Electric current is proportional to voltage divided by resistance.
7. Being cannot be nonbeing while it is being.
8. The majority party in Congress usually loses seats in the offyear election.
9. All the members of the jury were women.
10. The whole is greater than any of its parts.
11. Penicillin cures pneumonia.
12. Dogs bark.
13. "It is a truth universally acknowledged, that a single man in possession of a good fortune, must be in want of a wife." (Jane Austen, English novelist, *Pride and Prejudice*, chapter 1, first sentence)

Inductive Arguments in Context

Instructions

Find any inductive arguments that are contained in the following passages. (a) State the conclusion of the inductive argument. (b) State the premises of the inductive argument that are given in the passage. (c) Identify what kind of inductive argument is used. (d) State whether you think the induction is valid or invalid. Remember that there are no rules for induction, as there are for deduction; so you will have to use your judgment here.

1. "The cow, the goat, and the deer are ruminants. The cow, the goat, and the deer are horned animals. Therefore, all horned animals are ruminants." (Adapted from Aristotle)

2. "The history of all hitherto existing society is the history of class struggles.

"Freeman and slave, patrician and plebeian, lord and serf, guild-master and journeyman, in a word, oppressor and oppressed, stood in constant opposition to one another, carried on an uninterrupted, now hidden, now open fight, a fight that each time ended, either in a revolutionary reconstitution of society at large, or in the common ruin of the contending classes.

"In the earlier epochs of history, we find almost everywhere a complicated arrangement of society into various orders, a manifold gradation of social rank. In ancient Rome we have patricians, knights, plebeians, slaves; in the Middle Ages, feudal lords, vassals, guild-masters, journeymen, apprentices, serfs; in almost all of these classes, again, subordinate gradations.

"The modern bourgeois society that has sprouted from the ruins of feudal society has not done away with class antagonisms. It has but established new classes, new conditions of oppression, new forms of struggle in place of the old ones.

"Our epoch, the epoch of the bourgeoisie, possesses, however, this distinct feature: it has simplified class antagonisms. Society as a whole is more and more splitting up into two great hostile camps, into two great classes directly facing each other—Bourgeoisie and Proletariat." (Karl Marx and Friedrich. Engels, 19th-cen. revolutionaries, *Communist Manifesto*, 1848)

3. "Now it is scarcely possible to conceive how the aggregates of dissimilar particles should be so uniformly the same. If some of the particles of water were heavier than others; if a parcel of the liquid on any occasion were constituted principally of these heavier particles, it must be supposed to affect

the specific gravity of the mass, a circumstance not known. Similar observations may be made on other substances. Therefore, we may conclude that *the ultimate particles of all homogeneous bodies are perfectly alike in weight, figure*, etc. In other words, every particle of water is like every other particle of water; every particle of hydrogen is like every other particle of hydrogen, etc." (John Dalton, 19th-cen. English chemist who propounded the modern atomic theory)

4. "After this I inquired in general into what is essential to the truth and certainty of a proposition; for since I had discovered one proposition which I knew to be true, I thought that I must likewise be able to discover the ground of this certitude. And as I observed that in the words 'I think, therefore I am,' there is nothing at all which gives me assurance of their truth beyond this, which I see very clearly that in order to think it is necessary to exist, I concluded that I might take, as a general rule, the principle that all the things which we very clearly and distinctly conceive are true." (René Descartes, 1596–1650, French philosopher, *Discourse on Method*, chapter 4)

5. "The chromosomes in our germ cells are not affected by any change that takes place within our body cells. What this means is that no change…made in us in our lifetimes…can be passed on to our children through the process of biological heredity." (Amram Scheinfeld, 20th-cen. American popular science writer)

6. "As the species of the same genus usually have, though by no means invariably, much similarity in habits and constitution, and always in structure, the struggle will generally be more severe between them, if they come into competition with each other, than between the species of distinct genera. We see this in the recent extension over parts of the United States of one species of swallow, having caused the decrease of another species. The recent increase of the missle-thrush in parts of Scotland has caused the decrease of the song-thrush. How frequently we hear of one species of rat taking the place of another species under the most different climates!" (Charles Darwin, 19th-cen. English evolutionist, *On the Origin of Species*)

7. "The…study examined 80 first graders at one, five, and eight months into the school year. Half attended reading classes stressing letter-sound correspondences and the blending of sounds that make up words [= phonics]; the rest attended classes emphasizing mainly the study of whole words within relevant stories.

"At all three intervals, children in the phonics group produced fewer er-

The Logic of Arguments

rors in reading words aloud, both with phonetically regular words, such as 'cut' and 'but,' and with exceptions, such as 'put.' Their reading performance also improved more dramatically over the school year than did that of the other children." (Bruce Bower, "Reading the Code, Reading the Whole," *Science News*, February 29, 1992)

8. "Decoration is not given to hide horrible things, but to decorate things already adorable. A mother does not give her child a blue bow because he is so ugly without it. A lover does not give a girl a necklace to hide her neck." (G. K. Chesterton, 20th-cen. English essayist, *Orthodoxy*, "The Flag of the World")

Complex Arguments

The Essentials

With this lesson we reach the goal toward which we have been proceeding throughout this book. Longer and well-developed arguments invariably contain both deductive and inductive reasoning. Considering longer arguments that contain both of these kinds of arguments as parts is a natural resting point for our consideration of verbal, Aristotelian formal logic.

Sympathetic and Critical Logical Analysis

What we can call "complex arguments" are arguments that combine deductive and inductive reasoning. In order to understand them, we need to discern how the deductive and inductive parts of such arguments fit together. Here there are no easy rules or mechanical techniques to follow, for a very simple reason: in order to see how the deductive and inductive parts of a well-developed argument fit together, we first have to determine, through our own intellectual judgment, which parts of such an argument are deductive and which are inductive. Only then can we see how an author puts these parts together. The general advice I can give you is straightforward, accomplished in five steps:

1. Look for conclusions. In a longer argument, there will be many of them.
2. Try to discern how these conclusions are related to each other. Does

one conclusion lead to another? Can you find the overall conclusion of the longer argument?

3. Go back to each conclusion and try to determine how the author argues for each one: deductively or inductively. This step will help you see where one conclusion is used as a premise leading to another conclusion, and distinguish such cases from those where the two conclusions are totally or widely separate from each other.

4. Go through these three steps repeatedly; this will allow you gradually to widen your vision until you get a grasp of the author's whole line of thought or, alternatively, move from a broad view of the whole to seeing how the parts fit into the whole.

5. All along the way, look at the arguments you have distinguished, determining whether they are deductive or inductive, and whether they are valid and sound.

Steps 1 to 5 are what I have called "sympathetic" reading or listening to the author (including yourself). You should be a sympathetic reader first; but once you have done that, you should become a critical reader or listener. Open-mindedness, followed by critique, of the thought of others or of yourself is the key to what is now called "critical thinking," but has since the time of the Stoics been called simply "logic" (*logos*).

Three Examples

This final step in our journey through logic is not wholly new; we have already been walking in this way for some time.

Example 1

The very first syllogism presented in this book took us directly into the logical terrain where we have ended. In Lesson 6 we began with this syllogism beloved of logic teachers for centuries:

All men are mortal.
Socrates is a man.
Therefore, Socrates is mortal.

In considering this example of deductive reasoning, we saw that there must be evidence supporting the major and minor premises; evidence absolutely is required if we are to know, not just believe, the conclusion. We have seen that evidence is established not by further deductive reasoning, but by inductive reasoning. First, we come to know the meaning of the concept or term "man" through inductive reasoning by beginning with our experience of individual humans. And we also come to know the major premise by beginning with knowing about the mortality of individual humans and generalizing inductively. Although at that point we did not focus on any of the many points we later took up, in going through the three acts of the mind, it was clear from the beginning (or should have been) that to understand even such a basic syllogism as this one would require *both* deductive and inductive reasoning.

Example 2

Problem Set 29 introduced a much longer and more complex argument, that of the English physician William Harvey, proving that the blood in the human body circulates owing to the pumping action of the heart. This tremendously important argument overturned views that physicians and scientists had held for 1,400 years. The argument falls into two parts. The three lines of deductive argument that Harvey outlines can be found in Problem Set 29. Here in Problem Set 33, no. 5, are found two of the more detailed inductive and experimental arguments Harvey used. His overall argument combines deductive and inductive reasoning, and it cannot be understood correctly until one sees how these two different kinds of argument fit together.

Example 3

A third and succinct example is found in Problem Set 33, no. 4: "All birds of the same species in every age and country, build their nests alike: In this we see the force of instinct. Men, in different times and places, frame their houses differently: Here we perceive the influence of reason and custom."

Inductive Reasoning

In his customarily clear way, the empiricist philosopher David Hume lays out two conclusions reached by inductive reasoning: (1) All birds of the same species build their nests alike; and (2) Humans living in different cultures and eras build their houses differently. Hume does not present examples supporting these two inductive conclusions, because the evidence is so obvious. Those who know even a bit about bird nests, say, from their youthful explorations, and who know a bit about humans living in different cultures, either directly or through reports, can see that these two inductive arguments are solid.

Deductive Reasoning

But Hume was a moral philosopher, more interested in the difference between the behavior of humans and animals. Birds of the same species building their nests in the same way, and doing many other things in the same way, is a premise leading deductively to the conclusion that the birds act on the basis of instincts that are species-specific, not done on the basis of individual or group cultural decisions. The argument is an enthymeme whose missing premise asserts that traits or actions that are the same for all members of a species do not result from choice. Such traits, like the color, shape, and size of individual birds in a given species, are natural. Actions characteristic of species, like how they mate and raise their young, what they eat, and how they build their nests, are also natural; they do not come from choice. But because they are actions rather than traits, they result from instinct. While a biologist might go into much more detail, Hume doesn't pause, because he is interested in contrasting birds with humans. One group of humans will build their houses quite differently from another group; sometimes even one individual human will build his house differently from everyone else. Why? Because human house-building is the result of the combined influence of individual reasoned choice and the kind of group reasoned choice we call culture.

Structure of Hume's Reasoning

Birds

Deductive syllogism:

> Animals acting in the same way act based on instinct.
> *Birds in a species build their nests (and perform other actions) in the same way.*
>> Therefore, birds act based on instinct.

Inductive reasoning (= proof of the minor premise):

> Birds in species X build their nests in the same way.
> And birds in species Y build their nests in the same way.
> *And birds in species Z build their nests in the same way.*
>> Therefore, birds in any species build their nests in the same way.

Humans

Deductive syllogism:

> Animals acting in different ways act based, not on instinct, but on "reason and custom."
>
> *Humans build their homes in different ways (either individually or culturally).*
>
>> Therefore, humans act based on "reason and custom."

Inductive reasoning (= proof of the minor premise):

> Greeks build their houses in way G.
>
> Pacific islanders build their houses in way P.
>
> *Americans build their houses in way A.*
>
>> Therefore, humans build their homes in different ways (either individually or culturally).

Problem Set 33: Complex Arguments

Arguments Including both Deduction and Induction

Instructions

The following arguments may include deduction, induction, or both. Analyze. Identify both deductive and inductive arguments. Then check them for validity.

1. "Animals do not possess a language in the true sense of the word. In the higher vertebrates, as also in insects, particularly in the socially living species of both great groups, every individual has a certain number of innate movements and sounds for expressing feelings. It has also innate ways of reacting to these signals whenever it sees or hears them in a fellow member of the species. The highly social species of birds such as the jackdaw or the greylag goose, have a complicated code of such signals which are uttered and understood by every bird without any previous experience. The perfect coordination of social behaviour which is brought about by these actions and reactions conveys to the human observer the impression that the birds are talking and understanding a language of their own. Of course, this purely innate signal code of an animal species differs fundamentally from human language, every word of which must be learned laboriously by the human child. Moreover, being a genetically fixed character of the species—just as much as any bodily charac-

ter—this socalled language is, for every individual animal species, ubiquitous in its distribution." (Konrad Lorenz, 20th-cen. Austrian zoologist)

2. "It may safely be pronounced, therefore, that population, when unchecked, goes on doubling itself every twenty-five years, or increases in a geometrical ratio.

"The rate according to which the productions of the earth may be supposed to increase, will not be so easy to determine. Of this, however, we may be perfectly certain, that the ratio of their increase in a limited territory must be of a totally different nature from the ratio of the increase of population. A thousand millions are just as easily doubled every twenty-five years by the power of population as a thousand. But the food to support the increase from the greater number will by no means be obtained with the same facility. Man is necessarily confined in room. When acre has been added to acre till all the fertile land is occupied, the yearly increase of food must depend upon the melioration of the land already in possession. This is a fund, which from the nature of all soils, instead of increasing, must be gradually diminishing. But population, could it be supplied with food, would go on with unexhausted vigour; and the increase of one period would furnish the power of a greater increase the next, and this without any limit." (Thomas Malthus, 19th-cen. Anglican cleric, political economist, and population studies expert, *An Essay on the Principle of Population*)

3. "Thanks to a vast number of observations, we know that anyone transported from sea level to a high altitude shows symptoms of mountain sickness. After a few weeks these symptoms disappear; the person has become acclimatized. The examination of the blood then shows that the red corpuscles have greatly multiplied. It is thus legitimate to deduce that the organism adjusts itself to the rarefaction of oxygen in the atmosphere by increasing the quantity of hemoglobin capable of stabilizing this gas. This brings to light many aspects of the law of adaptation." (Alexis Carrel, 20th-cen. French surgeon and biologist, Nobel Prize, 1923)

4. "All birds of the same species in every age and country, build their nests alike: In this we see the force of instinct. Men, in different times and places, frame their houses differently: Here we perceive the influence of reason and custom." (David Hume, 18th-cen. Scots philosopher, *An Enquiry into the Principles of Morals*, 1751)

5. *Introduction*: Problem Set 29, no. 4 in the last section, "Classic Arguments," contains Harvey's overall conclusion, that the heart is a pump that

circulates blood through the body, and also his preliminary statement of the three lines of argument he proposes to use to prove his conclusion. Here we present two of Harvey's more detailed arguments.

In order to understand these arguments, it is helpful to know a bit about the views of Galen (2nd cen. A.D.), which had been accepted for centuries, but Harvey was rejecting. Galen was the first physician to realize that there were significant differences between the venal and arterial systems of human blood, though he went too far in thinking they were essentially two separate systems. He thought that the dark bluish-red blood in the system of veins was distinct in nature and function from the bright red blood found in the arterial system. The veins contained blood made in the liver, he thought, which was combined with air from the lungs, and distributed via the veins in order to produce *nourishment and growth* in the body's various organs. The blood in the arterial system, by contrast, he thought was made in the heart, it did not contain air, and it was distributed via the arteries to the organs of the muscular system, to produce *motion*. The movement of blood in both systems was caused by a kind of ebb and flow like the tides of the sea (Galen's example), the motions of the heart being an *effect* of the motion of this whole system, *not* its cause. So in both systems, blood flowed in both directions. Recognizing the importance of air, which enters the body through the lungs, for nourishment, growth, and also motion, Galen posited that in the heart the thick wall of the septum that separated the two blood systems was the only place where there could be some connection between them, so he hypothesized that air seeped across the septum through invisible channels from the venal to the arterial system, though in fact, there is no such connection across the septum."

Here is Harvey' argument:

"Chapter 10: *The first thesis.*

"So far our first thesis is confirmed, whether the issue be referred to argument or to experiment and dissection, namely, that the blood is constantly poured into the arteries in larger quantities than it can be supplied by the food [the view of Galen]; so that the whole [amount of blood] passing through in a short space of time, it is necessary that the blood perform a circuit, that it return to where it had set out.

"But if anyone shall here object ... let us here conclude with a single example, confirming all that has been said, and from which everyone may obtain conviction through the testimony of his own eyes.

"If a live snake be laid open, the heart will be seen pulsating quietly, dis-

tinctly, for more than an hour, moving like a worm, contracting in its longi-
tudinal dimensions (for it is oblong in shape), and propelling its contents.
It becomes a paler color in the systole [contraction], of a deeper tint in the
diastole [dilation]; and ... everything takes place more slowly and is more distinct [than in higher animals]. This point in particular may be observed more
clearly than the noonday sun: the vena cava enters the heart at its lower part,
the artery quits it at the superior part. If the vein is now seized either with
forceps or between the finger that the thumb, and the course of the blood for
some space below the heart interrupted, you will perceive the part that inter-
venes between the fingers and the heart almost immediately become empty,
the blood being exhausted by the action of the heart. At the same time, the
heart will become of a much paler color, even in its state of dilation, than it
was before. It is also smaller than at first, from the lack of blood. And then it
begins to beat more slowly, so that it seems at length as if it were about to die.
But when the impediment to the flow of blood is removed, instantly the color
and the size of the heart are restored.

"If, on the contrary, the artery instead of the vein is compressed or tied,
you will observe the part between the obstacle and the heart, and the heart
itself, to become inordinately distended, to assume a deep purple or even grey-
blue color, and at length to be so much oppressed with blood that you will
believe it about to be choked. But when the obstacle is removed, all things
immediately return to their natural state and color, size, and impulse.

"Here then we have evidence of two kinds of death: extinction from deficiency, and suffocation from excess. Examples of both have now been set
before you, and you have had the opportunity of viewing with your own eyes
the truth about the heart for which I contend."

"Chapter 11: *The second thesis is demonstrated.*

"Now let anyone make an experiment upon the arm of a man, using such
a band as is employed in blood-letting.... Under such circumstances, let a ligature be put around the extremity and drawn as tightly as can be borne. It will
first be perceived that below the ligature, neither in the wrist nor anywhere
else, do the *arteries* pulsate, at the same time that immediately above the ligature the artery begins to rise higher at each diastole, to throb more violently,
and to swell.... After the bandage has been kept on for some short time in this
way, let it be slackened a little, brought to that state or term of medium tightness which is used in bleeding, and it will be seen that the whole hand and
arm will instantly become deeply colored and distended, and the *veins* show

themselves tumid and knotted. After ten or twelve pulses of the artery, the hand will be perceived excessively distended, injected, gorged with blood....

"From these facts it is easy for every careful observer to learn that the blood enters an extremity by the *arteries*...but when the pressure is diminished, as it is with the band for blood-letting, it is manifest that the blood is instantly thrown in with force, for then the hand begins to swell....

"It therefore plainly appears that the ligature prevents the return of the blood through the *veins* to the parts above it, and maintains those beneath it in a state of permanent distension. But the arteries, in spite of its pressure, and under the force and impulse of the heart, send on the blood from the internal parts of the body to the parts below the ligature. And herein consists the difference between the tight and the medium ligature: the former not only prevents the passage of the blood in the *veins*, but also in the *arteries*; the latter, however, while it does not prevent the force of the pulse [in the arteries] from extending below it, and so propelling the blood to the extremities of the body, it does compress the *veins*, and greatly or altogether impedes the return of the blood through them....

"Farther, when the ligature goes from extreme tightness to being moderately relaxed, we see the veins below the ligature instantly swell up and become gorged, while the arteries continue unaffected. This is an obvious indication that the blood *passes from the arteries into the veins*, and not from the veins into the arteries. And it also indicates there is either an anastomosis [connection] of the two orders of vessels [arteries and veins], or porosities in the flesh and solid parts generally that are permeable to the blood." (William Harvey, *On the Motion of the Heart and Blood in Animals*, 1628)

6. "Are essence and existence the same in God?"

"Response: I answer that God is not just his own essence, as shown in the preceding article, but also his own existence. This may be shown in several ways.

"First, whatever a thing has besides its essence must be caused either by the constituent principles of that essence, like a property that necessarily accompanies a species, as the ability to laugh is a property of a human, and is caused by the constituent principles of its species, or it is caused by some exterior agent, as heat is caused in water by fire. Consequently, if the existence of a thing is different from its essence, this existence must be caused, either by some exterior agent or by its essential principles. Now it is impossible for a thing's existence to be caused by its essential constituent principles, for nothing suffices to cause its own existence, if its existence is caused. Therefore that thing, whose existence differs from its essence, must have its existence caused by another. But this cannot be true of God, since we call God the first efficient cause. Therefore, it is impossible that in God existence should differ from essence.

"Second, existence is that which makes every form or nature actual, for goodness or humanity are said to be actual, only because they are said to exist. Therefore, existence must be compared with essence, if the latter is distinct, as actuality to potentiality. Therefore, since in God there is no potentiality, as shown above, it follows that in him essence does not differ from existence. Therefore, his essence is his existence.

"Third, because, just as that which has fire, but is not itself fire, is on fire by participation, so that which has existence but is not existence, is a being by participation. But God is his own essence, as shown above. Therefore, if he were not his own existence, he would not be a being through himself, but he would be a participated being. But then he would not be the first being, which is absurd. Consequently, God is his own existence, and not merely his own essence." (Thomas Aquinas, *Summa Theologaie* I, q, 3, a. 4)

7. "Among aristocratic peoples, families remain for centuries in the same condition, and often in the same place. That, so to speak, makes all generations contemporaries. A man almost always knows his ancestors and respects them; he believes he already sees his grandsons, and he loves them. He willingly assumes his duty toward both, and he often happens to sacrifice his personal enjoyments for these beings who are no more or who do not yet exist.

"Aristocratic institutions have, moreover, the effect of tying each man closely to several of his fellow citizens.

"Since classes are very distinct and unchanging within an aristocratic people, each class becomes for the one who is part of it a kind of small country, more visible and dearer than the large one.

"Because, in aristocratic societies, all citizens are placed in fixed positions, some above others, each citizen always sees above him a man whose protection he needs, and below he finds another whose help he can claim.

"So men who live in aristocratic centuries are almost always tied in a close way to something that is located outside of themselves, and they are often disposed to forget themselves. It is true that, in these same centuries, the general notion of fellow is obscure, and that you scarcely think to lay down your life for the cause of humanity; but you often sacrifice yourself for certain men.

"In democratic centuries, on the contrary, when the duties of each individual toward the species are much clearer, devotion toward one man becomes more rare; the bond of human affections expands and relaxes.

"Among democratic peoples, new families emerge constantly out of nothing, others constantly fall back into nothing, and all those that remain change face; the thread of time is broken at every moment, and the trace of the generations fades. You easily forget those who preceded you, and you have no idea about those who will follow you. Only those closest to you are of interest.

"Since each class is coming closer to the others and is mingling with them, its members become indifferent and like strangers to each other. Aristocracy had made all citizens into a long chain that went from the peasant up to the king; democracy breaks the chain and sets each link apart.

"As conditions become equal, a greater number of individuals will be found who, no longer rich enough or powerful enough to exercise a great influence over the fate of their fellows, have nonetheless acquired or preserved enough enlightenment and wealth to be able to be sufficient for themselves. The latter owe nothing to anyone, they expect nothing so to speak from anyone; they are always accustomed to consider themselves in isolation, and they readily imagine that their entire destiny is in their hands.

"Thus, not only does democracy make each man forget his ancestors, but it hides his descendants from him and separates him from his contemporaries; it constantly leads him back toward himself alone and threatens finally to enclose him entirely within the solitude of his own heart. (Alexis de Tocqueville, *Democracy in America*, volume II, part 2, chapter 2)

8. "The condition of England, on which many pamphlets are now in the course of publication, and many thoughts unpublished are going on in every reflective head, is justly regarded as one of the most ominous, and withal one of the strangest, ever seen in this world. England is full of wealth, of multifarious produce, supply for human want in every kind; yet England is dying of inanition.

"With unabated bounty the land of England blooms and grows; waving with yellow harvests; thick-studded with workshops, industrial implements, with fifteen millions of workers, understood to be the strongest, the cunningest and the willingest our Earth ever had; these men are here; the work they have done, the fruit they have realised is here, abundant, exuberant on every hand of us: and behold, some baleful fiat as of Enchantment has gone forth, saying, 'Touch it not, ye workers, ye master-workers, ye master-idlers; none of you can touch it, no man of you shall be the better for it; this is enchanted fruit!' On the poor workers such fiat falls first, in its rudest shape; but on the rich masterworkers too it falls; neither can the rich master-idlers, nor any richest or highest man escape, but all are like to be brought low with it, and made 'poor' enough, in the money-sense or a far fataller one.

"Of these successful skillful workers some two millions, it is now counted, sit in Workhouses, Poor-law Prisons; or have 'out-door relief' flung over the wall to them,—the workhouse Bastille being filled to bursting, and the strong Poor-law broken asunder by a stronger. They sit there, these many months now; their hope of deliverance as yet small. In workhouses, pleasantly so named, because work cannot be done in them. Twelve hundred thousand workers in England alone; their cunning right-hand lamed, lying idle in their sorrowful bosom; their hopes, outlooks, share of this fair world, shut in by narrow walls. They sit there, pent up, as in a kind of horrid enchantment; glad to be imprisoned and enchanted, that they may not perish starved.

"The picturesque Tourist, in a sunny autumn day, through this bounteous realm of England, describes the Union Workhouse on his path. 'Passing by the Workhouse of St. Ives in Huntingdonshire, on a bright day last autumn,' says the picturesque Tourist, 'I saw sitting on wooden benches, in front of their Bastille and within their ringwall and its railings, some half-hundred or more of these men. Tall robust figures, young mostly or of middle age; of honest countenance, many of them thoughtful and even intelligent-looking men. They sat there, near by one another; but in a kind of torpor, especially in a silence, which was very striking. In silence: for, alas, what word was to be said? An Earth all lying round, crying, Come and till me, come and reap me;—yet we here sit enchanted! In the eyes and brows of these men hung the gloomiest expression, not of anger, but of grief and shame and manifold inarticulate distress and weariness; they returned my glance with a glance that seemed to say, "Do not look at us. We sit enchanted here, we know not why. The Sun shines and the Earth calls; and, by the governing Powers and Impotences of this England, we are forbidden to obey. It is impossible, they tell us!"'

"There was something that reminded me of Dante's Hell in the look of all this; and I rode swiftly away."(Thomas Carlyle, *Past and Present*, chapter 1, "Midas," 1843.)

Answers to Selected Problems

Problem Set 1: Grammar Review

Identifying the Eight Parts of Speech

Parts of speech are identified for some of the problems:

4. I (PN) heard (V) you (PN) were leaving (V).

7. Give (V) the (Adj) man (N) your (Adj) money (N).

13. The (Adj) dog ((N) chased (V) the (Adj) rabbit (N) into (P) the (Adj) woods (N) down (P) the (Adj) road (N).

18. Trotting (V) down (Prep) the (Adj) road (N) in (P) a (Adj) red (Adj) collar (N), I (PN) spotted (V) the (Adj) dog (N).

21. Death (N) is (V) the (Adj) black (Adj) camel (N), which (PN) stands (V) at (P) every (Adj) man's (N) gate (N). (Arab proverb)

24. It (PN) is (V pt 1) a (Adj) truth (N) universally (Adv) acknowledged (V pt 2), that (C) a (Adj) single (Adj) man (N) in (P) possession (N) of (P) a (Adj) good (Adj) fortune (N), must be (V) in (P) want (N) of (Prep) a (Adj) wife (N). (Jane Austen)

Diagramming Sentences

4.

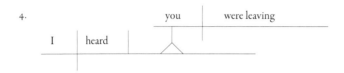

7.

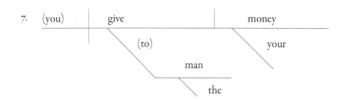

13.

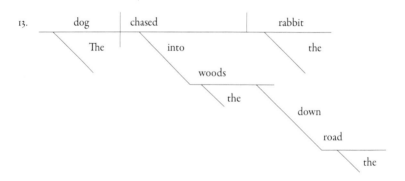

18.

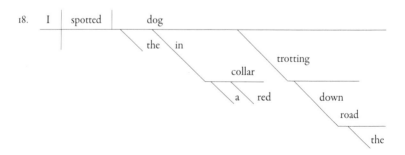

21.

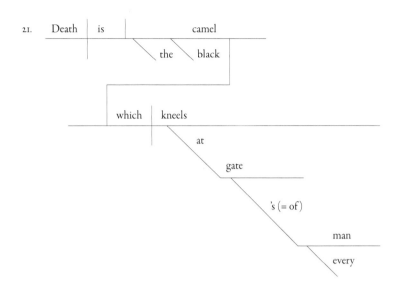

Problem Set 4: The Three Appeals

1. Benjamin Franklin

Answers

    a. Members of the executive branch of the federal government under the US Constitution should *not* be paid salaries.

    b. Primarily ethical appeal.

2. Edmund Burke

Answers:

    a. The French Revolution has been a complete disaster, because it ushered in rule of France by inferior, ignorant, and ignoble men.

    b. Primarily emotional appeal, by focusing on Marie Antoinette as Dauphiness (wife of the heir to the throne), who was later, when Queen of France, dethroned and beheaded at the guillotine, during the Revolution.

5. Leonard Spector

Answers

   a. Proliferation of nuclear weapons should be stopped.
   b. Rational appeal. The topic engenders emotions, but Spector offers rational arguments for his conclusion.

Problem Set 5: Problem Solving

1. a. In the tropics, why are machines such as taxi-cabs so prone to rust?
    b. In the tropics, the high humidity of the air makes metal machinery such as in taxi-cabs prone to rust.
    c. The tropics are humid and rain frequently: there is always water in the air. Rusting happens when the oxygen in the atmosphere oxidizes the iron in the metal of the car, to produce iron oxide or "rust." The process speeds up when there is water (H_2O) in the air, and it speeds up even more when there is salt in the water, as happens near the ocean.

4. a. What about the earth's atmosphere promotes the many life-forms?
    b. The atmosphere of Earth protects **life on Earth** by acting as a barrier protecting the earth and by containing important chemicals necessary for life.
    c. The atmosphere acts as a barrier in three ways: (1) by absorbing **ultraviolet solar radiation** to prevent it from getting to the earth's surface; (2) by warming the surface through heat retention (**greenhouse effect**); and (3) by reducing **temperature** extremes between **day** and **night** (**diurnal temperature variation**). The atmosphere also contains chemicals that are necessary for life, such as carbon dioxide for plants, and oxygen for animals.

Problem Set 6: Three Acts of the Mind

1. a. Terms: (1) Socrates; (2) Man; (3) Mortal/will die
    b. Propositions: (1) Socrates is a man. (2) Men are mortal. (3) Socrates is mortal/will die.
    c. Argument: All men are mortal. Socrates is a man. Therefore, Socrates is mortal.

4. a. Terms: (1) Existing (created) things. (2) Creator. (3) Good. (4) Unchangeably good. (5) Supremely good. (6) Changeably good.
    b. Propositions: (1) Existing (created) things are good. (2) Creator of existing things is supremely good. (3) Created things are not supremely and unchangeably good. (4) Created things are changeably good.
    c. Argument: (1) Creator of existing (created) things is supremely good. (2) Existing (created) things are good. (3) Therefore, created things are not supremely and unchangeably good. (4) Therefore, created things are changeably good. (5) Therefore, goodness of existing (created) things is subject to increase and decrease.

Problem Set 7: Signs

Kinds of Signs

1. Conventional, instrumental.   7. Conventional, instrumental.
4. Natural, instrumental.   10. Natural, formal.

Identifying Signs in Prose

1. (a) Sign: picture of a cat; thing signified: cat. (b) "Reader": dog. (c) Conventional, instrumental.

Individuals, Collections, and Universals

1. Collection
4. Individual
8. Universal

Problem Set 8: Recognizing and Using Categories

Terms and Their Aristotelian Categories

1. when	8. quality	15. passion/undergoing
2. relation	12. action	21. posture
3. substance	14. quality	27. action

Identifying Specific Categories

1. blue—color
4. sound—quality (1st sense)
8. killing—action

Problem Set 9: Argument Using Division

James Madison's Argument in *Federalist* No. 10

1. How to control the influence of factions
2. A large, federal republic, with multiple branches at the federal level (executive, legislative, judicial), and multiple levels of government (federal, state, local) is the best type of government to control factions. This type of government is better than monarchy, democracy, single level republic, single branch republic, or small republic.
3. Madison's argument begins with two important divisions:

   Ways to control influence of factions:

   I. Remove Faction's Causes
       A. Destroy liberty: No, this produces tyranny.
       B. Give citizens the same passions, interests, opinions. Impossible; contra human nature.
   II. Control Faction's Effects
       A. In a democracy.
       B. In a republic.

   See if you can add further subdivisions under II.

4. The following central terms need definition. Find Madison's definitions (when he gives one) and then restate them in your own words:

   1. Faction   4. Liberty
   2. Democracy   5. Tyranny
   3. Republic

Problem Set 10: Recognizing Essence, Property, and Accident

From Genus to Species

    2. bird: cardinal, eagle

    5. number: real (-10, $5/3$) vs. imaginary (contains I = square root of -1).
        Real numbers include: rational (5, -4, $4/3$) vs. irrational (sq. root of 2, π)

From Species to Genus

    1. monkey: primate; animal; living thing.

    7. gold: color; quality.

Distinguishing Essence, Property, Accident

    1. accident   16. property

    5. property   20. genus

    7. difference

Describing Things Using the Predicables

    1. rabbit: (a) animal, (b) hops, (c) in the field.

    9. fear: (a) emotion, passion, (b) usually makes us concerned, usually makes us act, (c) of my uncle.

    13. sweet: (a) quality, sensible, (b) perceived through tongue or nose, (c) being tasted by me right now, combined with orange color in my popsicle.

Problem Set 11: The Four Causes

Identifying all Four Causes of a Thing

    1. hammer
    matter: metal, wood
    form: long handle, heavy head or "hammerness"
    agent: craftsman or worker, using tools such as forge, a dye, and a lathe
    end/purpose: strike another thing, e.g., nail.

4. spider

matter: body with exoskeleton, segments, jointed appendages such as legs, internal organs

form: air-breathing internal structure, eight legs, fangs for injecting venom

agent: parent spiders: male and female

end/purpose: live like a spider should: hunting, web-spinning, eating, growing, reproducing

10. hydrogen

matter: protons, electrons and subatomic particles that make them up

form: structure of one proton and one electron (and maybe a couple neutrons)

agent: normally from breakown of compounds, e.g., from water through electrolysis

end/purpose: combination with other elements to form physical objects; burns readily

Problem Set 12: Definitions

Kinds of Definition of Man—That Is, the Human

1. Real, descriptive definition (property).
3. Real, logical definition.
5. Real, causal definition (efficient cause).
7. Nominal definition.
9. Real, descriptive definition (property).
15. Real, descriptive definition (accident).
18. Real, descriptive definition (accident).

Kinds of Definitions

1. Real, causal, final cause.
4. Real, causal, formal cause.
5. Real, causal, efficient and final causes.
10. Real—descriptive, accident.

Analyzing More Sophisticated Definitions

1. (a) Democracy.
    (b) 1. "Eternal justice ruling through the people."
    (c) 1. Causal definition: formal (eternal justice) and efficient ("ruling through the people").
    (b) 2. "Supremacy of man over his accidents."
    (c) 2. Descriptive definition.
    (b) 3. "The will of the people."
    (c) 3. Causal definition: efficient cause.

4. (a) Democracy.
    (b) experiment in government; only counts votes, doesn't weigh them.
    (c) Descriptive (property).

7. (a) Money; (b) "Metal pieces"; (c) Causal definition, material.
    (a) Money; (b) "Goods that can be had in exchange for it";
        (c) Causal definition, final cause.
    (a) Money; (b) "power of purchasing"; (c) Causal definition, formal cause.

Problem Set 13: Statements and Propositions

Distinguishing Kinds of Propositions

1. Categorical	13. Conjunction
5. Conditional	18. Conditional
9. Conjunction	19. Statement, but not a proposition.
11. Disjunction	21. Conditional

Problem Set 14: Basic Categorical Propositions

Four Kinds of Categorical Propositions

1. A	4. O
2. I	8. I
3. E	12. E

Problem Set 15: Advanced Categorical Propositions

Recognizing More Difficult Categorical Propositions

1. I	9. A	21. E	26. I	37. A
3. A	13. A	22. O	27. O	44. O
5. A	17. E	25. O	30. E	

Problem Set 16: Propositions in Context

Identifying Categorical Propositions in Prose

Propositions are quoted in the form they have in the quotation. Then the proposition's type (A, I, E, or O) is given. Rewriting each categorical proposition in simplified form is left to you.

1. "In short, I say …"

   a. "… as a city we are the school of Hellas." A
   b. "I doubt if the world can produce a man, who where he has only himself to depend upon, is equal to so many emergencies and graced by so happy a versatility as the Athenian." E
   c. "Rather, the admiration of the present and succeeding ages will be ours." A
   d. "… we have forced every sea and land to be the highway of our daring,…" A
   e. "… and everywhere, whether for evil or for good, we have left imperishable monuments behind us." A

5. "To suppose that the eye…."

   a. "To suppose that the eye with all its inimitable contrivances… seems, I confess, absurd in the highest degree." A
   b. "The difficulty of believing that a perfect and complex eye… should not be considered subversive of the theory." E

7. "With savages, the weak…."

   a. "With savages, the weak in body or mind are soon eliminated." A
   b. "… and those that survive commonly exhibit a vigorous state of health." I

c. "We civilized men, on the other hand, do our utmost to check the process of elimination." A

d. "No one who has attended to the breeding of domestic animals will doubt that this must be highly injurious to the race of man." E

Problem Set 17: Euler and Venn Diagrams of Propositions

Learning to Draw Diagrams of Propositions

5. None of the chimpanzees have been fed.

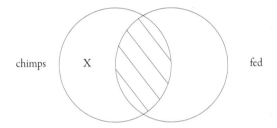

6. All airplanes are human artifacts.

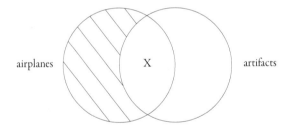

13. Not all the tires on my car are worn.

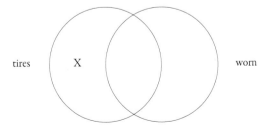

Problem Set 18: Opposition

Learning to Recognize Different Kinds of Opposition

1. Subcontrary; Undetermined   8. Subimplication; Undetermined
2. Contradictory; False   18. Contradictory; True
5. Contrary; Undetermined

Creating Opposites

2. (a) Subimplicant: All hummingbirds are large. False.
   (b) Subcontrary: Some hummingbirds are not large. Undetermined

5. (a) Subimplicant: All politicians are dishonest. Undetermined.
   (b) Subcontrary: Some politicians are not dishonest. Undetermined.

6. (a) Contradictory: Some apples are not red. True.
   (b) Contrary: No apples are red. Undetermined.

Inferences Using Opposition

2. There are two different inferences.

   a. If (1) "no neutrons are charged" (T), then (2) "Some neutrons are charged" (F). Contradictory; Valid.
   b. If (1) "no neutrons are charged" (T), then (3) "All neutrons are charged" (F). Contrary; Valid.

Problem Set 19: Conversion

Converting Categorical Propositions

1. Some Americans are Texans.
4. No converse.
7. Some pretty things are cats.
10. Some slow-growing trees are mesquite trees.
14. No converse.
17. Some things with powerful hind legs are frogs.

23. Rewritten: (a) "Everything beautiful is also true" and (b) "everything true is also beautiful." If Keats meant that (b) follows from (a), this immediate inference is invalid. He probably meant each is true independently and was not making an inference.

Problem Set 20: Obversion and Advanced Manipulations

Obversion

1. No sports are unstrenuous (or better: easy).
2. All humans are imperfect.
3. Some Texans are not dishonest.
4. Some Texans are dishonest.
6. Some caves are not uninhabitable. (The opposite of "habitable" is not "inhabitable" nor "unhabitable.")
8. No games are unorganized (or disorganized).
13. No iguana is harmful.

Advanced Manipulations

8. All games are organized.

   1. Obverse: No games are unorganized. (o)
   2. Then convert: No unorganized things are games. (c)
   3. Then obvert: All unorganized things are non-games. (o)
   4. Then convert: Some non-games are unorganized. (c)

Problem Set 21: Hypothetical Propositions

Learning to Symbolize Hypothetical Propositions

4. $(S_p \cdot P_p)$
7. $(S_p \rightarrow \sim S_k)$
14. $(\sim S_k \cdot P_k) \rightarrow \sim P_s$

Symbolizing with Your Own Symbols

1. $(G \rightarrow L)$ 8. $\sim(A_p \cdot A_r)$ 17. $(Cw \cdot C_s)$
4. $(L \vee \sim L)$ 12. $(R_s \rightarrow M_d)$ 21. $(\sim R_b \rightarrow L_b)$

Problem Set 22: Advanced Hypothetical Propositions

Advanced Conditional Propositions

1. $(J = (J_m \cdot A))$ 9. $(\sim G \rightarrow \sim L)$
3. $(\sim C \rightarrow \sim V)$ or $(V \rightarrow C)$ 15. $\sim G \rightarrow \sim (J \cdot M)$
7. $(\sim G \rightarrow \sim L)$ 20. $S \rightarrow [B \rightarrow (K \rightarrow M)]$
8. $(G \rightarrow L)$

Advanced Conditional Propositions in Prose

3. $(\sim P_c \vee \sim P_q) \rightarrow (P_q \vee V_p)$
   $(\sim P_c \vee \sim P_q) \rightarrow (\sim P_q \rightarrow V_p)$
6. $S_m \vee S_l \vee S_t$
   $\sim (S_l \vee S_t)$
   Therefore, S_t
11. $(\sim 25 \vee \sim 7_c \vee \sim S) \rightarrow \sim R$ or $\sim (25 \cdot 7_c \cdot S) \rightarrow \sim R$

Problem Set 23: Distinguishing Deductive from Inductive Reasoning

Drawing *Conclusions* Deductively or Inductively

1. Induction.   10. Deduction.
3. Deduction.   12. Both deduction and induction.
6. Induction.

Distinguishing Deductive from Inductive *Arguments*

1. Rusting machinery in tropics
   a. Machinery made of iron, a component of steel, rusts because of oxidation from humid air.
   b. two.
   c. (1) inductive: Iron rusts through oxidation, which is accomplished by transfer of oxygen from O_2 and H_2O particles in the air to iron (Fe), forming iron oxide or rust; (2) deductive: Machinery in trop-

ics rusts more, because machinery in tropics is in high humidity air, the source of oxidation; and high humidity air, the source of oxidation, causes more rusting.

2. Marx/Engels

a. All human history is a history of class struggles.

b. one

c. inductive

6. Scheinfeld

a. Bodily changes that happen during our lifetime cannot be inherited by our children.

b. one

c. inductive

Problem Set 24: Identifying Categorical Syllogisms

Syllogisms in Standard Form

1. Minor term: cheetahs
   Minor premise: All cheetahs are animals.
   Major term: living things
   Major premise: All animals are living things.
   Middle term: animals
   Conclusion: All cheetahs are living things.
   Figure: First
   Mood: AAA

4. Minor term: pillow
   Minor premise: Every pillow is soft.
   Major term: stone
   Major premise: No stones are soft.
   Middle term: soft
   Conclusion: No pillow is a stone.
   Figure: Second
   Mood: EAE

Syllogisms in Normal Prose

3. Minor term: Houstonians
   Minor Premise: No Houstonians are Frenchmen
   Major term: logical
   Major premise: All Frenchmen are logical.
   Middle term: Frenchmen
   Conclusion: No Houstonians are logical.
   Figure: First
   Mood: AEE

5. Minor term: friendly guys
   Minor Premise: Some socialists are friendly guys.
   Major term: Democrats
   Major premise: Some Democrats are socialists.
   Middle term: socialists
   Conclusion: Some friendly guys are Democrats.
   Figure: Four
   Mood: III

Problem Set 25: Validity of Categorical Syllogisms

Using the Rules to Determine Validity

1. Major term: humans
   Middle term: rational
   Minor term: people who failed the test
   Figure: Second
   Mood: AEE
   V/I: Invalid
   Rule violated: Rule 1, Equivocal term: "rational"

3. Major term: well-trained
   Middle term: cops
   Minor term: firemen
   Figure: First
   Mood: AEE

V/I: Invalid
Rule violated: Rule 3, illicit major term.

6. Major term: fishermen
Middle term: sea lover
Minor term: Texan
Figure: Second
Mood: AII
V/I: Invalid
Rule violated: Rule 2, Undistributed middle term

13. Major term: used
Middle term: dishes
Minor term: washed
Figure: Third
Mood: AII
V/I: Valid
Rule violated: none

Problem Set 26: Categorical Syllogisms in Prose

Using the Rules to Determine Validity

1. Major premise: Everyone who wears army shoes was in the army.
Minor premise: My mother wears army shoes.
Conclusion: My mother was in the army.
Figure: First
Mood: AAA
V/I: Valid
Rule violated: None

4. Major premise: All Frenchmen are logical.
Minor Premise: No Texans are Frenchmen.
Conclusion: No Texans are logical.
Figure: First
Mood: AEE
V/I: Invalid
Rule violated: Rule 3, Illicit major term.

11. Major premise: All menaces to society are people who fail in their obligations to society.
    Minor Premise: All poor mechanics are people who fail in their obligations to society.
    Conclusion: All poor mechanics are menaces to society.
    Figure: Second
    Mood: AAA
    V/I: Invalid
    Rule violated: Rule 2, Undistributed middle term.

15. Major premise: No apes are angels.
    Minor Premise: No philosophers are apes.
    Conclusion: No philosophers are angels.1.
    Figure: First
    Mood: EEE
    V/I: Invalid
    Rule violated: Rule 4

Problem Set 27: Venn Diagrams of Syllogisms

Determining Validity Using Venn Diagrams

1. Every fisherman loves the sea.

   Some Houstonians are fishermen.

   Therefore, some Houstonians love the sea.

   Valid

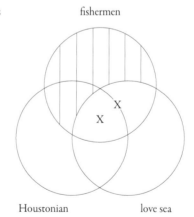

fishermen

Houstonian   love sea

2. Every fisherman loves the sea.

No drug dealer is a fisherman

Therefore, no drug dealer loves the sea.

Invalid

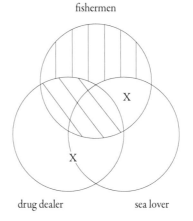

fishermen

drug dealer   sea lover

5. All patriots are voters.

Some citizens are not voters.

Therefore, some citizens are not patriots.

Valid

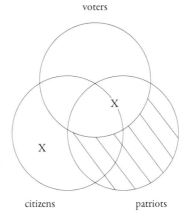

voters

citizens   patriots

8. Frenchmen are very logical and, in view of the fact the Texans are not Frenchmen, we may conclude that they are not very logical.

Invalid

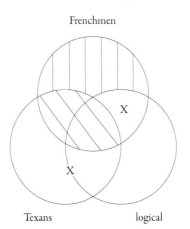

Frenchmen

Texans   logical

Problem Set 28: Enthymemes and Epicheiremas
Identifying and Evaluating Enthymemes and Epicheiremas

1. Type: Enthymeme (third order)
   Major premise: All gentlemen hold open car doors for ladies.
   Minor premise: Edward is a gentleman.
   Conclusion: [Edward holds open car doors for ladies.]
   Figure: First
   Mood: AAA
   V/I: Valid

6. Type: Enthymeme and Epicheirema
   Major premise: [All people who are like wolves should be removed.]
   Minor premise: All the political party leaders are like wolves.
   Conclusion: All the political party leaders should be removed.
   Proof of major: None
   Proof of minor: Party leaders prey on small beasts (= minor people in society).
   Figure: First
   Mood: AAA
   V/I: Valid

11. Type: Enthymeme *and* Epicheirema
    First interpretation:
    Major premise: Everything that can handle information can think.
    Minor premise: Some machines can handle information.
    Conclusion: Some machines can think.
    Proof of major: None
    Proof of minor: Some machines can calculate, conclude, and choose.
    Figure: First
    Mood: AAA
    V/I: Valid. But the major premise is false.

    Second interpretation:
    Major premise: Everything that can think can handle information.
    Minor premise: Some machines can handle information.
    Conclusion: Some machines can think.
    Proof of major: None

Proof of minor: Some machines can calculate, conclude, and choose.
Figure: Second
Mood: AAA
V/I: Invalid
Rule: Rule 2, undistributed middle term.
Major premise is true, but argument is invalid.
Conclusion: In either case, the argument is *unsound*.

16. Type: Enthymeme (third order)
    Major premise: All nations without souls are nations that cannot live.
    Minor premise: All nations without a conscience are nations without
    a soul.
    Conclusion: All nations without a conscience are nations that
    cannot live.
    Figure: First
    Mood: AAA
    V/I: Valid

Written during World War II when Churchill was Prime Minister of
Great Britain. The conclusion was about Nazi Germany; but Churchill said
this when the Germans were winning the war and the British were losing.
Since the premises are true, the syllogism is also sound.

23. Type: Epicheirema
    Major premise: All violations of the laws of nature are impossible.
    Minor premise: All miracles are violations of the laws of nature.
    Conclusion: All miracles are impossible.
    Proof of major premise: Experience has established the laws of nature.
    Proof of minor premise: None
    Figure: First
    Mood: AAA
    V/I: Valid
    Sound: Unsound. The first issue is whether or not the major premise
        is true. On Hume's own principles, we cannot know the major
        premise for sure, since experience cannot give us sure knowledge of
        causality in nature. Experience only gives us conjunction of events;
        we supply the idea of causal connections from our own customary
        ways of thinking. This is the import of his famous billiard ball ex-
        ample. The second issue is whether miracles really violate the laws

of nature. Hume takes the laws of nature to allow no exceptions, even though on his principles we can't know this for sure. Those who hold miracles are possible say that the laws of nature hold for the most part, but exceptions are possible, at least for God, who made the laws of nature. So something cannot really be a horse and a rose at the same time, but something can look like a horse or a rose, while really being something else. This is the explanation of how transubstantiation works. What was bread and still looks like bread has been made into a different substance—the body of Christ—while retaining the accidental features that make it look like bread, even though it isn't. No human can accomplish this feat, but on Catholic doctrine God can. Since Hume didn't believe God exists, quite naturally he denied miracles are possible.

26. Type: Epicheirema and Enthymeme

Major premise: No power of magnetism is correlative to the mass of the thing attracted.

Minor premise: All the power of gravity is correlative to the mass of the thing attracted.

Conclusion: No power of gravity is the [same as the] power of magnetism.

Proof of major premise: Magnets do not attract bodies based on their mass.

Proof of minor premise: Power of gravity changes with the mass of the thing attracted.

Figure: Second

Mood: EAE

V/I: Valid

Problem Set 29: Longer Categorical Arguments

Diagramming Arguments: Succint Arguments

3. a. Business conditions will improve.
   b. Corporate profits will increase.
   c. Stock prices will increase.
   d. Therefore, invest in the stock market now.

5. a. Gas burns easily.
   b. Carrying gas in car is dangerous.
   c. Gas engine moves car very fast.
   d. Gas has terrible explosive power.
   e. Don't carry a can of gas in your car

Longer Arguments

Instructions

The propositions in these arguments are indicated by letters. The diagrams show how they are arranged in the argument.

3. a. Marijuana produces mild euphoria.
   b. Marijuana not detrimental to health.
   c. Legalize marijuana.
   d. Tobacco leads to cancer.
   e. Surgeon General warnings against tobacco.
   f. Tobacco is detrimental to health.
   g. Ban tobacco.
   h. Legalize marijuana and ban tobacco.

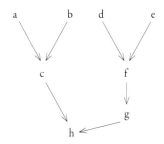

7. a. Human groups are made up of individuals.
   b. Psychological traits of groups are *caused* by traits of individuals.
   c. Psychological traits of groups are same traits as those of individuals.
   d. Analogy: study of individuals is *like* studying an object under a microscope.
   e. Psychology of individual provides details of group psychology.
   f. Study of individuals give *empirical* basis for study of groups.
   g. We should study individual psychology in order to understand group psychology.

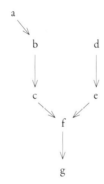

10. a. Moynihan: number of signals used by vertebrates: from 10 in fish to 37 in Rhesus monkey.
    b. Number of signals in social insects, esp. bees and ants: 10 to 20.
    c. Number of "signals" employed by animals is severely limited.
    d. Number of "signals" employed by humans is virtually unlimited.
    e. Radical difference in communication using "signals" between humans and animals.
    f. Radical difference in nature between humans and animals.

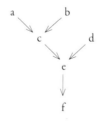

Classic Arguments

Instructions

The propositions in these arguments are indicated by letters. The diagrams show how they are arranged in the argument.

1. Machiavelli
   a. Men act out of self-interest, they are "ungrateful, fickle, false, cowards, covetous.
   b. Prince relies on love of his subjects for his benefits to them.
   c. Prince relies on fear of his subjects about his punishment of them.
   d. Citizens obey the Prince when their self-interest and love of the Prince coincide.
   e. Citizens disobey the Prince when their self-interest and love of the Prince differ.
   f. Citizens sometimes disobey the Prince.
   g. Citizens obey the prince out of self-interest, to avoid punishment.
   h. Citizens never disobey the Prince.
   i. It is better for the Prince to be feared than loved.

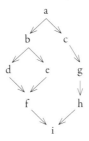

6. Marshall, *Marbury v. Madison*
   a. In a particular case, if there is opposition between a particular law and the Constitution, which takes precedence: the particular law passed by Congress or the Constitution?
   b. If Constitution is superior to "any ordinary act of the Legislature," then Constitution takes precedence.
   c. If a court denies this priority of the Constitution, then...
   d. An act contrary to the Constitution is obligatory, because following a particular law.

e. Legislature can over-ride the Constitution, just as one particular law can over-ride a previous law.

f. Gives the legislative branch "real omnipotence" over the other two branches.

g. Constitution prescribes legal limits by Courts but allows those limits to be "passed at pleasure."

h. The American *written* Constitution "reduces to nothing."

i. [Therefore, the nature of the Constitution requires the courts give Constitution preference over law enacted by the Legislature which are contrary to the Constitution itself.]

j. [The determination of Constitutionality is reserved to the judicial branch, not the legislative or executive. The judicial branch alone has the right and duty to determine whether or not a particular law is Constitutional]

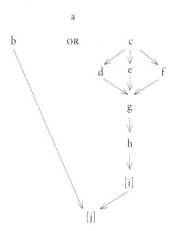

Problem Set 30: Hypothetical Arguments

Conditional Arguments

2.

$$G \rightarrow T$$

$$G$$

Therefore   T

Valid

7.
$$B \to \sim OS$$
$$\sim OS$$

Therefore   B

Invalid

Hypothetical Arguments in Prose

1. E = Evolution theory is true
    LF = lower fossils are less complex than higher fossils

$$E \to LF$$
$$LF$$

Therefore   E

Invalid.

Comment: This is why scientific experiments need to be repeated many times. The evidence does not demonstrate the conclusion for sure, but it offers evidence that the theory is true. Evidence "validates" the theory; the more evidence the greater the support of the theory.

5. Int = money draws interest Int_A = Aunt Alberta's money draws interest

    Inv = money is invested Inv_A = Aunt Alberta's money was invested

$$\sim Inv \to \sim Int$$
$$Inv_A$$

Therefore Int_A

Invalid

7. D = I am deceived.
    E = I exist.

$$D \to E$$
$$D$$

Therefore   E

15.   2 = A man serves two masters

H = hate one

L = love the other

$$\frac{2 \rightarrow (H \ \& \ L)}{\sim(H \ \& \ L)}$$

Therefore, $\sim$2

Valid

$\sim$(H & L) is not stating a fact, since we can hate one and love the other, but is stating a moral principle according to Jesus. You ought not to hate, but if you try to serve two masters, you will hate one of them.

Problem Set 31: Standardized Test–Style Argument

Logic Games–Style Question

Explanations and answers given in chapter 31.

Problem Set 32: Induction

Distinguishing Inductive from Deductive Arguments

1. Deduction   4. Induction

2. Induction   7. Both ways

Different Kinds of Inductions

1. partial enumerative induction

3. complete enumerative induction

7. abstractive induction

10. abstractive induction

Inductive Arguments in Context

2. Marx and Engels
    a. Inductive conclusion: "The history of all hitherto existing society is the history of class struggles.... in a word, oppressor and oppressed."
    b. Premises are examples of classes opposed to each other:
        (1) freeman and slave.
        (2) patrician and plebeian.
        (3) lord and serf.
        (4) guild-master and journeyman.
    c. Type: partial enumerative induction.

5. Scheinfeld.
    a. Inductive conclusion: "Chromosomes in our germ cells are not affected by any change that takes place within our body cells" during our lifetime.
    b. Type: partial enumerative induction
    c. Deductive conclusion: "no change ... made in us in our lifetimes ... can be passed on to our children through the process of biological heredity."
    d. Deductive argument: not given.

7. Phonics vs. whole-word reading.
    a. Inductive conclusion: Children using phonics learned to read aloud better.
    b. Type: Partial enumerative induction.
    c. Deductive conclusion: [Phonics should be used to teach children to read.]
    d. Deductive argument: not given

Problem Set 33: Complex Arguments

Three examples are presented and analyzed in the chapter.

Appendixes

The final part of this book contains two appendixes. First comes a chronology of major logicians, along with their works devoted, partly or wholly, to logic. The reason for including this appendix is to give a sense of the importance and long history of the kind of "verbal" or "Aristotelian" logic presented in this textbook. The second appendix lists a number of logic textbooks written over the last century that present such a "verbal" logic in textbook form. It is designed to show that, as important as symbolic logic has become for advanced studies in many areas, the utility of "verbal" logic for teaching a first, undergraduate course in logic is still recognized. Indeed, this recognition has grown over the last few decades.

Chronology of Logicians and Their Logical Works

Classical Greek Philosophers

Plato (d. 347 B.C.)

Student of Socrates, after whose death in 399 B.C. Plato began writing dialogues in defense of Socrates and his kind of "philosophy" or "love of wisdom." He did not distinguish logic as a branch of knowledge, but did separate the well-reasoned thought of the "philosopher" from the erroneous thought of the "sophist."

Logical/Rhetorical Works

Euthydemus (ca. 384 B.C.); *Gorgias* (ca. 380); *Republic* (ca. 380), which charts the progression from ignorance to wisdom; *Theatetus* (ca. 369); *Sophist* (ca. 360).

Aristotle (384–22 B.C.)

Born in Stagira, Macedonia, he moved to Athens and stayed in Plato's Academy for twenty years (367–47), returned home, taught Alexander the Great beginning in 343, and then founded the Lyceum, his school in Athens.

He distinguished areas of knowledge he called "arts" and "sciences," each a systematic study of a particular subject or topic, designed for classes he taught. Logic is an "art," not a "science," because it is a set of skills applicable in every area of knowledge. Each of his surviving works, completed between 347 and 322 B.C., set out his thought in one of the different disciplines. His logic is contained in six books. The present textbook presents the kind of "verbal" logic Aristotle invented.

Logical/Rhetorical Works

Formal logic: By distinguishing the form of thought and discourse from its content, later called its "matter," Aristotle could distinguish logic from the other intellectual disciplines.

Categories: First act of the mind: conceptualization of terms.

On Interpretation: Second act of the mind: mental judgments producing statements and propositions.

Prior Analytics: Third act of the mind, the structure or form of valid and invalid deductive reasoning.

Material logic: Includes logical consideration of content (or matter), focusing on how certain or uncertain the conclusions derived by reasoning are.

Posterior Analytics: Demonstrative reasoning, producing the kind of necessary and certain conclusions proven in an Aristotelian "science."

Topics: Aristotle's first attempt at a logic textbook, covering dialectical or probable reasoning. Organized on the model of "technical" manuals of earlier rhetoricians.

On Sophistical Refutations: The kind of errors found in sophistical reasoning.

Rhetorical Works:

Poetics: The way literature, especially poetry, can lead us to theoretical truths, especially about human life.

Rhetoric: The oldest surviving textbook of rhetoric, which shows how the "art" of rhetoric produces practical, persuasive discourse. Rhetorical reasoning need not be sophistical, as Plato had thought.

There are many English translations of the works of Plato and Aristotle. Greek and English translations in *Loeb Classical Library*. Greek texts in *Thesaurus linguae Graecae*, http://stephanus.tlg.uci.edu.

Hellenistic Philosophers and Logicians: The Stoics

Greek

They raised logic from an "art" to a "science," by dividing philosophy into three areas: physics, ethics, and logic, which concentrated on hypothetical rather than categorical syllogisms. Stoicism had begun with three Greek philosophers: **Zeno** (d. 262 B.C.), **Cleanthes** (d. 232 B.C.), and **Chrysippus** (d. ca. 206 B.C.), only pieces of whose works still exist. The book of **Diogenes Laertius** (fl. ca. 250 A.D.), *The Lives and Views of the Most Eminent Philosophers*, is our main source for their doctrines. Greek and English translation, *Loeb Classical Library*.

Roman

Cicero (d. 44 B.C.)

Lawyer and politician; last and greatest of the defenders of the Roman Republic.

Logical/rhetorical works: Rhetoric: *On Invention* and *On the Orator*. Philosophy: *On the Ends of Good and Evil Deeds* and *On Duties*.

Seneca (d. 65 A.D.): Advisor to the Roman emperor Nero, who forced him to commit suicide.

Logical/rhetorical works: *Epistles*, universally admired over the centuries, for their style and their display of Stoic logic, rhetoric, and ethics.

There are many translations of the works of Cicero and Seneca. Latin and English translations in *Loeb Classical Library*.

Commentators on Aristotle

In the ancient Western world there were two major centers of philosophical study, Athens and Alexandria, Egypt. From the time of Socrates, Athens attracted philosophers from throughout the world. In 176, Emperor Marcus

Aurelius established chairs in Athens for the four traditional philosophical schools: Platonic, Peripatetic (Aristotelian), Stoic, and Epicurean.

In 332 B.C., Alexander the Great had founded a city named after himself in Egypt, Alexandria, which became a second center of Greek learning, with its great library, under the Ptolemaic dynasty, begun by Ptolemy I Soter, one of the three Greek generals of Alexander who divided among themselves the vast territories he had conquered. Alexandrian philosophers organized the works of Plato and Aristotle into a sequence of courses. First came systematic study of the works of Aristotle, in this order: logic, mathematics, physical sciences, ethics, and metaphysics. Second came reading various dialogues of Plato. Most of the works of these Greek commentators have not survived.

The schools in Athens lasted until 529, when they were closed for religious reasons, by the Roman emperor Justinian, a Christian. At that point some philosophers from Athens and Alexandria migrated to the school of Gundeshapur, in the Persian Sasanian Empire, east of the confluence of the Tigris and Euphrates rivers, invited by Emperor Khosraw (Chosroes) I (r. 531–79). There the Greek philosophers mixed with Nestorian Christians, Persian Zoroastrians, Manichaeans, and Indian scholars. Even when the armies of the Muslim Caliph Umar defeated the Sasanians in 638, the school at Gundeshapur lasted and became the model for the "House of Wisdom" created by Caliph Ma'mun (r. 813–33) at the Abbasid capital, the new "round city" of Baghdad, upstream the Tigris from Gundeshapur.

Greek Commentators on Aristotle, before Plotinus (d. 270 A.D.), Founder of neo-Platonism

Greek texts of commentators: H. Diels (general editor), *Commentaria in Aristotelem Graeca* (Berlin: 1882–1909); and *Thesaurus Linguae Grecae*: http://stephanus.tlg.uci.edu. English translations are now available in the series *Ancient Commentators on Aristotle*, http://www.ancientcommentators .org.uk/, general editor Sir Richard Sorabji.

Andronicus of Rhodes (fl. ca. 60 B.C.).

Organized the entire corpus of Aristotle's works into the form we have now.

Alexander of Aphrodisias (d. 220)

Studied and taught in Athens. The only major commentator whose work preceded the influence of neo-Platonism, he interpreted *Aristoteles ex Aristotele*.

Logical/rhetorical works: Commentaries on *Prior Analytics*, bk. 1; *Topics*; *Sophistical Refutations*.

Greek Neo-Platonic Commentators on Aristotle

Porphyry (d. 305)

Studied in Athens, then in Rome with Plotinus. Student and biographer of Plotinus, he preserved and organized the writings of Plotinus.

Logical works: *Introduction* to Aristotle's Logic; *Commentary on the Categories*

Iamblichus (d. 320):Studied under Porphyry, taught in Syria.

Themistius (d. ca. 350).Constantinople. Orator and philosopher, supported by Emperor Julian the Apostate (r. 361-3).

Logical work: *Epitome of the Posterior Analytics*.

Syrianus (d. 435).

Athens.

Proclus (d. 485)

Studied in Alexandria, taught in Athens.
Systematic work: *Elements of Theology*

Ammonius (d. 520)

Studied in Athens, taught in Alexandria.
Logical works: commentaries on *Categories* and *On Interpretation*

Simplicius (d. ca. 560)

Studied in Alexandria under Ammonius and in Athens under Damascius. Taught likely in Alexandria until banished from the Roman Empire by Justinian in 529 for his paganism, whence he fled to the patronage of King Choesroes in Persia.

Logical work: commentary on *Categories*.

John Philoponus (d. 570)

Studied in Alexandria under Ammonius and taught there. As a Christian, he was not banned from the empire.

Logical works: commentaries on *Categories* and *Posterior Analytics*.

The works in this section were translated into Latin and influenced the Christian Scholastic thinkers, listed below.

Latin Neo-Platonic Commentator on Aristotle

Boethius (d. 526)

Roman patrician who lived after the death of the last Roman emperor in the West, Romulus Augustulus (d. 476), while the Ostrogoth King Odoacer ruled Italy (r. 493–526). Since Romans no longer knew Greek, he conceived the idea of translating the works of Plato and Aristotle into Latin, but managed to get no further than Aristotle's logic. These translations were the only Aristotelian works known in the Latin West until the twelfth century translations of the works of Aristotle and the Muslim Aristotelian Avicenna. Odoacer appointed Boethius to the high post of "master of the offices," but eventually put him in prison, where he managed to compose his masterful *Consolation of Philosophy* before being executed.

Logical works: Boethius translated all of Aristotle's logical works, except for the *Posterior Analytics*, composed commentaries on them, and also wrote his own works on their contents. They quickly became available in the Latin West. Available at *Christian Latin Texts*: http://www.brepolis.net/.

Medieval Arabic and Jewish Philosophers

Al-Farabi (d. 980–81)

Called the "second Master," after Aristotle, because devoted to presenting accurately the thought of Aristotle to the Islamic world. He wrote numerous commentaries and treatises on logic, only two of which are currently available in English. In line with the "Alexandrian" school, he thought the views of Plato and Aristotle complemented each other. He organized his synthetic works covering the whole of reality, however, using the traditional neo-Platonic circle of things emanating from, and then returning to, the one God.

Logical/rhetorical works: Al-Fârâbî (ca. 870–950), *Al-mantiq 'inda al-Fârâbî*, ed. al-'Ajam, Rafîq and Majid Fakhry, 4 vols. (Beirut: Dar al-Mashriq, 1985–87); Al-Fârâbî, *al-mantiqiyyât lil-Fârâbî*, ed. Dânishpazuh Muhammad Taqî, 3 vols. (Qumm: Matba'at Bahman, 1987–89); Lahcen E. Ezzaher, ed., "Alfarabi's *Book of Rhetoric*: An Arabic-English translation of Alfarabi's Commentary on Aristotle's Rhetoric," *Rhetorica* 26, no. 4 (2008): 347–91; Joep Lameer, *Al-Fârâbî and Aristotelian Syllogistics: Greek Theory and Islamic Practice* (Leiden: Brill, 1994).

Synthetic philosophical works, available in English translation: *Views of the Inhabitants of the Perfect State*; *The Political Regime*, also called *On the Principles of Being*; *Harmony of the Views of the Divine Plato and Aristotle*.

Ibn Sina (Avicenna) (d. 1037)

If al-Farabi was the master of the details of Aristotle's philosophy and logic, Avicenna was the first philosopher since Aristotle himself to write synthetic works incorporating the full range of philosophy; and he did this not once but four times. Each of these works is arranged to cover all four parts of the Alexandrian course of Aristotelian philosophy: logic, physics, mathematics, and metaphysics. And the logic parts contain all eight sections of Alexandrian logic: Porphyry's *Introduction*; *Categories*; *Propositions*; *Syllogism*; *Demonstration*; *Dialectic*; *Sophistic*; *Rhetoric*; and *Poetics*. But Avicenna refused merely to comment on Aristotle; instead he offered his own thought, heavily influenced by Aristotle, but on some central points quite different.

His four synthetic works: *The Book of Healing* (*Shifâ'*), translated into Latin in the twelfth century and heavily influential on the Christian scholastic thinkers beginning in the thirteenth century; *The Deliverance* (*Najât*); *Philosophy for Ala-al-Dawla*; and *Pointers and Reminders* (*Al-Ishârât wa-al-Tanbîhât*).

Logical works available in English translation: Ibn Sina, *Avicenna's Deliverance: Logic* (from al-Najât), trans., ed. Asad Q. Ahmed (Karachi: Oxford University Press, 2011); Ibn Sina, *The Metaphysics of "The Healing"* (*al-Shifâ'*), trans. M. Marmura (Provo, Utah: Brigham Young University, 2005; Ibn Sina, *Remarks and Admonitions*, part 1, *Logic*, trans. Shams C. Inati (Toronto: Pontifical Institute of Mediaeval Studies, 1984).

Ibn Rushd (Averroes) (d. 1198)

While al-Farabi and Avicenna lived in the Middle East, Averroes lived in Spain, which had been conquered by Muslim warriors in 711. By profession a judge of Islamic law (*fiqh* and *sharia*), he was by avocation a philosopher. He thought Avicenna's philosophy had been infected by introducing religious ideas into philosophy, so in order to rectify this mistake he composed a series of line-by-line commentaries on almost all the works of Aristotle. This task was important, because in his view, along with most Arabic philosophers, religious ideas contained "truth for the unintelligent masses," while philosophy offered truth for the intellectual and moral elite. In logic, he wrote commentaries on all the logical works of Aristotle. His commentaries were translated into Latin and heavily influenced the Christian scholastic thinkers.

Logical/rhetorical works: line-by-line commentaries on Aristotle's *Categories*, *On Interpretation*, *Prior Analytics*, *Posterior Analytics*, *Topics*, *Sophistical Refutations*, *Rhetoric*, and *Poetics*.

Commentaries on Aristotle available in Latin translation: *Aristotelis opera cum Averrois commentariis*, 12 vols. (Venetiis: Apud Junctas, 1562–74).

Maimonides (d. 1204)

Moses ben Maimon, called Maimonides, was a contemporary of Averroes. Born in 1138, his family lost their legal status as "people of the book" (*dhimmi*) and eventually left Spain, settling in Egypt around 1168. He was a physician who wrote medical works; as a Jewish leader he wrote the *Mishna Torah*, a comprehensive code of Jewish law; and as a philosopher he wrote the *Guide for the Perplexed*—that is, those struggling to reconcile religious faith with philosophy, which was translated into Latin and read by the Christian scholastics.

Logical work: *The Words of Logic*, which explains the technical terminology used in logic, following al-Farabi.

Medieval Christian Scholastics

The works of Aristotle himself, along with the writings of the Greek commentators and the commentaries and original works of Avicenna, Averroes, and Maimonides, were translated into Latin in the hundred years from 1150 to 1250. Their effect was nothing short of revolutionary in the sciences, philosophy, the liberal arts, especially logic, and even in theology.

The university as we now know it was created in Western Europe toward the end of the twelfth century, and early in the thirteenth came to be called a "university of masters and students" (*universitas magistrorum et scholarium*): "university" because one corporate entity, like a guild of craftsmen, whose teachers were called "masters," on the same model, while students were like apprentices and were called "scholars," from *schola* or "school." Then, as now, university education was divided into two levels. Undergraduate education in the "school of arts" originally focused on the seven "liberal arts": the *trivium* of grammar, logic, and rhetoric, and the *quadrivium* of geometry and astronomy, arithmetic and music. But with the translation of the works of Aristotle and his Greek and Arabic commentators, his many "sciences" were added to this curriculum. The medieval universities had graduate schools in three areas: theology, medicine, and law. The approach to learning in all faculties was called "scholastic," originally a term of praise, but in the hands of Renaissance humanists, followed by "Enlightenment" thinkers, it was gradually turned into one of disapprobation.

Peter Abelard (1079–1142)

The major logician of the twelfth century. First taught logic and then theology in Paris during the period of Cathedral schools, before the creation of universities. Attempted to change theological writing from commentary on Scripture to theological treatises applying logic to understanding the truths of revelation. Unfortunately, his knowledge of Aristotle was limited to the works translated by Boethius; but he was a forerunner of the "scholastic" thought to come.

Petrus Hispanus (Peter of Spain) (Thirteenth Century)

Summulae logicales, written 1220–50. Scholastic logic textbook, widely used from the thirteenth to seventeenth centuries. Divided into two parts: "the logic of the ancients" or Aristotelian logic, which focuses on reasoning, the third act of the mind; and secondly "the logic of the moderns" [= medieval logicians], which focuses on the properties of "terms," the first act of the mind, and is now called "terminist logic." This second part contains the beginnings of numerous medieval innovations, some of which anticipate developments in contemporary logic. Widely used in universities until replaced by the *Port Royal Logic*: Peter of Spain, *Summaries of Logic*, Text, trans., introduction, and notes Brian P. Copenhaver, with Calvin Normore and Terence Parsons (Oxford: Oxford University Press, 2014).

The major logicians in the Scholastic period, however, were Masters of Theology or of Arts in the university.

Thomas Aquinas, OP (1224/5–74)

Along with Plato, Aristotle, and Avicenna, one of the supreme philosophers of world culture, by profession he was a Master of Theology. But he embraced the rediscovered works of Aristotle, and is arguably the best of all of the commentators on Aristotle.

Logical Works: Commentaries on Aristotle's *On Interpretation* and *Posterior Analytics*.

Many English translations; also available at website: *Past Masters*. Latin works available at *corpus thomisticum*: http://www.corpusthomisticum.org

John Duns Scotus, OFM (ca. 1266–1308)

The major Franciscan philosopher of the thirteenth and early fourteenth centuries.

Logical Works: *Questions* on *Porphyry's Introduction*, on Aristotle's *Categories*, *On Interpretation*, and *Sophistical Refutations*. Latin texts, Wadding edition, online: http://www.sydneypenner.ca/os/scotus.shtml

William Ockham, OFM (ca. 1285–1347)

His nominalism or conceptualism, the metaphysical and epistemological view that universals are merely terms or concepts in the mind, led Ockham to concentrate on logic more than previous scholastic philosophers.

Logical Works: *Expositions* of Porphyry, *Introduction (Isagoge),* and of Aristotle, *Categories, On Interpretation,* and *Sophistic Refutations* (written 1321–24); *Summa of Logic* (written 1323–25). His masterwork, a systematic treatment of logic and semantics, arranged following the traditional order, but with many innovations: part 1, Logic of terms; part 2, Logic of propositions, focusing on "supposition" or the way the subject "stands under" the predicate;

part 3: Logic of arguments, divided into 3.1, syllogisms, both assertoric and modal, 3.2, demonstrative syllogisms, 3.3, consequences: which covers implications found in both propositions and arguments, 3.4: fallacies. Latin works: William of Ockham, *Opera philosophica et theologica*, ed. Gedeon Gál, et al., 17 vols. (St. Bonaventure, N.Y.: The Franciscan Institute, 1967–88). Various sections of the *Summa of Logic* have been translated by Alfred Freddoso, John Longaway, Michael Loux, and Henry Schurman.

Jean Buridan (before 1300–ca. 1358)

Remained a Master of Arts at the University of Paris for his whole career, unlike most scholastic philosophers who proceeded to become theologians. But this did not prevent him from twice becoming rector of the whole University of Paris. He wrote commentaries on most of the works of Aristotle, but his most important work was the *Summulae de dialectica*, which began as a commentary on Peter of Spain's *Summulae logicales*.

Logical work: *Summulae de dialectica*, a comprehensive work designed to show that the logical works of Aristotle are consistent with the *via moderna* or "terminist logic": Treatise I: propositions; Treatises II–IV: terms—their signification, supposition, and use in propositions; Treatise V: syllogisms; Treatise VI: topics or probable arguments; Treatise VII: fallacious arguments; and Treatise VIII: demonstrative arguments. English translation: Gyula Klima, trans., *John Buridan: "Summulae de Dialectica"* (New Haven and London: Yale University Press: 2001).

Renaissance

Lorenzo Valla (ca. 1407–57)

Humanist, the title of whose book *Repastinatio dialecticae et philosophiae* (*Digging up again the fields of dialectic and philosophy*), shows his rejection of philosophy, and its scholastic logic, and his preference for dialectical and rhetorical argumentation.

Petrus Ramus (1515–72)

Aristotelice animadversiones, dialecticae institutiones (*Attacks on Aristotle, Promotion of Dialectic*) (1543). Humanist and anti-scholastic who rejected logic in favor of rhetoric. Fought to remove from the university curriculum Peter of Spain's *Summulae logicales*, saying it failed to make him "more judicious in my studies of history and antiquity, nor more skilled in disputation, nor more competent at writing poetry, nor indeed more competent at anything at all" (*Scholae in liberales artes*, Basel, 1569).

Giacomo Zabarella (1533–89)

Opera logica, Venice 1578. Main representative of a thriving Renaissance Aristotelianism at the University of Padua. Especially concerned with the application of logic to natural science.

Modern (1650 to 1850)

Antoine Arnauld and Pierre Nicole

La Logique ou l'art de penser, usually called the *Port-Royal Logic*. English translation: Arnauld and Nicole, *Logic or the Art of Thinking*, trans. Jill V. Buroker (New York: Cambridge University Press, 1996). Follows Aristotle's organization of logic based on the three acts of the mind: concepts, judgments, arguments, but, following Descartes, adds a fourth part on "method." Limits sound arguments to rationalistic deductions, independent of sense experience.

Richard Whately

Elements of Logic (1826) and *Elements of Rhetoric* (1828). Following the Aristotelian tradition, and the *Port Royal Logic* in particular, Whately held that deductive argument was the sounder mode of reasoning than induction.

J. S. Mill (1806–73)

A System of Logic. 1834. Reply to Whately, Mill's empiricist philosophy led him to embrace inductive reasoning, for which he set out five "rules of thumb" to guide inductions, later called "Mill's Methods." But he abandoned the intuitive insight traditionally thought necessary to perfect inductive reasoning and achieve certain knowledge. He denied that syllogistic reasoning produces new knowledge: "Nothing ever was, or can be proved by syllogism which was not known, or assumed to be known, before" (*System* VII:183). So we gain no new knowledge using standard syllogistic inferences, such as "All men are mortal; Socrates is a man; therefore, Socrates is mortal," because the conclusion has already been asserted in the major premise.

Contemporary Symbolic Logic (1850 to Present)

George Boole (1815–64)

Mathematical Analysis of Logic (1847), *The Laws of Thought* (1854). First logician to move logic from its verbal language to a mathematical style language, that of algebra.

Augustus de Morgan (1806–71)

On the Syllogism and Other Writings, ed. Peter Heath, 1966. Works originally published 1846–62. Further developed the algebraic language of logic.

John Venn (1834–1923)

Symbolic Logic (1881), reprinted 1971. Took a second step toward mathematical logic, beyond Boole and de Morgan. Invented "Venn diagrams" in order to set the logic of verbal language into a second mathematical "language," that of geometric forms—namely, circles that represent classes of things. Intersecting circles are used to represent geometrically the language of verbal terms, propositions, and deductive arguments.

Gottlob Frege (1848–1925)

Rechnungsmethoden, die sich auf eine Erweiterung des Grössenbegriffes gründen. Jena: Friedrich Frommann, 1874. Translation by H. Kaal, *Methods of Calculation Based on an Extension of the Concept of Quantity*, in Gottlob Frege, *Collected Papers on Mathematics, Logic, and Philosophy*, ed. B. McGuinness (Oxford: 1984), 56–92.

In the following crucial passage, Frege separates arithmetic from the quantities of real things and bases it on logic; and then, following Kant, Frege claims logic is based purely in the mind, not taken from the contours of reality:

> According to the old conception, length appears as something material which fills the straight line between its end points and at the same time prevents an-

other thing from penetrating into its space by its rigidity. In adding quantities, we are therefore forced to place one quantity against another. Something similar holds for surfaces and solid contents. The introduction of negative quantities made a dent in this conception, and imaginary quantities made it completely impossible. Now all that matters is the point of origin and the end point—the idea of filling the space has been completely lost. All that has remained is certain general properties of addition, which now emerge as the essential characteristic marks of quantity. The concept has thus gradually freed itself from intuition [= sense experience] and made itself independent. This is quite unobjectionable, especially since its earlier intuitive character was at bottom mere appearance. Bounded straight lines and planes enclosed by curves can certainly be intuited, but what is quantitative about them, what is common to lengths and surfaces, escapes our intuition.... There is accordingly a noteworthy difference between geometry and arithmetic in the way in which their fundamental principles are grounded. The elements of all geometrical constructions are intuitions, and geometry refers to intuition as the source of its axioms. Since the object of arithmetic does not have an intuitive character, its fundamental propositions cannot stem from intuition. (Frege, *Collected Papers*, 56)

Alfred North Whitehead (1861–1947) and Bertrand Russell (1872–1970)

Principia Mathematica, 3 vols. (1910, 1912, 1913). Pioneering work that for the first time set out the content of symbolic logic in systematic order. Inspired by Frege's insight that mathematical truths are a subset of logical truths, Whitehead and Russell then proved the theorems of mathematical logic through logical deduction from a set of fundamental axioms, thus creating an "axiomatic system." This system was designed to show that mathematical truths have a secure foundation in logic, rather than the quantitative features of reality, as Aristotle had affirmed; and further, that the truths of logic itself are independent of the reality we experience empirically.

Appendix 2

A Selection of English-Language Textbooks in Logic

This selection of textbooks is weighted toward Verbal or Aristotelian logic. Textbooks are classified as treating: Verbal logic, Symbolic logic, or Both.

Byerly, T. Ryan. *Introducing Logic and Critical Thinking*. Grand Rapids, Mich.: Baker Academic, 2017. Both.

Clarke, Richard F., SJ. *Logic*. London: Green, 1921. Verbal.

Coffey, Peter. *The Science of Logic: An Inquiry into the Principles of Accurate Thought and Scientific Method*. 2 vols. New York: P. Smith, 1938. Verbal.

Connell, Richard J. *Logical Analysis*. Winona, Minn.: St. Mary's College Press, 1981. Verbal.

Copi, I. M., and C. Cohen. *Introduction to Logic*. 11th ed. London and New York: Routledge, 2002. Both.

Corbett, Edward P. J. *Classical Rhetoric for the Modern Student*. 3rd ed. New York: Oxford, 1999. Verbal.

Cotter, Anthony Charles, SJ. "Logic." In *The ABC of Scholastic Philosophy*, Heusenstamm: Editiones Scholasticae, 1947. Reprinted, New Brunswick: Transaction, 2012. 43–122. Verbal.

Dewey, John. *Logic: The Theory of Enquiry*. New York: Holt, 1938. Verbal.

Gensler, Harry J. *Introduction to Logic*. London and New York: Routledge, 2002. Both.

Hurley, Patrick J. *A Concise Introduction to Logic*. Stamford, CN: Cengage Learning, 2008. Both.

Joseph, H. W. B. *An Introduction to Logic*. Oxford: Clarendon, 1916. Verbal.

Kelley, David. *The Art of Reasoning*. 3rd ed. New York and London: Norton,1998. Both.

Kreeft, Peter. *Socratic Logic: Socratic Method Platonic Questions*. South Bend, Ind.: St. Augustine's Press, 2005. Verbal.

Kreyche, Robert. *Logic for Undergraduates*. New York: Holt, Rinehart, Winston, 1970. Both.

Maritain, Jacques. *Formal Logic*. Translated by Imelda Choquette. New York: Sheed and Ward, 1937. Verbal.

Oesterle, John A. *Logic: The Art of Defining and Reasoning*. New York: Prentice Hall, 1952. Verbal.

Parry, William, and Edward Hacker. *Aristotelian Logic*. Albany, N.Y.: SUNY Press, 1991. Verbal.

Sider, Theodore. *Logic for Philosophy*. Oxford and New York: Oxford University Press, 2010. Symbolic.

Smith, Vincent E. *The Elements of Logic*. Milwaukee: Bruce, 1957. Verbal.

Sommers, Fred. *The Logic of Natural Language*. Oxford: Clarendon, 1982. Verbal.

Spangler, Mary Michael. *Logic: An Aristotelian Approach*. 2nd ed. Lanham, Md.: University Press of America, 1993. Verbal.

Sullivan, Daniel J. *Fundamentals of Logic*. New York: Macmillan, 1963. Verbal.

Sullivan, Scott M. *An Introduction to Traditional Logic: Classical Reasoning for Contemporary Minds*. North Charleston, S.C.: Booksurge, 2005. Verbal.

Weston, Anthony. *A Rulebook for Arguments*. 5th ed. Indianapolis, Ind.: Hackett, 2017. Verbal.

Bibliography

Aesop. *The Complete Fables*. Translated by Olivia Temple and Robert Temple. London: Penguin, 2003.

al-Qushayrī, Muslim ibn al-Ḥajjāj. *Ṣaḥīḥ Muslim: Being Traditions of the Sayings and Doings of the Prophet Muhammad as Narrated by His Companions and Compiled under the Title al-Jāmiʿ-uṣ-ṣaḥīḥ*. Translated by Abdul Hameed Siddiqui. 4 vols. Lahore: Sh. Muhammad Ashraf, 1971–75.

Aquinas, Thomas. Latin texts of all works available at *Corpus thomisticum*: http://www.corpusthomisticum.org.

———. *Aquinas on Matter and Form and the Elements: A Translation and Interpretation of the De principiis naturae and the De mixtione elementorum of St. Thomas Aquinas*. Translated by Joseph Bobik. Notre Dame, Ind.: University of Notre Dame Press, 1998. [Electronic resource.]

———. *Aristotle: On Interpretation; Commentary by St. Thomas and Cajetan*. Translated by Jean T. Oesterle. Milwaukee, Wisc.: Marquette University Press, 1962.

———. *Commentary on Aristotle's Nicomachean Ethics*. Translated by C. I. Litzinger. Notre Dame, Ind.: Dumb Ox, 1993.

———. *Commentary on Aristotle's Posterior Analytics: A Translation of Aquinas's Commentary and of the Latin Text of Aristotle*. Translated by Richard Berquist. Notre Dame, Ind.: Dumb Ox, 2007.

———. *Commentary on Aristotle's Physics*. Translated by Richard J. Blackwell, Richard J. Spath, and W. Edmund Thirlkel. Notre Dame, Ind.: Dumb Ox, 1999.

———. *The Division and Methods of the Sciences: Questions V and VI of his Commentary on the De Trinitate of Boethius*. Translated, with introduction and notes by Armand Maurer. Toronto: Pontifical Institute of Mediaeval Studies, 1986.

Aristotle. Greek text of all works available at *Thesaurus Linguae Graecae*: http://stephanus.tlg.uci.edu.

————. *The Basic Works of Aristotle*. Edited by Richard McKeon. New York: Random House, 1941. By arrangement with Oxford University Press. Reprint: New York: Modern Library, 2001. Contains selected works in the first Oxford translation, ed. W. D. Ross.

————. *The Complete Works of Aristotle: The Revised Oxford Translation*. Edited by Jonathan Barnes. Bollingen 71. Princeton, N.J.: Princeton University Press, 1995. Contains translations of all the works of Aristotle, mainly from the first Oxford translation, ed. W. D. Ross.

————. *Metaphysics*. Translated by W. D. Ross. In McKeon, *Basic Works of Aristotle*, 681–926. Also in Barnes, *Complete Works of Aristotle*, translated by W. D. Ross, 2:1552–1728.

————. *Nicomachean Ethics*. Translated by W. D. Ross. In McKeon, *Basic Works of Aristotle*, 927–1112, and in *Barnes, Complete Works of Aristotle*, 2:1729–1867.

————. *On Interpretation*. Translated by E. M. Edghill. In McKeon, *Basic Works of Aristotle*, 38–61, and in Barnes, *Complete Works of Aristotle*, translated by J. L. Ackrill, 1:25–38.

————. *On the Soul*. Translated by J. A. Smith. In McKeon, *Basic Works of Aristotle*, 533–603, and in Barnes, *Complete Works of Aristotle*, translated by J. A. Smith, 1:641–92.

————. *Physics*. Translated by R. P. Hardie and R. K. Gaye. In McKeon, *Basic Works of Aristotle*, 213–394, and in Barnes, *Complete Works of Aristotle*, translated by R. P. Hardie and R. K. Gaye, 1:315–446.

————. *Politics*. Translated by Benjamin Jowett. In McKeon, *Basic Works of Aristotle*, 1113–16, and in Barnes, *Complete Works of Aristotle*, translated by Benjamin Jowett, 2:1986–2129.

————. *Posterior Analytics*. Translated by G. R. G. Mure. In McKeon, *Basic Works of Aristotle*, 213–394, and in Barnes, *Complete Works of Aristotle*, translated by Jonathan Barnes, 1:114–66.

————. *Prior Analytics*. Translated by A. J. Jenkinson. In McKeon, *Basic Works of Aristotle*, 62–107, and in Barnes, *Complete Works of Aristotle*, translated by A. J. Jenkinson, 1:39–113.

————. *Rhetoric*. Translated by W. Rhys Roberts. In McKeon, *Basic Works of Aristotle*, 1317–1451, and in Barnes, *Complete Works of Aristotle*, translated by W. Rhys Roberts, 2:2152–2269.

Atkins, Robert C., and Shirley Linde. *Dr. Atkins' Super-Energy Diet*. New York: Bantam, 1977.

Augustine. *Confessions*. Translated by F. J. Sheed. 2nd ed. Indianapolis: Hackett, 2007.

————. *On the Trinity*. Translated by Edmund Hill. Brooklyn, N.Y.: New City Press, 2002.

Austen, Jane. *Persuasion*. Edited, with an introduction and notes by Gillian Beer. London: Penguin, 2006.

————. *Pride and Prejudice*. Edited, with an introduction and notes by Vivien Jones. London: Penguin, 2006.

Averroes [Ibn Rushd]. *Aristotelis opera cum Averrois comentariis* [Works of Aristotle with the Commentaries of Averroes]. Venetiis apud Junctas: 1562–74. Translated from the Arabic into Latin in 12 volumes. Reprint. Frankfurt: Minerva, 1962. Latin translation from the Arabic.

Avicenna [Ibn Sina]. *Remarks and Admonitions* [Ishârât wa-al-tanbîhât]. Part 1, *Logic*. Translated by Shams Constantine Inati. Toronto: Pontifical Institute of Mediaeval Studies, 1984.

————. *Avicenna's Deliverance: Logic* [al-Najât: al-Mantiq]. Translation and Notes by Asad Q. Ahmed. Studies in Islamic Philosophy. Oxford and New York: Oxford University Press, 2011.

Berkeley, Edmund C. *Giant Brains or Machines That Think*. New York: Wiley; London: Chapman and Hall, 1949.

Bidinoto, Robert James, ed. *Criminal Justice? The Legal System versus Individual Responsibility*. 2nd ed. Irvington, N.Y.: Foundation for Economic Education, 1995.

Bridger, Bobby. *Buffalo Bill and Sitting Bull: Inventing the Wild West*. Austin: University of Texas Press; Chesham: Combined Academic, 2003.

Burke, Edmund. *Reflections on the Revolution in France*. Indianapolis: Liberty Fund, 1999.

Burr, Aaron. *Memoirs of Aaron Burr*. Edited by Matthew L. Davis. 2 vols. New York: Harper, 1837.

Byerly, T. Ryan. *Introducing Logic and Critical Thinking*. Grand Rapids, Mich.: Baker, 2017.

Byron, George Gordon. *The Complete Poetical Works*. Edited by Jerome J. McGann. 7 vols. Oxford: Clarendon Press; New York: Oxford University Press, 1991.

Carlyle, Thomas. *Past and Present*. In *Complete Works of Thomas Carlyle*. New York: Collier, 1901.

—————. *On Heroes, Hero-Worship, and the Heroic in History*. Notes and introduction by Michael K. Goldberg; text established by Michael K. Goldberg, Joel J. Brattin, and Mark Engel. Berkeley: University of California Press, 1993.

Carnap, Rudolph. *Logical Syntax of Language*. Translated by Amethe Smeaton (Countess von Zepplin). Oxford: Routledge, 2001. Originally published in 1937.

Carrel, Alexis. *Man, the Unknown* [L'Homme, cet inconnu]. New York: Harper and Brothers, 1939.

Cassirer, Ernst. *The Philosophy of Symbolic Forms*. Vol. 1, *Language* [Philosophie der symbolischen Formen. Erster Teil, Die Sprache]. Translated by Ralph Manheim. New Haven: Yale University Press, 1955.

Chesterton, G. K. *What's Wrong with the World*. London: Sheed and Ward, 1956.

—————. *The Autobiography*. San Francisco: Ignatius Press, 2005.

Christine de Pizan. *The Book of the City of Ladies*. Translated by Rosalind Brown-Grant. London: Penguin Books, 1999.

Churchill, Winston. *The Second World War*. 6 vols. Boston: Houghton Mifflin, 1948–53.

—————. *Winston S. Churchill: His Complete Speeches, 1897–1963*. 8 vols. Edited by Robert R. James. New York: Chelsea House, 1974.

Clarke, Richard F., SJ. *Logic*. London: Green, 1921.

Coffey, Peter. *The Science of Logic: An Inquiry into the Principles of Accurate Thought and Scientific Method*. 2 vols. New York: P. Smith, 1938.

Coleridge, Samuel Taylor. *The Collected Works of Samuel Taylor Coleridge*. Vol. 7, *Biographia literaria*. Edited by J. Engell and W. J. Bate. Bollingen series. London: Routledge; Princeton, N.J.: Princeton University Press, 1969–87.

Connell, Richard J. *Logical Analysis*. 2nd ed. Winona, Minn.: St. Mary's College Press, 1981.

Conrad, Josef. *The Nigger of the "Narcissus" and Other Stories*. Edited by J. H. Stape and Allan H. Simmons. Penguin Classics. London: Penguin, 2007.

Copi, Irving M., and Carl Cohen. *Introduction to Logic*. 11th ed. New York: Routledge, 2002.

Corbett, Edward P. J. *Classical Rhetoric for the Modern Student*. 3rd ed. New York: Oxford University Press, 1990.

Cotter, Anthony Charles, SJ. "Logic." In *The ABC of Scholastic Philosophy*, 43–122. Heusenstamm: Editiones Scholasticae, 2012. Originally published in 1947.

Cullman, Oscar. *Immortality of the Soul or Resurrection of the Dead*. London: Epworth Press, 1958.

Dalton, John. "Experimental Essays: Essays 1–4." In *Memoirs of the Literary and Philosophical Society of Manchester*. 2nd ed., 1802, 5:535–602.

———. *A New System of Chemical Philosophy*. Vol. 1. London: Bickerstaff, 1808.

Darwin, Charles. *On the Origin of Species by Means of Natural Selection; The Descent of Man and Selection in Relation to Sex*. 2nd ed. Great Books of the Western World. Chicago: Encyclopaedia Britannica, 1990.

Deely, John. *The Basics of Semiotics*. Bloomington: Indiana University Press, 1990.

de Montaigne, Michel. *The Complete Works: Essays, Travel Journal, Letters*. Translated by Donald M. Frame. New York: Knopf, 2003.

Desmet, Ronald, and Andrew David Irvine. "Alfred North Whitehead." In *The Stanford Encyclopedia of Philosophy* (Fall 2018 edition), edited by Edward N. Zalta. https://plato.stanford.edu/archives/fall2018/entries/whitehead/.

Descartes, Renée. *Discourse on Method and Meditations on First Philosophy*. Translated by Donald Cress. 4th ed. Indianapolis: Hackett, 1998.

de Tocqueville, Alexis. *Democracy in America*. Edited by Eduardo Nolla. Translated by James T. Schleifer. Indianapolis: Liberty Fund, 2012.

Dewey, John. *Logic, the Theory of Enquiry*. New York, H. Holt, 1938.

———. *Reconstruction in Philosophy*. Boston: Beacon Press, 1957.

Dostoevsky, Fyodor. *Notes from Underground*. Translated and annotated by Richard Pevear and Larissa Volokhonsky. New York: Alfred A. Knopf, 1993.

Dutton, Denis. "Plausibility and Aesthetic Interpretation." *Canadian Journal of Philosophy* 7 (1977): 327–40.

Einstein, Albert. "Geometry and Experience." In *The Collected Papers of Albert Einstein*. Vol. 7, *The Berlin Years: Writings, 1918–1921*, translated by Alfred Engel. Princeton, N.J.: Princeton University Press, 2002.

Emerson, Ralph Waldo. *Essays and Lectures*. New York: Literary Classics of the United States, 1983.

Fitzgerald, F. Scott. *The Great Gatsby*. New York: Scribner's, 1925.

Florey, Kitty Burns. *Sister Bernadette's Barking Dog*. New York: Houghton Mifflin, 2006.

Fourier, Jean Baptiste Joseph. *Analytical Theory of Heat* [1878]. Translated by Alexander Freeman. Cambridge: Cambridge University Press, 2009. Originally published in 1878.

Faraday, Michael. *Experimental Researches in Electricity*. Great Books of the Western World 45. Chicago: Encyclopaedia Britannica, 1955.

Frege, Gottlob. "Methods of Calculation Based on an Extension of the Concept of Quantity" [Rechnungsmethoden, die sich auf eine Erweiterung des Grössenbegriffes gründen].

Translated by H. Kaal. In *Collected Papers on Mathematics, Logic, and Philosophy*, edited by B. McGuinness, 56–92. Oxford: Oxford University Press, 1984.

Fromm, Erich. *Escape from Freedom*. New York: Farrar and Rinehart, 1941.

Gensler, Harry J. *Introduction to Logic*. 3rd ed. New York: Routledge, 2017.

Giaever, Ivar. "Global Warming Revisited." Lecture, 65th Lindau Nobel Laureate Conference, July 1, 2015. In Great Books of the Western World 6. Chicago: Encyclopaedia Britannica, 2015.

Gill, Eric. *Autobiography*. New York: Devin-Adair, 1941.

Hamilton, Alexander, James Madison, and John Jay. *The Federalist Papers*. Edited and with an introduction by Ian Shapiro; with essays by John Dunn, Donald L. Horowitz, and Eileen Hunt Botting. New Haven: Yale University Press, 2009.

Harvey, William. *On the Motion of the Heart and Blood in Animals*. Translated by Robert Willis (1844). Great Books of the Western World. Chicago: Encyclopaedia Brittanica, 1952.

Hazlitt, William. "On Wit and Humor." In *Lectures on the English Comic Writers*. Everyman's Library. London: Dent; New York: Dutton, 1967.

Herbert, George. *English Poems of George Herbert*. London: Longmans Green, 1902.

Herodotus. *The History of Herodotus*. Translated by George Rawlinson. Great Books of the Western World 6. Chicago: Encyclopaedia Britannica, 1955.

Hoffmeyer, Jesper. *Biosemiotics*. Scranton, Pa.: University of Scranton, 2008.

Homer. *The Iliad*. Translated by E. V. Rieu. Penguin Classics. London: Penguin, 1950.

Hume, David. *An Enquiry Concerning the Principles of Morals*. Edited by Tom L. Beauchamp. The Clarendon edition of the Works of David Hume. Oxford: Clarendon Press; Oxford and New York: Oxford University Press, 1998.

———. *An Enquiry Concerning Human Understanding*. Edited by Stephen Buckle. Cambridge and New York: Cambridge University Press, 2007.

Hurley, Patrick J. *A Concise Introduction to Logic*. 10th ed. Belmont, Calif.: Thomson Wadsworth, 2008.

Hutchins, Robert. "Morals, Religion, and Higher Education." In *The University of Chicago Round Table*, January 15, 1950, 29.

Huxley, Aldous. *Ends and Means*. New York: Routledge, 2017.

James, Henry. *The Portrait of a Lady*. Oxford: World's Classics, 1981.

Johnson, Samuel. *The History of Rasselas, Prince of Abissinia*. Edited, with an introduction and notes by Paul Goring. Penguin Classics. London: Penguin, 2007.

Joseph, H. W. B. *An Introduction to Logic*. Oxford: Clarendon Press, 1916.

Kant, Immanuel. *Prolegomena to Any Future Metaphysics*. Translated by James W. Ellington. 2nd ed. Indianapolis: Hackett, 2002.

Kelley, David. *The Art of Reasoning*. 4th ed. New York: Norton, 2014.

Kitto, H. D. F. *The Greeks*. New York: Routledge, 2017.

Kreeft, Peter. *Socratic Logic: Socratic Method Platonic Questions*. South Bend, Ind.: St. Augustine's Press, 2005.

Kreyche, Robert. *Logic for Undergraduates*. New York: Holt, Rinehart, Winston, 1970.

Laks, André, and Glenn Most. "Gorgias." In *Early Greek Philosophy*, vol. 8, *Sophists*, edited and translated by André Laks and Glenn Most. Cambridge, Mass.: Loeb Classical Library, 2014.

Langer, Suzanne K. *Philosophy in a New Key: A Study in the Symbolism of Reason, Rite, and Art*. Cambridge, Mass.: Harvard University Press, 1979.

Lavoisier, Antoine Laurent. *Elements of Chemistry*. Translated by Robert Kerr. New York: Dover, 1965.

Leibniz, Gottfried Wilhelm. *Leibniz: Political Writings*. Edited by Patrick Riley. Cambridge: Cambridge University Press, 1988.

Locke, John. *An Essay Concerning Human Understanding*. Edited, with a foreword by Peter H. Nidditch. Oxford: Clarendon Press; New York: Oxford University Press, 1979.

Machiavelli, Niccolo. *The Prince and the Discourses*. *The Prince* translated by Luigi Ricci, revised by E. R. P. Vincent. *The Discourses* translated by Christian E. Detmold. New York: Modern Library, 1940.

Madison, James. *The Constitutional Convention: A Narrative History; From the Notes of James Madison*. Edited by Edward J. Larson and Michael P. Winship. New York: Modern Library, 2005.

Malthus, Thomas Robert. *An Essay on the Principle of Population, or, a View of Its Past and Present Effects on Human Happiness: With an Inquiry into Our Prospects Respecting the Future Removal or Mitigation of the Evils Which It Occasions* [1803]. Cambridge and New York: Cambridge University Press, 1989.

Maritain, Jacques. *Formal Logic* [Petite logique]. Translated by Imelda Choquette. New York: Sheed and Ward, 1946.

Marx, Karl, and Friedrich Engels. *Manifesto of the Communist Party*. Authorized English Translation. Edited and annotated by Friedrich Engels. Chicago: Charles H. Kerr, 1888.

Montague, W. P. *The Ways of Things: A Philosophy of Knowledge, Nature, and Value*. New York: Prentice Hall, 1940.

Newton, Isaac. *Mathematical Principles of Natural Philosophy: Optics*. Translated by Silvanus P. Thompson. Great Books of the Western World. Chicago: Encyclopaedia Britannica, 1990.

Nietzsche, Friederich. *Joyful Wisdom*. Translated by Thomas Common. Poetry versions by Paul V. Cohn and Maude D. Petre. New York: Ungar, 1960.

Oesterle, John A. *Logic: The Art of Defining and Reasoning*. New York: Prentice-Hall, 1952.

Orwell, George. *1984*. New York: Harcourt, Brace, 1949.

Parry, William, and Edward Hacker. *Aristotelian Logic*. Albany: State University of New York Press, 1991.

Perrow, Charles. *Complex Organizations: A Critical Essay*. 3rd ed. Battleboro, Vt.: Echo Point, 2014.

Pilon, Roger. "Restoring Constitutional Government." Cato Institute. *Cato's Letters*, no. 9 (1995).

Plato. Greek texts of all works available at *Thesaurus Linguae Graecae: http://stephanus.tlg.uci.edu*.

————. *Complete Works*. Edited by John M. Cooper and D. S. Hutchinson. Indianapolis: Hackett, 1994.

————. *Five Dialogues*. "Euthyphro," "Apology," "Crito," "Meno," "Phaedo." 2nd ed. Translated by G. M. A. Grube. Revised by John M. Cooper. Indianapolis: Hackett, 2002.

Pope, Alexander. *Miscellanies in Verse and Prose*. London: Printed for John Thomas, 1744. http://name.umdl.umich.edu/004898469.0001.000.

Reed, Alonzo, and Brainerd Kellogg. *Higher Lessons in English*. 1877. Now available electronically at https://manybooks.net/titles/reedalonetexto4hilesıo.html.

Plutarch. *Lives of the Noble Greeks and Romans*. Greek with English translation by Bernadotte Perrin. 11 vols. Loeb Classical Library. Cambridge, Mass.: Harvard University Press, 1914–28.

Porphyry. *Isagoge* [Introduction] / *Porphyry the Phoenician*. Translated by Edward W. Warren. Toronto: Pontifical Institute of Mediaeval Studies, 1975.

Riegel, Jeffrey. "Confucius." In *The Stanford Encyclopedia of Philosophy* (Summer 2013 Edition). Edited by Edward N. Zalta. https://plato.stanford.edu/archives/sum2013/entries/confucius/.

Russell, Bertrand, and Alfred North Whitehead. *Principia Mathematica*. 3 vols. Cambridge: Cambridge University Press, 1910, 1912, 1913.

Santayana, George. *The Sense of Beauty*. New York: Scribner's, 1896.

Shakespeare, William. *The Arden Shakespeare Complete Works*. Edited by Richard Proudfoot, Ann Thompson, and David Scott Kastan. London: Arden Shakespeare, 2001.

Scheinfeld, Amram. *Your Heredity and Environment*. Philadelphia: Lippencott, 1964.

Sider, Theodore. *Logic for Philosophy*. Oxford: Oxford University Press, 2010.

Siderits, Mark. "Buddha." *The Stanford Encyclopedia of Philosophy*. Spring 2015 Edition. Edited by Edward N. Zalta. https://plato.stanford.edu/archives/spr2015/entries/buddha/.

Smith, Adam. *An Inquiry into the Nature and Causes of the Wealth of Nations*. Great Books of the Western World 39. Chicago: Encyclopaedia Britannica, 1955.

Smith, Vincent E. *The Elements of Logic*. Milwaukee: Bruce, 1957.

Sommers, Fred. *The Logic of Natural Language*. Oxford: Clarendon Press; New York: Oxford University Press, 1982.

Spangler, Mary Michael. *Logic: An Aristotelian Approach*. 2nd ed. Lanham, Md.: University Press of America, 1986.

Stone, Jon R. *Routledge Book of World Proverbs*. New York: Routledge, 2006.

Sullivan, Daniel J. *Fundamentals of Logic*. New York: McGraw Hill, 1963.

Sullivan, Scott M. *An Introduction to Traditional Logic: Classical Reasoning for Contemporary Minds*. 2nd ed. North Charleston, S.C.: Booksurge, 2006.

Symonds, Percival M. *The Dynamics of Human Adjustment*. New York: Praeger, 1946.

Teresa of Ávila. *Collected Works of St. Teresa of Ávila*. Translated by Kieran Kavanaugh and Otilio Rodriguez. 2 vols. Washington, D.C.: ICS Publications, 1980, 2012.

Thoreau, Henry David. *Walden, and Other Writings*. New York: Modern Library, 1992.

Thucydides. *The Landmark Thucydides: A Comprehensive Guide to "The Peloponnesian War."* Edited by Robert Strassler. Introduction by Victor Davis Hanson. Rev. translation of Richard Crawley. New York: Free Press, 2008.

Tolstoy, Leo. *War and Peace.* Translated by Louise Maude and Aylmer Maude. Great Books of the Western World 15. Chicago: Encyclopaedia Britannica, 1990.

Toynbee, Arnold. *Civilization on Trial.* New York: Oxford University Press, 1948.

Tkacz, Michael, and George Watson. *The Art of Reasoning: An Interactive Introduction to Traditional Logic.* 2nd ed. Dubuque, Iowa: Kendall Hunt, 2008.

Watson, James D. *The Double Helix: A Personal Account of the Discovery of the Structure of DNA.* New York: Atheneum, 1968.

Welty, Eudora. *On Writing.* New York: Modern Library, 2002.

Weston, Anthony. *A Rulebook for Arguments.* 5th ed. Indianapolis: Hackett, 2017.

Wilson, E. O. "Animal Communication." *Scientific American*, September 1972, 53–60.

Wilson, James Q., and Richard J. Herrnstein. *Crime and Human Nature.* New York: Simon and Schuster, 1985.

Index of Names

Index of Subjects